Thon

Companion to the

Summa Theologica

Book 1

Volume 1

Revelation Insight Publishing Co.

Dear Reader

1 Corinthians 2: 7-15. We speak the hidden mystical wisdom of God, which God ordained before the world unto our Glory, Which none of the princes of this world knew, for had they known it, they would not have crucified the Lord of Glory. But, as it is written, eye has not seen, nor ear heard, neither has it entered into the Heart of man to conceive the things, which God has prepared for them that Love him. However, God has revealed them unto us by His Spirit, for the Spirit searches all things, yes, and the deep things of God. For what man knows the things of a man, save the spirit of a man, which is in him? Even so, the thing of God knows no man, but the Spirit of God. Now we have received, not the Spirit of this world, but the Spirit, which is of God; that we might know the things that are freely given us of God. Which things also we speak, not in your words which man's wisdom teaches, but which the, Holy Spirit teaches, comparing spiritual things with Spiritual. However, the natural man receives not the things of the Spirit of God, for they are foolishness unto him, neither can he know them, because they are spiritually discerned. Nevertheless, he that is spiritual judges or discerns all things.

Companion to the
Summa Theologica
by
Walter Farrell O.P.

The Complete Unabridged Text
Re-edited for Today's Reader

Volume 1
Thomas Aquinas Library

Behold I stand at the door and knock, if anyone hears my voice and opens the door; I will come in and dine with him, and he with Me. He who overcomes, I will grant to sit down with Me on My throne, as I also overcame and with My Father on His throne. " Rev 3: 20-21

ISBN# 978-0-9823301-6-6

Library of Congress Cataloging in Publication Data.
2009927245

BISAC # REL067110

Printed and bound in the USA

E-Mail: Mystic@Orthodox.com

A COMPANION TO THE SUMMA
VOLUME I

ARCHITECT OF THE UNIVERSE
Corresponding to the *Summa Theologica, Ia Part*

Thomas Aquinas Library Introduction

These are designed and presented to accent a fine library of the essentials required for further in depth investigation of this genre.

The focus of this series is to provide today's reader with the essentials of background and investigative writings that are a part of our Christian heritage. The selected written works are a culmination of screening the best of this genre from the numerous documents, which are available. We selected these works based on a number of factors. The greatest impact upon the body of Christ, their insight of the genre and their related impact on other writers and the feasibility of this text to be used as a guide, in a standalone application. They are the primary indicators used, coupled with other factors in making our selection.

Each text in this series is a premier stand-alone text in this genre. The intended corpus of works pooled together make for a reference library rivaling that of some great monastery or university library on this subject. These are re-edited for today's reader. These writings are not abridged, they are the complete text, completely redone in grammar, syntax, verbiage, and other literary components to ensure the spirit of these works are not lost in these important changes.

For many of these texts, this is the first time they are available in this format and to these standards. These are not a scholarly reference work edition. For that purpose, there are other publications available. This series is intended for those who have a fundamental familiarity with the subject, and some of the writers. The intent is to address the needs of the readers who are journeying forward on their quest in union with God.

There are other selections to be added as certain texts are processed. Please look forward to these great works in print, audio and E-book formats at your local bookstore, although us directly.

Staff at **Revelation - Insight**

Aquinas Library Series Forward

The staff at "Revelation-Insight" presents this series. The objective of this particular series is to provide the focused reader, student, and others who have a need to go beyond the fundamental basics and achieve something more. This series was designed to provide you with the necessary tools by Thomas Aquinas to have a ready answer to foundational subject matter and answers to key and essential portions of various philosophical and theological works.

These tools will come in the form of apologies, a historical reference, systematic theology and various dissertations. This particular work, which is more than an overview of the accumulative life's effort and its varied formularies; it is an insightful guide. Presenting you with the essential and fundamental key elements required in answering a bevy of questions and perhaps summarizing the information with a need for a deeper explanation.

Throughout this series, there will be additions, which could be considered not simply a reference work but much more, and indeed that is our aim. By, providing you with much more than you intended upon receiving and yet not to the point of becoming overwhelmed. This is our pledge to you the consumer, to always bring to you in a palatable formula and format. To the student, a ready reference, to the reader, to educate through pertinent information, to the educator an essential reference tool for all avenues and venues. This is what we inspire to become for you the consumer. Many times libraries have bits and pieces spread across numerous volumes, requiring numerous hours to comb through. This series is designed and produced to provide you with the correct and proper information you need to come to grasp and obtain a sure foundation in your understanding your history belief events, leading up to its current formulary. Since history is what it is, and the facts remain self evident, in this series, we will not subscribe nor slant our presentations, following particular denominations. We will present these as straightforward as numbers are in a math equation. The rational is the numbers and the equation is what it is. There is no need to interpret. There is only one way to solve, one way to proceed, and only one correct answer to grasp.

Editor's Notes

Rational, Method and Aim of This Modernization

The intention of this book is not for the scholar. Instead, it is for the pilgrim who does not have access, to such works. It is for such individuals, that this edition has been prepared. My aim has been to make Aquinas's meaning clear to the modern reader with as little alteration of the available texts as possible. I have modernized the spelling, have simplified long and involved constructions, and have tried to illuminate the meaning by careful punctuation. I have dealt sparingly with the vocabulary, striving to keep some of the words likely to be understood.

I am aware that by my modernization, I have laid myself open to criticism in many directions. I strove for consistency, and tried solely to retain as far as possible the simplicity and charm of the original spirit and intent

I could not, nor will I attempt to alter this authors' works. I concur in my small effort, which is based upon his efforts. I will however add that the majority of this work has some editorial alterations solely for readability purposes. My intention is to solidify the meaning. As many will attest, this composition and some of its siblings are quite intense and are neither easily understood nor digested in their original. I trust this will enhance the readability of this monumental masterpiece.

This text is presented in its entirety. It remains unabridged.

This text carries it a style quite similar in grammar, expression, and phraseology that many early writers used. The complexity and other factors hint of this particular flavor. This effort follows Aristotle's, a.k.a. the philosopher's, format Nevertheless, I cannot begin to express what an impact this has had on me as I begin to edit this material. I am only a quarter of the way through this work and I feel and see such insight and reverence, which I have rarely seen before on such a minute and focused topic.

Aquinas is one who regardless of your placement on your spiritual journey. Aquinas is the basis for so much of what we have come to regard as dogma. This work is essential to not only understanding Aquinas's other works, but also our own journey. These issues, which he presents are not only fundamental, for many they are stumbling blocks, for others, they tend to be work around issues. These writings are the basics and yet essential works out of the plethora of works Aquinas has written. These are by no means the end all of him. They are merely the tip of a large glacier, which seems to forever be moving us forward.

A Locksmith

In time, much of this topic, enquiry and understanding will be relegated to the immortals as we plunged into the Dark Ages. It will not reemerge into the fore front until the likes of an equal intellectual Titan begins to bellow. This is none other than Thomas Aquinas, a prodigy, under the tutelage of Albert Magnus, a.k.a. Albert the Great, of the Cologne University. Aquinas is one of the few, who not only undertake this extraordinary issue to task, but will also bear fruit in this endeavor.

A Cipher and Mirror

a) The statement, "Reason is the handmaid of enlightenment."
b) "After what I have experienced, all that I have written are as straw."

The first comes to us from the Leviathan "Summa Theologica." [Aquinas 1.79.2] The second is just a few months prior to his death, it was not written, but intimately shared with a traveling monk. What is left in between has caused me to vacillate between the two and find the center portal, by which I may enter and ascend and pass on a discourse.

First, to dismiss Thomas Aquinas, is to dismiss the existence of the Empire State building when visiting, passing through or merely flying over NYC, you cannot mistake, nor fail to perceive its eminent presence among its contemporizes scraping against the skyline, more importantly, nor can you ignore its landmark heritage. The same applies to Thomas, his written efforts, and his rightful place among the School of Titans.

In this initial effort it is debuted by Walter Farrell's colossal undertaking of Synthesizing Thomas's Summa Theologica into a modern variation, making it relative to our world, environment and issues.

Peace be with you.

Brother Smith SGS 2009'

Introduction

Who is he?   Walter Farrell was a Dominican Theologian who, like Thomas in addressing his colloquies, attempted to provide a thorough understanding of this leviathan for the laity in a modern perspective of the original work coming into print by 1938.

What is objective?   *Walter* attempts in these four books to treat and address the fundamentals of interpretation, using classic avenues of rhetoric and its siblings. He then applies this to understanding some of the fundamental issues, which continue to plaque many even today. This work has broad implications regarding man in his relationship with God. This effort, like its true narrative remains unrivaled.

The benefits of the work: This is a multifaceted response. Each of the above themes resonates in any scriptural interpreter. The lay out, progression is a three part progression of general overview, "Quid Pro Quo" format. The idea is to have you come to a quick overview of rhetoric and interpretation and then present you with a paper to skim through and find your way with supportive measures. Aquinas's work however, is not one to be taken lightly as you will see as you delve deeper into this matrix. It takes on a much more personal and manifested performance and experience, which I have not found, evidenced within another writer.

I am not sure of any other collection of his, which has such an underlying motive and yet, addresses the subject with the intensity as these four accomplish. We believe as you begin your journey beyond the neighborhood, and venture out, you will find this work indeed an essential work and a masterpiece in itself. In the last work presented here, Walter, using Thomas's work, addresses and hammers away at supporting and defining God's will and our will, righteousness and evil.

This works is of such great importance to our relationship with God. Our understanding of how God works and allows certain, events to transpire. To date, there is no other work assemblage as there is within this volume, which you are holding. To deny Aquinas, is to dismiss so much of what we have come to believe. Regardless of what faith denomination you are affiliated with, his works are the foundation of many seminaries and universities. This phase begins a bit stronger and tougher elements for the pilgrim. This phase will bring the pilgrim into the path and provide nourishment, rest, and shelter on their spiritual journey through these works.

Once again, I would like to caution you in this assembled work. In keeping as close to his style, it is problematic to edit. He is quite skillful in rhetoric, his points are quite accurate. While working through this arrangement, you will discover, uncover, and become face to face with many issues, which perhaps were inadequately assumed, presented, and believed. Aquinas/ Farrell will call you in for questioning and seek a resolution to your ideas.

A Companion to the Summa, Volume 1

📖 CHAPTER I -- THE WISE MAN'S BOOK 📖
(Q. 1)

1. The wise man and his book,

  (a) The man,

     (1) Objections to Thomas.

     (2) A picture of Thomas.

  (b) His book,

     (1) Objections to it,

        a. Seven hundred years old.

        b. Ponderous.

        c. In a dead, scientific language.

     (2) The nature of the book,

        a. Its wise nature.

        b. Its personal nature.

     (3) Aim and division of the book.

2. The place of divine wisdom in human life,

  (a) Its necessity.

  (b) Its role in human activity,

     (1) A divine science--its object.

     (2) Its place among the sciences.

(3) Its character as wisdom.

(4) Its subject matter.

(5) Its method.

Conclusion,

1. Pertinence of the man and his book to the twentieth century,

(a) The man,

(1) His interests -- the perfection of God and the perfectibility of man.

(2) His battles -- in defense of God and man.

(3) His love.

a. Its constant basis.

b. Its ardor.

(b) His book -- an antidote for poisons,

(1) Of superficiality.

(2) Of provincialism.

2. A philosophy of life,

(a) The meaning of life -- ultimate answers.

(b) The goal of life a plan of action.

(c) The exemplar of living -- a way of life.

CHAPTER I

📖 THE WISE MAN'S BOOK 📖

(Q. 1)

The wise man and his book

It is not hard to admire St. Thomas Aquinas immovably caught in the splendor of a stained-glass window; it is easy to pay tribute to his *Summa Theologica* as long as it remains high on a bookshelf giving character to a library. Under these circumstances, we of the twenty first century can read about them both, talk about them enthusiastically, but pretty much leave them both alone. To have Thomas walking among us, his book opened on our desks for serious study, now that is altogether something else.

Objections to Thomas

If Thomas were to drop into a twenty first century club, or a twenty first century pub for that matter, he would, of course, be judged by twenty first century standards. By those standards he could expect no rousing welcome; he might be tolerated in an amused fashion, but certainly no one would get chummy with him. He lived in the wrong place, for his home was a cloister and to us a cloister is much more puzzling than a healthy appendix. He lived in the wrong age, long, long before the modern age of progress, in the very middle of the Middle Ages. His occupation was totally without interest to us. He was a professor and a writer of books; his researches uncovered no new vitamins or explosives, he had nothing to say about earning more pay, he neither attacked God nor debunked man and society, but he had a good deal to say about truth, goodness, love and God. His books had no scarlet pages, no profanity, no biological realism in perfumed words, no substitute for thinking, and no escape from life. Far from rejecting the past, the man actually revered old things!

Personally he was impossible. Bonds of blood closely tied his family to the royalty of all Europe, bad enough in itself; but Thomas, turning aside from the soldierly preoccupations of his brothers, became (although not without a fight) a begging friar. To get the full force of this last on the modern mind, it must be put cumulatively; he was a friar and a beggar. The man himself was an abstract thinker, a cold, ruthless logician proceeding with machine-like precision and heartlessness from principle to conclusion regardless of consequences. He had no passion in him, for he was a saint; no heart, for he clung stubbornly to truth; no imagination, for he was a metaphysician; no humanity, for he fled from the world.

If a particle of this were true of Thomas, he would certainly have no place in the lives of men of our age; if even less of it were true, he would belong, not in a stained-glass window, but in a museum. There are no people farther apart than saints and freaks; and this picture makes Thomas out a gigantic freak.

A Picture of Thomas

This picture of Thomas is worse than a caricature; it is a defamation of the man. There is no refuting the fact that Thomas was a friar; the best defense of that calling was not the one he wrote but the one he lived. It is not at all the same thing to fly from the world and to fly from men. For those who fly from men will die from the spiritual anemia induced by the feeble diet and the narrow confines of the cell of self. While those who stand by men, although flying from the world, will be crucified by both, and consider the crucifixion a price well worth paying for. Thomas has had his crucifixion down through the ages; perhaps the most bitter is the modern one of complete misunderstanding of his character.

We come close to the truth when we see Thomas as an eager youngster plunging into the pursuit of truth at the heels of the greatest master of his time. We are digging beneath his inscrutable surface when we see him holding on to that youthful zest in the way peculiar to the saints, supplementing native genius by labors even his great strength could not stand until, before fifty, his life was burned out. Throughout that short life he dreamed great dreams, impossible dreams, and did all a man could do to make those dreams come true; coming to the end of his life he was forced to admit, as we all are, that the accomplishment fell far short of his dreams, that all he had written seemed as so much straw.

Thomas was eminently human. He had a great natural capacity for love. Bonaventure could have testified to this, or the sisters of Thomas who went into his tower room to talk him out of the convent and came out themselves talked into the convent. He acquired a knowledge of human nature in no small degree from his treks up and down, back and forth, in a Europe, which knew little delicacy in its revelations of human nature. That knowledge was deepened, enriched by a love of God and a zeal for souls that made his every breath, even his dying one, a wind scattering truth broadcast through a hungry world, which eventually would reap the harvest of so prodigal a sowing.

He had indeed fled from the world, but not from men. This man was not without passion, he was on fire; his heart was not empty, it was overflowing; he was a metaphysician in the fullest sense of the word, which means he was a poet and a pioneer with enough imagination and equal courage to step over the edge of the world and into the darkness. This man doesn't belong in a museum; he doesn't belong in a stained-glass window; his place is with the daring ones, at the head of the crowd, with the ones who have the courage to be men.

700 Years Old Objections

Still, his supreme book is seven hundred years old. It might, you say, be of historical interest to a collector, of whom the rules do not oblige to read the books he cherishes, and might be enthused about it. Still, the world has come a long way in seven hundred years. Thomas was not a prophet; what could he know of our intellectual advancement. Every age has its own problems; what did Thomas have to do with democracy as against dictatorship, with unemployment, planned economy, or mechanized war? His book was medieval; our age certainly is not. His was an age of speculation, ours of observation; his of approximation, ours of accuracy; his of faith, ours of reason; his a leisurely age, ours one of speed. So we might go on, fondling the contrasts that are only half-true and omitting the essential consideration, namely, that seven hundred years has not changed the model of human nature.

A list of the problems dealt with in the *Summa* might as easily have been drawn from the schools of Greece, the libraries of modern universities, or, indeed, from the hearts and minds of men of any age. There is, for example, the problem of good and evil; of being and becoming; of change or evolution; of the goal of man; of knowledge; of God; of property; of the state; of pleasure; of duty; of the origin of the world, and so on. If the *Summa* of St. Thomas has anything worthwhile to say on these subjects, it is of interest to an age tortured as ours is with the lack of answers to the fundamental problems of humanity. As a matter of fact, St. Thomas was much too human to turn out a work useless to humanity, much too close to the hearts of men and women to have dealt with these problems in an abstract way that would be of interest only to the academic mind.

Objections, Ponderous

The book is ponderous, five folio volumes of closely packed print, and more closely packed thought. We are not of that by-gone age that would accept such a formidable work as an intellectual challenge, to prove it was not as inferior as it felt. We are rather of the age of headlines, compendiums, outlines and summaries. We must have reviews of the week, in pictures for the really rushed; summary magazines do our digesting for us, columnists do our peeking for us commissions do our fact-finding. For ourselves, we are always in a hurry.

Yet, a three-volume novel is not too much for us, or even a one-volume romance of twelve hundred pages. We do face pages and pages of reports, platforms, speeches, and statistics. We are of the age of heroically persevering scientific research. It cannot be that we are afraid of work. It is more likely that we demand some tangible fruits as the goal inspiring us to the expenditure of so much mental or physical labor. And it would be hard to quarrel with this eminently hardheaded attitude towards life or books. St. Thomas meets such a challenge with his usual overwhelming answer. It is not the age of his work, its ponderous size, even its medieval dress that repels the layman; but the unfounded opinion that this work is not worth the labor involved in becoming acquainted with it, the results of that labor are not pertinent to an age startlingly different from the age in which the *Summa Theologica* was written.

Objections, Dead Languages

The dress of the book has been changed; live languages have wrapped their attractive folds about it. Not that such a change was so very necessary; it is difficult to hide the beauty of youth behind the thin disguise of outmoded style. Only a superficial observer could have missed the allure of the *Summa*. It was written with enthusiasm for the enthusiastic, for the beginners who face light-heartedly the agony of the first step. There is about the book much of the eagerness of youth. It attacks the highest problems with a gay heart and sublime confidence; it meets the rebuff of mystery with youth's resiliency; it accepts the sweeping conclusions of truth with youth's idealism, youth's willingness to sacrifice. It aims at high goals with all the vigor of the great heart of youth.

The Nature of the Book

The humanity and perennial modernity of the *Summa* is the skeleton whose flesh and blood is the culture of all the ages. Within this book is the compressed essence of truth ground from the Oriental and Greek philosophies, from Socrates, Plato and Aristotle, from the Fathers and from those long thousand years that went into the making of scholasticism. Yet it is not a mere compendium of past achievement, a mausoleum of masters long since dead; rather it is the descendant of a noble line, worthy of the blood it bears. The hard won truth of man's earliest search for wisdom passed through a filter in Aquinas that barred nothing but the dregs, which would poison the drink.

The Book is Wise

Perhaps this last is one of the supreme benefits of contact with the *Summa Theologica*; the constant communication with one of the greatest minds of all time through the medium of his greatest work. The contents of the *Summa* had been preparing in the angry reply of a giant intellect through all of a lifetime. We can even see the slow steps of purification by glancing at Thomas' earlier works seeing the hesitating agreement, or carefully conditioned disagreement, with the thought of his masters. Later the bold statement of his own solutions does not balk at disagreement with the older scholastics, with Albert, Bonaventure, Augustine and the Fathers, with Plato and Aristotle. Agreements, wherever found, are even more startling. Here, in the full fruit of great genius, there is an economy of word and concept that is deceiving, a few lines of the *Summa* often equal pages of an earlier work and yet leave us puzzled as to what has been omitted. Frequently the marvel is not what has been so well said but what has been so well left unsaid. A principle is presented to us bowing down with human implications, but presented delicately, with a profound respect for the intellect of the reader, like a poem barely suggesting a sublime picture, or an early English drama without scenery. When a word either way might have upset the delicate balance of truth, might indicate an unjustified emphasis, might mislead the reader, that word is not said.

Its Personal Nature

St. Thomas sat down to write his greatest book as a typist might pull the cover off her typewriter and begin the transcribing of her notes. He too, was unabashed by the task before him; he approached it with serene simplicity, unimpressed with the importance of his work. Yet, his serenity and simplicity were the eternal expression of the confidence inspired by genius and sanctity. He admits, off-handedly in his extremely brief Prologue, that he intends to expose all that pertains to the Christian religion. In view of what he actually did, that meant that he intended to wander the corridors of eternity, and to neglect no item in the existing universe. His gaze would focus on the crystalline beauty of the angelic world; his step would not falter before the mysterious realms of the human heart; nor would he be confused by the pettiness and magnificence of the mind of man. He would make a thorough investigation of the animal as well as of the angelic side of the human image of God. The origin, end and make-up of the physical world he would treat as profoundly as the birth, life, death and resurrection of God made man. The mystery and misery of sin were to be well within his field; and, of course, the supernatural instrumentality of the sacraments, the riches of the whole life of grace.

The Aim of the Book

Thomas, faced with the abundance of his material, did not hope merely to toss it before the minds of men; he expected to expose all this adequately, lucidly, and as briefly as the matter permitted. Moreover, he was not aiming at an increase in the intellectual jowls of the well cared for specialists in philosophy and theology; he had in mind, rather, the underfed, the starving, the little ones, beginners who had gone hungry too long. He expected to avoid all that would confuse the thinking of these little ones that would impede their progress that might contribute to their discouragement. The thing seemed important enough to this first professor of the age of Universities for an explicit statement of the instruments he had forged to bring it about, order above all, simplicity, and the ruthless elimination of useless questions, arguments and repetitions.

The Division of the Book

The laziest man in the world might draw up a plan such as this. In fact, lazy men are usually prolific in their production of plans, perhaps the better to relish their idleness. The astonishing thing about Thomas' project is that it came very close indeed to complete accomplishment, so close as to leave the onlookers breathless before the massive beauty of this intellectual cathedral, oblivious of its unfinished sacristy. The only thing that could stop it stopped Thomas' project. He died while in the midst of his treatment of the sacrament of Penance.

The plan of the *Summa* is as simple as the statement of its aims by Thomas. The first part treats about God, both in Himself and as the principle from which the angelic, the human and the purely physical world take their rise; the second part treats of man's movement back to the source from which he came; the third, of the means or the road which he travels to that goal and the home that waits for him at the end of the road.

It is the first part of the *Summa*, which will occupy us throughout this volume. After a preliminary question, the burden of the rest of this chapter, we shall investigate the existence of the one God; then the inner life of the one true God, or the mystery of the Trinity; the rest of this volume will be taken up with a study of the angels, of men and of the world, for thus only can we have the full story of the procession of creatures from God. This latter part of the present volume will not involve argument about angels on the head of a pin; Thomas had no room for stupid questions. Nevertheless, it will involve the study and appreciation of the entire world, not merely the material part of it; of all of man, not merely the animal part of him; of the entire angelic world, not cynically amused caricatures of it. The pictures this study hangs in the minds of men will be strikingly different from those that today too often clutter the mind and shatter the heart. Man will not be found pictured here as a frightened god perched on the barren summit of a world in chaos. Nor will he be seen as no different in kind from the rest of the animals, his oddly human capacities for politics and poetry here are not only accidental differences, which set him off from the beasts no more essentially than the fact that he is somewhat more fastidious about his bath. God will not have the hurried, harassed look of a timidly ineffective man; these angels will not be gliding around languidly looking for a holy card on which to set ablaze. All these pictures have no inspiration in the world of reality; and it is only with reality that we are engaged in this volume.

It is extremely important, at the very outset, that we lay hold firmly on these two facts, Thomas, all his life, was a relentless searcher for reality, a ruthless enemy of falsehood; and his supreme work was a book of supernatural theology. In our own time, it has become the fashion to divorce theology from reason and so to destroy any conviction of its relation to reality. As for the supernatural, well that is an insult to our self-sufficiency not to be lightly suffered by an intelligent man. It is not too hard to understand the modern's impatience with the supernatural, for man has always been proud; but only the intellectual suicide of positivism could be so absurd as to limit the horizons of a man's mind to what he can uncover by the methods of science. This last has no need of rational refutation for the positivist contradicts himself in the denials that make up his doctrine; he advocates a way of death, rather than of life, for life cannot be lived on a basis of denials, it must be fled from. Men are intolerant of the cowardice of escape; they are sympathetic towards a spirit of independence, even exaggerated independence, although they, and everyone else, are barred from expressing that sympathy when the independence reaches the stage of voluntary confinement.

It is unquestionably true that man, left to his own devices, can gather a tremendous amount of information; so much, in fact, as to be smothered under the pile of facts he has heaped upon his own head. He can even, through the patient labor of the years; acquire something of wisdom's understanding of the pattern of things, of the distinction between details and essentials, of goals and means to those goals. The point that is overlooked too often is that a man simply cannot wait so long for the advent of wisdom. He has to know these things from the beginning he has a human life to live through all the years that are demanded for the personal achievement of the long view of the wise man; and, for by far the greater number of men, the mind, the heart, the hands are well occupied in winning a livelihood from a grudging mother earth. To be quite frank, there are many men who will never arrive at wisdom under their own power if they live to be a hundred and have absolutely nothing to do but think. To be equally frank, it must be admitted that the wisest of men are going to make mistakes.

This matter of human goals that give the directions for human living is much too important to run such risks. This knowledge cannot wait, it cannot be restricted to a few, it cannot be punctuated by error; if we are content to have it so, it is only because we assume the unimportance of the human individual, the meaninglessness of human life, the certitude of long life, the indifference of truth. All of these assumptions are false. Because they are, man, even in those things that are not strictly above his human powers, must have help. He can assert his absolute independence only at the cost of compromising his knowledge of reality and, ultimately, at the cost of failure in the living of human life. He must accept truth from the source of truth; and be thankful the truth is given him.

Necessity of Wisdom

All this would be true if man's life were to be fulfilled by a goal within the grasp of his natural powers. When we face the fact that the only goal of man is above all nature, the eternal vision of God, we see something of the desperate necessity for a divine revelation that will give him knowledge of that goal and the means by which he can arrive at it.

The illusion of independence can be bought at much too high a price. It could logically demand that we swim oceans rather than depend on a ship-builder and a navigator that we toddle through blizzards naked until we can make our own clothes that we fly by flapping our arms. Whatever the price paid, when we examine the thing in an honest light, the wonder is that we bought such a shoddy product at all; the certainty is that we have been badly cheated. There is nothing so completely useless as the illusion that we are self-sufficient, for there is nothing so completely false.

We must have wisdom from the beginning of life. It cannot be our own; nor is it sufficient if it is some other human being's. It must be divine, for only God is wise from the beginning. To begin life with the wisdom lent us by divinity, and end it by possessing that wisdom; to meet the charges at each station of life with a divinely minted coin; to see the road that stretches before us through the far seeing eyes of God, this is not an insult to human nature, it is an ennoblement of it.

A Divine Science -- Its Object

In this atmosphere of nobility theology draws its first breath of life, for the deposit of divinely revealed truth constitutes the life principle of all theological science. If philosophy, as the apex of natural intellectual effort, has deserved the name of human wisdom, then theology is rightly called divine wisdom. All of its varied fabric is given solid substance by the thread of divinity that is woven into it; if we unravel that complex fabric, that single thread will always lead back to God, the source of truth and the goal of it. Without that thread of divinity, theology is a name given to a crazy quilt that, paradoxically, is devoid not only of beauty but of variety, monotonous with the gray monotony of despair. It has nothing of wisdom about it, for it has nothing of meaning about it. Now drawing its life-blood from the source of all order, theology is vibrant with such significance as man would not have dared to dream, with divine significance for creatures who hardly dare to face human life let alone dream of living divine life.

To speak of theology as a science may sound blasphemous to modern ears. Indeed, it is blasphemous if we restrict science to the treasure buried in the physical world, a treasure to be unearthed only by the pickaxe and spade of the experimental method. However, if we take science, as it should be taken, in the larger sense of ripe knowledge plucked from principles that escape the blight of doubt, we can hardly mistake theology as a clever imitation of a live science, to be put under glass as a tribute not to its life but to its artificiality. We can, with an easy mind, expose it to the weather to live its rugged, vibrant life; let the rainfall on it and the wind tug at it, the sun shine on it and its enemies drag their tiny bodies over its broad branches. It will live; its roots are deep enough, its leaves broad enough, its branches high enough; it will live, although many hybrids die beside it.

Theology's Place Among the Sciences

Theology is no mongrel in the pack of sciences. Like every other science, it has its proper, and utterly distinctive, field the field of revealable truths. Its paraphernalia is totally inadequate to furnish it with its principles, so, in common with all other sciences, it gets the principles with which it starts and on which it depends from some other source. The philosopher, with no human science above him, accepts without question the self-evident principles his reason discloses to him or he ceases to be a philosopher. The theologian accepts his principles, not from the science of the physicist, the mathematician or the philosopher, but from the science of God and the saints. No science proves its own principles; nor does theology. But the principles of every other science are susceptible, with the help of another science or directly from nature, of clear vision by the human mind; theology alone accepts principles too clear to be seen by any mind but the mind of God. It believes its principles on the authority of the Truth incapable of error or falsehood.

Let us suppose that a great university invited all the sciences, in person, to dinner. Where should theology be seated, between the practical and the speculative sciences? Well, the thing is more practical than domestic economy for it deals with the most practical of things the goal of a man and the roads to the goal; at the same time it is more speculative than metaphysics for it handles truths that are divine.

It might take the grapefruit with the speculative sciences, move over to an empty chair for the soup with the practical sciences, back to its original place for the fish, and so on; a little fatiguing, perhaps, but then what can be done? Like many another person with an insoluble problem, the hostess will shelve it and pretend it does not exist, for the moment anyhow. Now about places, who will get the first place and who will slide humbly into the welcome obscurity of the seat far down the table? In the speculative section the question will have to be settled on the certitude of the science and the nobility of its subject matter. Theology jumps down from that mental shelf to worry the hostess, it would be hard to find a more noble subject matter than divinity or to compare the certitude achieved by a human mind to the certitude of the divine word. But the method! Yes, the others may be a little uppish on the question of method, but then how can we make a particular method the norm of precedence; is this a scientific dinner or a meeting of a secret society?

Very well, give theology the first place among the speculative sciences; at least that settles the question of where theology will sit. In the practical section, precedence will be determined by the ultimateness of the end served by the particular science. Obviously medicine will sit above domestic economy, but does it go above or below politics? We can settle that later; what is the very last end served by any science; theology again! The only solution is to sit theology in the very center with the speculative sciences descending on the right and the practical on the left, hoping, of course, that no wit brings up the matter of the sheep and the goats; but enough of the dinner. Abandoning the figurative language and getting down to hard facts, it is true that the findings of the other sciences seem much more certain to us than the conclusions of theology. This is true, but the flame of an acetylene torch is not less bright because it blinds us, less visible because we must see it through smoked glasses; nor is the divine truth less certain because it is too clear for our eyes, it is not less sure because we have to see it through the obscure glass of faith. It is also true that theology uses philosophy; but that is not because the pillars of divine truth need so much bolstering, it is rather because of the comfort our weakness derives from the clasping hand of philosophy. We will come back to this matter of philosophy later on in this chapter.

Theology's Character as Wisdom

It is difficult to conjure up a picture of a rollicking theologian. Perhaps there have been such, but the odds are against it. Not that theology demands that its disciples all have long, white beards; but it does seem to demand that its youngest masters be old and its oldest masters be young. Perhaps all this is because of the bouquet that wisdom throws off as we warm the word in the hollow of our hands. We do associate wisdom with old age, not because the mind of the old is keener, the heart more eager, but because the tired feet have wandered enough to know the highroad from a bypath, the old eyes have seen enough, to know a trifle from the gem for which a man must sell all he has, because the old hands have worked at tasks enough to know the ephemeral from the enduring. Old age should know more of the answers, it should see more of the pattern, and it should escape more of the confusion of the terrific detail of life. Theology is wisdom, old with the agelessness of eternity; but young with the youth of an eternal beginning.

The wise man to be consulted for the answers about the new house that is going up is the architect, not the bricklayer; if he does not know the reasons for things, there aren't any. He may be stupid in many other lines, but in this one, because he is master of the ultimate purposes of the building, he is wise; in any line, this knowledge of ultimate purposes brings wisdom. When the knowledge is of the last of all purposes, it brings that wisdom that needs no qualification; by it a man is simply wise. This will be the man who knows the answers that really matter; these are the answers for, which the theologian exists.

Theology's Subject Matter

For the theologian treats of nothing except in relation to the first beginning and the last end. He is in the intellectual order what the saint is in the practical order, a man wholly engaged with God. A general order covering the activity of the two men need suffer no single change in phrasing, "begin this task at once, work at it ceaselessly, and finish it in eternity." For the love of God is not to be encompassed in a lifetime, neither is the knowledge of God. However far afield the mind or the heart may seem to have wandered, both are engaged with God Himself or with the things that pertain to God as Beginning or as End. The saint knows the important answers by the quick intuition that has its deep roots in love, the theologian, by the reasoned argument that has its roots deep in study. When study and love are united to make a saint of a theologian, God has been exceptionally kind to men.

It is into the book of just such a man that we are timidly edging our way. There is a definite reassurance in the fact that Thomas insisted that reason roll up its sleeves and get down to its hardest task; this brings back the first day's study of any science. Moreover he has adopted the fully developed form of that similar method of Socrates; and what is more familiar than a question? The double flattery of a question is hard to resist; the contentedly ignorant and the insufferably omniscient never ask a question, while the fool is asked a question only by mistake. A question, after all, is the movement of a mind in search of truth and there is nothing so pleasant to disseminate as truth. Children and scholars are living question marks and, as Thomas wrote for childish scholars, it was right that every article of his book be a question demanding a straight answer. To clarify the issue, an opponent, fictitious or real, is introduced each time with so forceful a presentation of objections as to cause a little anxiety in the heart of a follower of Thomas.

Method of Theology

The body of the articles throughout concentrates on the work of explaining, illustrating, persuading, refuting and, where possible, proving. Thomas, of course, does not argue about theology's principles; no science does that. The inferior sciences depend on their superiors to take care of the borrowed principles; metaphysics, without a superior, will argue about its principles with an opponent who grants some of them; with an opponent who denies all of them it can do nothing but refute the denial, exposing its falsity. The procedure is the same in theology, with the added assurance that every objection in denial has its answer for these principles rest on the immutable truth of God.

Still, there is plenty of room for argument in theology beneath the principles; nor has there ever been a slackening of that argumentation that destroys error, preserves truth and uncovers still more of truth. Here philosophy is put to work in earnest; here human reason is employed to its fullest strength; for here is a task worthy of the great potentialities of the mind of a man. As a reward for this backbreaking labor, theology restricts the field of possible philosophical error, releasing this flood of conserved energy into the channels of real philosophical investigation. Philosophy is not substituted for, it is not destroyed, not diluted; for grace does not destroy nature, it perfects it. It is not superseded by a higher wisdom; it is consecrated by that higher wisdom.

Conclusion, Thomas' Interests

This consecration and perfection of nature by grace was a dominant note in the life of Thomas. He could never close his ears to its challenge. From the beginning his mind and heart were complete captives to the enticement of the perfection of God; he fought his mother, his sisters, his brothers that he might be freer to pursue it and, in the race to embrace it, nobility of family, wealth and power, the world itself were cast off as so much dead weight slowing his steps. He read the book of the world with all the intense concentration and genius of his great mind; he pondered the divinely revealed secrets like a miser fondling his gold. As the years passed and virtue mounted he plunged deeper and deeper into that infinite perfection and was more and more overwhelmed by it.

Knowing God so well, he knew himself the better. Not only himself, but all men; it was not for nothing that the divine plans had him tramping up and down the roads of Europe in an age when a friar was the beloved priest of scullery maid and princess, of peasant and prince. A dull-witted man with no human sympathy could hardly go through such an experience without acquiring a deep knowledge of human nature; and Thomas has not been accused, since the grotesque accusation of his student days, of being dull witted or unsympathetic. He read the secrets of the human heart, his own and the hearts of others, seeing their pettiness, cowardice, smug mediocrity and even viciousness, he saw how far they could get from God; but seeing, too, their high hopes, their dogged courage, their quick remorse and unselfish loyalty, he saw how close they could come to God. On this double theme the symphony of his life developed, the perfection of God and the perfectibility of man.

In Defense of God and Man

From his first appearance in a professor's chair Thomas was embroiled in intellectual battle; that battle continued all of his life; nor is it finished yet. It was, and is, a battle in defense of God and of man. Thomas would not stand by and see God torn down from His divine throne; he could not stand by and see the image of God defaced on earth. God is perfect and man can be perfected; any lessening of the perfection of God is a denial of Him and any lessening of the potentialities of man is a denial of humanity. These two truths must stand whatever the cost of their defense, God is divine and man is capable of a share in divine life. One cannot be attacked without the other going by the board; and at no time in history have both come under so ceaseless a fire as in our own time.

His Love

The genius of Thomas could have put up no such fight as it did without the driving force of a love to match its greatness. A love so great, so utterly selfless, so impervious to the allure of every other love could be nothing short of the divine love whose full flower goes by the name of sanctity. Thomas, from the beginning, was head over heels in love with God; to the end his love's great problem was not to hold a fickle lover but to find the means of spending himself enough to give expression to that love. He came as close to solving that problem as is given to man on earth.

Certainly Thomas placed no conditions on his love. He did not cautiously arrange emergency exits in case love's demands became too inconvenient. There were no limits of time, of strength, of thought, of surrender involved in this divine contract. Rather that love was a searing flame that consumed the man that hurled him into a whirlwind of labor that knew no lull until death stopped that great heart. Love such as this may seem a strange thing in a world that has adopted security as a watchword. But only by love such as this will a man ever again come so close to other men and be so intimately joined to God; only on this condition will humanity ever again have such a champion and God such an apostle.

Antidote to Poisons

In his book Thomas offers the twentieth century love and truth; but the love cannot be reveled in until the truth has been mastered. This truth comes as a rather violent antidote to the two modern poisons of intellectual superficiality and naturalistic provincialism.

Superficiality

Another name for that intellectual superficiality is intellectual laziness. It consists in that easy grasping at the first and partial answer, breeding smug satisfaction and a shallowness that will not float an idea. This book looks to the last and the adequate answer, the answer that awes and humiliates, the answer that will intrigue a man's mind for a lifetime and direct his actions beyond the limits of life. Thomas' effort for beginners was not directed to the cultivation of the ability to quote others; its aim was to develop the capacity to think for oneself. His is not an emphasis of facts to the neglect of wisdom; his book cannot be read as a memory exercise. Laying it aside after some careful reading, we cannot dismiss it with such remarks as, "how interesting, how odd." It will hit us between the eyes, or it will not touch us at all, for the ultimate answers cannot be looked at without deep personal reverberations.

Provincialism of Naturalism

Against the provincialism of naturalism, Thomas discovers the meaning of the natural world by frankly stepping into the supernatural; he discovers the perfect fulfillment of man by refusing to accept man as the perfect fulfillment of the universe; his book rejects the modernist's contempt for the past by offering cultural contact with the wisdom of the ages and with one of the greatest intellects the world has yet seen.

Life's Meaning, Goal and Exemplar

This man is not to be framed in a stained-glass window; his book is not a library decoration. This is a man and a book providentially designed for the needs of the twentieth century. Certainly no age has greater need for ultimate answers, for a plan of action, for an exemplar of human living; for no age has had less conception of the meaning of life, the things that go into successful living, the manner in which human life must be lived to be successful. In his three great divisions of this book, Thomas gives us precisely these things, a study of the divine architect and His completed work; a study of the goal of human life and the human actions by which that goal is attained; a study of the God who became man that men might become like unto God.

📖 CHAPTER II -- HE WHO IS 📖
(Q. 2)

1. Beginners and the beginning,

   (a) The mystery and difficulty of beginnings.

   (b) Difficulty for beginners.

   (c) Reasons for a beginning,

      (1) Their modernity,

         a. Objections against them.

         b. Their perennial strength.

      (2) Their completeness.

2. Preliminary notions to proof of the beginning,

   (a) Potentiality and actuality.

   (b) Change, potential, process and product.

   (c) Limitations of proofs of existence.

3. The five proofs,

   (a) From passivity -- motion.

   (b) From activity -- causality.

   (c) From defectibility -- contingency.

   (d) From perfection -- participation.

   (e) From order -- finality.

4. Characteristics of the proofs,

(a) A posteriori arguments.

(b) Not cumulative but independently sufficient.

(c) Strictly limited to the evidence.

(d) Foundations of the deductive tract   on the nature of God.

Conclusion,

> 1. Significance of the proofs.
>
> 2. Real mystery of beginnings.
>
> 3. Allegedly non-mysterious substitutes.

📖 CHAPTER II 📖

HE WHO IS

(Q. 2)

It is more than the perennial vigor of human hope that makes human life a long process of constant beginnings. A beginning never becomes a prosaic thing, although we see its counterparts on all sides every day; it is in itself glamorous, enticing, irresistible, for it is in itself mysterious. The feeble spark of young life in a mother's womb, the first tentative plan of the architect, the first step of the infant, the first scribbled words of a book fascinate us. They swing open doors and we cannot resist straining our eyes to peer down the long corridors of the future they reveal to us. It is not an explanation of this attraction to say that this moment of beginning is tightly packed with love's rewards, love's labors and love's hopes. It is all of this; but it is much more. It is that inexplicable thing that we call mystery, the thing that calls our minds out on the long road along whose winding way the explanation of the mystery may be found.

The mystery and difficulty of beginnings

The woman who gives birth to a child is not only a cause of a wondrous effect; she herself has become what she was not before, a mother. It is not only the marble under the sculptor's chisel that has become something new; the sculptor has undergone a process of becoming in producing his masterpiece, he has fulfilled a formerly unfulfilled capacity within himself. For in these human beginnings the process of becoming wraps its arms around both cause and effect to pile wonder on wonder and yet leave the mystery intact, the mystery of the beginning of that which becomes both in the cause and the effect, the mystery of the beginning not of becoming but of being itself.

Difficulty for Beginners

Beginnings are not only mysterious they are also difficult. Perhaps it is because they are mysterious that beginnings are so hard; at least, it is a fact that it is always difficult to begin at the beginning. That is a divine way of doing things, the divine way that made the Son of God start human life as an infant. For divinity itself is the Beginning and is naturally careful of beginnings, even of human beginnings, which are, but fragments gathered up from the feasts of the past. Surely the Catholic Doctor must be careful, even exhaustively careful, of beginnings, so careful that his works must be aimed, not merely at the learned or saintly, but at those humble beginners who are his particular care as an exponent of the things that pertain to God.

Reasons for a Beginning

Beginnings are hard for us even when we ourselves are capable, the material on which we work is apt, and the work we have to do is no more than to coax to full bloom hidden beauties in the material and in ourselves. To our minds, the uncreated beginning faced the extreme difficulty, not of drawing out hidden powers, but of establishing, that which is. Beginners in the way of God, which is to say beginners in the way of human living, face a man-made difficulty that springs from the reluctance of their teachers to begin at the beginning, a difficulty that is only hinted at when we call it a lack of order in the presentation of truth. That reluctance is not difficult to understand, there is an attractive, although completely false, air of excitement in dodging difficulty, shutting one's eyes to mystery and plunging into the middle of things.

Objections

That excitement has so gripped the modern mind that the beginning of things has become irritating to the point of consuming much of modern energy just in the elimination of it. These reasons for a beginning, which are sometimes called the proofs for the existence of God, have been excluded on the grounds that the human intellect cannot be trusted outside the boundaries of direct sense experience. Of course, many other objections have been made to them, scientific objections, such as their pitiful dependence on an Aristotelian science long since defunct; they are not the product of scientific investigation; they are in evident conflict with the history of religion and the theory of evolution, both of which show that the Christian God is a very modern luxury.

If the philosopher's patience is worn thin enough, he may protest that the results of such proofs are meaningless, devoid of qualitative content; which means this philosopher has been much too lazy to think. In desperation, the philosopher may simply toss the proofs out the window regardless of their truth or falsehood; the God they speak of is of no value or service to humanity. And this will be a philosopher who takes all the important things for granted.

Their Perennial Strength

These proofs may be a nuisance to one who tries, philosophically, to keep up with the times at whatever cost; but they cannot be denied modernity if by modern we mean to occupy a place in the minds and words of men of our day. They are strong enough, independent enough to live through this age and all ages. They ask no favors. They ask only what cannot be denied -- and then make the most of it.

Specifically these proofs for the existence of God start with a simplicity worthy of the divinity they demonstrate, demanding just two things, a fact evident to the senses and the first principles of the intellect. Understand, now, this sensible fact is not carefully selected, difficult to see or subject to controversy; but an obvious, tangible reality of experience, such a fact as the wink of an eye, the birth of a child, the withering of a leaf, the beauty of a face or the smooth flight of a bird. The first principles of knowledge demanded are only those fundamentals without which intellectual operation of any kind is impossible, the principles which are the rock bottom of being as well as of thought and without which science itself is invalid, nay unthinkable. In thoroughly modern fashion, these reasons proceed carefully, cautiously, adhering strictly to the evidence in hand. They are not dependent on a system of science, a weight of tradition or subjective dispositions to make their way in the world. They are genuine.

Their Completeness

The proofs for the existence of God do not belong on the dubious fringe of philosophy but in a place of honor; they have fought a bitter battle in defense of the intellect of man. A complete treatment of the existence of a beginning of things must always be a three-sided fight, which must be won on all fronts, or the intellect is lost. On one side are the champions of the ineptitude of man who insist that man's one distinctive power of intellect has no intrinsic value; of course it cannot prove the existence of God. At the opposite extreme is the camp of optimists and emotionalists, one group insisting the existence of God needs no proof since it is self-evident, the other tacitly admitting the intellectual incapacity of man but holding for an emotional assurance of the Supreme Being. In the middle, carrying the brunt of the offensive today, are those who champion man by destroying God, claiming there is no God, at least no such God as the Christians worship.

The fight is bitter; this is because not all men and women have the appetite for fighting, or the time and ability to carry on the fight to the end, and because so very much hangs on the outcome of the battle, infallible authority has come forth to protect those who by force of circumstance are non-combatants. By that authority, the man who cannot follow the intricacies of proof, either by reason of inability or lack of leisured time, knows beyond question that the reason of man, by its own power, can certainly know the existence of God and that God, the Supreme Being, certainly exists.

The gesture of authority is necessary, not because the truth it defends is beyond the range of the guns of reason, but because it is essential that *every* man *knows* of God's existence for his individual life, just as it is essential for the world about man that God *exists*. The thinker who has seen and grasped the proof has no need of authority; he holds that truth by a clear insight into a natural truth. This man can prove the existence of God; by that proof he has also shown that the existence of God is not self-evident, it does not rest on an emotional assurance, it does not escape the powers of the mind of man. It is a proved fact.

Preliminary Notions

Of course this man did not arrive at the proof of the existence of God effortlessly, as he might come to the point of raising a beard. The proof demands hard work, the hard work of thinking; certainly this man would have to have some preliminary notions accurately in mind before he could take a step towards the proof itself.

Potentiality and Actuality

There is, for instance, the simple, but decidedly abstract notion of potentiality and actuality, a notion that is perhaps grasped more easily by seeing it in the complex notion of change. Let us look at these notions in a rather clumsy example. Let us take a large, perfectly plain block of marble; then put a sculptor to work on it and have him make a statue of that block of marble. We say, rightly, that in the original marble block there is the potentiality of becoming a statue, the principle or aptitude for receiving this further perfection, the quality of being changed. It may be worth noting that by "perfection" here we mean any respect in which a thing can be completed or become more determinate in its being. When the process is complete, that potentiality has been realized, the marble block has become a statue.

Change, Potential, Process and Product

We call this process of realizing potentialities "becoming," and whole philosophies have been built upon it. More simply, we call it "change;" in its positive form we give it the name of "development." Whatever we call it, it is nothing more or less than the motion from potentiality to actuality, from the mere capability of receiving perfection to the perfection received. This is motion in its widest sense; it takes place in every change, of canvas and tubes of paint into a masterpiece, of a farmhand into a doctor of medicine, of an acorn into an oak, as well as in a journey from Chicago to New York. Obviously, this process of change involves three things:

(1) a potential or starting point, which is prior to the change and contains the potentiality, a thing which is already something but with the capacity for becoming something else, for receiving an added perfection

(2) the reality of the process or movement of change, which proceeds from the potential to the actual

(3) the product of the change, the actual needed perfection.

It is essential that we hold fast to the obvious fact of a distinct difference between the potentiality and its goal of realization. If this difference is denied, we are forced into a denial of both ends of a change, potentialities and actualities, or into an identification of these two. In either case we are in the impossible position of holding to a motion as eerie as a faceless smile, a motion that has come from nowhere and goes nowhere, or of holding to the absurdity that contradictories are identical, that there is no distinction between the undeveloped and the developed, between farmhands and doctors, marble blocks and statues.

The particular value of clarity in this notion of change lies in the fact that it brings out the complete necessity of explaining every realized potentiality, every perfection, by an explanation external to the realized potentiality itself. It makes more obvious the truth that a developed perfection is not its own explanation, it has not developed itself, nor is it explained by the potentiality, which it perfected.

Another value, for our purpose of proving the existence of God, is had from the difference this process of becoming, or change, brings out between the action of God and of creatures. It is on the basis of this process of becoming that we argue from effects to causes in created causes and their effects. Where the cause is divine, the fundamental question remains the same, that is, the explanation of a perfection that is not self-explanatory, that has not produced itself. In this latter case, however, it is not a question of a cause drawing a potentiality to perfection, but of a cause producing that which possesses the potentialities. In a word, the question in this case is not of the cause of becoming (or change) but of the cause of being itself; the transition is not from potentiality to actualization of potentiality, but from non-being to being.

Limitations

One other preliminary notion that must be clarified before proceeding to the actual proofs for the existence of God is the limitation of all proofs for existence. As a matter of fact, there are only two possibilities for proof of the existence of anything, the direct proof offered by sense experience, such as a man has of the existence of a door by ramming his nose against it; and the inferential or a posteriori proof, such as a detective might have of the existence of a murderer when he finds an armless paralytic dangling on a four-foot rope from a rafter fifteen feet above the floor. The detective, by his type of proof, may never come to more than an extremely great probability because it may be impossible to rule out all possibilities other than murder. Where it is possible to rule out all other possibilities, this proof by inference, the a posteriori proof, gives complete certitude.

No other proof of existence is possible, no a priori proof is valid, because existence in no way enters into the very nature of created things; we cannot argue from the nature of things to their existence, as we can argue from the nature of man to the spirituality of his soul. As we shall see, when the proof for God's existence is completed, existence does enter into the very nature of God; but we cannot presuppose that when starting off on the task of proving God does exist. In other words, a conclusion about existence cannot be drawn from premises, which do not assert the existence of anything; to assert the existence of something in the conclusion of a line of reasoning, you must assert the existence of something somewhere among the premises.

Ontological "Proofs"

The contrary is the sophism inherent in all a priori or ontological proofs for God's existence, the sophism which Kant attributed to all proofs for God's existence. He argued that some concept of God is essential at the start of any proof for the existence of God and such a concept includes the notion of

God's existence. Kant is right, of course, in maintaining that some concept of God is necessary from the very beginning of these proofs; after all, the proofs are trying to prove *something*. However, it is quite enough, for the purpose of the proofs, that that concept be no more than a statement of the absence of contradiction between God and existence; in other words, that concept, required to begin the proofs, need be no more than a construct which demands only the possibility of the union of the subject and predicate in the proposition "God exists."

Experience assures us emphatically that we *do* not have a direct sense knowledge of God's existence. When, in the course of this volume, we learn more about the divine nature, we shall see why we cannot have a sense knowledge of God. For the present, it is sufficient to accept the dictum of experience and concentrate our efforts along the only line of proof left open to us, the inferential or a posteriori proof, the proof of the cause from the effects.

The Five Proofs, the First Proof from Passivity -- Motion

The first proof proceeds from the fact of motion or, to put the same thing in another way, from the fact of the passivity of things. Its extremely simple formulation can be made in these terms, because nothing that is moved moves or changes itself, the unquestionable fact of movement or change in the world about us, forces us to conclude to the existence of a first mover who is not himself moved. That is all of the proof. Its very brevity is reason enough for a somewhat lengthy explanation of it.

The phrase, "nothing moves or changes itself," means only that a thing cannot be, relative to the same goal, merely movable and already moved, merely changeable and already changed; for the starting point and the goal of the process of becoming are necessarily different. The mere aptitude for receiving motion is not its own completion. The common sense fundamental back of this phrase, then, is simply that what is not possessed cannot be bestowed; and the very notion of potentiality is the absence of perfection that can be possessed but so far is not, for, unless we maintain that contraries are identical, a potentiality is not its actualization.

Actually this argument goes back a step farther, beyond the cause of change to the cause of that which is changed, back of the cause of becoming to the cause of being. For the immediate cause of change alone is itself in the process of becoming by its very causality; the mover of a potentially movable thing is himself moved by the very movement by which he moves this thing, he becomes something other than he was. The peddler does something to himself as well as to his pushcart when he bends his strength to its movement. Unless we come to a cause that produces that which is subject to change, to a cause that does not itself become something other than it was, the process of becoming or change cannot start. Briefly, what is in question here is not the process of motion, but the existence of that perfection, which is motion.

It is obvious, then, that the term "mover" is used of the first and of secondary movers not in an identical, but only in a proportional, sense; for the first mover is the cause of being and is himself unchanged, while secondary movers are causes of change and are themselves changed in their action. It is to this unique first mover that the argument concludes.

A not uncommon fallacy today is to suppose that since this particular movement is caused by another, this latter by another, and so on, there is no need for further explanation since it is taken for granted that the world is eternal. From this point of view, since you can never come to the end of the chain of movers, there is no mystery about the present movement. The fallacy lies in the fact that without a beginning the whole thing could not start; no one of these previous movers is sufficient explanation of itself and its effect on others, yet a sufficient explanation must be found if the fact of movement is to be intelligible, if we are not to have something coming from nothing. The haze of distance or the weight of time does not do away with the necessity of explanation any more than they offer a positive explanation. To be satisfied with this is to be satisfied with the removal of the question to more obscure quarters, comforted by its consequent vagueness. The plain fact is that unless we come to a mover that is in no way dependent we have not explained the existence of the movers who are undoubtedly dependent either for their actual movement or for the power to move, where the effects are patently present the cause ultimately explaining them is not to be denied.

Two things are to be particularly noted about this first proof for the existence of God, the narrowness of the conclusion and the independence of the argument from the element of time. The argument adheres rigidly to the limits of its premises; it concludes to a first mover unmoved, and to nothing more. There is nothing more, which can be concluded from the sensible fact of motion with which the argument started. This is because there is movement; there is a cause of cosmic movement, which is itself unmoved. The argument is not a sputtering flame to be extinguished by the simple expedient of blanketing it with centuries. There is no question here of movement beginning in time. It is not a question of a present reality demanding a cause in the past. It is simply a question of the universe as given, movement or change as experienced, and the conclusion that such a movement or change is unintelligible without a first mover communicating movement to all things. Time makes no difference. If the eternity of the world were to be proven tomorrow beyond all doubt, this proof would be in no way affected; the fact of change is there, the effect is with us, and its cause cannot be denied.

The background for the other four proofs is exactly the same as for this first one. Keeping the preliminary notions, explained above, well in mind and holding to the detailed explanation of this first proof, the others can be seen readily. The point at issue is always the same, the existence of perfection that did not previously exist.

The Second Proof, from Activity -- Causality

The second proof proceeds from causality or the activity of things. Here it is a question of the existence of an efficient cause, the external agent by whose operation a thing exists, the question of the existence of the hen that laid an egg, of the thunderbolt, which struck a man dead, the storm that has battered a ship into helplessness. The starting point is again the sensible world.

We see in that sensible world an order of efficient causes dependent one on the other for their causality the powder which propels the shell, which in turn crashes into a storage tank of gasoline, and this throwing out a sheet of flame in the heart of a city, and so on. We find nothing that is the cause of itself. Precisely because of this impossibility of a cause causing itself, the efficient causes of the sensible world force the conclusion upon us that a first efficient cause exists, which is itself uncaused.

Here it is said that it is impossible for a cause to cause itself for the same fundamental reason as was exposed in the first argument, namely, because the starting point and the goal of change, the potentiality and its realization, cannot be identical. Otherwise we are identifying opposites, saying that the potentiality is the actuality. Here again, as in the first proof, the argument is really stronger than it looks; for the only alternative is not merely identifying opposites, it is identifying non-reality with reality, non-being with being, for the transition is not from potentiality to actuality but from the purely privative condition of nothingness to existence. Here again it must be noted that the term "cause" is used, not identically, but proportionally, of the first and secondary causes.

A difficulty may be offered to this argument, the difficulty of living causes where the dependence is not so immediately obvious. And the answer is that no one living cause explains the efficacy of the species to which it belongs and from which it derives its power to cause. Yet that efficacy must have its explanation. Infinite regress get us nowhere, without the first uncaused cause there will be no effects produced by any cause no matter how many eons are placed between the beginning of things and the world of today. It is not a question of time, nor is the question made more difficult by adding on a few million years to the age of the world. Again attention must be called to the strict adherence of the conclusion to the evidence in hand, the argument concludes to the existence of a cause that is itself uncaused, nothing more. Either of these two arguments is sufficient to demonstrate the existence of God; their effectiveness is not a matter of accumulative evidence. They are merely different angles, shafts of light focusing on the same spectacle of divinity but taking their rise from different starting points in the sensible world.

The Third Proof, from Defectibility -- Contingency

The third proof proceeds from our experience of the contingency or defectibility of things. It can be stated briefly like this, if any beings exist whose essence is not one with their existence (that is, which are contingent), then a being exists whose essence is its existence (that is, an absolutely necessary being). The fact is that in the world about us we see things that can have or lose existence, that begin to exist and cease to exist, that are born and die. If everything were of this nature that is if existence is not essentially natural to anything, then nothing would ever exist; which is patently false in view of the existing world. The argument proceeds, as do the preceding ones, if things are capable of beginning to exist or of ceasing to exist, then, since they do in fact exist and cease to exist, that capability is fulfilled, that potentiality is realized, and a potentiality cannot realize itself. Much less can nothingness produce that which is the subject of realized potentialities.

The objection of physically necessary substances is answered, as was the fundamental objection to the preceding arguments. No such physically necessary being explains its own necessity but *receives it* (an actualized potentiality). So the necessity of the species is not explained by the species itself; "a multitude of contingent things do not make a necessary thing any more than a multitude of idiots make one intelligent man." This necessity must be explained by a necessary being that does not *receive* necessity, but that is its necessity. Again the element of time makes no difference. An infinite chain of beings that *receive* their necessity, or of beings which are not necessary, neither complicates nor explains the difficulty; it merely attempts to dodge the problem by hiding under the accumulation of immediate causes or the accumulation of the years.

These first three proofs have argued to the existence of God from the passivity, the activity and the contingency of things. The fourth proof argues from the perfection of things. Yet, the argument still proceeds from the world of reality, not necessarily the world of sense experience, sense impressions, but nonetheless from the world of reality. For the real world also includes the things we understand as well as the things we feel, such things as love, justice, friendship, things that we can never grow in the garden or meet on the street but which are, for all that, decidedly realities.

The perfections in question here are only the absolute perfections that carry the note of perfection in themselves, not the relative which are perfections only because of their order to something else. Examples of such absolute perfections are animality, rationality, life, existence. And these can be roughly classified by stressing the point that they are in themselves either strictly limited or completely limitless.

As examples of the strictly limited, we may mention animality or humanity. A man is no less an animal than a lion; nor has a sickly boy less humanity than a strapping giant. These things imply definitely fixed limits. They either are or are not fully possessed; there is never any question of having a little or a great deal of them. To exceed or to fall away from the fixed limit means the complete loss of that perfection. As examples of the limitless perfections, there is life, goodness, existence, and so on. If there are limits to these perfections in this or that individual or species, the limitation does not come from the perfection itself. We note the source of the limitation in our very manner of speech when we speak of *human* life and *animal* life, although it never occurs to us to speak of *human* rationality or *animal* animality.

Since it is precisely from these unlimited perfections that the proof of the existence of God proceeds, it may be worthwhile pointing out some of their characteristics. Perhaps the most noticeable is that these perfections are possessed by different kinds of being in an analogous, not an identical, way; thus, for instance, we speak of a good stone, a good fruit, a good horse or a good professor according as each has its due perfection. Obviously the goodness of the professor is not identically the same as the goodness of fruit. There is proportionality there, but not identity. The second particularly noteworthy characteristic is that these perfections are realizable in different degrees; thus, in the course of one lifetime a man may be bad, of mediocre virtue, of more than average virtue, and ultimately a saint.

The Fourth Proof, from Perfection -- Participation

The fourth proof for the existence of God can be stated succinctly. In the world about us we see these perfections existing in things in greater and lesser degrees, that is, we see things that are more and less good, more and less true, and so on; we see life within human limits, animal limits, plant limits. Now these limited degrees of limitless perfections can be explained only by the existence of something to which these perfections pertain in their fullness, something which does not possess this or that degree of goodness, truth, life, but which is, by its very nature, limitless goodness, limitless truth, and limitless life.

Certainly these limited degrees of limitless perfections are not explained by the natures, which possess them. For what flows from the essential principles of a nature is had in its fullness; humanity is not something a man achieves after a long struggle. Moreover, perfections which flow from nature does not vary, the spoiled lapdog is no less an animal as the days pass, the puppy does not grow into his animality. Yet, as a matter of fact, in the world about us these limitless perfections of goodness, life and the rest are not had in their fullness and they vary with an infinite variety.

The explanation, then, must be sought outside of the natures, which possess a limited edition of a limitless virtue, that is, in some extrinsic source, which has the perfection perfectly. Otherwise we meet the fundamental obstacle erected by an identification of contraries, of a potentiality bringing about its own realization, indeed, of the absence of perfection bringing about the presence of perfection. In a word, these limited editions of limitless virtues are *received* virtues; in the ultimate analysis, they are explicable only by some being who has not received them but to whom they belong, in their limitlessness, by the very nature of that being. Nor is this a question of a jump from the ideal to the real order. These effects, human life, the goodness of a man, are decidedly in the real order. It is not a matter of having an ideal rule by which we may measure these perfections; but of having a real, existing cause by whose action these realities have been brought into being.

This fourth proof proceeded from multiplicity to unity, from the multiplicity of shared or received perfections to the unity of essentially possessed perfection. The fifth proof proceeds from an ordered multiplicity to an ordering unity. The order of the world, which is at the starting point of this proof, furnished one of the most constant evidences of the existence of God to men through the ages. It appealed to Greek poets and philosophers; in unphilosophic form it was preserved in the Sacred Writings of the Jewish heritage; primitive peoples appealed to it in their origin myths. It has been not only one of the most ancient of the proofs but one of the most popular. It has been accepted as genuine by the uneducated who were unable to follow its philosophical implications; and, at the same time, was the only proof given a measure of respect by the great Kant.

It was perhaps to be expected that modern philosophy, with its contempt for the past should most strenuously assail this particular proof. Some will say that it was destroyed by the theory of evolution which, telling a tale of the process of development, made unnecessary all explanation of the beginning of that process. Again, the facts of reality are said to be adequately explained by blind chance or by necessity. We shall look at these last two modern (and ancient) objections more closely after we have seen the proof itself.

The Fifth Proof, from Order -- Finality

The fifth proof for the existence of God proceeds just as the other four have, demanding no more, resting on just as solid a foundation. It has the same starting point of facts in the world in which we live; it makes use of the same fundamental principle of reason and of things, namely, that opposites are not identical. Here the point in question is the existence of an order; the search for its explanation leads us to a supreme intelligence.

The argument might be phrased briefly like this. In the world about us we see things devoid of intelligence acting for an end, a fact which is evident from their always, or generally, acting in the same orderly way to attain that which is best for them. Evidently these actions are placed, not by accident, but on purpose. As things devoid of intelligence do not act for an end unless they be directed by some intelligence, we must conclude that a supreme intelligence exists which directs all natural things to their end.

An immediately obvious difficulty against this argument seems to be that it presumes the order of the world; this order is by no means a fact of experience. If there is such an order in the world, we have not discovered it yet. As a matter of fact, this objection has its roots in the lush soil of confusion, the confusion of external and internal finality. To solve the mystery of external finality we would have to know all the answers to such questions as the external reason for the bite of a mosquito, the existence of a snake, the destruction wrought by a hurricane. We simply do not know these things; certainly we do not know all of them and probably we never shall. It is asking a good deal to demand an exhaustive measurement of divine plans by such an instrument as the mind of a man. As a matter of fact, we do not have to plumb the mystery of external finality for the purposes of this argument.

It is quite sufficient that we establish the fact of internal finality that we can and do know without a doubt. We do know that the eye is constructed for purposes of seeing, the car for hearing; that a mosquito bites for purposes of nourishment that the snake's fangs are weapons of defense, and so on. Knowledge such as this is sufficient for the starting point of this fifth proof for the existence of God. Indeed, only one such instance of internal finality would give grounds enough for the proof. This fact of internal finality is quite sufficient to absolve this argument from the charge of anthropomorphism, which some philosophers have leveled against it. The argument does not demand that we search the soul of a snake or a mosquito to unearth motives, intentions or plans; it asks merely that we recognize the fact of a constant order of cause to effect.

This internal order is not to be explained by chance. Such an explanation is an insult to common sense, my ear might just as well have turned out to be an organ of smell; on such grounds, is it not surprising that so many animals have ears? The ratio of the chances for a simultaneous chance development of the thirteen conditions immediately necessary for sight has been figured out as 9,999,985 to 15; yet the thing happens every day!

Putting aside the appeal of common sense, which is strangely suspect by the modern philosopher, the explanation of the order of the world by chance is philosophically unsound. Certainly chance exists. It is just chance that a bald-headed man is caught in a thunder-shower without his hat; but obviously if there were no reason for his being out, no reason for the shower, the heavy drops would not now be smacking off the smooth surface of his head. In other words, the very existence of chance presupposes the existence of the essential; chance is no more than the clash of two causes attempting to pursue their own purposive ways; it is an accident which happens to the essential, not which explains or does away with the essential. If everything happens by chance, then all nature is reduced to the level of the accidental; things are not essentially what they are, but only accidentally so, the mirage may melt away before the groping fingers of our mind.

Such an explanation is no explanation at all; it is a contradiction. It is the by now familiar absurdity of explaining the perfect by the imperfect, the greater by the less, order by the lack of order. To put it bluntly, it identifies opposites potentiality with its realization or potentiality with the lack of all being. Additionally, we are faced with the old dilemma of denying the potentialities of the medical student and the perfections of the doctor or of denying the difference between the two; that is, we are back to the impossible attempt to deny facts.

The modern, intent on dodging the infinite, is not at all dashed by the breakdown of an explanation, which he will confidently use again as soon as the thunder of reason's guns has died down. For the moment he solves the problem by denying it, the order of the world is explained by the necessity of nature; God is unnecessary because the world is self-sufficient. In plain language, this means that order is discernible in the world, science can continue with its investigation of this order, because things are what they are; this is their nature, they are determined by necessary physical laws to this way of being and of acting, nature itself supplies the necessary determination.

No real question is solved by pretending it does not exist, and this is a real question. The solution offered on the grounds of necessity merely pushes the question back. Where is the source of this determination, this necessary inclination to determined action? What is the source of the necessity of nature and of physical laws? Obviously it does not explain itself; chance will not do as an explanation; the only possible solution is a cause above nature, an intelligence that is supreme. Not any intelligence will do. For if that intelligence is not supreme, then it is not intelligence but a nature which *has* intelligence, that is, a nature determined, inclined, ordered to know; and we have the same problem all over again -- whence comes this determination, this inclination, this order? This ultimately explanatory intelligence must *be*, not *have*, intelligence; it must not be ordered to knowing but must be its own knowledge.

A Posteriori Arguments

Such are the proofs for the existence of God. They have their foundations deep in the solid earth while their superstructure sweeps up to the heights of divinity. These proofs are not airy abstractions, they are not vague constructs made to substitute, in the dim light of argumentation, for solid reality. They are inferential proofs, a posteriori proofs, inductions based on the facts of the sensible world and the first principles of reason. The facts upon which they are based are in no sense disputed facts; given the movement of an eyelash, the perfection of a stone or the contingency of a sigh, these proofs hold. Surely, in all common sense, the foundation asked from the senses for these proofs cannot be denied.

On the other hand, the principle of reason involved in these proofs is no less indisputable. It cannot be denied without the denial of all intellectual activities, without the denial of the world of reality; indeed, it cannot be denied without being affirmed. For this principle is simply that a thing is what it is, a thing cannot be and not be at the same time, it cannot be itself and something else; in other words, the principle insists that differences are not identities, that potentialities are not their actualizations, that non-being is not identical with being.

Independently Sufficient

The philosopher who, for reasons best known to himself, decides to challenge these proofs has entered a war of cosmic proportions; fortunately for himself, he cannot win. Such a victory would be his own annihilation. These proofs are not aimed at a cumulative effect; they are totally different from the mass of arguments gathered in support of the hypothesis of evolution, they are not the frail threads woven into the strong cloth of a prosecuting attorney's circumstantial argument. From all of them or from any one of them, the existence of God is established; from any one of them as a starting point, it can be shown that God is existence itself, the perfect being, *ens a se*.

Strictly Limited to Evidence

No fault can be found with their procedure, for they adhere rigidly to the evidence in hand and conclude within the proper limits of this evidence. The knowledge they give is not that of probability, not even of very high probability; rather it is knowledge of metaphysical certitude, excluding every other possibility, leaving only the first mover, the first cause, the necessary being and so on as the ultimate answer to the facts of the world of reality.

Implications

That these proofs have been shrugged off as meaningless to men, devoid of qualitative content, is something the thinking man will always be unable to understand; and for the very good reason that such an attitude is unintelligible. The following chapters will bring out at length the implications of these notions; but without further elaboration these arguments bow down under the weight of the ripe fruit of profound significance. Thus, for instance, the fact of the existence of a first unmoved mover means that there is no movement, from the crushing force of a tidal wave to the rise and fall of a breast in sleep which does not depend every instant on God; there is no change, from the imperceptible coloring of a leaf in autumn to the upheaval of a social revolution in which God does not play a major part. The existence of a first uncaused cause means that in the swaying struggle of men's lives, the triumphs of their greatest thoughts and works, their masterpieces, their literature, their architecture, the soarings of the poet or the crisp command of the soldier, there is no instant from which God can be excluded. No walls are thick enough, no wastes lonely enough, no army powerful enough, no governmental edict sweeping enough, no hatred bitter enough to exclude the action of the first cause.

Significance of the Proofs

The existence of an absolutely necessary being means there is a divine sustaining hand whose withdrawal means annihilation; it means that we cannot contact anything of reality without confronting divinity; that God is closer to us than we are to ourselves, that every moment of life, every particle of dust, every stitch of a garment is permeated with divinity or it could not continue to be. That there is an all perfect being means that all the beauty, the love, the goodness that lift the heart of a man out of himself are but shadows of the infinite on the pool of life, vague hints of the ineffable that lies at the beginning and end of life. That a supreme intelligence exists makes it plain that the hairs of our head are indeed numbered; that there is no step, no breath, no success or failure that is without its meaning, without its place in a divine plan, a supreme order, that necessarily goes beyond the human mind's power of assimilation.

Real Mystery of Beginnings

These proofs may be attacked as wild abstractions of reason without solid foundation or as cold reasonings that have no meaning, no interest to men. Both accusations are completely false, these are scientific proofs based on the world of reality; they are of an inexhaustible significance and interest to men. If the truth were honestly faced, it would be evident that the real grounds for the modern unease in their presence is the fact that they lead the mind of men to the ultimate mystery. Every beginning is mysterious because every beginning has a drop of the exotic perfume of divinity on its garments.

Every beginning is a bridge spanning the chasm between what can be and what is, by its very existence proclaiming the perfection and the mystery of its builder, the ultimate Beginning who laid the foundations upon which every such bridge must be built. The most prosaic beginning intrigues our mind. For the humblest beginning poses a question that only divinity answers and only divinity can fully understand that answer. By a beginning something has come into being that did not exist before; it is a sleight of hand trick, a bit of magic that cannot be true, a mouse giving birth to a mountain unless we come to the Beginning that never began and always is, to the limitlessness that explains the limited, to the utterly independent which is the sole support of the dependent. When we have arrived at that ultimate answer, we are face to face with the incomprehensible precisely because we are in the presence of the limitless.

Non-Mysterious Substitutes

To the man who confusedly identifies human excellence with absolute supremacy, this sort of thing is intolerable; what overflows the measure of the human mind simply cannot exist, for this would be a refutation of the excellence of man. Some other solution must be had, something not mysterious, something that can be weighed, measured and put in its place by the human god of the universe. It may be this man will try to satisfy his mind, and his heart, by the absurdities of order explained by chance, by the blindness of necessity that has no source, or the deceit of substituting a process for an explanation. But such things can satisfy the mind of a man only by destroying it; they do not solve the problem of a beginning, they dodge it, deny it, destroy it, whereas the mind of man can be satisfied only with an answer. If we are to have that answer, we must face the fact of mystery, for mystery can be eliminated only at the cost of eliminating the beginning and so eliminating all that follows from that beginning. Perhaps, some day, the modern man will learn that mystery is not the prison of the mind of man it is his home.

📖 CHAPTER III -- THE INEFFABLE 📖
(Q. 3-11)

1. Limitations of speech,

    (a) By the violence of passion.

    (b) By the ignorance of listeners.

    (c) By the sublimity of the concept.

2. Philosophy's unspeakables,

    (A) The unknown God of the Christians,

        (1) The enemy of modern politics.

        (2) The feeble governor.

        (3) The pious hypocrite.

        (4) The out-dated divinity.

        (5) The stranger to a changed world,

            a. A world of new knowledge and interests.

            b. A world of new philosophy.

            c. A world in flux.

    (B) The unknown man,

        (1) Not a corrupt puppet but a supreme lord.

        (2) But a vulnerable, ignorant, despairing lord.

3. The ineffable God,

   (A) The obvious perfections of God in general.

   (B) The perfections in detail,

      (1) The simplicity of God.

      (2) The perfection of God,

            a. The difficulty of incompatibility.

            b. Virtual, formal and eminent perfection.

      (3) The goodness of God.

      (4) The infinity and ubiquity of God.

      (5) The immutability and eternity of God.

      (6) The unity of God.

4. Unspeakable modern gods,

   (A) A subjective god.

   (B) A finite god.

   (C) An undeveloped god.

   (D) A pantheistic god.

Conclusion,

      1. The crisis of the ages.

      2. The modern choice.

      3. Evaluation of the choice.

📖 CHAPTER III -- THE INEFFABLE 📖
(Q. 1-11)

Limitations of Speech

Undoubtedly there is some advantage in a blind man's inability to watch with anxious impotence as his words tread their dangerous way to the mind of another, plodding ineptly, their frail strength weighed down with the heavy burden of thought. Yet, then neither can he detect the garbling of the message, the complete perversion of misunderstanding or the meaninglessness of a word that has lost its burden on the way. Therefore, of course he misses the incalculable advantage of rushing a host of other messengers immediately in the hope that one will make the crossing safely, of supplementing the gawky word with a swift flash of an eye, the grace of a smile, the sincerity of a gesture that say so much more than will fit into a word.

That words are poor messengers is evidenced by the wholehearted support we give them whenever such support is possible. Where the words must stand alone, in a letter, a telegram, a book, we put them down in fear and trembling; but then, they are the best messengers we have, so we make the most of them. Where they actually break down we are brought up short in the realization of our helpless dependence on them.

Violence of Passion

Indeed, they do break down. The man who is so angry he sputters may be so angry he is incapable of forming words; or it may be he can find no words staunch enough to contain the thunderbolts he would like to hurl. Certainly a man consumed by hate is silenced by a bitterness too great for words; the coward is a victim of nameless fears, fears so deep and so violent that they will never have a name. These passions, and many others, stir up within a man the literally unspeakable things, things that pass beyond the boundaries of speech and so are necessarily imprisoned in the heart of their victim; his fight against them must always be a lonely battle.

Ignorance of Listeners

A tourist, whose rugged independence forces him to abandon the protective offices of his guide, soon discovers a quite different example of the breakdown of words. He may ruin his disposition and hoarsen his voice before it dawns on him, but eventually he will come to recognize the fact that shouted words in his own language do not solve the difficulty. In the same line, but much more befuddling, is the professor's difficulty when his words bounce off his students as although they were wearing thought proof vests, when example, illustration, contrast, synonymous repetition do nothing at all to the wall of blankness that protects their minds from his incursions. However, these difficulties of communication are not insuperable; time, patience and work should clear them up. There is yet another case of the breakdown of words that no amount of effort can overcome.

Sublimity of the Concept

A feeble example of the impossibility of squeezing the ineffable into the confines of words is had in the almost tangible silence that envelopes a moment of crucial parting of those whom love has made one, that moment when we put the whole burden of speech into a tight, lingering handshake, a desperate embrace, or the hopeless silence of tears. Here there are things to be communicated, but things too sacred, too deep, too wide for words. Moreover, there is that mysterious moment of intellectual maturity when reason's intuition sees antinomies merge and still remain distinct, an insight that must always remain utterly personal because it surpasses words. Nevertheless, if human love and human knowledge of created things reach heights too sublime for the plodding steps of words, obviously human love and human knowledge of the limitlessness of the uncreated soar to levels where words are almost a profanity of the concepts they might attempt to express. A light can be so bright that it destroys sight, a sound so loud it deafens the ears; and there can be a truth so great it defies the messengers of truth, which are words; and that truth is the truth about God.

Philosophy's Unspeakables

There is, then, an infinite chasm between the unspeakable things that are too base, too irrational for words and the ineffable things that are too high, too intelligible for the framework of speech. The chasm, however, does not stop the modern philosopher who has had so much practice identifying contradictories and laughing logic out of court. He has bridged the chasm by making the ineffable divinity an unspeakable thing.

The Christians' Unknown God

The picture he draws of the Christian God is revolting enough to drive any man to atheism; but the paint he uses for the picture is not squeezed from the tubes of facts, rather it is the free-flowing, bodiless stuff of an imagination gone wild. To him the Christian God is the embodiment of tyrannical absolutism. In our modern political ideas there is no room for this sort of thing; men can no longer be looked on as the slaves, the puppets of a Caesar-like God living in epicurean felicity while his underlings drag out their lives in misery. What kind of a god is this, they say, who governs less wisely than a dishonest member of a corrupt political machine? Their god must be constantly striving, however unsuccessfully, against evil, or they will disown him. They have no sympathy for the hypocritical god who covers an essential corruption of man with the bright cloak of trust, leaving the essential rottenness untouched. If god is not battling against evil, even physical evil, but rather is pretending that the evil is not there, then he isn't much of a god and we shall get along without him.

Outdated

The modern philosopher protests so much against God that he creates the suspicion he is having a hard time convincing himself; the longer and louder he protests, the more unsound are the reasons he offers. He argues, for instance, that God should be, if not as variable as fashions at least as changing as the ages. So in one age an idea of God is completely satisfying while, in the succeeding ages, an entirely new one is necessary to satisfy men. No belief retains its divinity unchanged through different generations; our race has changed, so our God must change. The Christian idea of God is old fashioned, an aloof, rigid idea; it is the notion of a God incapable of participation in human affairs, sublimely above them and, at least as far as concrete evidence is concerned, not so intimately worried about them.

A World in Flux

Our world has changed. The views of the men and women of that world have changed. Our instruments of investigation are vastly improved, our methods of inquiry are better, more accurate; and the particular interests involved are quite different, for the things we seek and discover were not objects of inquiry for our Christian ancestors. We need a new god. Our philosophy today is different; philosophers today are not Theo-centric but homocentric. Their chief interest is not God but man; they have a new conception of the supernatural, the bible and Christ. Of course that conception does not leave much of the supernatural, of the bible or of Christ; but it has the one indispensable quality, it is new. To match it, we must have a new concept of god. Moreover, we envision the world as dynamic, reality as dynamic; the world and reality are not stable but a mysterious flow sweeping on to yet unsuspected perfections. The absolute God of the Christians simply will not do for this changed point of view.

Not a Puppet but a Lord

The plastic surgeon of philosophy who does not hesitate to do a face-lifting job on God could hardly be content with man as God made him. The finished product would move the mother of men to deny her parenthood indignantly; and no one could blame her. Man is no longer the puppet and slave of God; he is the supreme lord of the world. Apparently there is no medium. Yet, for all his exalted position, he is a bedraggled figure. Physical evil, sickness and death, are his supreme misfortunes; that is to say, he is so highly vulnerable that he must slink through life in terror of ill health, a blow on the head or the crack of a gun which would utterly destroy him and his happiness. He is an ignorant fellow, his knowledge limited to a suspicious acceptance of history, the cluttering details of science and the vague findings of the collective judgment of men, although he may get an irrational lift out of that emotional thing called religious experience.

If this ignorant, frightened creature exercises his unhappy privilege of looking beyond the sunset of today his eyes focus on the goal of all his terrified living oblivion; and the gates are thrown wide to despair.

A Despairing Lord

The philosophical plastic surgeon may run his caressing eyes fondly over the product of his surgery; certainly no one else can, least of all a philosopher whose chief interest is truth. This is much too high a price to pay that the modern philosopher be happy. This monster he has created is not a Christian man, indeed is not any kind of man. The corruption allegedly fixed on man by Christianity got much too late a start to deserve the name Christian; Christianity began before the sixteenth century. The philosophical plastic surgeon started out to remove a blemish that was non-existent and ended by utterly disfiguring the image of God whose treasures were so deeply buried within the impregnable fortress of his soul as to be secure from all but himself, whose mind could leap the boundaries of sense, of time and space, whose goal was eternal life, a goal worth much more than the struggles, failures, discouragements and dashed hopes that have to be faced in the living of life. This unspeakable thing created by modern philosophy is not man as we know him, as men and God have known him from the beginning.

Still less are the God modern philosophy attacks, the God whose existence Thomas proved in the preceding chapter of this volume. As Thomas knew Him, the God of the Christian was not a being from whom a reasonable man would recoil in horror; rather this God is a being to enthrall the heart of a man, a being for whom man would leave all things and lose his life to have all things and to save his life. This is the God whose ineffable nature and divine messages engaged the minds and hearts of Fathers, doctors and theologians down the centuries; who was the inspiration of the saints, the courage of the martyrs, the purity of the virgins, the charity of all men; this was the God who came from Mary's womb to die on the Cross that men might have more abundant life.

The Ineffable God

Such a God is well worth the knowing. In this chapter we propose to give a rough description of Him, a description adequate enough to allow us to recognize divinity, yet totally inadequate from the point of view of the rich personality of God. Just as we might describe a man by talking of his dark hair, his blue eyes, his long swinging stride yet know full well that only deep acquaintance, solid friendship and even the full consecration of love can make that man really well known, so we describe God as simple, utterly perfect, good, infinite, present everywhere, unchangeable, eternal, one; knowing well that only eternal vision and unending love can dissipate the haze which shrouds divinity's heights from the mind of men.

God's Perfections in General

This list of divine perfections is by no means exhaustive. We shall learn more of God as we progress further and further with the analysis of the divine nature. This is merely the brief, muttered formula of introduction. There is much still to be said of God's knowledge, of His will, His mercy, His providence and His justice, all these will be taken up in the succeeding chapters of this book.

The particular attributes selected for treatment in this chapter were chosen as the most obvious implications in view of the proof for the existence of God in the last chapter, the proof of the existence of a first unmoved mover, the first uncaused cause, the absolutely necessary being, the absolutely perfect being, the supreme intelligence at the root of the order of the world.

It is to be noted that our knowledge of these divine perfections is not arrived at by way of "religious experience," they are not the projections of faith states, of self-hypnotism, they are not the ethereal transports of the poet or the rich imaginings of pious souls; they are not the result of an outlook, an age, a political or scientific theory. They are rigid deductions, implications from an established fact. The additional implication here, is to be taken in its full strong sense, the sense of being contained, wrapped up in what has been previously established. There are, it is true, other senses of the word, senses that have about them the unhealthy pallor of a slyness, a cowardice, of an uncleanness that shirk the bright sunlight of direct speech to haunt the alleys of suggestion, hints, indirect or double-meaning speech.

The sense in which we are using the word here is as bright as sunlight on sand, as clean as the smell of the sea; the sense in which, for example, the motherhood of Mary is implied in the statement "Christ was the son of Man." In this same sense it follows that, since I am a man, I am a rational animal; since this person is a woman, she is not a man. These are inescapable implications whose validity rests entirely on the validity of their foundation.

Simplicity

The most obvious implication from the proofs for the existence of God is that God is in no sense a composite or complex being; He is wholly simple. Before going on to establish the obvious character of this divine attribute of simplicity, it might be well to admit frankly that we have done such strange, contradictory things to simplicity that God might consider this particular attribute a dubious compliment. There is a great difference between the simple things we pity or patronize for their simplicity and the simple things to which we pay the tribute of profound respect and admiration. A simple-minded man is one who, through lack of ability or opportunity, does not know any better; whereas a richly simple gown is the result of supreme ability and unlimited opportunities. The simplicity of the child's essay is altogether different from the simplicity of the literary craftsman's easy grace with words. In the one case we see simplicity as the mark of imperfection, in the other, as the stamp of genius; in both cases we are right, but it must be seen that we are using the word simple in decidedly different senses.

Simplicity is a badge of imperfection and will remain so in the world of created things where perfection must be measured in terms of potentialities and their realization. Man stands at the peak of the physical universe precisely because of his rich potentialities; his life is richer, fuller, as more of those potentialities are realized, as even greater potentialities are acquired, in a word, in proportion to the increased complexity of his life. He may cast an envious glance at a cat sleeping in a sunny window; life is so simple for a cat. However, the envy is not real; no man wants to spend his life curled up in sleep, particularly in a window.

Nevertheless, this rich potentiality, the very basis of the complexity, which makes up the perfection of created things, is itself a statement of imperfection. It implies imperfection; it is a declaration that something can still be had, that there is a void still to be filled up by someone something else. The being who has no potentialities, but only pure actuality, who is the source of all potentiality, alone escapes the stigma of imperfection and is free of the basic element of complexity. This being is utterly and completely simple; this is the being who receives nothing but gives all things. The simplicity we so admire and respect in created things, the simplicity that smacks of genius, is not really simplicity at all but the appearance of simplicity; men have succeeded in giving to rich complexity a smooth unity by a perfect coordination to a single end and we salute the faint image of divinity thus produced.

To say that God is of simple means, in the concrete, that He is in no sense composite. He is not, nor has a body; He is not a golden calf or a painted idol. He does not have divinity as man has humanity; He is divinity. His nature is not a cup filled to overflowing with existence, He is not full of life; He is existence, He is life. There are no family quarrels of the gods; there is nothing in God upon which to base a difference in divine nature. He does not grow fat or thin or red in the face; His thought is not a procession of concepts as ours is, for there is nothing accidental, transient, unessential in God. Because He is simple He cannot enter into composition with others as sugar does with coffee or oxygen with hydrogen; He cannot be immersed in the inert mass of matter like Bergson's *élan vital*, expending His divine life fighting free with all the agony of a boy fighting his way out of sleep. God is simple because He is the *first* the completely *independent* source of all being.

Perfection

One of the greatest concentrations of perfection the world has seen was to be found in that small house of Nazareth when Gabriel saluted the Immaculate Virgin; yet even in this sublime company there was the specter of imperfection, which is limitation that haunts all creation. The angel had the potentialities of successive thought that all eternity would not exhaust; the virgin had the undeveloped potentialities of mind and heart that are the task as well as the glory of human nature; both had the imperfection inherent in the limited character of their respective nature, for the angelic no less than the human nature has its boundaries fixed. The most intimate glimpse of the limitless perfection of God given to man on this earth is to be had in the picture of the Madonna with the divine child in her arms; for there is all the perfection of human nature along with its inevitable limitation, but there also is the unfathomable abyss of the boundless source of all perfection.

There is simply no place for imperfection in God. In Him, there are no potentialities to be realized, as all potentialities must be realized, by something other than themselves. He is absolutely independent because He is first; all others depend on this first cause Who cannot depend on any other without ceasing to be first. More than that, He has in Himself the perfections of everything else that ever has; ever will, indeed, that ever could exist. Unless He is their cause they cannot be; He cannot be the cause of perfections that are not in some way already His.

Virtually, Formally and Eminently

When we come down to detail, the argument for the utter perfection of God seems to involve insuperable difficulties. If we try to picture God as a combination of the ferocity of a wolf and the pathetic friendliness of a dachshund, the beauty of youth and the serenity of age, the grandeur of a sunset and the peace of night we shall drive ourselves insane. Still, why should we try this sort of thing in our thought concerning the divinity when we are so careful to avoid it in our thought of the created universe? We know that a father contains within himself all the perfections of the human nature of his son and in exactly the same way; if we had to put this in a technical phrase, any journeyman philosopher could tell us that these perfections were possessed formally. We are quite sure an acorn contains the perfections of an oak; but we do not try to picture the oak's huge trunk and stubborn leaves as packed into the tiny confines of an acorn. We know these perfections do not exist in the acorn in the same way as in the oak; they are had, not formally, but virtually, radically, in the acorn. We do not hesitate to attribute the perfections of a poem to its author; but we do not make the absurd mistake of expecting the poet's mind to get musty, yellow with age, or covered with dust on a library shelf. It is not the poet that leaps out of the frightened child's mouth in elocution class. In this case the poet possesses the perfections of his poem but in a completely superior manner, eminently.

It is in this last fashion, eminently, that the perfections of all creation are found in God; He is the cause of them all, they exist in Him, not virtually, not identically, but eminently. The conclusion that all reality is godlike is quite true. What we see in the world of existence, of beauty, of goodness, of grace and all the rest is had from God, Who is overflowing with perfection. These creatures share, and participate in the perfection of God. This was a truth close to the heart of Francis of Assisi and Martin de Porres, a truth that made all irrational creation and the whole world of men a lover's note to be read slowly, tenderly, repeatedly, to be treasured caressingly until the writer in person made plain all the beauties that could not be squeezed between the lines. It is right that the strength of a storm at sea, the innocence of a child, the calm of a country twilight should stir us to the depths of our being for these are shadows of divinity passing by.

It might be well to note here, for accuracy's sake, that we speak of divine attributes in a double sense, often without realizing the distinction. Thus when we state these attributes positively, such as simplicity and perfection, we are speaking only by way of analogy; that is, we do not mean to attribute these things to God in exactly the same way in which they belong to men but in an infinitely superior manner. On the other hand, when we state them negatively, insisting, for example, that God is incomposite and devoid of all imperfection, we are talking literally, univocally, and expect our words to be taken without qualification.

Goodness

Another caution that may not be amiss is that we have an entirely accurate notion of the particular attribute under discussion. Thus, to speak of the goodness of God in the sense of sanctimoniousness is to divorce the discussion from reality, as, well as to flavor it distastefully. The notion of goodness adds nothing to being but the smack of desirability, that is, a thing can be good, desirable, only insofar as it is possible or thought to be possible; it can be pursued and enjoyed only insofar as it has being. We do not desire an automobile that can be folded up and dropped into a purse. We can see the advantage of a servant with five arms, but we do not advertise for such a one. We do, however, have a real desire for real things for friends, a ham sandwich, new clothes, and knowledge. It is this smack of desirability that goodness adds to being, which is at the root of all activity.

Activity, then, is striving for the desirable thing, for something good; boredom, on the other hand, is the absence of knowledge of, and interest in the good and is the nearest approach to stagnation to be found among living things. As a matter of fact, everything in the world has its desirable something, its goal. Concretely that goal is the completion, the perfection, the complete fulfillment of the particular creature; every creature is good in proportion as it is, it is better in proportion as it has approached its goal. Briefly, a thing is good insofar as it is real. Bluff, defect, incapacity have nothing desirable about them because there is nothing real about them. Yet, He Who is the cause of all reality, the perfect Being, is the highest goodness for He is the most real Being. Not that He has goodness; rather He is goodness, as He is reality. On His goodness all other goodness is modeled, from His goodness all other goodness proceeds; all other goodness is a similitude, a participation, a limited miniature of the limitless goodness of God.

Because of the smack of desirability which goodness adds to being, God is most desirable, most lovable. So true is this that everything in the universe hustles eagerly to this goal of goodness, each in its own way, man with alert steps along the dangerous road of knowledge and love, brutes with the unerring aim of instinct, the inanimate world with the blind, plodding step of physical necessity devoid of all knowledge. For each creature in the universe is spurred on to action by the goal of its own perfection, a goal, which is nothing but a similitude, an image, a mirroring of the goodness of God.

Infinity

No limits are to be placed on the goodness of God, as no limits are to be assigned to any other divine attribute. How can you have a fence with nothing, absolutely nothing, on the other side of it? What is there of reality, that God will not have, to mark the spot where the fence must begin? Limitation is essentially a declaration of potentialities achieved or potentialities capable of achievement; without potentiality limitation is a contradiction in terms. Additionally, there can be no potentiality in God, for potentiality is a declaration of dependence. God has not received existence within the limits of a human, an animal or an angelic nature; He has not received at all, He is. The idea of reception is the idea of change, of potentiality actualized, of perfection within limits, something that our proof for His existence forced us to exclude from God. He is infinite, and He alone; for He alone is first, receiving from no one, giving to all.

Ubiquity-Omnipresence

In a very real sense, this utterly limitless God overflows the limits of the universe. He is everywhere within it, yet not contained by it. Everything in the universe comes from God; existence is His proper effect. Where anything exists, there is God. Understand, now, this is not merely a matter of God first giving existence and then abandoning the universe to its fate; He does not give us a pat on the back as we leave the corner of nothingness to jump into the ring of life, leaving us to take the blows while He shouts advice that takes none of the sting out of the blows. Existence belongs to God; as long as existence endures, there is the hand of God sustaining it as a mother supports her infant or the throat of a singer sustains his song. God is everywhere, and only God; for only God is the infinite, the first cause explaining every existent thing.

The ubiquity of God, in common with all the divine perfections, is not a cold, abstract thing meaningless to men. Its significance for human living is inexhaustible. In the concrete, it means, for instance, that God is in the surge of the sea, the quiet peace of hills and valleys, the cool refreshment of rain, the hard drive of wind-driven snow. In the cities He is in the bustling of crowds, the roar of traffic, the struggle for pleasure, for life, for happiness, in the majesty of towering buildings. In homes He is not to be excluded from the tired, drowsy hours of night, the hurried activity of morning, from the love and quarrels, the secret worries and unquestioning devotion, the sacrifice and peace that saturates a home. In every individual one of us, God is more intimately present than we are to ourselves. Every existing thing within us demands not only the existence of God but also His constant presence, from every rush of blood from our hearts to every wish, every thought, and every act. In other words, everything that is real must have God there as the explanation, the foundation, the cause of every moment of its reality.

Thomas puts this all succinctly and beautifully when he says that God is in the world, in everything and everyone in the world, by His essence, causing all things, by His presence, all things being naked and open to the eye of this intelligent cause, by His power on which everything depends, to which everything is subject.

There is in this conception a majesty that transforms the earth. The mistaken exaggerations of Eastern philosophy made men walk carefully lest, treading on a living thing, they tread on the soul of a man. We have no fear of treading neither on the soul of man nor on God; but we do live in a world vibrant with divinity. We can give a real reverence to every being because within it, supporting its very existence is the living God Himself. There is terror in this conception, the terror of moving in an atmosphere pervaded with divinity, of being ourselves wrapped about with divinity, penetrated with the infinite. There is also courage and comfort here to be had from no other source. We bar the world in general from everything but the surface of our lives; friends are allowed to enter a few rooms of our palace; love throws open the gates as far as it is given us to open them, as wide as physical signs or clumsy, stumbling, inadequate words can open our souls, as wide as sacrifice and devotion can keep those gates open. Only God can walk freely about the innermost corridors of our being. And He does. Unless He is there, we could not be.

The pessimistic pantheism of the East, to which our modern philosophy edges closer every day, distorted the truth of the intimate presence of God to the point of identifying everything with divinity. On such premises there were good grounds for pessimism. All distortions are false; this one is as absurdly false as the identification of my image in a mirror with myself or the inability to see any difference between the poet and his poem. None of the things created by God are divine; rather they are the mirrors of divinity, the effects of the divine cause that depend every instant on that cause for their reality.

Immutability

Nor is this intimate presence of God in the world to be mistaken for that tortured, twisting, developing god of the moderns that fights its way towards perfection through the struggle of the universe, changing as we change, getting better as we improve. God is altogether unchangeable. For what is change but the realization of a potentiality, the receiving of something new or the loss of something old. In God there can be no potentiality, nothing to be lost, nothing to be gained. He is pure actuality, pure being, possessing all things. He is beyond change and He alone; for He alone is first, dependent on no other, free of all potentiality.

To the modern philosopher this notion makes God completely static; if this is true, then this is a dull, stagnating, deteriorating God. His reason is not dissimilar from the reasons for a New Yorker's distaste for travel, an

Englishman's tolerance of the continent or an American tourist's amusement at the strange antics of the rest of the world. In his own little world of creatures, the modern philosopher sees clearly that there must be change for progress that immutability is closely akin to stagnation and deterioration. The point is that he is provincial enough to judge everything, even God, by the standards of that created world. It is true that change is inseparable from perfection in the world of unrealized potentialities; but it is also true that such a world is inconceivable without a Being of pure actuality; a Being Who is pure activity, Who has no potentiality, no possibility of losing or gaining but is a white flame of perfection. Such a Being is not in a state of static inertia; His is an activity so intense that change of any kind is impossible to it.

Eternity

This God did not begin; He cannot end. For both beginning and end proclaim a change, a reception or a loss, an imperfection, a dependence. He is eternal and He alone; eternal with that absolute, complete eternity of a divinely unchangeable Being.

Unity

Obviously there is only one such God. More than one demands some ground for difference something one would have and another lack; this God lacks nothing. Where would infinity stop, which has no limits that another infinity might begin? How could there be beginning or end, limitation, to the infinite perfection and pure act that is God? He is one, distinct from the world of finite, limited creatures, yet intimately within it. In the beautiful words of the Divine Office, "To the King of ages, the immortal, invisible, the only God be honor and glory forever and ever."

Unspeakable Modern Gods

This is the God rejected by modern philosophers. Caught by the glitter of their words, thousands of men and women have turned their backs on the only God and their faces to the gods of modern philosophy. What is offered to them?

A Subjective God

One group of philosophers suggests a subjective god, one of our own manufacture. To some of these, such a god would be no more than a projection of our subconscious states or of our social and racial instincts. The god-makers would be, for the most part, the weak, the oppressed, the downcast; for such a god is offered by way of compensation for inferiority. The superior man, they say, does not need this sop; but for the others, who still remain children, it is necessary that they have some enduring symbol of parental shelter to which they may run when life becomes too much for them. Others of this group suggest a deification of humanity, the spirit of a people, of the world of humanity, or of living beings taken in their associated and ideal experiences. This conception of divinity, says one of these philosophers, is best expressed by such terms as "alma mate" or "Uncle Sam!" Still others advise that we make our divinity of a quality of the world peculiarly akin to ourselves; or perhaps the material best suited is the higher reality on which we lay hold when we comprehend a truth or obey a noble impulse. These are the doctrines American universities are swallowing whole!

A Finite God

A second group of philosophers cast their vote for a finite god, not a subjective god, but one who needs our help, who is sustained by the world, whose interests are at stake in the world. God cannot be infinite, omnipotent, a static absolute if he is to work and make a difference to us. They will have a god who began but will never end; one who is not a creator, not infinite; but one, who began with the human race, grows with it, an ideal gathering up to itself the achievements of humanity.

In the last analysis, both of these are stark atheism, the name of god is a cover-all to hide the ugly body of doctrine; both are violently opposed to the solid facts. In both, there is a pathetic note, a note of weakness and of fear. The thesis paints a picture of lonely men trying to find comfort in a crowd, bundling themselves together with their fellows in the hope that somehow they will add up, not to a number of men, but to divinity; and it paints a picture of men who are not only weak but who are searching desperately for an escape from the fear of life, the fear of liberty, the fear of action.

An Undeveloped God

The third group takes a further step towards madness in advocating a kind of fluid, undeveloped god. God is the perfect in process; the principle of all struggling towards perfection through matter; yet this principle is fluid for everything real is a process of becoming. Others, within the group, insist that god is the next higher step, the empirical quality just above the highest we know; divinity, in other words, is the mechanical rabbit that lures human greyhounds into running their hearts out in a hopeless race. Maybe this undeveloped god is the finite world with its nisus[1] towards deity; maybe this god is evolution, maybe it is the spirit of rational order. Make it anything you like; but do not dare to make it divine!

A Pantheistic God

The fourth group of modern philosophers comes out frankly for a pantheistic god. Some say God is the life force identical with man and the universe. Others, not covering their shame with a blush of words, insist there is no ontological [2] separation of one being from another; and this, if it means anything, means I am my dog and my dog is God just as I am. The connection between God and the universe is an organic one.

These last two groups represent the brutal pessimism of the Orient not yet carried to its logical conclusion; logically, these opinions should lead to utter despair and offer self-destruction as the goal of human life. Both are open violations of the facts; on such a basis, obviously the universe could not exist. It is important to remember that all four of these modern ideas of God are sponsored by men of learning, honored in their universities, hailed as leaders of thought.

---

[1] This means to a goal aimed at or achieved.

[2] The school of thought concerning "being".

Crisis of the Ages

God has been crucial to the thought and life of all ages, not only the existence of God, but knowledge of Him, love and hatred of Him. Men of all ages have had to think a great deal about God, for men of all ages have had to think a great deal about a goal to which they might direct their lives. To many men in many ages, the crisis has been one of loyalty, of the heart rather than the head; the difficulty has been in resisting the lure of the world's tempting byways, and of holding fast to the path they knew to be the true one. This crisis will never be absent from the lives of men for it is the crisis of sin. Some men have failed to meet that crisis with any courage. Others will meet the same failure, but their difficulty, and the difficulty of all the sorry ones who follow after them, has not been in finding the courage to admit the truth of God and His law, but the courage to live up to the truth they admitted even although it condemned them.

The Modern Choice

In our day, as in all days, the crisis of loyalty, the crisis of sin exists. But today, on an increasingly alarming scale, men are being forced to meet another crisis, the crisis of choice, the crisis of the head more than of the heart. It is being made difficult for them to know the true God, let alone give Him their hearts, for modern leaders have set up false gods and demanded, with all the influence of their position, their learning, their skill in words, that men bow down and adore.

Evaluation

Saying that he is offered a human god, an inhuman god and the divine God might sum up the choice offered to the man of the twentieth century. The human god is the product of subjective sentiment or of communal huddling together to the destruction of personality, a god that takes the alternative forms of personal sentiment, humanitarianism or of absolutism. The inhuman god may be the intangibility of a process under the name of evolution or the absurdity of pantheism. The divine God is the Christian God some of whose attributes we have looked at in this chapter. There is, of course, no rational choice between these three. The first two have no foundation in reality or reason; they are flagrant violations of fact arrived at only as a result of the denial of reality, of reason, of the supernatural, while the last is an inescapable truth.

The choice, from man's point of view, can be stated in concrete terms. One gives immediate and complete oblivion in the crushing force of an absolutism where the individual is less than a cog, or in the vague future of the race in the name of humanity to the denial of men; the second is a matter of hiding from life in the sweet nothings of subjectivism with its promise of sure oblivion after death; the third insists on the dignity of man's personality, on its eternally vital character, it demands that man, fully responsible and with eyes wide open, carve out a personal destiny that can never end. This last is the only God, simple, perfect, infinite, unchangeable, supporting the universe and present in the depth of all that is.

◫ CHAPTER IV ◫

THE VISION OF GOD
(Q. 12-18)

1. End of the myth of man's omniscience,

    (a) The fact and its causes.
    (b) Laymen and this fact.
    (c) Philosophers and this fact.

2. Answers to the question of God's omniscience,

    (a) Negative answers,

        (l) The lazy answer -- Agnosticism.

        (2) The timid answer -- Naturalism.

        (3) The cowardly answer -- Psychological mechanism.

        (4) The proud answer -- Idealism.

    (b) Affirmative answer.

3. The Knowledge of God,

    (a) He knows Himself,

        (1) The fact.

        (2) The manner of this knowledge.

    (b) He knows everything else,

        (1) Actual and possible things.

        (2) Evil.

        (3) Infinite thoughts of angels and men.

THE VISION OF GOD
(Q. 1-11)

End of the Myth of Man's Omniscience

Not so many years ago the very educated man got up from his breakfast and turned to his researches as joyously as a child hurrying to play with the toys Christmas showered on him. It seemed that the world and all its secrets had been handed to men as castles, towers, cranes and bridges are handed to a child in the gift of a structural toy; all that was necessary was that men work patiently piecing things together and eventually they would know all things knowable. Surely no one would be mean enough to give them such a toy with some of the pieces missing; it was entirely incredible that not all the mysteries could be reconstructed from this shiny array of unlimited possibilities. So the very learned labored happily in their playrooms; and saturated with their own contentment, they were very polite to all the rest of the poor ignorant men who still talked of the inscrutable knowledge of God, the mystery of the supernatural, the intangible, spiritual truths of philosophy.

Since then someone has told these happy creatures that there is no Santa Claus. Their naive world is crumbling about their ears; and it becomes more evident, day-by-day, that some of the pieces were missing, countless pieces. Today we are not quite so sure of the sweep of our own knowledge, not at all certain that we know it all. The mechanism of the nineteenth century, the happy theory that made the gears of the world and the metallic clanking of laws almost audible, has definitely broken down; with its collapse came wholesale confusion among the better educated. Today that confusion has not been lessened by the progress of the sciences, it has been immeasurably increased; while physics and biology seem to point more and more in the direction of the purposive and the idealistic, the modern psychologies look more and more to the purposeless, the irrational, and the mechanical.

Laymen and this Fact

Such conflicting results have given pause to the brash confidence of our fathers; they have humbled us a little, slowed up our process of conclusion considerably. We are proceeding with the caution of the spoiled child after his first week in a public school. The confusion and humiliation have been good for us. A tragic note in the whole affair is that the ordinary man and woman have been completely deprived of a proper share in this confusion and humiliation. Their ordinary sources of information proceed on the old mechanistic basis as if nothing had happened, as if, somehow, they had been water-proofed against the seepage of such scandalous uncertainty from the higher levels; to the layman, the implications of the old mechanism are still established facts, he is polite or pitying to those who are not scientifically up to date, and his life is aimed earnestly at grotesque goals that enjoy a macabre existence now that the mind that sponsored them has retracted.

Philosophers and this Fact

The layman do not need to feel too lonely in his ignorance; hordes of modern philosophers are right at his side patronizing the rest of men for their unscientific neglect of the new truths that are already decrepit. At least this confusion of the mechanistic basis of life has not produced any great clarity of thought among modern philosophers. They still retain that frigid politeness and bored tolerance, characteristic of nineteenth century scholarship, in the face of such problems as the knowledge of God, of the soul, of absolute morality and all the rest of the things outside the reach of science. Perhaps the one outstanding evidence of the crash of mechanism has been a slightly more sympathetic attitude towards other explanations; that and a bewildering variety of answers to all the questions that matter.

Negative Answers, the Lazy Answer -- Agnosticism

Take, for instance, the question of God's knowledge. The modern agnostic evades the problem by shrugging his shoulders and confessing a complete ignorance, a complete inability to know the answer. Such tactics may conserve his intellectual energy, but only at the price of a flat contradiction of the facts; for surely we can know the existence, and something of the nature, of a cause from its effects, we can form some idea of the knowledge of a poet from his poem, the knowledge of an engineer from his bridge. It is not too much of an effort to raise the mind from the poem to the poet, from the bridge to the engineer, from the world to God.

The Timid Answer -- Naturalism

Certainly the naturalist is not lazy. He hustles along the road of knowledge like a boy hurrying past a cemetery at night, whistling to prove he is not afraid. Yet, he is afraid, afraid to go beyond what his hands cannot touch. He states that science and the experimental method are the only sources of truth. In either form he is contradicting the facts that he himself must live by, every day facts like our knowledge of love, of justice, of friendship, which are slippery things to slide under a microscope.

The Cowardly Answer -- Psychological Mechanism

At least naturalism tries to put up a bold front. Mechanistic psychology has quit the fight altogether; it has given up the task of facing human life with all its possibilities of failure and defeat, with all its burden of responsibilities. It is willing to surrender all man's claims to humanity, to bury his head in sub-human muck. Of course it will have nothing to do with the problem of God's knowledge.

The Proud Answer -- Idealism

The idealist is not a bluffer, neither is he a coward; he is blind. He cannot see the world, let alone raise the eyes of his mind to the cause of the world. As far as he is concerned, man can know only what is in his own mind; he can know of God only in so far as he is a part of God, or is God. He invites all men and women, not to share his blindness, but to set up havens of darkness of their own where, with no truth intruding to interrupt the game, they can play at being God, or a part of God.

All of these people agree that we can know nothing of the knowledge of God. If their particular explanations are not appealing, a man might try, without stepping outside the boundaries of a negative answer, the despair of the evolutionist's answer, that men are the only part of the life process enjoying intelligence, our knowledge is all there is. Or he might embrace the narrow provincialism of the pragmatist, the humanitarian and the humanist, the men who have little time for God because of their consuming interest in men, or who have time enough only to agree that, whatever God knows, He certainly does not know all things.

All of these opinions might be summed up in terms of the last chapter, where we saw that the world today gives us a choice between a human and an inhuman god, whereas the facts demand a divine God. For these men the question of God's knowledge is reduced to this, what can a human or a less than human god know? Obviously such a god cannot have divine knowledge.

Affirmative Answer

The affirmative answer to the question of God's omniscience is not, as has been alleged, a dream wish, the urging of the unconscious or the surging of a dumb life force; it is not made up of the sentimentalities of subjectivism; it is not mere poetry, although it surpasses the beauty and nobility of great poetry. It is not vague, hesitant, and theoretic. Above all it is not a denial of the facts. It is objectively valid, proceeding from the solidly proved fact of the existence of a first mover, a first cause, a necessary being, a perfect being, a supreme intelligence; it is simply the admission of the implications that necessarily flow from these proved truths. To admit such implications means no more than to refuse to deny the facts themselves.

The Knowledge of God, He Knows Himself

Obviously we cannot deny God knowledge of Himself without making Him less than divine. A man who knows nothing about himself needs medical attention and rest; plainly he is sick, a victim of amnesia. A man who gets himself mixed up with someone else, who imagines, for instance, that he is Napoleon or the archangel Gabriel, is evidently insane. If God is not sick or insane, He knows Himself; if, as has been shown, He is completely perfect, then He knows Himself perfectly, for ignorance of self is certainly an imperfection.

The Manner of this Knowledge

To put this truth more philosophically, we may point out that knowledge is the result of a union between the knower and the thing known. No matter how tempting the intellectual fare served by a teacher, the pupils remain immune to knowledge until such a time as their intellects touch this intellectual food. Knowledge cannot be poured into a student's head; if, as the fathers of modern philosophy maintained, there is an unbridgeable chasm between the world and the intellect, then knowledge is forever impossible. We have already proved that God is supreme intelligence; for knowledge of Himself then, all that is necessary is that He be present to His own intellect, a condition, which His divine simplicity makes it impossible to avoid. He is supremely real, therefore supremely intelligible; He is supreme intelligence, therefore supremely intelligent; He is utterly simple, so that the union of intelligible and intelligence is absolute, complete.

He Knows Everything else, Actual and Possible Things

An obvious difficulty presents itself from the fact that we do not leave our intellects at home when we go for a walk; we are certainly present to ourselves, yet we pick up the facts about ourselves like spectators. The fact is that our mere physical existence does not make us present to our intellects in the only way things can be in our intellects, that is, not physically but intelligibly, intentionally. We are potentially, not actually, intelligible to ourselves; we must judge ourselves, as we do of other men, by the activities we see ourselves engaging in. Perhaps we could sum up both the question of knowledge and of intelligibility by pointing out that all determination is a limitation both of the degree of knowledge and of intelligibility. Because the eye is determined to no one color It can see them all; if, through the instrumentality of green glasses, we determine our eyes to one color, then we can see nothing else. If a being is absolutely determined to one form, as is a plant to its own form, then it can have no knowledge whatever; if it is indetermined in the sense of being able to receive the forms of other things through sense images, as is the animal, then it can have sense knowledge; if it is free of determination to such an extent as to be able to receive all forms as intellectual concepts, then the wide horizons of the intellectual knowledge of men and angels are opened up; while if there is no determination, no limitation, whatever, as in God, there we have supreme intelligence and supreme intelligibility. There is much more to be known about an animal than there is about a plant, for the animal is less determined, less limited; there is more to be known about man than about animals, much more to be known about angels than about men. As for God, well, in the unending act of our vision of God we shall never be finished learning what there is to be known about His absolutely unlimited reality.

The frightened penitent, after his first disastrous bout with passion, can say with real honesty, "I don't know what made me do it; I never do such things." Our mask of nonchalant complacency often hides real astonishment as the thought runs through our minds, "I didn't know I had it in me." We can and do surprise ourselves, for better or for worse. However, if we picture God as gazing in astonishment at the ludicrous results of His creation we've entirely missed the comprehensive character of the knowledge of God; God cannot surprise Himself, He cannot be ignorant of anything about Himself without being imperfect and He cannot be imperfect without ceasing to be God.

That God should know all about Himself seems fair enough. That He should know all about everything else, particularly about ourselves, is an altogether different and decidedly disconcerting thing. Still, we make no objection to an architect's knowledge of a house he has designed nor to a poet's knowledge of his poem. God is the architect of the universe; He needs no instruction on the product of His creative act. He is the cause of everything of course He knows all that is.

Nor is this knowledge gathered by His peering out a window of Heaven. He needs only to look at Himself. The puzzle in this is, not that it should be so, but that we should be puzzled by its being so. The mystery of a weekend guest finding his way to the kitchen in the dark is cleared up as soon as we discover that he is the architect who designed the house. We are not at all surprised that the poet is able to explain the thought of his poem without a glance at it. Why, then, should God have to grub about the corners of the world or employ an intelligence staff to keep informed of what is going on? He knows Himself perfectly, so He knows how far His powers extend, how far they have been exercised, how far they will be exercised; all that is His product. Everything that exists was made according to the plan of the divine architect, made to the scale laid down by the mind of God; a sinner's rupture of diplomatic relations with divinity does not deprive God of a source of information. God sees men and women as they walk down the street, not by waiting for them to turn His corner, but as they and their every step exist in the divine mind. Nor is this an indirect or vague knowledge. Every instant of existence, every bit of reality is immediately dependent on the divine cause; moreover, every item of perfection in the universe is an imperfect mirroring of the unblemished perfection of divinity. Knowing the perfect perfectly, God knows immediately all the shades of imperfection, of limited sharing of that perfection; otherwise His very knowledge of Himself is imperfect.

This all embracing divine knowledge is the cause of all existing things, past, present and future, for they exist because of the model in the mind of the divine architect joined to the divine decree which called them from nothingness. As we have seen, in the second chapter of this book, there is no other explanation of the world about us. God's knowledge of existing things, then, is not had by reasoning closely from a principle to a conclusion. He does not forecast them as an astronomer foretells an eclipse of the moon; God is eternal, the divine model is eternal, the divine decree is eternal and this eternity encompasses time like a cloak thrown about it. In one glance at His divine self, everything is naked and open to the eyes of God.

Evil

To say that God knows all possible things, things that could have been but will not be, is only to insist on God's knowledge of the extent of His power, His comprehensive knowledge of His own perfection; for unless He knows in how many ways His perfections can be shared, imitated, mirrored by creation, He does not fully know Himself. There is absolutely nothing that can escape the mind of God. The thoughts of men and angels run the length of an endless road with a speed beyond measure; but the road is not long enough, nor the speed great enough to outdistance the divine mind upon which every thought, like every other reality, depends intimately, ceaselessly, ultimately. Evil is a gaping hole in reality; unless that hole is known, reality itself is not perfectly known. Obviously we do not know a man's face if we do not know the hole in the middle of it, we do not know a fence unless we are also cognizant of the boards missing from it here and there. Evil is a defect, a privation of good; God's perfect knowledge of good necessarily includes a knowledge of the way in which good can be or is defective.

Future Conditioned Things

Even the knowledge of those future conditioned things that might happen but do not is at the fingertips of God. The debutante of five years ago has had her mind made up for years to devote herself to marriage, if someone asked her; as the years go on, with the condition still unfulfilled, hope does not die in God's heart. He has not been on tenterhooks all this time; the very condition which hides in the halls of the future depends upon the first cause of all that is or can be, not only upon its own proximate causes.

The Unvarying Character of this Knowledge

If God is completely above all change, as He certainly is, then He does not forget things, His knowledge does not ebb and flow, He does not acquire new knowledge by keeping His eyes open, through long periods of concentration, or by eavesdropping. In a sense there are many ideas in the mind of God, in the sense, that is, that God knows many, indeed, all things; but He knows these things through His own divinely simple essence, not through a multitude of concepts. More accurately, He is His intelligence. His knowledge; and He is the immutable first.

We can sum up all this doctrine on the knowledge of God in the one profound statement, God is truth. For truth is in an intellect when that intellect knows a thing as it really is; truth is in a thing, when it measures up to the intellect which caused it; God's essence not only measures up to His intellect, it *is* His intellect; God's intellect not only knows His essence, it *is* His essence. This is the immutable first truth, the foundation of all other truths. Every other truth participates in this first truth or ceases to be truth, the world of reality as it measures up to the divine exemplar; created minds when, measuring up to the world of reality, they get a glimpse of the divine exemplar. When we touch upon truth we are in the shadow of divinity; when we embrace it, we are ennobled by the contact to a degree easily recognizable by all men. In the world of reason, love of truth produces the philosopher; in the world of affairs it produces the gentleman; in the world of grace it produces the saint. The respect given these men is the spontaneous tribute given to divine messengers. Humanity doffs its cap or makes its curtsey and goes its way with renewed hope; God is truth.

Some Sources of Modern Difficulties

Thus far, in exploring the divine knowledge, we have used only the compasses and guidebooks of philosophy. All that has been said is an inevitable implication of the proof for the existence of God. The mind of man can go thus far unaided, although there is authority at hand to help those who are prevented by circumstance from following the philosophical argument. Yet the contrast between the modern philosophical limitation or denial of divine knowledge and the all including sweep of divine knowledge we have portrayed is so great as to be a little ludicrous. Even more striking is the determined, and patent, resistance against the acceptance of a really divine knowledge in God. If reason can come to grasp the fact of this divine knowledge, why does the reason of so many highly trained men make such a desperate fight against this truth of reason?

The thing is puzzling. Certainly we cannot uncover reasons to justify this modern stand, for there are no valid arguments to justify an attack on truth. We may, however, be able to understand it to some extent by seeing something of the very human weaknesses that creep in to color the thoughts of men. There are a great number of these, perhaps for the most part not fully realized. Thus, for example, an understandable conceit or intellectual pride may move a man to blind boasting about the human mind, as when he insists that the mind of man, as the peak of evolution, is the measuring stick of all knowledge, the supreme rule which simply cannot admit a superior; on the other hand, the same pride may be at the root of a pathetic eagerness to deny all intellectuality, all validity of the intellectual efforts of man. In this last case, the evident weakness of our best efforts has so discouraged the modern thinker that he indulges in the petty gesture of despair that strives to chainman down to the world of animals; at least here he can be the biggest frog in the pond. Surely some of this resistance to truth can be traced to a timid snobbery evident in the mob fear of obstructing the wheels of progress, of not paying the full reward of worship to the scientific method, of being old-fashioned. Certainly fear plays its part. We like to have a few dark corners in which to stow away the unpleasant litter of life; human life, without a basement or an attic where things can be hidden away and forgotten, is a fearful thing. To have to stand up, in the clear light of our own knowledge and the much clearer light of another's perfect knowledge, and face the responsibilities of all our actions every minute of every day, admit they clang out in the halls of eternity for all time, this is a bit too much to demand of human courage.

Perhaps the most seductive element in this resistance is the apparent comfort, the alluring softness of the doctrines of psychological mechanism, evolution and positivism; they assure us that we are as free as a bird, which is to say that we are not free at all. We are offered escape from responsibility at the cost of our humanity. The subjective sentimentalities of the various forms of humanism are the deceptive resemblances of a decadent nobility; their superficial interest in man has the appearance of nobility, but without nobility's mind and heart. For communal groupings of men and their aspirations which leave the individual out of consideration, losing him in a fog or crushing him in a crowd, have no solid claim to the respect of men; the individual must not, cannot, be lost, not even a hair of his head is unimportant enough not to be numbered. To attack the truth of God in the name of man on this basis may be sentimentally attractive in some strange way; but the attraction is a soft, decadent, effeminate thing, repulsive to the touch.

Man's Knowledge of God, the Effects of God

God knows us inside and out because He made us. What do we know of God? In attacking this question, we can safely put aside the modern aberrations of a man-made, a human or an inhuman god and honestly face the facts; after all, these things have been sufficiently refuted in the second chapter of this book. In the light of the facts and the proofs already offered, it must be clear that we can know God from the world as we know an author from his book, as we know any cause from its effects. This is the sole knowledge we have been using thus far in our discussion on the nature and attributes of God. We have seen that it necessarily involves the removal of the limitation or imperfection of the creature from our concept of the perfections of God; it means the tracing of every perfection in the universe to God, but understanding these perfections to be analogically in God, in an eminent fashion, somewhat as the beauty of a poem is in a poet. This is rock bottom knowledge. It is absolutely dependable; it starts from the most indisputable of facts and goes no farther than those facts allow, or rather than those facts insist upon.

Revelation

From what this solidly certain knowledge has told us of God, it is immediately evident that God can tell us things about Himself. We have seen Him as supremely intelligent, knowing Himself perfectly, the first truth. Obviously then, He cannot deceive Himself. Clearly God cannot be guilty of silly boasting or a downright lie; He is truth itself. He can tell us things about Himself; and those things will always be true. This is the knowledge of God, which comes to us by way of revelation.

Direct Vision of God

There is yet another possibility. Can man know God, not indirectly through his effects, not darkly through faith in revelation, but clearly, openly, directly, face to face, through the immediate union of his intellect to the divine essence? The very question itself is a refutation of the idea that God is a fictional sop given in kindly pity to the little weak ones unable to munch the solid food of truth; it is not the weak, the defeated, the cowardly who advance boldly to peer at divinity itself, it is the violent who storm the kingdom of heaven for a direct vision of the beauty of God.

Possibility of this vision

Quite frankly, this idea of seeing God face to face is so high and bold that it probably would never have occurred to the mind of a man left to himself. The solid basis of the affirmative answer to the question is not the facts of the sensible world, not the firm steps of intellectual proof, but simply and solely the authority of God, the word of Him Who can neither deceive nor be deceived. [3] The supernatural is not to be reached by the instrumentality of any created thing; it is utterly, wholly above nature, the proper field of God.

From our side, once the possibility has been revealed to us, we can readily see how beautifully the vision harmonizes, perfects, completes our nature. For here is the ultimate quenching of our thirst to get at the cause of things, here the ultimate answer to our perpetual "why," here is the ultimate peace for that intellectual restlessness that refuses to be satisfied with anything the world of nature has to offer. Here is a fulfillment of our potentialities for all truth, a fulfillment so great that its abundance can be accommodated only by the gift of still greater potentialities within us. In this vision is the goal of our searching, the home for our wandering feet, the quiet for our clamoring heart; only God can offer us these things, and only by this vision can we directly, immediately come home to God.

Coming down to particulars and attempting to be objective about the question, we take John Jones as the average man. How is he going to see God? He has a fine, sharp pair of eyes, but they will be of no help to him; God is not a body and so not to be seen with bodily eyes. John Jones has a good enough mind when he can whip up the energy to use it; but again, this is not sufficient. How can God be seen through any image or concept? What finite concept can show us the infinite God as He is in Himself? Before this infinite essence all the natural powers of our intellect are as helpless as the eyes of an owl in the midday sun; this light is too bright to be seen in its undiminished brilliance by the eyes of our minds. What is known is in the mind of the knower in the way that is peculiarly proper to him. So a man can know sand and sugar; in a sense these are in his mind, not scratching or scarring it but ennobled by it, lifted up to its immaterial, universal level. In the same way a man must know all other things; what is beneath him must be lifted up to his level, what is above him must be dragged down to his level and taken apart that it might be carried through the narrow door of a human mind. God, brought down to the level of the human mind, is not God seen as

---

[3] Sacred Scripture gives explicit testimony to this direct vision, I John, ch. 3, 5. 2, "We shall see him as he is." Matt. ch. 5, 5. 8, "Blessed are the clean of heart for they shall see God." Cf. Matt. ch. 18, 5. 10; I Cor. ch. 13, 5. 12. The definitions of the Church are no less explicit, thus the Constitution Benedictus Deus of Benedict XII (Denzinger, Enchiridion Symbolorum, #530), ". . . they (the dead) see the divine essence by an intuitive vision, face to face, without the medium of any other creature; but the divine essence shows itself immediately to them, nakedly, clearly, openly...." Cf. Council of Florence (Ibid., #693).

He is in himself. For this, the human mind must be lifted to a higher level as a child is hoisted up to see over a crowd; our mind must be lifted up to the heights of divinity and by the strength of One Who is divine; that supernatural help given to the mind of man in order that it might see God is called by theologians, "the light of glory"

Object of this Vision, the Divine Essence and all Formally Contained in it.

Perched thus on the shoulder of God, head and shoulders over the world, we look at a sight that opens our eyes wide with awe, and which will keep them so for all of eternity. By this vision we see the unveiled beauty of God; not just a shining part of it, not an unending succession of its splendors, but all of it at once. It can be no other way, for God is simple; you must see all of Him or see Him not at all. The magnificence of that beauty is eternity's secret; the eye has not seen, nor has the ear heard, nor has it entered the mind of man to conceive it. Some faint shadow of it is thrown across our lives; however, in the glimpses we get into the gallantry of courage, the splendor of love, the sincerity of sacrifice. In the knowledge of what these faint, distorted images of divinity can do to our heart we have a foretaste of the rapture of the blessed in heaven. There, it will not be the image but the original; we shall see all of it, although our finite minds, even with divine help, will never be able to exhaust, to comprehend the infinitude of that divine perfection.

The Perfections of Creatures

As a matter of fact, we shall see a great deal we missed on earth for in heaven our insight into the perfections of creatures will not be limited to territory of a few squares in a city, of a few miles in a country or of a few years of life. God has in Himself all the perfections of creatures, the full story of the thoughts, hopes, and struggles of those closest to our heart, a detailed account of the complicated laws of the universe. All these we shall see, not exhaustively, for that would be to comprehend the plans of God; not equally, but in proportion to the degree of that supernatural help which is the light of glory; not by images or concepts, but as God sees them, in His very essence. We shall see them, not bit by bit, day by day, year by year, but all at once. This however, is the work of heaven and the proper material of the second and fourth volumes of this work.

The Achievement of this Vision

Earlier in this chapter it was said that the contrast between the affirmative and negative answers to the question of God's knowledge was so great as to be ludicrous. When we turn to the implications of these two answers for the living of human life, the contrast is utterly tragic, so tragic indeed, that the choice made by the modern thinker numbs the mind with its horror. Only a kind of madness could lead men into even a moment's hesitation between the two answers.

Freedom and Savery

The one answer sets a man free; the other enslaves him. In the divine knowledge, as we have portrayed it, we have an invitation to enjoy the utmost limits of our possibilities. We are not only privileged to wander up and down the highways of the universe finding knowledge where we can, our mind is given wings to soar to heights undreamed of by any mind in nature. The modern philosopher limits our possibilities of knowledge to the sense level of a high grade animal; he not only puts the mind in the limited area of nature's jail, forbidding its flight to the heights of divinity, he builds a partition across the cell, further narrowing the space. There, we can pace back and forth until we have driven ourselves insane.

Inspiration and Despair

The one answer to the question of divine knowledge is an inspiration; the other is a condemnation to despair. The one throws open the gates of all desire, putting no limits to what we can desire because it puts no limits to what we can know. It offers us the completion of our human nature, its fulfillment; it assigns reasons for individual dignity, for individual self-respect, for a personal goal and so for a life with a distinctive personal meaning. The other offers us the opposite of all these things. We are counseled to lose ourselves in a mass, a process, a group; to strive for an impersonal goal, to live a meaningless life of bitter, hopeless striving to inevitable defeat and oblivion.

Humility and Conceit

The one answer confers on us the nobility of humility's truth; the other wraps us about with the pettiness of conceit. The one demands a recognition of our responsibilities, our privileges, our possibilities, our realities; yes, and of our failures, our defeats, our dangers, the battle we must face. It also sees the possibility of success and of a victory well worth all the danger, the struggle, and all the intermediate failures. The other invites us to eat our meals by candle light in order to create the theatrical air of romance, to destroy the mirrors about the house that we might the better hug the illusion of our peerless beauty, to close our eyes that we might contemplate only the illusion of our beauty and might the better deny perfection to everything else.

Courage and Fear

The one is a courageous answer. Only a brave man can face his life knowing how open every detail of it is to the eyes of God. Only a very brave man, with a full knowledge of his own defects, could aim at a direct vision of God. Bravery is not without its compensations, particularly in this matter. For the brave answer does give a meaning to things, it brings the assurance that an intelligence is directing the world and everything in it. This brave man knows what it is all about, where he is going, and why and how. The other answer is so timid an answer as to be despairing. The man who has made this answer his own faces the terror of the unknown, a terror increased by the conviction that this unknown is unknowable, or even is devoid of all meaning. The world he faces has all the terror of darkness where light would reveal worse horror, the terror of blind, resistless force, of being hopelessly at the mercy of the unfeeling sweep of the elements or of a god gone mad.

The Vision of God and Life

There is much truth in the statement that man cannot see God and live. Surely he cannot know God and merely plod through the bare routine of existence; he cannot know God and not have his heart moved to high things by the vision of the horizons of hope, of courage, of golden goals such knowledge opens up to him. He cannot know God and miss the greatness of man. It is even more profoundly true that man cannot live without seeing God, for he cannot see man in the vague twilight of a godless world, he cannot see a goal towards which life can advance, and he cannot see an instrument of action that will not crumble in his hands. Perhaps the greatest horror of this murky world is not what cannot be seen, but what can be seen, for it is a world divorced from the first truth and so devoid of all truth.

📖 CHAPTER V 📖

THE WILL OF GOD
(Q. 19-21)

1. The mainspring of action,

   (a) The nature of appetite.   (b) The boundaries of desire.

2. Two views of the appetite of God,

   (a) A denial. (b) A distortion. (c) Sources of these views,

   (1) A perversion of knowledge.

   (2) A double difficulty,

   a. The difficulty of human freedom.

   b. The difficulty of evil and suffering.

3. The existence of the will of God,

   (a) The proof. (b) Supremacy of this divine will.

4. The nature of the will of God,

   (a) Its objects,

   (1) Necessary object.

   (2) Free objects.

   (b) Its characteristics,

   (1) Cause of all things.

   (2) Infallible.

   (3) Invariable.

5. The difficulty of human freedom,

    (a) Preliminary notions to the solution of the difficulty,

    (b) Precision of the question and of Possible results.

    (c) Solution,

        (1) Definition of freedom.

        (2) Proof that the divine will is the cause of freedom,

            a. Indirect proof.

            b. Direct proof.

6. The love of God.

7. The justice and mercy of God.

Conclusion,

1. The erroneous views of the will of God,

    (a) Their significance for men.

    (b) Their common bond.

2. Significance of the truth of the will of God,

    (a) For freedom.

    (b) For love.

    (c) For justice.

    (d) For mercy.

THE WILL OF GOD

(Q. 19-21)

The Mainspring of Action

In a practical world, such as ours, everyone knows that it is not the dreamers who make dreams come true. Activity is necessary for achievement; it is absolutely essential for life. The bird that is too timid to risk the first flight from the nest will die from its very devotion to security, the tree that is too sickly to sink its roots deep enough to find moisture will wither away from its very conservation of energy. We have learned well the lesson that the price of life is activity, so well, in fact, that we are tempted to quit life's school as soon as we have passed this kindergarten test. Many men and women of our age have framed their kindergarten diploma and proudly opened up an office for the living of life; the shingle they displayed to the world proclaimed them to be doers, apostles of activity, zealots devoted to progress, to more and bigger and busier days.

The Nature of Appetite

Their restless content might have been undisturbed were it not for the frequency of that pungent modern question, "so what?" A man might twiddle his thumbs just or the sake of doing something; but he will certainly not go hungry just for the sake of doing something, he will not wear down the hours with his labors, or face a sneering mob from the height of a cross. Stifling the dreamer and shattering his dreams do not solve life's mysteries. Process, change, progress, activity are not bugle calls rousing men from inertia; they are man's answer to the fundamental challenge of the desirable thing. There is something deeper than activity, which is activity's cause; there is something beyond activity, which is its goal. There is, deep in the heart of a man, a spring which can be released only by the ethereal touch of a dream; resultant activity, begun by the touch of a dream, rushes to the materialization of that dream and beyond, to its enjoyment, unless the dream was not worth the dreaming.

In other words, activity is not limited to process, change or striving; it goes beyond to the possession of the desirable thing that was at its root. Man does not run for the sake of getting out of breath, he does not live for the sake of consuming life, the days of his search are not filled with a dread of the search being successful. In all this he is at one with the world in which he lives. In everything, there is a tendency or inclination towards that desirable thing which is self-perfection and what pertains to that perfection, to its achievement and its enjoyment.

The Boundaries of Desire

The general term for this inclination is appetite and it responds to the impact of desirability as the intellect responds to truth. In the animals it is sense appetite; in intelligent beings it is will. By a kind of courtesy, easy to those in superior positions but uncommon, we extend the term to the whole of inanimate and plant creation and there call it natural appetite. It is to be well understood that this is merely courtesy, for appetite always follows the lead of knowledge and never out distances its guide; these things have no knowledge of their own and so, strictly speaking, no appetite. They do, however, have a determination to a single course of activity. A plant, pushing its roots deeper in dry weather, is following the knowledge of God impressed on its very nature; but without knowledge of the thing it seeks and with the invariability of inviolable physical law. A dog sniffing for his buried bone has at least the flashlight of sense knowledge lighting up little patches of the path his appetite runs along; while a man, seeking social position, happiness, love or truth walks in the broad daylight of intellectual knowledge that makes plain the beginning, the end and the space between.

Two Views of the Appetite of God
a Denial --a Distortion

It would seem hard to deny activity in the world in which we live, although it has been done; granted activity, it would seem impossible to deny the desire necessarily behind that activity and the organ of desire which is called appetite. With activity and appetite present in the world, inevitably men's minds turned to the question of activity and appetite in God; in fact, it has been as impossible for men to keep their minds off the question of the will of God as to avoid the question of the existence of God. The answers, affirmative or negative, have repercussions for human life so momentous as to make any attempted detour around them a palpable child's game of pretense. This thing must be settled, for on its solution depends the whole complexion of the life of man.

Sources of these Views

The variety of answers offered by the ages of human thought is overpowering. Yet, then, that is not surprising, one absolutely certain result of an open forum on any question put to men is this same dazzling variety. In this matter the various erroneous answers can be roughly reduced to two, the completely negative answer and the answer, which distorts divinity by ascribing to God an appetite other than a divine one. Both these answers are rightly based on the truth that appetite is blind, deaf and dumb, unable to take a step in any direction until knowledge takes it by the hand. If, as the first sort maintains, there was neither intellect nor knowledge until our own human variety mysteriously appeared, or if even now there is no such thing as the spiritual faculty of intellect with its shafts of knowledge piercing the armor of time and sense, then obviously there can be no intellectual appetite, no will in God. Love, desire and love's faculty of will are ruled out of the universe, above all they are ruled out of the Creator of the universe, the world and men are delivered over to a mysterious but plainly blind force, which cannot be brought before the bar of reason. On the other hand, if, as the others say, God is a man-made product with an intellect cut down to human measure, obviously the will of God can wear any human cast-offs but looks ridiculous in the flowing robes of divinity.

The moderns, who make the human will and human love the source of the divine, offer men a synthetic product that was meant to be flattering but which, in fact, is as disillusioning as a candid camera shot or an impromptu voice recording. From their synthetic divine will it is obvious that some of these champions of men lose themselves in sentimentalities unworthy of even human love; they shudder at pain and evil, dream of life in terms of sweetness, soft music, gentle sighs and insist upon a god who exudes the milder emotions Others, with a frank touch of autobiography, grant God only a feeble, struggling, often failing will and love for men; with such a god they can be quite friendly, or they can even feel sorry for him. The very numerous champions of masses of men at the cost of the individuals necessarily limit the object of all will and all love to a crowd; will is a prerogative, not of men, not of individuals, not of persons but of communities. If God is to have a will, then He must, some way or another, be a crowd, a mass, a community.

A Perversion of Knowledge

Both the denials and the distortions have their explanations if not their excuses. There is, on the intellectual side, the same perversion of scientific findings to support unscientific conclusions, conclusions completely outside the field of science, that is to be found in the modern treatment of God's existence and His knowledge; the same conceit which refuses to bend the intellect of man to any superior also refuses to admit any will higher than the will of man. Behind that conceit is the mistaken notion that such an admission degrades man, reduces him to the level of a slave or a puppet.

Double Difficulty, Human Freedom, Evil and Suffering

On the moral side, the explanations of these modern errors have a dangerously enticing appeal. The existence of a divine will involves, on our part, a subjection which glories in truth, a loyalty that is achieved only by sacrifice, and a love which is contemptuous of caution; such things are easily shirked by an age whose theme is self and whose password is safety first. Then, too, the existence of a divine will seems to set up an irreconcilable conflict with human freedom. If this divine will is supreme, how can our human will wander where it chooses, how can we resist the divine, how are we masters of ourselves? This is a difficulty of the first order and we shall treat it at some length in this present chapter. Another difficulty, of proportions nearly as serious, is that of evil and suffering. If an infinitely good and powerful God has a supreme will, why do evil and suffering exist at all A human governor tries his utmost to overcome these things and fails because his will is limited, his power is finite; where there is no limit, no weakness, there should be no evil and no suffering. This difficulty will be met at length in the next chapter of this book. Here let it be frankly admitted that both these difficulties are decidedly real and that they have played, and still do play, a part in man's reluctance to admit a truly divine will in God.

Existence of the Will of God
The proof

Yet, in the name of common sense and evident facts, a divine will cannot be denied to God. Will, or intellectual appetite, is the mainspring, the motive or driving force in intelligent beings; in the second chapter of this book we have proven that God is intelligent, a proof that proceeded from the fact of His divine action. It is true that there can be a driving force without intrinsic knowledge; we do not insist that a hurricane plans the last detail of its destructive venture, although, as we have seen and shall see at greater length, even that last detail is marked down on the blueprints of a supreme intelligence. Yet it is impossible to have intelligence without will, as impossible as having being without a goal for its existence. If intellect could be conceived of without will, it would be aloof, cold, futile, sterile, barren; where, in fact, great intelligence is found complemented by a puny will we find that personification of futility, the timid soul. Briefly, whatever is has a goal of its being and an appetite, which reaches out to attain or enjoy that goal; the facts of the world demand the existence of God.

Supremacy of the Divine Will

In view of what we have seen demanded by the facts of the nature of God and His attributes, the absence of all potentiality, all limitation, the infinitude of His perfection. It is obvious that we cannot treat the divine will as a distant and abjectly poor relation. The very notion of God is destroyed as soon as dependence is introduced into it; to attribute anything but complete supremacy, complete perfection to the divine will is to contradict the evidence of the facts adduced above in the second chapter, it is to make God not the first, not the source of all else, not the absolutely Perfect being that the world of things tells us He is. To put the fact of the divine will with complete accuracy, we must say, not that God has a will, but rather that He is His will as He is His intelligence; for the notion of "having" is inseparable from the notion of potentiality, of a received perfection, of dependence.

The Nature of the Will of God
Its Objects, Necessary Object

It is no reflection on the supremacy of the divine will to insist that it is not free in all its willing, just as it is no reflection on the human will to recognize the fact that a man necessarily, not freely, wills his perfection, his happiness. Rather in man, this essential embrace, by his will of its adequate object is the source of all his activity, the explanation of all his striving; that unappeasable hunger, which he cannot deny, therefore he gives all of his actions a nobility borrowed from the goal, which the will cannot refuse to desire. In God, also, the divine will cannot refuse the one object adequate to its infinite perfection; God cannot refuse to will His own supreme goodness. Nor is this laying down the law to God; it is merely insisting that in God, the supreme Truth, there is no room for the absurdity of a contradiction. God cannot be guilty of the stupidity of thinking that there is some rival to infinite goodness, something more desirable than the supremely desirable. The supreme Intelligence cannot act against intelligence as He would have to in order to refuse to will His own goodness. Again the human parallel may help to make this clear, even in our grossest desires, we cannot tend to evil as such, although here we do make a serious mistake as to the desirable thing; we always, without exception, act in the name of the good, of the perfect, of happiness.

Free Objects

In the human order, the necessary acts of the will, dealing with the goal and its essential means, make up the bare house of our activity; the rugs, furniture, pictures and the multitude of delightfully unnecessary but warmly personal objects that make a home of the house are the free acts that so crowd our every day. There is, thank God, in the very nature of appetite the inclination, not only to possess the desirable, but to give it away; not only to have the goal but to share it. When that inclination is frustrated the activity of man begins to have the bitter taste of the sweat of a slave, when, for instance, purely mechanical instruments make it impossible to put the stamp of his intelligence on his work or to sign it with the flourish of his utterly distinctive personality; or when the perverted outlook of an age makes it vulgar of him to share the splendor of his human life with his children.

Its Characteristics

In God the field of these warmly personal free acts is unlimited. God is His perfection. He is His end; there is no divine striving for perfection unattained. All else other than His divine goodness is freely willed, although, of course, it is willed in reference, not contradiction, to that divine goodness. Our conviction of this divine freedom finds daily expression. It would be silly to pour our prayers over the concrete foundations of a machine; a crisis drives us to our knees, but not because God is helpless to do anything for us; our gasp for help or smile of thanks is not directed to a being who is tied hand and foot. We are convinced that God can help us.

Cause of All Things

Of course this help of God is not something that has about it the embarrassed surprise of a yawn or the irritating suddenness of a stumble; in this, as in all His actions, God acts as an intelligent being. For ourselves, we have no trouble distinguishing between a thoughtless word and the malicious dig; the first slipped out on us, the second was a deliberate product of our intellect and our will. The first was stupid, the second, maliciously intelligent. For it is only insofar as our acts indeed do flow from a deliberate will, the will guided by intelligence, that we give them the name of intelligent acts. In God, then, the cause of all His effects, which is to say the cause of everything, is His will acting in conjunction with his intellect; for God does not operate by necessary determination or at the urge of a blind force but as the supremely intelligent first agent.

Infallible

The very fact of the necessary priority of divine action, and so of the intellect and will as sources of divine action, makes plain the complete infallibility of the will of God. Where absolutely everything depends on God in its causality, where can one find a cause that can hinder the divine action? What is there that escapes the divine support, the first mover, the first cause? What is there that is outside the order of the divine plan? This divine will must be universally efficacious or it cannot be divine, and its divinity cannot be denied without open contradiction to the facts of the world, which proclaims the existence of divinity.

Invariable

The will of God is universally efficacious; it is not only infallible, it is invariable, not hesitating, retreating and plunging ahead, but immutable. For, as we have seen, there can be no change in God. The idea that God paces the floor trying to make up His mind is as absurd as the notion that He has His ear cocked to the latest news flash from the radio or spends eternity tearing open cablegrams on the state of the world. How, then, can we seriously entertain hope in our prayers? God is omniscient; His will is supreme, eternal, unchanging. What is the use of praying?

The Difficulty of Human Freedom--Preliminary Notions

The objection has a history almost as old as the life of man; and no doubt, a future that will stretch to time's last instant. Its full answer will be found in the third volume of this work where the subject of prayer is treated at some length. Here we can do no more than indicate two diverse angles of that answer. The objection argues that God wills all things and His will is supremely efficacious; there is, then, no reason for our praying. We cannot change the will of God; if He wills this or that particular thing, we shall get it whether we pray or not. On the same grounds we might argue for the amputation of all human arms. We have been foolishly spending money for generations to cover those arms with sleeves, whereas the arms are totally unnecessary; why lift a cup of tea to your face if God wills you to have it? No doubt it will jump up and splash all over you. Now do not sit there too long waiting for God to pour the tea down your throat. The fundamental reason why we pray is the same as the reason for our taking a personal part in the solution of the transportation problem involved in eating, namely, that God has given us a part in the great dignity of causality. God is the first cause but His causality does not destroy all other causality; rather it produces and guarantees the effectiveness of secondary causes, we are secondary causes, not only in the physical order, but also in the moral order; the bending of our elbow fulfils a condition, of our nourishment in the physical order and prayer fulfils a condition of achievement in the moral order. The precise causality of prayer is not unlike the causality of a fertilizer scattered over a field, keeping the moral and physical orders distinct; the fertilizer does not produce the grain but it does play its part, prayer does not produce the effect desired but it, too, plays its part, a dispositively[4] efficient part in the government of the world of men.

The other point to be noticed here about prayer is the odd fixity with which we concentrate our attention on only one, and usually a lesser, result of prayer. No doubt it is our tendency for the gaudy attractiveness of the immediate and sensible that explains our lack of appreciation for the merit that is the constant fruit of prayer and that makes us take lightly the peace and strength that come from lifting the mind and heart to communion with the infinite. However, all this is gone into at greater length in the third volume. A major point that must be made here is that the infallibility, the supreme efficacy and absolute changelessness of the will of God do not conflict with our freedom; they *cause that freedom.*

Preliminary Notions to the Solution

Before plunging into the discussion of the difficulty of human freedom in the face of the universal efficacy of the divine will, it is well to understand what is at stake in this discussion; it is above all necessary to understand what is not at stake. The whole discussion takes its rise from the juxtaposition of two truths. The important thing to remember here is that they are both truths; the validity of neither is under question; the effort of the discussion is not aimed at establishing either one or the other of these truths. Beyond and above the

---

[4] In law, this is a motion to allow the proceeding in favor of another part or view; typically it is a preemptive move for an appellate decision.

present discussion, altogether apart from it in their validity, stand the truths of the freedom of man and the supremacy of the will of God. Both of them can be proven beyond all doubt by human reason; both of them are vouched for by divine authority. Whatever the intricacies of the discussion, these two truths must not be lost sight of; they are the beacons that flash out the guiding light, which alone can preserve the discussion from serious errors; they are not the rocks upon which the human mind may be shipwrecked, above all they are not the ships threatened by the tempest of the discussion.

Considerable space has already been consumed in this chapter in showing, from human reason alone, the infallible supremacy of the will of God; there is no need to repeat that argumentation here. The truth of human freedom is clear from the shouted acclaim of common sense, which recognizes it in every human action; that itself, should be proof enough. If more proof is demanded, that proof is readily supplied. The fact of man's possession of intelligence is quickly seen From the most casual scrutiny of any man's actions, you will find a knowledge of such intangible, timeless things as relationships, of means to end, of part to whole and so on; such spiritual things as justice and love; such universal things as being, or even of divinity itself. A knowledge that escapes the limits of matter, time, sense is not the product of a sensible faculty of knowing but of a spiritual faculty of intellect. As knowledge measures and limits appetite, such timeless, immaterial, spiritual knowledge as a man possesses sets free his appetite from the appeal of the material, the particular, the sensible. It holds out to the will of man the universal good and, by that fact, enlightens man's will to the defect of limitation in every other desirable thing.

Precision of the Question

The precise question involved in the difficulty we are discussing here is not, "Can man be free if God's will is supremely infallible; can God's will be supreme if men are free?" Rather it is, "*How* are men free since God's will is supreme and infallible; *how* is God's will supreme and infallible since men are free?" The question, you see, is not one of the fact of these truths but of the fact of their harmony and the manner of this fact; whatever the answer, the fact of freedom in the human and supremacy in the divine will remain untouched.

One of the chief difficulties in the solution of this question is not unlike the chief difficulty moderns find in marriage. To the man or woman who expects marriage to produce an unceasing honeymoon, marriage is a complete failure; really the failure is on the part of the human agents, for marriage by its very nature was not meant to produce an unending honeymoon but to produce children who would live forever. To the man who approaches this discussion expecting the supremacy of God's will and man's freedom to be established or rejected, the whole discussion will be useless; it is not intended to establish or reject these truths but to show they are not in conflict.

In fact, even if the precise point at issue is adhered to and we were to come up with a completely satisfactory answer harmonizing the two truths, we would have every right to be as astonished as a boy who opened his fist to find the whole of the universe rolling about in the palm of his hand. For a completely satisfactory answer in this matter involves a comprehension of the infinite, it demands no less than that we fully understand the divine action. That a human mind can comprehend the limitless divinity is a contradiction much more absurd than that a boy can hold the universe in his hand. What we can expect, and attain, in this discussion is just this, the manifestation of the fact that these truths do not contradict each other that their mutual truth is not against reason, that the difficulties offered against them can be answered. One last word of caution; the explanation, which will be offered here is a theological one, and so a solution offered by human minds. It is reason doing its best with a difficulty; but its results are not to be compared to the validity of the two truths of the freedom of man and the supremacy of the divine will.

Solution, Definition of Freedom

To come to the point of this discussion, we may describe the freedom in question as the choice, devoid of necessity, of the means to an end. If there are a hundred theatres in town, I am free to choose to go to any one of them; if there is only one, I am still free in the matter of going to a cinema for I can choose either to go or stay at home. This free choice, therefore, is a change, a motion from the capacity to choose to actual choice, from indetermination to determination. Obviously the capacity remains under its determination, that is, I can leave the theatre any time I like; but I cannot be determined to a choice and free to choose at the same time, I cannot leave the theatre and stay there at the same time. *All attempts to explain this fact of human freedom on rounds other than divine action destroy that freedom and establish fatalism.*[5]

5

Proof that the Divine Will is the Cause of Freedom
Indirect Proof

Take, for instance, the possibility of this determination to a choice coming from the inside, the possibility of the will moving itself to the choice with no other agent having any part in the affair. If the will moves itself from the capacity to choose to the actual choosing, three possibilities, all fatalistic, are left open.

1) The will is at the same time undetermined (as freedom demands) and determined (as choice requires); that is, the will is at the same time potentially choosing and actually choosing. This is the same contradiction as that involved in identifying the marble block with the statue it can become, or the medical student with the doctor he can become. All that this possibility asks of us is that we agree that determination comes from indetermination, that nothing, of itself, produces something.

2) Or the will is always determined, man is moved by some necessary instinct; and so all possibility of freedom is ruled out.

3) Or the will is never determined and so all possibility of action is ruled out. Take your choice; you may have any one of the three, but you cannot have freedom too.

If, on the other hand, we decide to try the possibility of the will being moved by some outside agency other than God, what have we? The will is moved or changed from mere capacity to choose to actual choice by some external object or set of circumstances; then, obviously, in the face of this object or of these circumstances, it must necessarily move. It is bound by the merciless chains of the external world, determined to this object or these circumstances; thus it cannot be free.

Since the will cannot move entirely of itself or be moved by any thing outside itself short of God and remain free, *yet it does move and is free*, God must move it to its choice. There is nothing else left to explain the facts.

Direct Proof

That proof is, however, indirect; and indirect proofs are as unsatisfying, although adequate, to the human mind as an indirect compliment is to human pride. The direct proof has nothing unsatisfying about it. God is the first cause; every movement, every reality depends upon Him. Take such an unassuming reality as a cough. We have not told the whole story, by a long shot, when we say that the cough depends on God. The cough might have been coldly deliberate, completely free; a cough, for instance, that substitutes for a sneer, that bridges the gap between thoughts, that throws down a smoke screen for embarrassment or waves a flag of warning. Again it might have been completely outside our control, a necessary thing, like the whoop we have been trying to choke down at least until the dramatic point of the sermon was passed. In each case, there was a cough; but in the one there was freedom, real freedom, in the other there was necessity, real necessity. Not only the cough but its freedom or its necessity must come from the first cause, from God, *for this freedom and this necessity are also realities*. In other words, not only the act but its mode, its freedom or its necessity, depends on God. The real modes of freedom or necessity, like all other realities, do not spring from nothingness. The causality of God, the first Cause, extends not merely to the act we perform, but to the mode of that act, its freedom or its necessity. *Unless God causes that freedom, it cannot exist.*

The universal efficacy of the divine will is not an obstacle to nor a destruction of human liberty, it is that liberty's sole explanation; just as it is the sole explanation of the necessity of a sunrise, the contingency of a laugh, so is it the sole explanation of the freedom of a prayer. To put the whole thing briefly, we may say that God is the cause of all existing natures and He is also the cause of all the acts of those natures. He, the First Mover, moves things according to the natures He has given them; it is man's nature, because he is rational, to move freely. How can God move man freely? Well, certainly nothing else can and the fact is there, testified to by our reason and God's own word. This is the solid fact of the harmony of these truths, As for the manner of the fact, how it can be done, to know that is to understand the divinity, to comprehend the infinitude of divine action. There precisely lies the mystery of the manner of the reconciliation of these two truths, a mystery that will forever be beyond the powers of the mind of man.

The Love of God

Perhaps the best approach to the act of God's will, which is love can be made through the love with which we are so intimately familiar, our own human love. Let it be said here, that the present brevity of treatment is by no means to be taken as an underestimation of human love; as a confirmation of this claim, let me point to the exhaustive examination of love in the second and third volumes of this work. For the present, it will suffice to point out the double love which runs through the life of a man, one, a movement of the sensitive appetite, is common to all the animals; the other, the movement of the will, is proper to intelligent beings. Evidence of the first is to be found in the movement of a man's appetite to food. In this sense love is the first of the passions and the foundation of all others; its characteristic note is one of assimilation, of absorption, of taking to one's self. It is properly called love for it is a movement of appetite towards its object, the good.

Rational love, which so sharply distinguishes man from the animals follows intellectual knowledge, whereas sense appetite primarily follows sense knowledge. This rational love extends to all the objects of human appetite, although its proper object is the universal good. Sometimes it approves and embraces the movement of the sense appetite, as when a man deliberately walks into a restaurant and orders a dinner; at other times it glowers at the sense appetite, as in the case of the smoker who so obediently follows the doctor's orders; again it may be quite independent of sense appetite, as when it insists that justice be respected, that love of God be cultivated or that sacrifice be made in love's name.

It too can be assimilative; the astounding thing about it is that it can also be utterly self-sacrificing. In this latter form, the form, which commands our immediate and complete respect, it means no more than to wish good to another and to do something about that wish if possible. It really amounts to an identification of wills between the lover and the one loved to the point of considering the loved one as another self. Hence, the language of love is sacrifice, generosity; the norm by which its depth can be judged is the extent of its unselfishness, the extent of its willingness to sacrifice. All of this is said succinctly when we say that this kind of love is a consecration to some one other than ourselves.

Since God has no body, there can be no question of passions in Him, none of that animal love whose management takes up so much of our time and energy. Yet, there is indeed question of the first act of the will following knowledge, that is, there is question of rational love in God. The fact of love in God should be immediately evident. We have shown, in this chapter, that God has a will and wills Himself, who is all goodness, and all other things; which is to say that God loves Himself and all other things. Moreover the fact of this love in God follows immediately from the fact of His possession of a will.

Abstract discussions of love usually leave us unmoved and reasonably so; we do not expect love to be lazy, vague or distantly impersonal. It should be endlessly busy, intensely thoughtful, deeply interested. Knowing this so well we ask, if we are of the modern skeptics, where is the evidence of God's love for men; or, if we are not skeptics but spoiled children, we wonder why God so often neglects to give us concrete tokens of His divine love. In both cases we are insisting that if God does not overwhelm us with fur coats, jewelry and tickets to the opera He clearly does not love us; the bread and butter of everyday existence does not count; they, in some mysterious way, are taken for granted as rightfully ours.

The love of God for men, and indeed for all things, passes even such cold-blooded tests as these with high honors even although we are not given a Bethlehem or a Calvary for every birthday. If love means to wish good to another as effectively as possible and God is the cause of all things, then obviously every individual perfection to be found in the world, in every thing in the world, is the kind of concrete proof this calculating lover demands. Perhaps the truth of this will be more evident if we keep in mind the striking difference between human and divine love. In our love we are like lovers of the beautiful, haunting art galleries. We do not cause the goodness we love; we discover it and sometimes, in our blindness, the search is long, even futile. God does not roam the world searching for someone worthy of His love, someone whose goodness He can recognize and honor by His love; for His love is a creative love, He causes all goodness other than His own. In a word, ours can be an extremely generous love, but it is always a love called forth by the goodness of the one we love; it can never, therefore, compare with the generosity of the divine love by which God, from His inscrutable goodness, calls into being from nothingness the very goodness that He loves. By His love He not only gives Himself to us; He gives us to ourselves.

Still using that concrete and extremely hardheaded test of love, it seems clear that God does not love all things equally. If He did, there would be no difference between the perfection of the things of the world, between an angleworm and a humming bird, for the perfection of the world is the precise effect of divine love. It should be equally clear that God loves men with a love altogether different from the love He has for animals. A woman, or anyone else for that matter, cannot have friendship for a Pekinese; no matter how tenderly she cares for the dog, what money she lavishes on his special food, how becoming the ribbons with which she adorns him, the dog is still only a dog and so incapable of returning intellectual love, incapable of becoming another self to this delicate lady. In fact, even the omnipotence of God cannot make a friend out of a dog. That privilege is reserved for men and angels; they can, and do, become the other selves of God.

The Justice and Mercy of God

While we do not find it at all difficult to focus our minds on the friendliness of God, there is often a real fear of even a momentary consideration of His justice, as although the two were somehow bitterly opposed. Yet a moment's consideration should make it evident to us that justice is not to be eliminated from the divinity; that, indeed, it would be tragic for us if God were not just. For, if justice means anything, it means the refusal to deny to anyone what is his due. The individual justice which is called commutative lies between equals, giving a man what is his own and towards his individual end; the social justice which is called distributive lies between rulers and their subjects, giving a man what is his own as a social being in order to his end as a part of the community. As man has this double end, so every creature, in a larger sense, has a double end, one as an individual, and the other as a part of that community which is the universe.

God is certainly just in the first sense of justice, that is, giving every creature what it should have by nature, the natural equipment to carry that creature to its own end; of course there can be no equality, and of course the benevolence of God is inextricable from even so large a conception of justice as this, for how could we lay claim to rights until we were first brought into being? Carrying the parallel further, we see that God gives every creature what is its due as part of the universe, that is, what this creature needs to play its part in that external order of the universe to God. More simply, God acts according to the divine wisdom and goodness by which the order of the world was laid out. Here again there is a gift behind the very notion of the divine justice; here again justice and love are inextricably mingled. If we keep that intermingling of justice and love well in mind, we can say that justice in God is nothing more or less than the truth; the living up, on God's part, to the divine model, the plan of the divine architect by which the nature and natural rights of everything were determined.

That act of love, which lies at the root of divine justice, if we were to single it out from the divine activities and give it a name, would be called divine mercy. Mercy, it must be understood, is not to be confused with sentimentality or that vague insult to man, which goes by the name of humanitarianism; it means that, moved by the misery of another, we take steps to alleviate that misery. It does not mean that we encourage a man in his crimes to keep him in good humor, that we pamper his weaknesses for fear he will pout, or that we hide him in a crowd so that his misery will be less disconcerting to our own dreams of a utopia. Perhaps one of the reasons for our confusion about mercy is our confusion about the nature of misery. In its most general sense, it means the privation of a perfection; as far as human misery is concerned. Quite obviously we cannot recognize it if we consider man as merely an animal, merely a comma in an interminable sentence, or merely a child who never reaches maturity. Under such circumstances, we cannot know what perfection is lacking to a man because we do not know what perfection is due him.

In a very real sense, then, the most complete misery would be the most complete lack of perfection. The act of creation, which brought things into existence is by that simple rule a supreme act of mercy. Divine mercy, then, is not contrary to but fills up and overflows the cup of divine justice. Divine mercy does not detract from or destroy divine justice; it lies beneath and goes beyond it. Wherever divine justice is found, divine mercy is there at the root of it; more than that, it is present tempering divine justice by giving much more perfection than any creature could justly lay claim to.

Conclusion

The Erroneous Views of the Will of God

Our age is not the first in which men tried to do strange things to the divine will. Centuries ago the attempt to rule divine love out of the consideration of men and of the world resulted in the pessimism of India and Persia; quite logically, such an attempt held out to men the supreme goal of personal nothingness and the supreme act of self-destruction. Quite logically, this attempt made human life a term of suffering and indignity to no personal goal. Centuries ago men tried to make gods, and the will of the gods, out of human stuff. The result was the cynicism and brutality of the late Roman decadence, the foul degradations of a pagan idolatry. Centuries ago men tried to make sentiment and softness supreme, tossing out the rigors of reality to make cloying love the highest value; out of this attempt came, not men, but delicate beasts.

Their Significance for Men

We have the parallels of these attempts present in our own time. We too have thinkers who deny the divine will; we too have thinkers who make divinity out of human stuff. The results of these attempts do not vary from age to age; they can be predicted with complete assurance, despair, brutality, and effeminacy.

Their Common Bond

From the individual man or woman's point of view, these attacks on divinity are not nearly so disparate as they seem at first glance. At least there is one common bond, which ties them into intimate unity as far as the individual man, or woman of any age is concerned; for all of them without exception, destroying God, obliterate His image. All of them, without exception, are violent attacks on the individual man as man; they push him aside, over the abyss of oblivion, with the crushing blow of despair, the mailed fist of brutality, or the subtly enticing gesture of corruption.

Significance of the Truth of the Will of God
for Freedom

This is not what men want. They want their individual freedom, the surrender and incredible labors of love; they cannot exist without justice; they cannot hope without mercy. These things are not to be found by abandoning God but by holding to Him at whatever cost. Here, in America, we are dedicated to the ideal of freedom and freedom is unintelligible without God, the real God Who is the sole cause of freedom. A world looking for freedom is a world looking for God. A world that looks for absorption in a life stream, in a process of change, in an absolute state, a "holistic" organism or the future of a race is not looking for freedom but for slavery; it is searching, not for God, but for oblivion. That, most likely, is precisely what such a world will find.

For Love

There is no hope for the love of men if there is no love in God; there can never be the destruction of love's solemn consecration in men as long as there is love of God. To trace love's roots to irrational depths of the subconscious, the biological necessity of an animal or the mistaken sentimentality of a fool is to obliterate human love. This sort of thing does not give birth to sacrifice, generosity, thoughtfulness, and undying consecration. The divine love gives rise to all these things in its image in human life. Men can love, and love in precisely this divine way, because by their very manhood they are images of God; without that divine love, man's tireless search for an object of love is doomed from its inception, for there is no goodness, which is not the fruit of the creative love of God.

For Justice

Where will justice find a home if the divine will be non-existent, if it is made of human stuff, if it is unjust? For justice is truth and like truth it is immutable; like all truth, it is intimately, immediately dependent on the first Truth, which is its source. Where there is no truth, justice is a fanatic's wishful dream; where there is a first truth, justice is a reality against, which the crimes of men dash themselves and are destroyed. Men can live if there is justice, although they fear it; if there is none, as there must be none without God, their fear becomes a reign of terror and human life an impossibility.

For Mercy

There is mercy among men because there is mercy in God, there is love in men because there is love in God and mercy is love at work in a crisis. Still, the bountiful mercy of men is never enough for the crises of men's lives, if for no other reason than that men can scratch only the surface of other men's lives. The crises that enter human life are not confined to the surface of life; indeed, the most tragic crises are those that take place in the depth of a man's soul, for there his richest perfections exist, there he can sustain the most serious losses. Only a mercy that can plunge its caressing hand into the depths of man's soul can relieve the misery that must be relieved if men are to face the long days of life; that is, only a mercy that extends its help as far as the love of God extends its beneficence, freedom, love, justice, mercy, these are things indispensable to the men and women of any age these are the fruits of the will of God.

📖 CHAPTER VI 📖

THE FATHER OF ALL
(Q. 22-26)

1. The paternal viewpoint,

    (a) Its responsibilities

    (b) Its privileges.

2. The children's viewpoint.

3. Viewpoint of the eternal Father,

    (a) The fact of Providence.

        (1) Direct proof.

        (2) Indirect proof.

    (b) Characteristics of Providence,

        (1) Universal.

        (2) Immediate,

            a. Distinction from government

            b. Relative immediacy of Providence and government.

4. The children's criticisms, objections against Providence,

    (a) Accident.

    (b) Necessity.

    (c) Physical evil.

    (d) Sin.

5. Power of the eternal Father,

    (a) The nature of omnipotence.

    (b) Its "limitations."

6. Happiness of the eternal Father,

    (a) Fact of God's happiness.

    (b) Its nature.

Conclusion,

   1. Answers to the children.

   2. A fatherless world.

   3. Children at home.

◻ CHAPTER VI ◻
FATHER OF ALL
(Q. 22-26)

The Paternal Viewpoint

At present, the day set-aside in tribute to father is a miniature, and firmly masculine, Christmas. When it escapes its present timid preliminary stage we shall no doubt erect a statue flatteringly expressive of fatherhood. Its sculptor will have to be of the stuff of genius; he will have to catch the fleet grace of motion imprison it in stone, as the Greeks did, without weighing own the swift feet of motion by the stolid strength of the stone. For the gray area jokes that swing about the traditional father pacing the corridors of a maternity hospital, are sparrows twittering on the side of a mountainous truth.

Perhaps the young father does not realize it, but those anxious hours outside a delivery room start him off on a life-long walk. All the rest of his days he will mentally pace corridors; all the rest of his days, the moments of the present, which seem so precious and fleeting to others, will be stupid strollers that block his path to the next hour, the next day, the next year upon, which so much depends; year after year he will stand on tiptoe, trying to peer over today's shoulder, craning his neck to see around the next corner, straining his eyes to see just a little beyond the horizon that limits the sure knowledge of a man.

Its Responsibilities

This last might, in fact, be a better, because more universal, motif for that statue of father, the figure of a man shading his eyes with his hands, his head tilted a little to increase the range of his sight, looking up and out, far out, scanning the future with the clear, responsible, judicious eyes of a sailor standing his watch. Such a symbol, freed of the note of anxiety but made formidable by the accent of responsibility, would show the intimate bond between the fatherhood of God and the fatherhood of man.

Both are providers, taking that word, not in its limited sense of a faithful wage-earner who furnishes bread and butter, but in its more proper sense of one who sees ahead, who copes not only with the present but also with the future. The eternal Father provides, in this sense, for all of the future; an earthly father, for that little piece of the future that is of such intimate concern to those given to his care. It is that correlative of providence the handing over of the lives of others to the hands of a man that is behind much of the panicky flight of the twentieth century from parenthood. "Splendor" is too noisy a word to describe the steady light of that quiet courage, which makes a man responsible for the care and nourishment of this mite of life during its long progress to the vigor of manhood; for the intellectual cultivation and discipline, which alone can guarantee freedom to this latest citizen of earth and heaven, for the mysterious unfolding of moral character that will either be a condemnation to hell now and forever, or the violence behind the storming of heaven. We can appreciate, to some little degree, the agony of remorse that fastens its iron grip on a neglectful father of an undernourished, crippled, sickly child; unless the experience becomes our very own, we shall never plumb the depths of sorrow in the heart of a man whose child has set its feet on a path unworthy of man.

Its Privileges

Paternity, in the ordinary course of affairs, richly repays a man for the responsibilities it imposes. There is literally a personal share reserved for the father in the strength, the beauty, the brilliance, and the sanctity of his children. Yet, long before these ultimate rewards are ripe for the reaping, there is a treasure too great to be risked outside the strong walls of a home; only the members of the family are privileged to peep into that treasure chest; no one has found the words to list its items. The absolute, unquestioning confidence, the unshakeable faith of a child burrows its way deep enough into the heart of a father to allow him a glimpse of what the unquestioning confidence and unshakeable faith of man does to the heart of God. It is not the appealing trick of a gesture, the impish attraction of a smile, the naiveté of a word that breaks down the barriers a man has built up to protect his heart; the child, asleep or awake, in smiles or in tears, its feet straining with excitement or dragging with fatigue, reduces the father to helpless devotion by its own joyous dependence. Neither would have it otherwise.

The Children's Viewpoint

There is probably no man so consistently misjudged as a father; and there are few judges more unfair than his own children. To the very young, he has an air of indifference, of preoccupation and impatience; for they are living in the present while he is straining his every faculty in the crucial struggle with the future, a future much more crowded with possible moral catastrophes for his children than with dangers of starvation, meager comfort or vanishing luxury. A little later on, the children will submit him to constant comparison with all his competitors who enter their field of acquaintance. Too often the rule of thumb is a purely material one. If his success, in terms of clothes, houses and cars, has been a mediocre one, he can thank God for his preoccupation with the future, which blinds him to the bitterness of silent condemnation, or the even greater bitterness of pity. Only much later, too late in fact, does he obtain the solid judgment that comes from an evaluation of his efforts to build men and women; a few solid blows from life quickly determine whether the training, the counsel and the example of home have built enough moral stamina in the children for the facing of life, or whether the soft flabbiness of neglect will make it necessary to hide from life through all of adult years.

Viewpoint of the Eternal Father

Of course the Eternal Father, Who is God, has not escaped this general misjudgment of fathers. Those of His children who are extremely young wholly engrossed with the toys of the present, find Him aloof, indifferent, and preoccupied. Why does He look ahead, providing for the long future of eternity, which is of no present interest to us, instead of drying our tears, repairing our toys, taking us in His lap and comforting us? He's not a father to us at all. The older children have looked around a bit. They have seen life, the outside of it, and are complacent in the naive sophistication, which that superficial view has given them. From their superior heights they pass judgment on the eternal Provider, pitying Him the miserable job He has done, roundly condemning Him as a complete failure, or even going the lengths of denying His paternity. The rough contacts of life may eventually scratch the glittering surface of that sophistication, the humiliation of failure may cut down the height of the judgment seat, memory's journey over the long road of the years may distinguish crumbling landmarks from those that endure; if that happens, the children mature and in their maturity pass a saner judgment on the Provider of men. The comforting thing about this long tale of misjudgments is that correction does not come too late, if it comes at all; this Provider is never beyond the reach of our apologies, never out of range of the whisper of our thanks.

The Fact of Providence

The denial of providence's long vision of the future to God is a childish misjudgment. It is only by burying our head in the presents mass of detail that we can blind ourselves to that providence; it shouts for our attention, whether we focus our eyes on the world we live in or on the God who made the world and us. In the second chapter of this book we have proved the existence of the supremely intelligent Cause of the world; to deny God's providence is to suppose that this supreme intelligence acted with less foresight than a half-wit; look at the thing honestly in its human framework. If our ordinary actions are intelligent, we know what we are going to do, or at least what we are going to try to do, before we start. An editor of a magazine does not cool his heels at a newsstand doggedly waiting to see what his magazine looks like and what it contains; he knew before the magazine went to press. The arrangement of the rooms in the house he has designed does not surprise the architect; if it does, he has been a very stupid architect indeed.

This is what can be expected of intelligences, this is what intelligence means, the ability to act for an end intelligently, selecting the best means, having in mind from the beginning the goal and the best way to attain that goal. In denying this to God we strip ourselves of intelligence, not only because such a position is stupid, but also because the divine is the only possible source of our own intelligence. Providence in God means no more than intelligent planning for divine action. It means that God acted intelligently in building the world and governing it. He knows where He is going and how, what this particular stone is for and where it belongs. To challenge this in God is to challenge the intelligence of God; and a challenge of divine intelligence is a challenge of the unquestionable facts of the world.

Direct Proof

Approaching the question of God's providence from the other side, the side of the world, we find every detail of the universe cast in the role of a friendly guide effusively anxious that we see the central truth of the fact of providence. In a previous chapter, the internal finality of the world was insisted upon, even although such insistence seemed to be laboring the obvious, the fact that the ear was ordered by its very nature to the one act of hearing, the eye to the one act of seeing and so on. It was made clear then that this internal finality demanded a supreme intelligence that it was not sufficiently accounted for by chance, by necessity, or by a limited intelligence. Now, as a matter of fact, such undeniable internal finality forces the mind to a recognition of an external finality, that is, to the recognition of an order to an end beyond the individuals, a world order to which each individual creature makes its own contribution.

A tree sinks its roots to search out minerals and moisture; it is not the minerals who climb the tree to pick apples. It is not the grass, which clips the sheep off short, but the other way around. When cows start to hit men on the head with a mallet, hang their haunches up to age and complain of the toughness of the human hide, it will be time enough to revise our ideas on the way of the world. As things stand now, it is the plant, which uses the mineral, the animal that uses the plant, and the man who uses the animal; that is, it is the superior being, which orders the inferior to its own superior end. In other words, the external end of the plant is the internal end of the animal; the plant furnishes the appropriate material, which makes possible the end for which the animal organism exists.

The obvious interaction of creatures in the world, their subordination one to another, necessarily means a subordination of their proper ends, one to another. Things do not sit glumly in this world like so many patients in a doctor's office, aloof, detached, encased in an impenetrable wrapping of individuality, with no reference to each other. Rather, their mere juxtaposition strikes up an intimate interrelation with all the totally unselfconscious abandon of a child among interested strangers. No one thing exists merely for itself or by itself; it is bound to things above it and below it, using the one, serving the other. Things, in other words, have an order to each other; there is an order, a finality, over and above the order to the immediate end of any one creature. There is a world order; the plan of that world order in the mind of God is called providence. For, obviously, that order, like all order, is the fruit of intelligence; it does not explain itself, but is explained only by an intelligence that cannot itself be part of that which it is ordering to the end of the world.

It is quite true that we cannot always trace the lines of that world plan. We do not know, for example, why a giant shell should have crashed into the church of St. Genevieve in Paris at the precise moment when it was most crowded; a great deal of speculation on the part of the author did not clear up the mystery of the collapse of the fictional bridge of San Luis Rey with these particular individuals on it. It is just as true that unauthorized interpreters of the divine mind have often invoked divine providence for reasons of personal vengeance or childish spite, to them, there is no doubt that the strained tonsils of a loud spoken neighbor or the financial failure of a bitter rival are evidences of God's smooth ordering of the world for their convenience. One great American news magazine mocks at a Chinese earthquake as a divine solution to a problem of overpopulation.

Still, why must we try to understand every detail? The element of mystery in the world order is not surprising. Our naiveté in demanding a complete copy of the divine plans, a copy adapted to our intelligence, is more than surprising, it is humiliating, with a clear knowledge of the mistakes our reasoning has led us into, of the misjudgments we have made, of the natural truths that leave our minds reeling, we pout because divinity is not made plain in tabloid form!

The mystery is there. The fact that it is a mystery gives us no more right to deny the fact, forced on us from so many different angles, than a wounded man has to deny his wound because he cannot trace the source of the bullet The order of the world is a fact that has struck the intelligence of the most ignorant of men as well as the most learned, the shepherds watching their flocks under the brilliance of an Eastern night as well as the astronomer watching the stars that shed that brilliance. The providence behind this order, the plan of the order in the mind of God, has not, consequently, been a matter of esoteric knowledge; it has been a common heritage of the human mind. The existence of that providence can be rigidly proved by unaided human reason, as we have seen; but, for the benefit of those who, for one reason or another, have not such a proof at hand and whose mind might be unsettled by the sophistries of agnostics or atheists, God Himself has revealed the existence of divine providence. Providence is a truth much too central to human living to be left to the sole support of a mind that stumbles with the grace of long practice and falls into the arms of fatigue as into the embrace of a life-long friend.

Indirect Proof

A psychologist may spin out a hypothesis that is, to him, as beautiful as a child is to its mother. Yet, if a consequence of that hypothesis is the denial of a soul, a mind and a free will to man, he must either chuck the hypothesis out the window or admit that he is merely playing with toys. Some psychologists have refused to do either one or the other when faced with this dilemma; but, then, neither did they act the part they had written for other men or, perhaps, quite unconsciously, they did that very thing. At any rate, every scientific hypothesis must be checked by comparing it and its consequences with the known facts, when such facts are at all available. Following the same technique with a denial of divine providence, it becomes obvious that such a denial will not stand for an instant even as a hypothesis, such a denial would mean that a supreme deity did not exist. This would not worry the antagonist of providence; but it would mean that neither he nor the world could exist for a moment. Moreover, it would mean a denial of all intellect, even of the intellect of the psychologist; for obviously, if the first intelligence does not exist, the secondary intelligences have no more chance to exist than the baby's squall without the baby. Imagine an expectant father walking the floor cuddling a squall while he awaits the arrival of the first child of the family! Yet we are behind the times when we protest that we cannot picture a psychologist cuddling his intellect while he awaits the evolution of the supreme intelligence.

A shallow cup held under a rushing flow of water will hardly catch more than a sip; called up on the carpet, it might argue, in the human way, that there was no more water or obviously it would have been filled to the brim. When we hold the human mind under the swift flow of infinite truth, it misses most of that truth and comes up with the truculent denial of all but what it has grasped. Under the shock of the truth that divine providence is absolutely universal, extending to the smallest detail of everything past, present and future, the mind of man is numbed. Reasoning readily shows that this means no more than that God works intelligently. Everything exists only insofar as He causes it, and, of course, He knows what He is doing. Still the truth leaves us as calm as a subnormal student in a calculus class; much more of it has splashed out of our mind than was held there.

Characteristics of Providence, Universal

There is a little more encouraging light in our eyes when it is pointed out that the knowledge of God has, roughly, the same relation to the universe that the architect's knowledge has to the house he planned; that is, the ordering of the effects of the first Cause to the end He intended is precisely as wide as the effects produced by the first Cause. Of course it is barely possible that a plumber with original ideas might set up a sink in the living room, to the complete surprise of the architect; the plans of God cannot, however, be wrecked, nor can the divine Architect make mistakes.

The truth about providence begins to seep through the rocky outer surface of our minds when we come down to details. We cannot be altogether unmoved by the realization that the sun rises and sets in this way and no other, with this exact, inviolable regularity, that rain always wets us, or fire burns us because they were so planned by God. It is because God made them that way that a sigh lasts only an instant while an angel lives forever, that a man is born and dies in a few years while the planets swing around their courses for millions and millions of years. That a man acts freely while the physical world about him follows inexorable physical laws is because God made him, and the world, that way; because the freedom he enjoys is a product of the same divine causality, which produced the necessity of the physical world. By this time we are beginning to see that the plan of God, like His causality, extends not merely to things that are, but to the way they are, not merely to what happens, but to how it happens. The very difference of things find their only full explanation in God.

Immediate, Distinction from Government

The difference between the extent of God's causality and ours becomes clearer when we advert to some of our own limitations. We can, for instance, make a dog come our way simply by pulling on the leash with sufficient strength; but we do not pretend to be responsible for the dog's acting in dog-like fashion. We can wrap a blanket around him, but we cannot stuff a bark down his throat. Our causality is necessarily limited to acting upon things; God's extends to the innermost principles of the natures of things. He is not merely responsible for the dog, but for the nature of the dog; He is not merely responsible for the nature, but for the way that nature acts whether necessarily, contingently or freely. Unless He is its cause, freedom can no more exist than can necessity. This insistence on the universality of the causality of God is very much to the point here for the plan of God, since He is intelligent, extends as far as His causality.

Relative immediacy of Providence and Government

The plan of God, going to this great detail, would account for the action of every creature in its rush to its own goal. Actually the universality of divine providence extends much further for the creature is not an isolated being, it lives in a world in which it plays, on however small a scale, its cosmic part. It is true that providence extends to the proper end of each being in the world; the plant and animal have the apparatus and organization calculated to accomplish their own preservation and growth to maturity. Over and above this, every living thing has a purpose to accomplish relative to the species, a duty to be done for which it is prepared with unfailing efficiency and regularity. This preparation, too, is in the plan of God. Moreover, each species is not an isolated affair. It, too, has its purpose, its taste to accomplish in the cosmic scheme of things, a purpose that may be described in a general way as the service of its superiors. Again it is prepared with complete efficiency and regularity for this cosmic end; this order to the world end in the mind of God is the plan or providence of God. Little wonder that our mind staggers under the impact of this truth. Little wonder that our eyes are dazzled whether we consider its divine attention to the minutest detail or its magnificent reach to the ends of the universe. It is as wide as the world, and wider, as wide, in fact, as the action of God. That is much too wide for the mind of man to embrace and hug to its breast.

The Children's Criticisms -- Objections Against Providence

We are children and God is our Father, our Provider. His eyes sweep the far horizons of the future, of eternity; ours are fixed on all-engrossing moments of the present. Some of us, not seeing our Father's far distant goals, decide that He is not much of a Father; even, perhaps, that we are orphans who not only have no father now, but never did have. This order about us and within us needs no further explanation than that which is offered by necessity or by accident, that is, by chance. Still others pity the efforts of our Father, pointing out the fact of physical evil as evidence that He has made a botch of His work as Provider; others positively condemn Him as a complete failure, a condemnation based on the existence of that moral evil which is called sin. These are the childish viewpoints of spoiled children, they do not need the Father; or they do not want the kind of Father Who tolerates suffering and sin.

If they were fairly reticent in their misjudgments, as decency would demand while they are still in their Father's house, they might be passed over in silence and left to life's hard maturing process. Of course they are not reticent; such children never are. They are bitter, critical, hastily unfair, dogmatically indocile and, above all, blatant. They must be dealt with firmly.

Accident

In the second chapter of this book we have seen the fallacy of the explanation of order by chance or necessity. Here it will be enough to recall that argumentation by noting that the explanation of order by chance violates common sense; we are not at all as happily surprised that the constituents of the eye add up to an organ of sight, as we are that a roll of the dice should turn up a seven. It is opposed to all scientific thought which refuses to admit it is unveiling a will-o'-the-wisp in discovering nature's laws. It is opposed to philosophic thought; we investigate airplane accidents; we do not make up schedules for them because we cannot conceive of the accidental as the regular course of affairs. Any devotee of horse racing would go bail for the statement that accidental results do not follow with monotonous regularity; any orchestra leader would resent the claim, if he understood what it meant, that chance unites a number of different causes in such a way as to produce, regularly, an effect that is essentially one and perfect; any amateur gardener would scoff at the notion that chance produces multiple and perfectly connected elements from a seed that is essentially one. For, to all these men, it is obvious that mere chance does not constitute the order of things, does not explain the regularity, the harmony, the efficacy of what science calls the natural action and interaction of creatures in the world.

Necessity

Necessity, the force of nature, the emergence of new elements or adaptation to surroundings do not offer an explanation; they merely push the problem back, hoping to bluff it into obscurity. How explain the necessity? What causes the adaptations or the emergence? The problem is exactly the same; it can be solved only in the name of a supreme intelligence or of sheer chance, and chance is absurd as an explanation.

Physical Evil

The problem of physical evil represents a much more serious difficulty against divine providence to us of the twentieth century. Some of the difficulty comes, no doubt, from the fact that it digs its way into our hearts as well as into our heads; and when we start thinking with our hearts we can call the product thinking only smilingly. Only a poet can talk this way without embarrassment. Much more of the difficulty comes from a faulty outlook, which is peculiarly ours. A close-up view can be much too close for comfort, much too close for truth; if we take an ant's eye-view of the world by standing on our heads we can be terrified of the things we ordinarily tread under foot, a blade of grass or a fallen leaf. When we stand on our heads to look at the world, of course the things close to our eyes will look enormous; of course we shall be blinded to everything but what is within range of our eyelashes. We might as well have no eyes at all, depending on our eyelashes as an ant depends on its feelers.

As regards physical evil, we are often standing on our heads when we make our judgments; we have our eyes glued so close to the material world that our values are ludicrously distorted. From this undignified position sickness, ill health, bodily injuries loom as major catastrophes. They are absolutely fatal to one who cannot see beyond the material world he has jammed against his eyes. They to seriously interfere with pleasure, with work, with family life. However, they do not impede the central activity of human life, the meriting of heaven; indeed, they often distinctly aid it. Why do you suppose that

Christ commanded men to take up a cross if suffering is a major evil? Why did He visit His saints by such diseases and physical agonies? Why did He flood the soul of His mother with sorrow? Why did He himself undergo such a terrible death at so early an age? These questions demand answers before we gamble everything on health and comfort.

To this upside down observer death has all the horror of complete and blank finality. If it means the end and collapse of achievement, the end of joy, the end of life, the end of love, it is a major tragedy. Now, if it is only the beginning of all these things, of all that will complete our happiness, and the end only of those things that rob us of happiness it ceases to be a dread terror stalking a man through all the byways of life. Loss of fortune, of friends the discovery of a love's falseness, all these are major tragedies only if we have made major ends of the things we lose by them. If we have glued our eyes to earth and neglect to look over the horizon into the infinity of the world of the spirit, we necessarily carry our heart on our sleeve; it will be crushed, battered, wounded, defaced, betrayed and broken. Because, you see, that is no place for a human heart.

Unquestionably God does cause physical evil, at the very least, through the operation of the natural laws of which He is the author. Sometimes, frequently enough to assure us of His providence, we can see the reason for the evil. We can understand that the plant must die to feed the animal; that animals must die to feed men; for we can understand the impossibility of order without subordination of one thing to another. We even see, now and then, how priceless was the suffering, which brought a man to his senses, toppling him from the insecure throne of self-sufficiency and setting him humbly about the business of making his way home. Of course we cannot see all the reasons, nor can we see reasons all the time. Still, what a tragic disappointment it would be if we could see God's plot so long before we had finished the book.

Sin

By far the most serious of the children's criticisms arises from the existence of sin. This difficulty clears up to a great extent when the exact nature of sin is accurately grasped; but, then, so penetrating an insight is a little too much to expect from children who refuse to grow up. Sin is, primarily, a privation, a lack of order to God in some act. Or, more simply, sin is a human act with a hole in it. Just as dough is not necessary to build up the pleasing and practical emptiness of a hole in a doughnut, so nothing positive is necessary to build up the pleasing and apparently practical emptiness of the hole in a human act.

The action of the first cause, God, is not demanded for this defect, precisely because it is a defect, a lack of something. The first cause must be responsible for everything that exists; the trouble with this bad human act is just that there is something that does not but should exist in it. In a word, for this defect, the human will needs no help from God.

Secondarily, there is a positive element in sin, the physical act itself; just as in the doughnut there is the positive element surrounding the hole. For this positive element we must go back, through the human will, to God. Look at it in the concrete. All a pickpocket does is put his hand into a pocket and extract a wallet. We do the same thing several times every day, although with none of the eager excitement enjoyed by the pickpocket. Physically considered there is nothing wrong with the acts indeed, from this physical point of view, the thief's extraction of a wallet is far superior in its smooth grace to the honest man's grumbling fumble. The difference is that the pickpocket puts his hand in someone else's pocket to take a wallet that is not his own. This is the precise defect of order. God is certainly the ultimate cause of the physical act in sin; He causes it by moving the human will freely to it. God does not cause the defect, the formal element that makes sin, sin; it is merely permitted, tolerated.

That brings us sharply against the problem of freedom. Why does God permit this defect? Why doesn't He make it impossible to sin? The answer to those questions is very, very simple, *because the nobility of man demands this permission.*

God could have made us physically incapable of violating the laws by which we are led to our goal; in such a case we might be beasts, or vegetables, or minerals. We would certainly not be men and women. He could have created us in possession of eternal happiness, but it would not have been so divinely generous of Him. For He would thus have robbed our lives of loyalty and victory, of the stubborn courage that drags us to our feet after a severe beating; of merit, responsibility, personal accomplishment, of faith and hope and the whole life of virtue; of the light of the life of Christ and the exquisite joy of fellowship in His sufferings. It has been well said that it is the possibility of sin that made possible the lives of the saints. Because men can lie, cheat, steal, kill, make beasts of themselves there is great merit in truth, honesty, justice, and chastity. Because we can hate so bitterly and live so selfishly, human love is the precious thing it is. It is only because the gates of hell are wide open for us that we can batter down the walls of heaven with our own fists.

Briefly, the terror of evil in the world springs from the heart of a coward. It is the normal echo of that effeminate attitude towards life that holds out, as life's ideal, uninterrupted coddling, endless days of petting, coaxing, and protection. This is the view of life that shrinks from sharing the weariness and discouragement of struggle, the glory of personal victory, because of the possibilities of failure.

Power of the Eternal Father

In this investigation of divine providence, we have simply been looking facts in the face. The direct glance of facts now push us one step farther along in our scrutiny of the nature of God, the further step to the acceptance of the rather terrifying truth that yet lies at the roots of our hope, the truth of God's omnipotence. Lest our wavering intellect, in spite of facts and irrefragable proof, should hesitate, trembling before the awfulness of such a concept, we have again the bolstering declaration of in fallible authority. Strictly speaking, however, authority is not necessary in this matter; our reason can handle this alone. In fact, once we understand what is meant by omnipotence, the intellect holds out open arms to embrace it.

The Nature of Omnipotence

Power is not attributed to God in the sense of the power of a canvas to be turned into a masterpiece. Such a principle of passive reception is an open confession of perfection not yet had, a thing inconceivable in God. Nor is divine power to be taken in the sense of the power of a painter to produce a masterpiece. Great as such power may be, it too, is kept humble by its necessary confession of imperfection; it, too, implies a change, a motion, and a passage from potentiality to actuality. It is a clear statement of help received, of dependence on another mover. God is completely independent, altogether unmoved.

Power in God must be understood in a sense that is unique, the sense of a principle of action on others, in itself implying no imperfection whatsoever. No example of it can be given for it exists nowhere outside of divinity. The power of creatures is no more than a shadow recording the presence of divine power.

However, starting from the world we know so well, we can rise up to some knowledge of divine omnipotence. In our world, creatures are principles of action that is they have power, in exact proportion to their own actuality, their own realized potentialities. Thus, for instance, I cannot teach others the art of ballet dancing because I do not have that knowledge; I can teach others only what I myself know. A man can put the stamp of intelligence upon his work only in the degree in which he possesses intelligence; he cannot generate angels, even if angels could be generated, because he does not himself enjoy angelic life. God, as we have already proven, is pure act, complete perfection. His power, then, is complete, as unlimited as His perfection, almighty.

Its "Limitations"

Divine omnipotence, then, means that God can do all things. The teasing, merry objections that are offered against this divine attribute are harmless things as long as we understand that they are meant to be funny and are not objections at all but contradictions in terms. With this clearly in mind we can, with the somewhat weary patience that is our only defense against a punster, sustain such questions as, can God make past things present? Can God make an object so big He cannot move it? Ect. In a way, these objections are an aid to a clear notion of omnipotence. They bring out its real meaning, namely, the power to do all that can be done, to make all that can be made; or, more simply, to do whatever does not involve a contradiction. What does involve a contradiction is not to be classified as impossible to some created cause, not to God's power, but impossible to itself. A circular square cannot be made; a soulless Frankenstein can never escape from the pages of fiction; a creature can never be infinite; for in all these there is contained an open contradiction.

Happiness of the Eternal Father, Fact of God's Happiness

There is one last question to be investigated in this analysis of the nature of God. a question that comes to us naturally as involving the high point of existence, is God happy? The question has seemed in very bad taste to the gloomy religionists of the past few centuries, the men and women who identified godliness with stern frowns or resigned sighs. To speak, or even speculate, on happiness in reference to divinity was as vulgar as gossip about the king's indigestion. On this basis, heaven should be pictured as a dreary front parlor exuding dignity with the angels tip-toeing in terror down the halls in dread expectation of the roaring anger of a God as wrathful as a victim of gout.

Its Nature

How such a notion ever came into being is totally inexplicable on rational grounds. A simple analysis of happiness shows that it demands an intellectual nature, the possession of a good, and a consciousness of that possession. Consequently a dog or a cat can never know happiness; it can be satisfied, its appetites quieted, but it cannot know that these appetites have been satisfied. The animal, in other words, is incapable of that reflexive act that enables us to look at ourselves. Obviously, a man may have much good and yet be thoroughly unhappy by the simple trick of concentrating on the things he does not have, or by cultivating a kind of unconsciousness of the goods he does possess. Nevertheless, it is utterly impossible for God to be unhappy, He is supreme intelligence, He is supreme goodness, He knows Himself, His goodness, perfectly with an eternal, uninterrupted act. Our happiness, then, like all our other perfections, is but the faintest rejection of the full, infinite, ineffable happiness of God. Gloom, grouches, bad temper or blues simply cannot have a place in God for sorrow, defect, imperfection are excluded by the very notion of divinity.

Our little share in that overflowing divine happiness makes up the eternal happiness of heaven. In fact, the happiness of God includes all other happiness; whatever desirability there is in any other happiness, whether that happiness be true or false, Preexisted complete and in a much more eminent, a divine, way in the happiness of God.

It seemed so important to St. Thomas that men see God as a happy God that he drew up a table of extremely rough parallels, in the hope that some little glimmer of the smile of God would light up the darkest days of human life. He made the parallel between the clear, penetrating, translucent beauty of human contemplative happiness and God's continuous contemplation of His own infinitely perfect divine nature and of all other natures; between the solid, substantial, creative happiness that belongs to the activity of men and the happiness of God's creation and government of the world. From what might be called earthly happiness, pleasure, riches, power, dignity, fame, he looked to the infinite joy of God in Himself and His creatures, to the infinite sufficiency of divinity, the divine omnipotence, the eternal kingdom of God, the universal admiration of the created world. The parallels are clumsy; but they should rule out of the minds of men the horrible caricature of a gloomy God.

The home over which so happy a Father presides is a grand place to live in. Wherever He is, is home. Now, while we are on the road, it is a makeshift affair, a tent thrown up for the night, but still home; when the journey of life is done with, that happy Father will give us the full happiness He has been planning for us all along the road, His eyes looking far down the future to eternity. It is, however, extremely difficult for the most provident, the happiest of Fathers to give happiness to carping, critical, unfair children. If they insist on misjudging their Father in the light of their childish minds and distorted information no one can do much of anything about it.

A little faith, a more docile acceptance of the long view of the Father, makes all the difference between happiness and misery. To accept that long view of providence does not involve a denial of that weakest of all intelligences, the human mind; it is not a slavish surrender of man's supreme faculty. True enough, the intellect of man has rights, rights which cannot be denied without a denial of our own manhood, of our claim to superiority to the irrational world. It has the right to demand that it be not violated, that these truths about the nature of God be not against reason not in contradiction to it. It also has limits, limits which are definitely those of a finite creature. It is violating itself when it expects or demands the comprehension of the infinite; it is being childish when it demands that the Father see no further than the smallest of His children.

Conclusion

The intellect is forced to the conclusions we have discussed in this chapter, forced by fact, by simple adherence to the fundamental laws of thought and of being. Those conclusions, moreover, are bolstered by infallible authority's crystal-clear pronouncements. The difficulties urged against these conclusions do not show there is any contradiction involved; there is nothing contrary to reason here, merely something above it. For there is mystery here, as there is mystery wherever the divine movement is involved; the comprehension of the mystery is possible only to the mind that can comprehend the infinite. We do make those difficulties seem more forceful, not by further argumentation, but by standing on our head, holding the world so close to our eyes that our whole scale of values is inverted; the difficulties seem enormous only when we blind ourselves to the truth.

Answers to the Children--A Fatherless World

It is fortunate for these ungrateful children that the violence of their misjudgments cannot destroy the benevolent paternity of God. The make-believe world they construct for themselves is a horrible habitation, but there is always the comforting knowledge that it is only make-believe. Pushing the Father aside as utterly incompetent, they take on their childish minds His work of running the house of the world, and break down before that work, as a man always breaks down before a job that is too big for him; they end up trying to escape from the house of the world to which they have denied all doors and windows. Some of them will deny the very existence of the Father, the very framework of the house of the world, pulling the walls down on their own heads to escape into chaos without order and without meaning. They are unbalanced children who insist that the toys of life are life's essentials; they are frightened children to whom despair is a playmate; they are children at war with God, with the world and above all with themselves, a war that breeds a hatred that looses its most deadly venom against the children themselves. They are the children of a Fatherless world.

Children at home

It is, thank God, only a world of their own distorted minds. In reality God's children are at home even during this rough passage to heaven. The walls of the house of the world are rough, unfinished, crude things; but within that home there is the serenity, the courage, the peace and self-respect that is the right of children, the product of a provident Father. In place of panic in the face of chaos, there is the calm quiet of children with perfect trust, for here is a Father whose provident eyes search the long horizons of eternity. Here there is no fear, no despair; for here the intelligence and power of the Father are assured. Failure, misfortune, discouragement, sickness, even sin itself have their meaning in the divine scheme of things. Here there is that sane balance that recognizes success, praise, high position, good fortune, health, as only steps in a divine plan, steps which are perhaps no more significant than their opposites. Here is peace for here is order; and the supreme self-respect, the supreme helpfulness to neighbor, that comes from sharing in that divine providence, from partaking in the dignity of causality, from being in command of our own souls with the future what we care to make it.

📖 CHAPTER VII -- THE INNER LIFE OF GOD 📖
(Q. 27-43)

1. Perception of life,

    (a) The sign of death.

    (b) The mark of life -- activity,

        (1) Transient activity -- root of a modern mistake.

        (2) Imminent activity

2. The scale of life,

    (a) The principle of gradation.

    (b) Concrete gradation of life, plant, animal, human, angelic.

3. Divine life,

    (a) As seen by man,

        (1) The fact of it.

        (2) The manner of it.

    (b) As seen he God.

    (c) As told to man by Cod,

        (1) Statement of the mystery of the Trinity.

        (2) Sole source of this knowledge.

        (3) Validity of this knowledge.

4. Reason and the mystery of the Trinity,

    (a) in generals

    (b) in particular,

        (1) Basis of the distinction of persons -- the Processions

        (2) Reality of the relations set up by the processions.

        (3) The classical illustration.

        (4) The divine persons.

Conclusion,

    1. Parodies of the Trinity,

    (a) Horror of death.

    (b) Fear of life.

    2. Thirst for life.

    3. Climax of life

📖 CHAPTER VII 📖
THE INNER LIFE OF GOD
(Q 27-43)

Perception of Life

Quiet is a calm refreshment of the soul if it is not too hushed. There is a reason behind a city boy's panicky restlessness in the stillness of his first night in the country; to him, whose days have been so crowded with clamor, no sound is audible. Although he may never admit it, he is frightened by such absolute quiet, as are all those whose ears are not attuned to the workings of their own souls; as frightened as all men are by those occasional moments of mental blankness that seem to dissect life with a stroke as ominously quiet as the blow of death.

The Sign of Death

Completely motionless waters, waters with no hope of activity in them, leave us uneasy; they are dead, or so close to death that the air above them is tainted, the depths beneath them unclean, their surface already in preparation as a breeding ground of unhealthily lush growth. We have, quite rightly, associated life with activity; we demand activity of anything that lives, we are disturbed at lack of activity or even at the lack of signs of activity. For we know that inactivity is the herald of death, the advance guard of decay. Perhaps it is the depth of our appetite for life that makes the signs of its opposite so repulsive. At any rate the fact remains that a corrupt vegetable pollutes our hands, destroys our appetite and speeds our departure. We cannot pass a dying tree unmoved unless we wear the equivalent of a blindfold; a man who is going to seed mentally or physically misses much of the distress and repulsion he awakens only because heroic virtue is not nearly so rare as the cynic thinks; a man who is corrupting morally is a source of contamination as obnoxious to healthy cleanness as a leaking sewer. Stagnancy, decay, rottenness anywhere, in any form, is repulsive; it sets up an unmistakable sign of the end of activity, it is the sign of death.

The Mark of Life – Activity

On the other hand, a brisk wind off a choppy sea injects new life into us. A buoyant step, the sharp, decisive click of a heel, or a laugh that skitters across the room and back like a scampering child, dissipates the fog of our sluggishness and awakens us from lethargy to a lighter, brighter, quicker life. Youth, with its vibrant life, has a beauty of its own, a clamorous, insistent beauty that will not be ignored. Freudian experts, who explain all light by darkness, would have it that thousands gather each fall to watch "a scampering boy with a ball" by way of enjoying vicarious thrills and triumphs; they forget that youth still preens itself before a glass and age enjoys the pleasant sadness of nostalgia. Age, too, has a beauty of its own, a quiet, penetrating, burning beauty that sets roaring fires in the heart of youth. A pair of eyes alive with ceaseless thought's clashing battle are not pushed from memory with a careless gesture; they are glowing coals that give comfort only to those who seek a flame. The lines and depths written on a man's face by the winds, storms and far horizons of long journeys over the seven seas of life offer wisdom's refuge to fellow travelers. The sure judgment, hand carved with weighted words, is the masterpiece of time and patience.

Life and activity are too intimately bound together for either to exist by itself. There may be some solid truth in our suspicion that life is activity, at least some kind of life. It is strange that the suspicion has not driven us to a closer inspection of activity; instead, we have neglected the vista opened by it and seized upon the most obvious activity, the activity involving change, as the synonym of life. As a result we have made change the cardinal virtue and placed becoming, the acquiring of perfection, above being or the having of perfection. We have described life as a process; no wonder so many pass it on the street without a nod of recognition.

Transient Activity – Root of a Modern Mistake

It is not strange that the magic of the craftsman should fascinate us. The child sits spellbound as the pies and cakes take shape under the deftly sure fingers of a cook; years later, the adult stands gaping as a building springs into being at the urging of steel-workers and masons. We have always had a personal pride in the human art of making things, even although our role is no more than that of a spectator. It is something to be proud of; but it is not the sum total of activity, this working to the perfection of something outside the worker himself. It is tangible, vivid, fascinating, but it is only transient activity, the least of the things life does.

Imminent Activity

There is another kind of activity that remains within the very agent who produces it, an activity obviously superior to that which passes outside and beyond him. The very purpose of the pies and cakes is precisely to furnish material for one such activity, the nutrition and growth that remain within the child who so eagerly devours them. The structure of steel and stone was made precisely to enclose a world of intricate plans, daring hopes, of knowledge and love and desire; it is no more than the servant of these things that yet remain within the head and heart of a man.

It is this latter activity, which is living activity, immanent activity, activity from within, and remaining within the agent. In a thousand ways we testify to this truth; but, on the crucial point, we throw out the testimony. The difference between the growth of crystals and the growth of a plant is admittedly the difference between the activity of the non-living and the living. A leaf stretching out to its full development on a tree is not nearly so active as the seared leaf buffeted by November winds; but the one is alive, the other is dead. Our very metaphors are confirmatory witnesses to the depth of this truth, a dead house is not lifeless because something has happened to the outside of it, but because something has gone out from within it; a dead face is a lantern without the inner flame; a dead heart is an empty one. It is immanent activity that is the mark of life.

The Scale of Life, the Principle of Gradation

This is so true that the scale of life can be accurately drawn up only on the basis of immanent activity, only on the principle that the greater the immanency of the activity the greater the life. In the concrete, this principle is immediately obvious. A plant's perfection of life consists precisely in the fact that its growth is from within and its three operations of generation, growth and nutrition are immanent operations. Its imperfections, which place it on the lowest scale of life, are precisely its defect, the material of its actions comes from the outside, the term of its activities continues apart from the plant; it may be moved from place to place, but will surely not stroll off for itself; and any arranging of means to its end will not be accomplished by concentrated study or agonizing worry on the part of the plant, it will come from the outside.

Concrete Gradation of Life, Plant, Animal, Human, Angelic

An animal has all the perfections of a plant, yet, additionally, has locomotion and sensible knowledge, these two being exactly proportioned and marking out the difference, say, between an oyster and an eagle. On the side of the imperfection of life, there is the fact that the term of the animal's activity is never within, it cannot reflect on itself, look to the goal over the head of the present; the term of its generation, its offspring, is always distinct in essence and operation; the determination of ends and means, things worth having and ways of getting these things, is always from the outside.

Going up a step higher, we find human life possessed of all of the immanent activity of plants and animals, with the inherent limitations of this activity; and, in addition, the marvelously immanent activity of human knowledge. The term of this activity, the fruit of a man's thought, is not to be wheeled about the park in a perambulator; it is immanent, taking up permanent residence within a man's own head. It is the man himself, not something outside of him, that determines the things worth having and the means of getting those things. Still, even this is not perfect life. The material of a man's thought comes from the outside, it is measured by the world of reality outside a man, and, while a man's thought stays within his own head, the term of a man's thought is still not the mind of a man. The emphasis of imperfection, here as all through the scale of life, is on the notion of external as opposed lo internal; what comes from the outside or goes to the outside is not so much from life's fullness as from its limitation. A clumsy example of our realization of this fact is to be had in the difference between our attitude towards a frail intellectual genius and a stalwart but moronic athlete; our pity goes, not to the one man's frailty but to the other man's lonely strength.

Yet obviously, from the very essential perfection of human life, there is room in the universe for yet more perfect life, for there is room for yet more perfect immanency of action. That next step lifts us to the angelic level where there is no question of growth, development, process or change; but where there is indeed question of vital activity. Here change ceases but the intensity of life increases. The world of the angels will be treated exhaustively later on in this volume; for the purposes of this chapter it will be enough to point out that an angel is as nearly an independent world in itself as it is possible for us to conceive within the world of nature, which is to say, within the essentially dependent world of creatures. Its movement from place to place is not to be compared to the effortless glide of a bird; it has about it the agile speed of thought, the closest approach among creatures to an illustration of the omnipresence of God. The angel does not have to endure the long, slow days of schooling, the back-breaking labor of thought, the tenacious effort of memory that so mark the progress of man's mind to its maturity; the angel does not gather ideas, it is created with them. There is no progressive accumulation of knowledge; knowledge is full and immanent from the first instant. The angel knows itself, not through some other medium, even so intimate a medium as its own acts as we do, but directly, immediately, immanently. Like man, the angel has its determination of ends and means from the inside not from the outside.

However, this is still not perfect life; there is still the element of the outside marking beyond all doubt a definite limitation of life's perfection. The angel's ideas still come from the outside, not from beneath it but from above it, for they are infused by God; it still moves from the consideration of one idea to that of another, a kind of passage from potentiality to actuality; its knowledge, while not measured by reality, is measured by something outside the angel, by the mind that measures reality, the mind of God; it is still dependent in its being and its activity on an outside source, the source of all being and all activity, the first Cause. The angel's knowledge, while intensely immanent, is still distinct from the mind of the angel; it is not so immanent as to be identical. There is, in a word, room for perfection far above that of the angels.

The rungs of the ladder of life are clearly marked. The lowest is that of the plants, for this is the least immanent in its activity; up a step is animal life; still higher is human life; nearing the top we come to angelic life. However, this is still not the peak of lifer for this is still not the peak of immanency; the mark of life still has some of the dross of externality in it. It is not absolutely pure. For that supreme degree of life, we must look to the divine.

Divine Life

From what we have seen of the existence and nature of God, it is plain that there is a divine life. God is the first cause Who sowed life so prodigally in the world; He must have it to give it. He is the supreme intelligence and intelligence is the highest form of immanent activity, that is, of life's activity. Again, life is one of those limitless perfections that is not had in its fullness by any creature, that can only be shared, participated, received in a definite mold by anyone less than God. It is not to be discovered in an analysis of the essential characteristics of any creature; only God *is* life.

As Seen by Man, the Fact of it

It is to be understood, of course, that divine life is infinitely superior to created life; that life is spoken of in God and in creatures only in an analogical sense, it is in God in an altogether eminent way. With that precaution in mind, a consideration of divine life in the terms in which we have been speaking of life in this chapter brings out sharply the perfection of divine life by focusing attention on the immanent activity of God. Here there is no question of the power from within to move from place to place; by His divine nature God is everywhere. There is no question of growth, nourishment, gradual attainment of perfection; God is eternally perfect. There is no dependence on things below Him, as there is in man; nor on things above Him, as in the angels. His mind is measured by no other mind, no other thing; He does not consider first one idea, then another; there is no distinction between the divine idea and the divine mind, for God is utterly simple. Divine activity, in other words, is absolutely immanent; which is to say, that divine life is absolutely perfect.

The Manner of it

This is a far cry from the modern blindness that sees the Christian God as too static, imperfect, stagnant, divorced from life, principally because there is no advance, in divine life, from the stage of short pants to long pants, from hair down to hair up. The argument, in its absurdly simple form, is that there is no life in God because there is no change in God. The real conclusion, of course, from the absence of change in God is that there is no imperfection in the divine life. This is life at its highest, most intense, most perfect degree, intellectual life, activity perfect in its immanency.

Thus far reason can take us, and no farther. This much man can see of God with his own eyes, and no more. By these steps man comes to the edge of the abyss that lies between the finite and the infinite; there he is halted by the very limitations of his nature. This is the threshold of the inner life of God; the inner secrets are God's and God's alone.

As Seen by God

To divine eyes, the mysterious inner life of God is completely clear; God can comprehend all its ineffable perfection, for the infinite alone can comprehend the infinite. This is knowledge that has been God's from all eternity and that will never belong to any other although all of an eternity is given to its contemplation and all the graciously tender thoughtfulness of God is exerted in unfolding the story to lesser minds.

We are humbled before these inscrutable truths, but not humiliated; rather we are exalted as a man of mediocre virtue is exalted by contact with heroic sanctity. What a tragic thing it would be if his paltry virtue were the highest peak to which the heart of man could aspired What a traffic, desperate thing it would be if our paltry minds could encompass all truth! What an inspiring thing it is for the heart of a man to know that there is inexhaustible beauty beyond the faint shadow that he can perceive; what an incredibly gracious thing it is that man should be given, as far as he can be given, the eyes of God to see beyond the shadow into the infinite reality!

As told to man by God--Statement of the Mystery of the Trinity

For God has not spoken of His mysteries in guarded whispers behind the locked gates of heaven, He has shared them, as far as they can be shared, with the least of intellects, the intellect of man. He has told us something of that ineffable inner life of His; and that something is almost too much for our minds to bear, like a joy that crowds the heart to the breaking point. The mystery of the Trinity, as God has told it to us, is the mystery of three divine persons, really distinct, in one and the same divine nature, coequal, coeternal, consubstantial, one God. Of these persons, the Second proceeds from the First by an eternal generation; the Third proceeds from the First and the Second by an eternal spiration.

Sole Source of this Knowledge

There is absolutely no way in which we could have come to this knowledge of ourselves. It had to be explained to us by God. It is told vaguely, dimly in the obscure words of the Old Testament, as although to prepare the mind for the terrific impact of so great a truth; then, in the New Testament, there is the clear statement both of the trinity of persons and their identity of nature; finally, in the declarations of the Church, the mystery is stated with a clear-cut brevity that staggers the mind. This is the only source of our knowledge of the Blessed Trinity,- the authority of God, only God could know of it, only God could tell of it; He has told us and we bend our minds in humbly grateful belief.

Validity of this Knowledge

The modern individuals, cannot understand why we accept a truth we cannot verify by our own intellects. To us, it does not seem a wisely superior thing to doubt that God, Who gave us the intellects by which we pan out flakes of golden truth, should give us nuggets beyond the capacities of our laborious panning process, indeed, beyond our wildest dreams of rich strikes. From whatever point of view we take, it is the doubt of these mysteries that needs explanation, not their belief. We can prove, and have proved, that God is supreme intelligence, the first truth; that, consequently, He is incapable of deceiving Himself or others, of being deceived by others. Why then doubt His word? Knowledge of God arrived at by reason from the world of reality is undoubtedly valid, as we have shown; should knowledge of Cod be less valid when it comes directly from God Himself? Or, to put the same truth in simpler terms is first hand knowledge necessarily to be classed as inferior to second hand knowledge? Yet surely the knowledge garnered from the effects of God in the world is second hand by comparison with knowledge coming directly from God. No, the fact that this knowledge comes to us as a completely free gift from God is not a reproach to its validity but a guarantee, a divine guarantee, of it.

Reason and the Mystery of the Trinity--In General

The Trinity is a mystery, no doubt about it. Unless we had been told of its existence, we would never have suspected such a thing. Moreover, now that we know that there is a Trinity, we cannot understand it. The one who attempts to unravel the mystery is in the position of a near-sighted person straining their eyes from the Eastern Shore of Maryland for a glimpse of Spain. We cannot probe the depths of the ocean of divinity with the foot-rule of the human intellect.

It may feel grand to adopt a righteously indignant attitude against mysteries, snatch up a hatchet and sally forth as a crusader dedicated to smashing the dark windows behind which mystery carries on its revels. Yet, why not start the crusade at home? Long before we have finished in nature, our hatchet will be dulled, our arm fatigued, our soul humbled enough to see that there are undreamed of truths in this world, undreamable truths in the world of divinity. What, for instance, do we know of electricity beyond the fact that it works and something of how it works? There is very much to be explained about radio beyond the mysterious selection of the dogged entertainers who use it as a medium of slipping into our houses. Over and above the realization that a red light gives us a choice between stopping our car and accepting a ticket, we know that it involves some 130,000,000 vibrations a second, but that is not much help. A culture developed from the brain or spinal cord of a mad dog will arrest the development of rabies; but no one knows why; ect, yet, we are surprised, indignantly surprised, that the divinity should propose truths beyond the capacities of our minds!

Ordinary common sense should tell us that this is a natural concomitant of the inevitable limitations of our nature. A small cup can hold only so much water, not the whole ocean. Our eyes can see only so much of the spectrum, not all of it, they can take in only so much light under pain of blindness; there are rays of light invisible to our eyes, sounds inaudible to our ears we take these limitations for granted. As our eyes are only human eyes, our ears only human ears, so our intellects are only human intellects, there are truths we cannot know by those intellects.

When such truths are made known to us by a superior intellect, there is not much we can do with them. Certainly we cannot prove them; we have little result from attempting to probe them; we can show they are not violations of reason that is that they do not involve contradictions, and we can dig up a few clumsy illustrations. Thus, for instance, we can show that the idea of three persons in one nature is not inconceivable; it is not the contradictory statement that the same thing is at the same time one and three. As a matter of fact, the exclusion of this often alleged contradiction against the truth of the Trinity is absurdly simple; all it involves is the manifestation of the fact that there is a distinction between person and nature. In the construction of a crossword puzzle, the principle *by which* the puzzle was drawn up is a human nature, but the principle *who* drew up the puzzle was John Jones. The first answers the question *why* such a thing was possible, no other nature engages in such activities; the second answers the question *who* did the work involved. The distinction is fairly obvious from a normal man's resentment of the inference that he is any less identically human than any other man as contrasted with his assured knowledge that there is no identity between his person and the person of any other man who has ever existed.

In the mystery of the Trinity, the persons are distinct from each other; but each one is identical with the divine nature, here the question is not one of conceptual possibility, assured by our perception of the distinction of person and nature in the world about us, but of fact.

Isn't this a violation of the mathematical principle that two things equal to a third are equal to each other? The Father is not distinct from the divine nature, the Son is not distinct from the divine nature, and therefore the Father is not distinct from the Son. The revealed truth is that although Father and Son are not distinct from the divine nature, they are distinct from each other; nor does that truth violate the mathematical principle in question here. Perhaps we can see the root of the confusion if we reflect that the qualities of action and passion are the same as immanent, but not the same as each other; for example, a blow in the face as given and the blow as received are the same as immanent, i.e. at the point of contact, but they are certainly distinct from each other under their own proper and formal conception. The Son, precisely as Son, is distinct from the Father, precisely as Father, although both are identical with the divine nature.

By way of illustration we hit upon such clumsy things as the merging of three flames into a single flame; the light of a candle, which is red, yellow and blue, yet one light; or the trunk of a tree springing from the roots and the fruit coming from both root and trunk, yet all three make up one tree. These are clumsy examples, examples that limp so badly that they are a hindrance, rather than a help, to the tranquility of our restless intellects. As has been insisted throughout this chapter, human reason cannot get much done with truths that are entirely proper to the mind of God. Perhaps the best procedure, in dealing with the Trinity, would be to single out the basic theological terms, subject them to analysis and illustration, so that we might be able to achieve an accurate statement of the mystery and maintain our slender intellectual foothold on the flowering truth of three divine persons in one divine nature.

Basis of the Distinction of Persons – The Processions

These basic terms, which enter into the very revelation of the mystery, can be reduced to three, *processions of origin, subsistent relations*, and *person*. Examining each of these in order we shall at least come to a knowledge of what the mystery of the Trinity does not involve and of what, therefore, we are precisely to believe in believing that mystery.

By faith we know that the Son proceeds from the Father, the Holy Spirit from the Father and the Son; that is, the Father is the principle of the Son, the Father and Son are one principle of the Holy Spirit. To have distinction we must have difference; and, since there is no difference whatever on the side of nature, the three Persons having the numerically same divine nature, the sole possibility of difference lies in the processions of one person from another. To our way of thinking, a principle is the cause of a thing. We cannot comprehend how one Person can proceed from another without depending in some way or another. This is precisely the heart of the mystery; this is precisely what we shall never understand. We can understand the meaning of the statement, the Father is not the cause of the Son, nor are the Father and Son the cause of the Holy Spirit. This is what we are to believe. There can be no relation of causality between the divine Persons for this would destroy the truth that they are all divine. The word "principle" is used because it signifies an order of origin in an absolute way, without determining a particular mode that would be foreign to the origin of the divine Persons. In a word, this term "principle" is invaluable because of its indefiniteness, because it hides a truth we cannot understand, shading our eyes from its splendor; it does not distort that truth. Procession, here, is not to be understood in the sense in which a word proceeds from a man's mouth to wander up and down the world, but, analogically, as an idea proceeds from the mind of a man but stays in his head. The divine processions are not processions to the outside but within divinity itself, with all that perfection of immanency that is uniquely God's.

Procession, then, in God is not as it is in the lowest creatures, that is, either by way of local movement or by way of cause proceeding to exterior effects. Rather it is in the order of the most perfect activity in its most perfect form, intellectual activity. In this order, what proceeds is not necessarily distinct from its source; indeed, the more perfectly it proceeds, the more closely it is one with its source, for the more perfect it is, the more immanent it is. The faith teaches us there are two of these processions in God, that of *generation*, by which the Son proceeds from the Father; and that of *spiration*, by which the Holy Spirit proceeds from the Father and the Son as from a common principle. We shall touch upon these again at a somewhat greater length later on in this chapter.

Reality of the Relations set up by the Processions

The point to be noted here is that these two processions set up relationships in God, the double relationship of paternity and filiations arising from generation; and the double relationship of active and passive spiration arising from the procession of the Holy Spirit from the Father and the Son. In our human order, a relation arising, say, from the anthropological classification of a man as Alpine, Mediterranean or Nordic, is purely a thing of the mind, a relation of reason; for it does not arise from the principles of the same nature. On the contrary, a man's relations to his end, to his acts, to his Creator are all real relations, arising from the very principles of his nature. A visitor to Washington, however short his stay, will certainly see the massive pillars of the Supreme Court building. By his glance at those pillars, a relation is set up between him and the pillars; on the side of the pillars that relation is a relation of reason, for the nature of pillars does not give rise to the relation brought about by being seen. In the divine order, the relations of paternity, filiation, active and passive spiration are real, not rational, relations, arising from the numerically same divine nature. As real they are distinct terms, paternity is not the same as filiation, nor is active spiration the same as passive spiration. They are real, they are intimately opposed, and, as entirely distinct from any relation in the created world, they subsist. The opposing relationships constitute the three divine persons, Father, Son and Holy Spirit. Only by such opposition of origin is there distinction in divine things; there are then, not four, but three divine persons since there is no opposition between active spiration and the relations set up by generation. All this is, of course, impossible to understand. The whole purpose of this exposition was not to make the mystery intelligible but rather to make clear wherein the mystery lies that our faith might embrace it. Nevertheless, our intellects are a restless, rowdy, independent lot; they chafe under the restraint of the incomprehensible, even although that restraint in reality is a release from the chains of the natural into the unsuspected freedom of the truths proper to God. The irritation is far from logical; but it is nonetheless quite universally human. If we can get some little grip on a mystery, even although it is by no more than our fingernails, we feel very much better. It was perhaps in recognition of this childish stubbornness, which is so common a human weakness that God moved men to conceive the most celebrated illustration of the trinity.

The Classical Illustration

It is to be remembered, however, that this is only an illustration; it is not to be taken literally, univocally. It limps because it compares the divine to the human; but it does give us that fingernail grip so necessary to pride. It goes like this. Life is activity. In the created world, it is a process of change, a process of attaining perfection or of using perfection attained. Still, throughout its keynote is immanency. The more perfect the immanency, the more perfect the life. The highest life, and consequently the most immanent activity, we know is intellectual. Coming to the absolutely perfect life of God, we can expect activity, the highest, the most perfect activity; hence activity of the most sublime immanency. Both from the fact of the perfection of the immanency of this activity and from the fact that God is pure intelligence, we can expect that His activity is intellectual activity, of which there are, to talk in our human fashion, only two principles, the intellect and the will.

The entirely immanent activity, then, from the side of the intellect of God, will be the knowledge of God, God knowing Himself. This knowledge depends in no way on anything or anyone outside of divinity, it is not measured; it proceeds to a term, God known, which is utterly perfect because utterly immanent. God knowing Himself is the principle from which proceeds the eternal Word of God, God known.

On the side of the will, which in us follows on knowledge, there is the eternal and immanent act of God's love. God, eternally knowing Himself perfectly with sublime immanence, generates the eternal Word, the Son, the perfection of the Father; the eternal and immanent breath of love of the Son for the Father and the Father for the Son is the Holy Spirit, the sign of divine love that subsists. The perfect immanency of these acts insists that no one of these three is distinct from the divine essence but entirely identical with it; the opposition of the relationships insists that they are distinct one from another. They are one God and three divine persons, consubstantial, coeternal, and coequal.

The Divine Persons

Father, Son and Holy Spirit are not called persons by a kind of poetic license; this is not figurative speech. They are persons. This is one point we can see clearly by clarifying our own notion of what a person is, shearing away the accidentals that the essential might stand out. A person, to put it as briefly as possible, is an individual intellectual substance, whatever kind of intellectual substance or in whatever way distinguished from other persons of the same nature; thus there are human persons, angelic persons, divine persons. The human person subsists in a human nature and is distinguished from all other human persons in the way proper to human nature, that is by signate matter; an angelic person subsists in an angelic nature and is distinguished from all other angelic persons in the way proper to angelic nature, that is, by a specific distinction; a divine person subsists in a divine nature and is distinguished from other divine persons in the way proper to divinity, that is, by the opposition of the relations of origin.

Sometimes we give these divine persons names that belong to them by reason of their divine nature; such names, for instance, as almighty, good, merciful. These names belong, not to any one person, but to all three for the numerically identical divine nature is common to all three. At other times, we address the divine persons by names that belong to them, not by reason of the divine nature, but by reason of the opposition of the relations of origin; such names, for instance, as Father, Son, Holy Spirit. These are completely proper names, the name of the Son cannot be given to the Holy Spirit, for title to it is by the relation of filiation, which is proper to the Son alone. It is worth noting that when we say the "Our Father" we are addressing the whole Trinity, not merely the first Person; for God is our Father, not by the eternal generation of the Son, but by creation which, like all external operations, is common to the three Persons.

One of the most reassuring things about the mystery of the Trinity is its incomprehensibility. It is grand to have so concrete an assurance that our minds do not tell the whole glorious story of intelligence, that the crumbs of truth we amass so laboriously are only crumbs, not the sum total of truth's banquet, that the feeble glow which hardly lights up a path for our own steps is not the light of the world. The concrete assurance of this incomprehensibility comes to the solitary human mind like the comfort of a lost child's discovery of its parents; with a joy too big for words and too deep for laughter, with rekindled hopes and the utter, unquestioning, eager surrender of faith.

Conclusion

Some children, however, seem to have been born disillusioned. Someone has told them the truth about Santa Claus and now they spend their days in pouting. They are determined to be happy with the introduction to the story of intelligence, to be surfeited with the crumbs of truth, to light up the world with the match they have just blown out. They will get along without God and His incomprehensible mysteries; above all they will have nothing to do with the Trinity. Yet they never quite make their renunciation stick. Although they abolish God and the Trinity, they make a travesty on the divinity and the divine persons.

Parodies of the Trinity

It is palpably true that the man who denies God makes a god of his own with much more piteous results than the amateur wood-carver ever produces; but there is reason behind the unreason, for every man must have a goal towards which he aims his life. It is not at all clear why man should also produce a burlesque of the Trinity in abandoning it; the fact is clear enough. He makes himself and his material world as unbegotten as the Father; his intellectual effort is concentrated on self and the material world, sometimes even to the extent of that intellectual effort producing the world; from this knowledge of self and the world, a knowledge that is necessarily streaked with broad bands of ignorance, arises an abiding love that leaves room for no rival. It is an attempt at the perfection of immanency without the perfection of life that must underlie immanency, a parody of divine self-sufficiency, which accomplishes eternity by overlooking the beginning and the end, a caricature, which ends in mere bustling, of the intensity of divine life.

Horror of Death

Even for the undemanding purposes of burlesque there are too many characters involved; one or the other must go. So eventually, either the world is pushed aside while a man wraps the folds of his being about himself and retires into the arid oblivion of solipsism; or the individual is pulled into the maw of the world to furnish the material for the nourishment of a mass. Whichever way the choice turns one of two, or perhaps both, characteristic qualities come to the surface. If it is the mass that absorbs the individual, then there is little horror of death for death has already become a living thing; but there is a panicky fear of human life, a haunting terror that paralyzes a man at the very thought of being alone, being responsible, of possessing a life with a meaning. On the other hand, where the individual excludes the world, there is apt to be a combination of the two, a horror of death and a fear of life; his very precautions against death, his watchwords of security and safety first, his revulsion from physical hardship and sacrifice, will make it impossible to drink deeply from the hearty cup of life. He is so afraid of death that he starts his dying in the prime of life; life is so precious a thing, he dare not handle it.

Fear of Life

The thing is logical enough. He has made a little trinity of himself; and no one knows better than he that that trinity is not a principle of undying life, that here there is no eternal grip on the elusive victory over death. He knows he has life only for an instant; why should he not fear death? He knows, as no one else knows, that life is too big for his little trinity, that it escapes his mind, his will, his hands; why should he not be afraid of life?

Thirst for Life -- Climax of Life

Obviously a man cannot be consumed with a thirst for life and cut himself off from the full perfection of divine life. Obviously a man cannot be in love with life and either pushes it coldly from him or try to enfold its intensity within himself. Thirst for life must mean thirst for that perfection of action which is described by immanency; or in plainer terms, thirst for life must mean thirst for God, thirst for that absolutely immanent activity of the Trinity. This is the eternal and perfect life of God, all other life is a participation of this divine life, all other activity is a participation of this activity. All other life, all other activity, is perfect in proportion as it approaches to that complete immanence of divine life. This is the climax of all life, the top of the scale of life, which is beyond all scales, the peak that is also the foundation, the beginning that is also the end.

📖 CHAPTER VIII – THE ARCHITECT AT WORK 📖
(Q. 44-49)

1. The story of the world

    (a) A story that must be told.

    (b) A story from which the architect cannot be omitted.

2. The unfolding of the story.

3. The cause of the world,

    (a) The fact of the cause.

    (b) The manner of the world's production,

        (1) Dualistic explanations

            a. A principle of perfection and of imperfection.

            b. A principle of good and of evil.

        (2) Monistic explanations,

            a.   Pantheism.

            b.   Evolution.

            c.   Creation.

4. The stuff of the world.

5. The model of the world,

    (a) Primary and secondary models.

    (b) Source of order and law.

6. The goal of the world,

  (a) Necessity of the goal.

  (b) Objections against the goal.

7. The variety of the world

8. The age of the world,

  (a) From reason.

  (b) From faith.

Conclusion

  1. Fictions and facts of the world.

  2. Purposes and failures of fiction.

  3. Comfort and significance of the facts.

▣ CHAPTER VIII ▣
THE ARCHITECT AT WORK
(Q 44-49)

The Story of the World

History has been described as a blend of art and philosophy. Too much history has been, in actual practice, a blend of fiction and fact. Whatever its components or mode of procedure, it usually makes for comfortable reading even when its matter is unpleasant; we can be calm, detached, judicious about it. After all, these men are not going to rise from the dead and challenge us to debate or duel; the past is securely dead and we can look on its face as securely as we would on the corpse of an enemy, totaling up its mistakes, jibing at its incompetencies, smiling at its pretensions, stifling its protests as easily and majestically as we silence a radio commentator.

A Story that must be Told

We can be entirely impersonal about history, that is, about most history. Detailed accounts of men, of nations, of races, even of hundreds of centuries can pass before our eyes, as thousands of cases pass before a judge's bench, leaving our lives untouched, our appetites unimpaired, our satisfaction with ourselves undisturbed. When we dig a little deeper and strike the rock bottom of the story of activity, it is an altogether different question; we cannot shrug off the fundamental history of the world for this is an intensely personal matter.

The mere contact of the world of reality with a human intellect arouses difficulties; and no one, as yet, has succeeded in avoiding that contact. Nor is it a matter of specialized difficulties particularly prepared for the palate of an historian or a philosopher; some of these difficulties plague the steps of every man and woman born into the world. They clamor for an answer with an insistence that is almost uncouth; they will not be put off, silenced, brushed aside and on their answer depends the whole course of human life in every age. Men have to know how the world came about; of what it was made; what was the model for this stupendous work; why it was made at all and when; whence comes the immense variety in the world and why; what keeps it going.

Clearly the answers to such questions cannot fall into the classification of a soothing bedtime story with which we calm our hearts in preparation for death, as we calm the children before sending them off to undergo the mysterious risk of sleep's oblivion. This cannot be the pleasant fiction with which we dissipate the isolation of a cold winter evening, peopling the house with shadowy guests. This is not a tale of the past buried with the past; it is a story of the past that molds the present. On the basis of it, men live their lives wisely or insanely, hopefully or despairingly, courageously or cringing in cowardice, successfully or in miserable failure.

A Story from which the Architect Cannot be Omitted.

It might reasonably be objected that this book, as a companion to the *Summa*, is a theological book. If that means anything, it means a book about God, why not stick to the proper subject matter of such a book and leave the consideration of the world to scientists and philosophers? It is certainly true that this is a theological book and that theology deals with God. Let the objector be assured that the proper subject matter of theology will be closely adhered to in this book, as it is in St. Thomas' masterpiece; here, as there, whatever the immediate matter of discussion, be it heaven or hell, sin or virtue, mud or stars, saint or sinner, the youth of the world or the agelessness of Cod, everything will be treated precisely in its reference to God.

It is less astonishing that a theological book should treat of the world than that a book about the world should attempt to omit a consideration of God. As a matter of fact, God has something to do with, some part to play in, the unfolding of every act in the drama of the universe. Indeed, nothing in the whole universe is adequately considered, nothing is truly seen, truly located, truly evaluated, until it is considered in relation to God. Like everything we say about God, calling Him the architect of the universe is decidedly inadequate. After all, an architect is responsible only for the form of the house; if he has left his plans handy, the construction of the house can get along very well without him. The house once finished, the architect slips away into the obscure regions of his office; the rest of the story of the house and the human drama that unfolds within it is completely outside the scope of a blueprint. God is the architect of the universe; but He is also its builders its sustainer, its governor, the source of its life, and its activity, its goal.

A philosopher looks at the world in the flickering light of human reason, tirelessly carrying on his endless search for the last answers as they are open to the human mind. Theology also looks for last answers. Still, it is much more than human wisdom. It is the supreme wisdom which, gazing down from the far horizons of eternity, with the background of infinite experience and under the floodlight of the first Truth gives that mellowed, rounded judgment that is the last, the adequate, the satisfying answer to the world and its smallest detail.

Theology has indeed something to say of the world. As a matter of fact, we started off our theological considerations with the world. That primary consideration, however, took the world merely as a starting point, a jumping-off-place for an expedition into divinity. We have not, as yet, attempted to consider the created world in itself; rather, talking a small, obvious fact of the world, such as the movement of an eyelash, the perfection of a stone, the order revealed in a human eye, we mounted to the heights of the life of God

The Unfolding of the Story

In this chapter we start a detailed examination of the world. A plunge into the mass of detail in that world might easily cost us proper perspective, trapping us into mistaking an anthill for a mountain. It will be much better to stand off a little, trying for a general view of the country we are about to invade, tracing its main outlines, fitting its salient features well in our minds, familiarizing ourselves with the topography of the country, at least in a rough fashion, before we set out on our journey. That general view is the goal of this present chapter.

Beginning with the next chapter, and continuing through all the rest of the book, we shall examine the world in detail. We shall look thoroughly into the spiritual world, the material world and into that doubly mysterious world that is part spirit and part material, the world of man. Throughout this chapter and all the others, we shall be considering God, not God as He is in Himself, His nature, the Trinity of divine person that has all been done; but God as creatures proceeded from Him. God the Creator and Governor of the world.

The Cause of the World

The story of the world is not a detective thriller. Consequently the purpose of such a story is not to confuse the mind, hide the answers, or appeal to impossible explanations. It is a story that must be told quickly, clearly and completely; for all men must have all of it accurately before they can begin the absorbing task of human living. Yet it is by no means a simple story; the created world it explains furnishes the philosopher with such fundamental problems as the many proceeding from the one without injury to that unity, and the action of the first cause, and purpose in a world too big for the philosopher's mind to grasp its plan. The difficulties of the man who is no philosopher and the mysteries that besiege the mind of the man who is trying hard to be a philosopher are not, as a matter of fact, wholly different things. They coalesce in the central problem of the cause of the created universe, what is its efficient cause and how does this cause work; what was its material cause; its formal or exemplary cause; its final cause or end? Along the lines of this fourfold question the story of the world must unfold.

The Fact of the Cause

In the second chapter of this book, we have seen that the efficient cause of the world can only be God. There we saw that the only possible explanation of the existence of the created world was a completely independent first cause upon which every creature, every activity, even motion, every mark of intelligence, every bit of order depends. The question here, then, is not one of God's existence and His first causality; rather it is a question of penetrating into the manner of operation of God. How did He work? How was the created world actually produced?

The Manner of the World's Production, Dualistic Explanations, a Principle of Perfection and of Imperfection

Many philosophers jumped at the obvious answer of dualism. There was much perfection in the world; and there was much imperfection. They proceeded to their solution as a man might conclude there was a masculine and a feminine influence at work in an apartment where one room was a model of neatness, everything folded and packed away so that nothing could be found, while another room showed a cluttered desk, heaped chairs and littered floors with everything in instant reach of one's hand. These philosophers decided that there were two first principles one of complete perfection, the other of complete imperfection; from the principle of imperfection, the principle of perfection worked out the creatures of the world. The solution was quick, obvious and worthless. As a matter of fact, there simply cannot be two first principles, as we have seen in treating of the existence of God. Moreover, this principle of imperfection, while dependent on another for every development, is yet independent in existence; which is like saying that a man has everything but humanity, or a dog lacks nothing but canine qualities A dependent first principle of being comes as close to reality as a hollow shell without an external surface.

A Principle of Good and of Evil

This, however, does not discourage the dualists. They come forth with another variety of solution that seems more plausible but, actually, is just as hopelessly contradictory. Because there was good in the world and also very much evil, and because evil is so unalterably opposed to good, the universe was explained by two principles, each supreme in its own field, one of good, the other of evil. These two do not work together, nor one upon the other, but against one another; good is the triumph of the principle of good, evil is a memorial of a battle where the principle of good was defeated by the principle of evil. It sometimes happens that the Christian truths of God and the devil are given this interpretation; perhaps Satan relishes this sort of thing, but it is empty of truth. Stills, truth must be a bitter dose to one in the devil's position.

Again the explanation is quick, obvious and worthless. A principle of evil supreme in its own field would be essentially evil, that is, it would have no good in it. That statement sounds rather solid, if a man stops thinking immediately. The trouble is that evil is not something positive, something one can put a finger on; the very essence of evil demands that it elude your finger, it is something missing, a defect. To have an evil at all, there must be a good capable of having holes in it for evil is precisely the hole in good. Immediately we concentrate on evil in any one order, the absurdity of a supreme evil becomes manifest. Evil, for instance, in the moral order, is a violation of reason, an unreasonable act; if, then, moral evil is absolutely complete, reason itself is destroyed to the destruction of the very possibility of moral evil. In a word, evil, if it is complete, destroys itself. Of course there is always something good to say about a bad thing; a filthy book will always have something good about it, it will be beautifully written, have a strong binding, or at least be cheap. There has to be something good in it or there could be nothing bad; the outstanding characteristic, then, of a first principle of evil would have to be, from the very nature of evil, its non-existence.

Evil cannot be a first principle for evil supposes good, in which alone it can exist; it cannot be independent, existing of itself, for that is its destruction. Moreover, evil does not appear suddenly, for no reason and from nowhere, like the words that pop out of a giddy, empty head. Evil must be brought about, it must have a cause. Of course it has no formal cause, it is the defect or privation of form to some degree. Neither has it a final cause, for it is essentially a privation of order to an end. To look for a material cause of evil does not mean looking for something from which to make evil, like hunting for the material for paper dolls; it means searching for some apt location for evil, a location that can be nothing else than a good. As for efficient cause, well, evil is always a by-product; it is never produced directly. It cannot be an efficient cause itself, for it is a defect; it cannot have an efficient cause, except indirectly, as the death of a carrot has its cause in the rabbit's direct action to nourish itself. In other words, evil's outstanding quality is one of complete dependence; whereas a first principle is outstandingly independent.

If we place evil in the human order as a first principle, we are establishing as a first cause either sin or punishment; for evil affecting man is either a defect of integrity or a defect in act, the first a punishment, at least of original sin, the second, sin itself. Strange qualities, indeed, to propose as ultimate explanations of anything; but as far as that goes, all dualism is strange, as strange as a myopic man stubbornly insisting that there is nothing beyond what he can see. That is, in fact, the fundamental error of dualism, it is near-sighted. It focuses on particular causes, blinds itself to universal causality; it cannot see over the hill, so there is nothing beyond the hill. It sees only particular effects and makes its sweeping judgment from them, or it sees the contrariety of particular causes and concludes to contrariety in the very fundamentals of causality. These are the blind who insist on leading others; the marvel is that they can find so many ditches to fall into.

Monistic Explanations

Dualism attempts to explain the diversity of the world by a diversity of principles; at the other extreme is monism, explaining that diversity on the basis of a single principle. Of its multiple forms, three, which are fundamental are worth detailed consideration.

Pantheism

Pantheism solves the problem by denying it. It is the original sin of Eastern philosophy and the proud child of ultra-modern American philosophical parents. To its mind there is no question of the world coming from God, or from anything else; the world is God, a manifestation of the absolute that is identical with it. The world is an internal evolution of the divine substance.

The ancient philosophers advanced this denial of the problem to avoid what seemed to them a rupture of the unity of being; it was an escape from the apparently unbridgeable chasm between the finite and the infinite, it side-stepped the apparent contradiction of the addition of Created beings to the sum of the infinite to the impossible total of more than infinite being. The moderns advance it as a necessity for the philosopher who would keep pace with science, as a means of the preservation of the unity and hierarchy of being, and as the essential condition for keeping knowledge where it belongs, in the realm of science. The older cause of this explanation of the universe was intellectual cowardice, in face of the difficulty of a solution, the problem was denied; this led, as most cowardice does, to still more awesome difficulties. The modern adoption of the same explanation is rather an intellectual betrayal, an assassination by strangulation of the one faculty that could recognize the problem and find an answer for it.

Both lead to the same absurdities, the identification of the perfect and the imperfect, the contingent and the necessary, the free and the forced, matter and spirit, animal and angel. Both have so perverted the intellect as to have it swallow calmly the identification of opposites, which normally nauseates it. In doing away with the difficulty they do away with God; in explaining away the necessity of the first cause, they destroy the cause itself. They do not meet the problem courageously; faced with it, they collapse and blow out their brains.

Evolution

The second monistic explanation is a widespread favorite today, the explanation of evolution. Let it be well understood that evolution, as an explanation of the universe, is not a working scientific hypothesis but a philosophic thesis; and it is precisely under its philosophical aspect that we are dealing with it here. Logically it is pantheism; it is admitted as such by many of its modern adherents. To others, that logical connection is not evident; they insist it is not pantheism, either because there is no God or because the god they admit has none of the attributes of the first cause, that is, their god has everything but divinity. We shall go into this philosophical evolution later on in this book, in treating of the origin of man.

For the present it will suffice to point out that evolution like pantheism, is not an explanation but a denial of all explanation. Some primary stuff, eternal or mysteriously giving birth to itself, slowly and inexorably developed, by chance and an equally mysterious environment, into the complicated world we know as the universe. Or, in another form, a mysterious life force, utterly imperfect, has blindly, necessarily surged its way up through matter, which is unexplained into the perfections we know to day. In this second form, there is no universe, no material world; only the process of perfection without a perfected substance, a process that does not stop long enough for us to know it. It is a river of undetermined origin ceaselessly flowing to undetermined seas; or, rather, the flowing without the river into seas without water.

Both these philosophical forms of evolution are very, very old; both have undergone face-lifting operations, both now travel by plane and dress in adolescent clothes to prove they are modern. The immediate, and modern, cause of this evolutionary explanation has undoubtedly been the mistaken effort to make a philosophy out of a scientific method. More profound reasons were the intellectual suicide of philosophy, following the devastating assumptions of a chasm between the mental and physical world, and the religious rationalism of Reformation times whose logical conclusion was the exaltation of human nature to the pinnacle of the universe by debasing it to the level of the material universe.

Whatever the explanation of its origin, evolution, as an answer to the questions evoked by the created world, fails. In its scientific form, it offers a highly plausible explanation of *how* the universe unfolded; in none of its forms does it offer an explanation of *why* the universe unfolded at all, or why and how there was a universe. A process is not an explanation but a demand for an explanation. Piling millions of years on a question does not smother the insistent query; it merely betrays fear of the question and despair of the answer. Slowing up the process to a hobbling pace does not change the problem nor its demand for a solution.

Creation

Creation, the third monistic explanation, is offered us by our faith and forced on us by our reason. It is commonly defined as "making something out of nothing;" a description that, while not inaccurate, is subject to misunderstanding. More properly, creation is defined as the production of an effect independently of any pre-existing subject; it is, in a word, the production of the whole being of a thing. The world was produced by the first cause in the way proper to that first cause, that is, with complete independence; if we maintain that there was anything upon which to depend, we have simply pushed the problem back and denied that this particular cause was first. Complete independence in action means production independently of any pre-existing subject.

The proofs for this explanation of the universe are those already given for the existence of God. For either this was the way things were produced or there are no things; there is no other way to account for the universe. Nor is this merely a question of accounting for the big things, mountains, continents, planets and stars; the question extends to the smallest of things, a speck of dust, the wink of an eye. One cries out the existence of the first cause and His mode of action, creation, as loudly as the other, or as all together. Either there is a first cause or there are no effects; either that first cause created (if He acted at all) or He is not first.

Though creation is the only reasonable explanation of the universe, men have consistently fought it throughout the ages. Such resistance to reason obviously needs clarification. One cause undoubtedly has been stiff-necked intellectual pride, which refuses to bow before a mystery; and creation, from the side of God, precisely as His divine action, is a mystery. It is the infinite operation of God, the same as His divine essence; the comprehension of this action of creation would be comprehension of divinity itself. We can prove the world cannot have come into existence any other way and we know it has come into existence; nor are we at all reasonable in rejecting creation on the grounds that all truths must fit into the mould of our finite minds. In fact, we confess to the unreasonableness of this demand in our easy acceptance of such mysteries as life, solar action on the planets and many others in the purely natural sphere.

Some men have seen creation as a glorified bit of magic, with God pulling worlds out of nothingness as a magician pulls rabbits out of a hat. The real difficulty here is not that something is produced from nothing; that, in fact, is a fundamental dogma of the evolutionary thesis on emergent perfections. The educated among the modern individuals do not shrink from this sort of thing; they rush to embrace it, especially if something is produced from nothing without adequate cause. Real intellectual repugnance lies rather in the admission of the production of something without a cause; in the mystery of creation, there are absolutely no grounds for this repugnance, for here the supreme cause is operating.

Other men hare rebelled at the effortless ease of God's action in creation, refusing to accept such a notion as the motionless action by which the universe sprang into being, the omnipotence of the whispered command of God. They would, no doubt, feel better if the work of creation had cost God effort. Yet these same men are fairly reasonable when the same philosophical principle is at stake in other matters. They do not chase flies with a spray of machine gun bullets nor close their fist to punch their way through a fog; in these cases, they see clearly that the dominance of the agent proportions the movement and effort necessary to his action. They expect an ant to stagger under the weight of a bit of grass; if a stalwart athlete staggers into a stadium under the same weight, they can be sure they are witnessing comedy or insanity. However, they rebel at the notion that absolute omnipotence should produce effects by mere command.

The creation of finite beings in no sense destroys the unity of being, as the pantheists feared. That unity is to I be found in God Who has all perfection eminently. Created beings do not add something to the sum total of being; they participate being. They do not limit the infinite, marking off the spot where the Creator ends and the creature begins; for limitation is not so much by points of distinction as it is by subsistence or independence. My being, for example, is not limited by the being of my hand or my arm, but rather limits their being. If the thousands who listen to an orator were dependent on him for their very being, then they would not limit his being, rather he would limit theirs for they are dependent on him, not he on them; precisely because these listeners are not dependent but independent of the orator, they do limit his being. If a search of the universe were to uncover one being independent of God, then there would be a limitation of God; until such a time, no multiplicity of created things adds to or limits the being of God.

There is one last point to be noted about creation. It is not only the only way in which the world could have come into existence, not only the only way in which the first cause could act to produce the world; it is an act uniquely proper to the first cause. Only God can produce something independently of any preexisting subject. This might be made clear by insisting that only a whole cause can produce the whole of being, that we can expect no more than partial effects from partial causes; and only God is a whole cause in the sense of possessing the full perfection of causality. The same truth comes out from a consideration of the effect of creation, namely, being. Thus a damp rag cannot produce all the modeled effects of a summer shower, for the rag only participates the sopping wetness, which belongs essentially to rain; in the same way, no total effect such as creation demands can be expected from a cause that only participates being.

We can push this truth still further to point out that not only can no secondary cause of itself create, absolutely nothing in the universe, from the highest angel to the least of things, can be used by God as the instrument of creation. The closest anyone or anything comes to taking part in creation is the human mother who cooperates with God in the production of His masterpiece of humanity; she prepares the material destined for union with a spiritual soul that can come into being only by the direct action of God. It is not divine snobbishness that excludes all created causes from creative activity; there simply is nothing in the act of creation for a created cause to do. Given a choice between a sponge and a hammer for the work of driving a nail, we would, of course, select the hammer as the proper instrument, knowing well that an instrument must have its proper effect or there is no sense in using it. It would be too much to expect the sponge to stiffen up sufficiently to drive the nail; that simply is not the effect of a sponge. It is much too much to expect a Created cause to produce its proper effect when there is nothing, absolutely nothing, on which it might produce that effect.

The stuff of the world

With the efficient cause of the world determined and something of its nature and manner of operation understood, the rest of the story of the world tumbles over itself in its eagerness to get down on the pages before we write finis to the book. If we appear to start off on another avenue in search of the stuff of the world or its model, we know very well that we are simply taking a circular stroll that will bring us back to the same delightful spot that is divinity.

The thought of our time almost makes it necessary to talk of the stuff of the world, the very phraseology implying, erroneously, that there was some pre-existent subject upon which divinity worked. In this erroneous sense, it is said that God Himself is the material cause, the stuff, of the world. Yet, this is to slip back into the unhealthy, primeval slime of pantheism or evolution where both God and the intellect must die to keep a monster alive. It is true that only God is the sufficient explanation of the existence of the material of the universe. Even though we take this material in the sense of extreme imperfection, which the philosophers designate by "prime matter," it must still be traced to the first cause, the more so because of its utter dependence. It is positively childish to picture the material of the universe as the stuff from which God fashioned the universe much as a child fashions muddies from a handful of mud. Moreover, that material is itself a part of the universe and can actually exist only as a part of the concrete things that make up that universe. It is not a prerequisite of creation but an effect of it; it is not something with which God must have started off, but something that must have started off from God's act of creation.

The Model of the World

The search for the model of the universe leads us even more directly to God. As intelligent effects do not pop out of nowhere without rhyme or reason, it is obvious that there must be a model for the universe. Now and then, when we drag our tired eyes above the dust and confusion of the moment to let the fresh winds of the future and the dry breezes of the past wash and refresh them, we catch some insight into the truth that only God could be the model of the universe. Some detail of the masterpiece, the minuteness of love's thoughtfulness, the magnitude of a mountain, the power of a smashing wind, brings out the genius of the craftsman and we are almost ready to fall down in adoration. If the model were anything other than God, then He would not be first, He would be dependent; that is, He would not be God.

Primary and Secondary Models

In spite of the suffering, the vice, the ugliness, the evil in the universe, the scale to which it is drawn, the plan upon which it is built, its blueprint is the eternal knowledge of Cod. It is not these defects that are difficult to explain; but the beauty, the joy, the perfection, the virtue, the happiness, the very existence of the universe can be conceived in no other way than as participations of that divine perfection. Who but God could know the possible participations of that divinity, the myriad mirrors that could reflect the divine excellence. We have seen this in some detail in an earlier chapter on the knowledge of God. Here it is only necessary to point out that the divine character of the model of the universe is not a denial of all other models. Of course an architect can have, in his mind, a model of the house he is building; of course a boy can choose a model upon, which he builds his character. These are not excluded but rather made possible by the fact that the supreme architect is in possession of the first and absolutely universal model to which everything in the universe responds.

Without such a model, the divine action would not be the intelligent operation of divine wisdom but the stupidly haphazard wanderings of a drunkard or an idiot; deter mined forms of things can come only from the determined plan of their maker. Even the so called "accidental" discoveries of scientific research are the inviolable results of a determined divine plan giving determined qualities to the elements that enter into that research. The scientist can repeat the "accident" again and again, precisely because the only accidental thing involved was his discovery that there was no accident at all.

Source of Law and Order

These divine ideas, the model of the universe, are, then, the source of all order, an order that extends not merely to the physical outlines of the universe but to the essential principles of all natures, to the details of all acts. This order, which brings the benediction of peace and precludes the chaos of madness, embraces not only the physical and spiritual world of being but also the moral world of men's acts. To all these worlds it gives standards as stable as the divine mind. It is as impossible for the morality of men's acts to fluctuate from age to age as it is for the nature of angels, of men or of water to change. The moral laws are not the result of a caprice, not even of a divine caprice; they cannot be changed even at the pleasure of God. That divine model of the universe is immutable; so also is His law, which is the ultimate root of the order which governs the universe, for the model is one of the roots of the law.

The Goal of the World

Why were these things of the universe created at all? Why did God extend His activity beyond divinity itself? What was His purpose; what is the end of it all? Surely there must have been some goal; God, above all cannot act for no reason at all for that would be a disorderly act, a violation of His divine intelligence. Rather, the absence of an end, the complete indetermination thus involved, would result in no act at all. An act does not saunter aimlessly about the universe, or about the walks of eternity; it is going some place or it does not start at all.

Necessity of the Goal

From what we know of the nature of God, it should be clear that there is only one goal, one end, possible to Him, if He acts at all, He must act for Himself. God created the universe for Himself; His goal was God; the end of the universe is the same as its beginning, God. Anything else is simply unthinkable. If God were working to a goal other than Himself, divine independence would be a myth as would the primacy of the first cause; God would, through the long life of the universe, be creeping up on something He lacked, mapping out a campaign for the capture of something outside Himself. There simply cannot be anything outside of God that does not come from Him, He cannot lack anything and still be God. Aside from the divine nature, the divine action cannot tolerate any other end than God, God, the absolutely perfect agent, must act in a perfect manner, not in the imperfect manner of an imperfect agent striving to perfect himself. The perfect agent, having all perfection, can act only for himself.

Objections Against the Goal

This truth has caused many a sniff at God by high-minded pagans. The idea! This is the God Who demands complete unselfishness and self-denial from us, yet, having all things, He cannot in the least of His works act for anything but Himself. This is a mean, petty, grasping God that a man can enjoy cheating. Like many another sniff, these protests of outraged nobility are entirely due to a misunderstanding; indignation stamps out, slamming the door, before it can be explained that the phrase "for himself" is equivocally used of man and God. A man, because he is an imperfect agent, reaches out to get something when he acts for himself; God, because He is a perfect agent, reaches out to give something away when He acts for Himself. We act to obtain or insure our perfection; God acts, in the only way He can act having all perfection, only to communicate His goodness. This is the perfect act, communication of goodness; this is the exact meaning of God acting for Himself.

Let us suppose these noble pagans had their way with God and He decided not to act for Himself, what would happen? Obviously, nothing would exist, for God cannot act any other way. Now on the impossible hypothesis that God created the world and then washed His hands of it, as an ultra-modern mother gives birth to a child then turns it over to household and institutional servants, what would happen? Such a world would not be directed to Him, men and creatures would push God entirely out of their lives, out of their actions. The result? A howling chaos; a world full of creatures with no possible end in view; heartless brutality; men remorselessly driven by a desire for love and knowledge of God, a desire doomed to hopeless frustration. The whole thing would be a humorless practical joke on a cosmic scale, a mass of whirling worlds going nowhere, like a man driving himself insane by marching about the living room in a perpetual circle.

For the perfection, the end, of anything is the same as its beginning; the effect comes from the cause faith something of the excellence of the cause, certainly no more, usually very much less and it approaches its perfection as it approaches the excellence of its cause. All things coming from God reach their perfection as they approach the divine likeness, which is the peak of that infinitesimal participation of divine perfection which makes them what they are.

The Variety of the World

The end or purpose of creation was to communicate the divine goodness so on every side of us we see something of the family likeness of God. The staggering variety of the universe is the result of divine ingenuity's struggle to paint, in the stiff medium of creatures, a likeness of the gracious beauty of God. Of course even the divine artist failed. No finite creature is capable of receiving all of divine goodness, no one creature is capable of perfectly mirroring that divine perfection. It is more perfectly mirrored through the multiplication of different species of creatures; but even indefinite multiplication through all of an eternity fails to give back an adequate likeness of the face of God. The divine likeness, perceptible to the keen eyes of a saint in the lowest creatures of the world, is like the image given back to a woman by the one faulty mirror in her room; the bewildering beauty and inconceivable variety of the angelic world gives the effect of many mirrors each giving back a particular view, but no one of them nor all of them together, do more than catch a mood, a passing gesture, the light of a smile. Worlds could have been multiplied, as mirrors can be multiplied, but the results would be no more adequate. Nor, for that matter, would they be any more disparate; whatever the number of worlds created, the whole of creation would still be bound tightly together by an order to the only possible end, God Himself. Whatever God does must be orderly and there can be only one principle of that order, one end, God.

The Age of the World, From Reason

The story of the world, as the story of the likeness of God on earth, is a beautiful story. It is also a long, long story; how long we do not know. Our faith assures us that it is not as long a story as eternity, that it is not coeternal with God. Many modern scientific discoveries are taken by their discoverers as proofs from reason of the beginnings of the world at some definite time, such discoveries, for example, as the breakdown of radio active substances, the laws of thermodynamics tending than equilibrium of energy, the account of the years graphically written in geological strata, and so on. These may indeed be indications of a *fact* and a decided embarrassment to those devotees of a scientific method as a philosophy who have found their place among the evolutionists. But these discoveries are not proofs of the *necessity of the fact*. Neither the eternity of the world nor its beginning in time can be proved by human reason.

From Faith

There is no place for such a proof to start. If we begin the argument from the side of God, there is the obvious fact that since this creative action was free and He existed from all eternity, He could have created from all eternity or He could have created in time. If we decide to build up the argument from the side of the created world itself, we are blocked by the fact that the essential natures within the world do not, in themselves, include any reference to or against time; they contain merely a reference to a cause, an insistence that they did not produce themselves. It is to be noticed, however, that even if the world were eternal, the problem of its cause would remain unchanged; the world's dependence would not be destroyed by its eternity, nor would its ageless existence make of it a first cause. In other words, the problem of the cause of the world is not to be dismissed by hiding it in the vast spaces of eternity any more than heaping the centuries upon it can destroy it. We can know without faith that the world has its causal beginning and what is its end; faith alone can assure us that it had its temporal beginning. Even so, the story of the world is a long, long story; a story that is never finished and never untold. It has been told from the beginning of the lives of men. In the telling, it has passed through the minds, the hearts and the hands of all the countless millions of men who have looked out upon the world up to this time. Some were simple, others sophisticated; there were wise men and very foolish men; cowards and men of courage; the far seeing and the blind; the humble and the proud. The story has done something to all these men; and many of them have done something to the story. The centuries still to unfold will not vary the variety of men who listen to the story and tell it to their children; it will do things to them and many of them will do things to the story.

Conclusion, Fictions and Facts of the World

The story, however, will not be changed; there will merely be some spurious versions of it circulated with great popularity for a moment, then the old, old story will go on. There are bound to be spurious versions, as there have been in the past, because the story itself will not be to the liking of everyone. For one reason or another, men make their own changes in the old tale, as if their telling of it could mold the world. To some, the beginning of the story will be absurd because they did not witness it; they will do away with the beginning and start in the middle. To others; the end will be too hard and strong a thing to face; they will do away with the end, keeping something of the end's gift of order, as a murderer will do away with a man but hold fast to his fortune. Others will be displeased with the way the world started and call on their own distorted imaginations for versions that are not so much mysterious as grotesque and absurd. Still others will be quite content with the world and the way it runs along, but insulted by the idea of an architect of it all; they will make the most of the house and laugh the architect into oblivion.

Purposes and Failures of Fiction

These, of course, are fictions, playthings of the mind of children whose greatest value is that they make no change in the facts. It is still true that the world had a beginning and has an end; that it sprang from nothing at the command of an omnipotent Creator. The madness and chaos that should flow From a causeless world whirling to no purpose clever crimes about; the despair that should saturate the lives of men in a meaningless world never displaces the hope established by the facts of the World. The fictions might have been concocted that the sophisticated might revel in their superiority, that the foolish might clown with impunity, that cowards might run away from life, the blind enjoy their darkness and the proud lord it over their little world. Still, it never is kindness that caters to and encourages the weakness of men; it is merely hurrying the half-reluctant suicide over the abyss he has been flitting with. The fictions fail as substitutes for the truth of the story of the world, for truth has no substitutes; the more heartily they are hugged to the breasts of men, the more completely do they betray men. In his heart, the superficial, cynical sophisticate has a deeper knowledge of his own pettiness than ever another man will have; the coward knows well his lack of courage; the blind, his lack of light; and the proud, the lowliness of the throne he occupies.

Comfort and Significance of the Facts

The story of the world is a hard story only to weak men who are very proud. To all others, it is the solid bedrock on which a man can build the towering spires of his human life. The omnipotent Creator is an assurance upon which a man can begin his life with the unwavering confidence of strong youth; the source of the world's material is a dash of common sense that protects man from the absurdities of modeled and hedonism, from irrational gloom and senseless ecstasy; the divine model is his explanation of the beauty, the order, the peace that links all of creation to the family of God. The goal of the world explains his present restlessness, his incredible hopes and courageous efforts, the values that make life a cheap coin to be spent extravagantly in the attainment of this last thing that gives meaning to the world, to life, to struggle and even to failure.

CHAPTER IX

THE ANGELIC WORLD
(Q. 50-53; 61)

1. Banishment of the angels,

    (a) By the ancestors of modern philosophy.

    (b) By the moderns,

        (1)Its reasons

        (2) Its effects.

2. The angels and the ages

3. Universality of belief in angels,

    (a) Testimony of men.

    (b) Testimony of philosophy.

    (c) Testimony of history.

        (1c) Explanation of this universality,

            (1) Primitive revelation.

            (2) Angelic effects.

            (3) Reason.

3. Existence of the angels,

    (a) From faith

    (b) From reason,

(1) From the perfection of the universe.

(2) From the imperfection of the human intellect.

4. Nature of the angels

   (a) Their simplicity.

   (b) Their incorruptibility.

   (c) Their variety and number.

5. Consequences of the angelic nature

   (a) In relation to bodies.

   (b) in relation to place.

   (c) in relation to movement.

Conclusion, 1.Companionship of the angels,

        (a) An inspiration.

        (b) An acceptance of the limits of man.

        (c) An insistence on the excellencies of man

   2. The appeal of the angels.

   3. Room for the angels.

Banishment of the Angels

As the modern society edits it, the first dreadful chapter in human history has been recast, the roles changed so that the victim is now victimizer. Originally the angels stood at the gates of Paradise, inexorable, their swords flaming, as the first man and woman trudged out of the Garden disconsolate to begin their long, lonely exile. Today it is the angel who is banished and man who stands, inexorable, his words a flaming sword, guarding the barriers of the world. Of course, an angel is a difficult person to get at, even with a flaming sword; but the moderns have done the best they could. If it were possible to imagine a bedraggled angel, the victim of the modern decree would be a sorry sight; for here there is no promise of a redemption or a Redeemer. Indeed, if the angels had to take this stern exile seriously, their lot would be much more serious than was that of Adam and Eve, the first man and woman were forbidden a corner of the earth and made to climb the hill to heaven; the angels, if the moderns had their way, would have no corner of the earth left to them, nor any place in heaven or in hell. They would be ruled out of existence.

By the Ancestors of Modern Philosophy

In the modern picture there is little room for an angel, however economic an angel might be with space. Certainly the immediate ancestors of our modern philosophers left little ground for angels to walk on, none to call their own. The materialism of the nineteenth century made a closed shop of the world, its machines purring along smoothly in a mechanical pride at their monopoly of the past, present and definitely predictable future. Machines and angels have little in common; and this was a completely mechanical world. No account could be taken by it of the angels for, by its own confession, it could handle only the material; the rest was ruled out of existence.

By the Moderns

The naturalism, which supported this machine-like world, identified the known with the seen, the observed; only that which could be weighed, measured, dissected was real. An angel was much too slippery to be real. Rationalism, at least in its earliest beginnings, admitted human reason and its immaterial character into the world of reality; but then it slammed shut the gates. There were no seats left, certainly none for a being that claimed superiority over that human spirit, Rationalism expected to destroy the angels by snubbing them; instead, it has come perilously close to destroying the human reason it professed to champion.

Its Reasons

The modern attitude is a jumble of all three of these views of reality. Some men, pushing naturalism to its logical extreme, deify science and so, of course, brush the angels aside impatiently. What can a scalpel, an atom smasher, or a list of cleverly arranged words do with an angel? There cannot be angels. A logical consequence of this is the denial of reason itself; reason, you see, has not as yet been strapped to an operating table. Their flag proclaimed them to be mechanistic and psycho-analytical psychologists but they were, none the less, pirates preying on humanity who made even that feeble offspring of spirituality, which rationalism spared walk the plank. The step was not far from the insistence on the absolute supremacy of reason to its complete extinction.

Today, many legions of men insist on the complete independence and supremacy of man, refusing to have anything to do with a creature, or even a God, superior to man. Modernity again bites off its nose to spite its face; the trick is so ingenious that we have not yet tired of it. To spite reason and extol the scientific method, reason is ruled out and so science is killed; to spite authority and rule mystery out of the universe, reason is elevated to the highest rung of the ladder and nothing is left for the ladder to stand on. The moderns have made the defense of man by putting him at the crown of existence, a kind of three-ring circus with no publicity barred; but when the noise dies down and the crowds file out, the hero of the whole performance is crawling about on all fours. Obviously angels have no place in such thinking as this; neither, for that matter, have men.

Its Effects

This modern contempt for things angelic has, as a matter of fact, had its effect on those who have no slightest doubt about the angelic world. Not that it has shaken their belief in any way; it has rather made them self-conscious about angels. They would hesitate to drag an angel out in public. Belief in angels is made to seem just a little childish, like believing in hobgoblins or Santa Claus; it is as although angels belonged in the world of make-believe that may be dissolved at any moment by the call to dinner. There is just the faintest odor of suspicion that by such belief we are not being entirely true to our reason, we are a little too credulous for manhood, a little too hopeful for an adult.

The angels and the Ages, Universality of belief in Angels Testimony of Men

If a Christian must have his angels, then he must stand off to one side of the modern world, in a sense sharing the banishment of the isolated angels. Yet, strangely enough, it is only in these last few centuries that an angel was made to feel like an outsider or the believer in angels to feel naively credulous. The anthropological findings on primitive man certainly indicate that an angel would have been taken for granted in the days of pre-history, at the very beginnings of human life. The belief in beings, superior to man and matter but inferior to God, was then almost universal. Sometimes these spirits were good, sometimes they were bad, at different times they were identified as belonging to a river, a tree, a rock, an animal. But their essential characteristics of immateriality, their superiority to man and inferiority to God, crop up as constant factors.

Testimony of Philosophy

As history grew up and began to scribble its account in the copybook that will never be filled, it found the world positively crowded with beings exhibiting these same angelic characteristics, beings who bore the names of spirits or demi-gods. The richness of Greek and Roman mythologies, to give just one instance, is evidence of this among the people themselves and in the literary expression of this popular attitude. Lest this be discounted on the grounds of popular ignorance, it might be well to notice that the philosophers did not escape this universal belief. Thales and Pythagoras placed them in the vestibule of the divine world; Socrates talked familiarly with one of them; Plato and his disciples filled the world with separated intelligences or secondary gods; to Aristotle they were the movers of the heavenly bodies. Indeed the angels are not newcomers to the world of men.

Testimony of History

Putting the popular accounts, mythology and philosophy to one side and coming to strict history, we find the most thoroughly authenticated and extrinsically corroborated of historical books, the Bible, parading the angels across almost every page. It was an angel that stayed the hand of Abraham, that slew the first-born of Egypt, that led the way to the Maccabean victories; the angel's message was a little too much for the aging Zachary but not for the maid of Galilee or her trusting husband; God Himself stooped to angelic comfort after the long days of desert fast and the long hours of Gethsemane's agony. Down through the centuries, the lives of the saints, not to be sniffed at even by the most historical of noses, have not found room enough for all the angelic details; nor were their writers seriously disturbed, knowing full well there would be all of heaven's eternity to listen to the full account.

Explanation of this Universality, Primitive Revelation

It is not the angels who are lonely in the world of men; rather it is the age that banishes the angels that finds itself a stranger among its fellows who have harbored human life. Such universal belief deserves better than to be treated contemptuously; surely it is too huge a thing to be cast off like a shawl by a shrug of the shoulders. At the very least, it deserves some examination, and considerable explanation. From the Catholic's point of view, the view of faith, a quite obvious explanation is primitive revelation; an explanation, by the way, that has many a likely looking corroboration in the folklore of primitive peoples with its accounts of a virgin birth, a creation, a flood and so on. This is one way of knowing about the angels, indeed one of the very best ways of knowing about anything, being told by the first truth Who can neither deceive nor be deceived and Who is the first cause of everything.

Angelic Effects

Putting aside the question of a primitive revelation, there are many facts pointing plainly to the existence of the angels. To the medieval mind, with its solid Catholic outlook on all of life, even angelic life, there was no particular difficulty connected with such things as Peter's release from prison or the collapse of the chains that had bound him, nor with the case of Peter of

Verona whose lonely cell was flooded by brilliant light long before the days of electricity and voices were heard talking to him as he prayed alone in his cell. Quite obviously the angels were responsible for these things. When one of the brethren was obsessed by the devil, it was not necessarily an epileptic fit nor congenital insanity; for after all there were devils and the fact remained that the afflicted one was returned to perfect normalcy through an ecclesiastical exorcism.

Reason

There is at least a suspicion creeping into the cynical modern mind that there is more to the world than bodies, more to thought than measurement, more to activity than the bouncing of electrons. A modern philosopher, for instance, admits in print that there are many psychical phenomena that have not been satisfactorily explained, giving as examples such things as authenticated activities of a room, the mischievous, cheap little tricks of poltergeist origin and so on. A long established psychical research laboratory in London, and a similar institute in Boston, frankly admits to numerous examples of things that defy explanation on the grounds of a materialistic philosophy. Indeed some modern scientists have been so overwhelmed by these phenomena as to go to ridiculous lengths of childish credulity in originating a cult that has often been a rich harvest field for knaves and tricksters.

Existence of the Angels

All this may or may not appeal to the mind of a man of today as a rational jumping-off-place of an argument in favor of the angels. There might, as a matter of fact, be serious difficulty from this angle in arguing to the activity of the good angels; such supra-human activity might be a direct divine effect. No such difficulty, however, presents itself in arguing to the activity and existence of the bad angels, the devils. For such satanic activity, while obviously supra-human, is just as obviously not divine; surely the divinity does not play the poltergeist's cheap tricks of breaking dishes, cuffing surprised victims or slipping in a sly pinch just for the devilment of it.

There is still another way of getting at the existence of the angels by reason alone, a solid enough way and old enough to have proved its solidity. Indeed, this was the method adopted by many a scientist with remarkably fruitful results; thus it was, for instance, that Descartes, arguing to the way other things had to be by the way things are, uncovered so many of the mysteries of the spectrum long before there was tangible evidence to support his theories; thus, too, the table of atomic weights was drawn up in neat completion long before many of the tardy elements had found their way into the narrow opening of a man's mind; it was in this way that Einstein proceeded in evolving his mathematical theories.

This way of arguing can bring out the possibility of angels, or even the sublime fittingness of angels in the ordered scheme of things; it cannot demonstrably show that they do exist There simply is no way in which we can set about proving the existence of angels a priori neither from the side of their cause, God, Who creates with complete freedom; nor from the side of the angels, His effect, who, like all other creatures, do not include existence in their very nature. Before setting out, then, on the arguments reason offers, it is to be noted emphatically that, for the Catholic, the solid grounds for the existence of the angels is the word of that first Intelligence, the source of all truth, i.e., the infallible revelation of God Himself assuring us of the existence of these supreme creatures of the created world.

From Faith

The importance of angels to human life may be estimated from the overwhelming character of the evidence of the revelation of their existence we have already spoken of the familiar frequency with which the angels stride through the pages of Scripture. These examples could be multiplied indefinitely, from the wandering visitors of Abram, through the unemployed Raphael's ready acceptance of a position as guide, to the business-like abruptness of Gabriel. Even more impressing is the part the angels played in the human life of God Himself, they heralded His birth, ministered to His weakness in the desert, comforted Him in His agony, announced His resurrection and on the mount of the Ascension drew the curtain after the short drama of His life that there be no mistake about its importance, the existence of the angels is reasserted in the earliest statements of belief, the creeds or symbols. The same truth is proclaimed again and again in the Councils in solemnly impressive language, "We firmly believe that there is one God, creator of all visible and invisible things, spiritual and corporal; Who by His omnipotent power from the beginning of time made both the spiritual and corporal creature, the angelic namely and the earthly, and then the human creature from both spirit and body." (Fourth Council of Lateran.)

In both Scripture and the Councils it is insisted that these angelic creatures are intellectual substances superior to men. These essential characteristics of the angelic nature have been stressed with complete universality by the Fathers, both Greek and Latin. This is the more remarkable in that there was no particular dispute about the angels and there were enough fundamental doctrines under heavy attack to occupy the hands and heads of all the Fathers all the time. It was as although each one considered his life and writings incomplete until he had paid his intellectual tribute to these big brothers of humanity.

From Reason

Down through the centuries, the angels were a subject to be cherished by every Catholic author. They played such an intimate part in the lives of Mary, her Son and the apostles, they took the beginnings of Christianity so much to heart that Christian authors, now that Christianity had grown up, frankly hailed the angels as the friends, the champions, the defenders they really were. It is not surprising, then, that the Doctors of the Church labored lovingly on their treatises on the angels. Thomas put such exquisite touches to the delicately firm lines of his tract as to merit the name "Angelic Doctor" and to have the tract draw the eye of every intellectual connoisseur by the sheer boldness, Penetration and beauty of its conception; its execution has left it unparalleled as the supreme treatment of the angels. That supremacy, however, has not discouraged theologians since his time from doing their bit towards establishing the angels solidly in the heart of Christians of every age.

From the Perfection of the Universe

To get back to the elusively inconclusive but subtly persuasive argument from reason, it might be well to point out that the angels do properly fall within the scope of a natural investigation. The angels are decidedly an integral part of the natural order because they are supra-human, some men have jumped to the conclusion that they are supernatural; it is a conceit that forgets that to a plant a worm might as reasonably seem supernatural, to a worm a dog, to a dog a man. When, in a rare moment, we emerge from pride's fog, it is not difficult for us to admit that we are not so utterly perfect as to make unthinkable a natural perfection superior to our own; especially in the morning before breakfast. It is from this obvious limitation of man and the clear perfection of the Author of man that the arguments of reason for the existence of angels proceed.

The first, and very beautiful, argument might be summed up in the dry words of the principle that the effect is perfect in proportion as it resembles or images its cause. The principle comes to life as soon as it is brought from the abstract to the concrete, we agree without demur to the contention that reflected light is more perfect as it can itself illumine others; knowledge is more perfect when it can enlighten others; love of God is more perfect in our hearts when we can set the hearts of others on fire. We cannot picture the perfect architect of the universe bungling the job; the universe, for God's purpose, is perfect. His purpose was the communication of His perfection, the manifestation of His goodness. Thus, things existing mirror the existence of God, things living give us a faint picture of the life of God; but of the operation of God, of His own most inner life, of the intellectual activity proper to Him we have no adequate image unless there be angels intellectual substances, independent of the world of matter, whose entirely immanent activity is one of intellect and will.

From the Imperfection of the Human Intellect

It is true that man does mirror God in some little way; compared to the creatures beneath him, man is far and away king. He seems infinitely above them by his power of thought and of love. Yet, even to our feeble eyes, there is a jagged gap between the operation of God and the operation of man. Man's spirit is incomplete without a body; he needs matter for the very stuff of his thought; in every action, every thought, he must use his material body; it is through the material that he attains his intellectual and moral perfection. What a contrast to the complete independence of spirit that is God's! If man stands at the peak of the created universe, the table of perfections is incomplete, there is existence, life, sense knowledge and love, intellectual knowledge and love dependent on matter; the missing grade is obvious intellectual life, knowledge and love completely independent of matter. A scientific mind meeting a similar situation in the scientific world has no hesitation in proclaiming the existence of the missing grade and setting out in search of it; the mind of man, scientific or otherwise, meeting the same situation in the wider world of the universe, has had even less hesitation in proclaiming the existence of angels. Nor has the search for them been far or long.

Whether a man preen himself, looking over the world with a proud eye, or debase himself, insisting on identification with the world beneath him by ingeniously devised camouflage, the fact remains that he is neither at the top nor the bottom of creation. He stands on the lowest rung of intellectuality. In him the native independence of intellectuality is walled about by the world of matter. This feeble flicker of intelligence in man itself proclaims the existence of a more perfect intelligence. In treating of the life of God, we have seen that intelligence does not of itself need the material of the physical world; to intelligence as such the material is accidental, something peculiar to intelligence as it exists in the composite we call man. This fact tells quite a story. It is accidental to animal life to flaunt wings; so we find some animals without wings. It is accidental to legs to be bowed; so we find some legs that are not bowlegs. It is accidental to living things to have legs, so we find some living things without legs. If, then, it is not essential, but rather accidental, to intelligence to be bound up in matter, there will be some intelligence, even created intelligence, independent of matter.

In fact we can push this farther, making it a more general argument, by insisting on the point that human intelligence is an imperfect grade of intelligence. In every class of beings, the imperfect presupposes the perfect, perfection is something posterior to perfection, something that happens to perfection, like the twisting of a word through a crooked mouth. The appearance of an imperfect grade assures us of the existence of the perfect grade of that perfection.

At any rate, our study of the different grades of life in which we traced the intrinsic activity of creatures up to the intrinsic activity of God that is the Trinity gives us more than room enough for an angel or two in the scheme of things. Certainly the story of creation would have been halted in the middle of a chapter if God had not produced angels. For all their high perfection, angels are not to be confused with God Himself. They are not uncaused, nor did they make themselves; they are not utterly self-sufficient. Rather, in common with all creatures, they are utterly dependent on the sustaining hand of God, which brought them into being and alone keeps them there. Their stupendous perfection is only a wavering silhouette of the infinite perfection of God. Theirs too, like our own, is a borrowed, a participated perfection, a loan made from the essential perfection that is divine.

Nature of the Angels

They were created in time, not from eternity; although any attempt to prove this statement is predestined to failure. This is one of those truths that are not material for proof but for belief; obviously, if the temporal beginning of the universe cannot be proven, the existence of any one thing in it cannot be dated with the stamp of eternity or time. Proceeding on faith's solid assurance of the temporal beginning of angelic life, theologians have no hesitation about plunging into the question of the relative time of the production of the angels, were they produced before, after, or simultaneously with the physical world? Again, reason cannot get very far. From the language of the definitions of the Church, and because they are such an integral part of the natural universe, Thomas concludes that the angels were created together with the physical world. Here reason is left entirely to itself; walking alone in this territory, it rapidly loses its swagger, its voice sinks to the whisper of an opinion and, while the darkness endures, humility is no effort. Thomas' opinion is reasonable where decision is impossible; although he stands opposed to the Greek Fathers, he is not alone, for his opinion is the quite natural universal opinion of the Latin Fathers.

Their Simplicity

Those superior intellectual substances, which we call angels do exist. What are they like? The picture that reason draws of them is necessarily negative. At least it is clear that they are not bulky giants whose great strength makes men look anemic. There can be no question of bulk in an angel for there is nothing material in an angel. Moreover the possibility of ever dissecting an angel is precluded by the fact that they are without matter, there is no inside and outside, top and bottom, fore and aft, arms and legs to an angel. This spiritual being, precisely because it is spiritual, is completely simple, utterly devoid of parts. In fact, an angel has not even that essential composition of matter and form so universal in all of nature beneath the angelic order; and this is no more than to insist again that these beings are spiritual, completely spiritual, altogether independent of the material. True, this conception comes hard to us because our minds are necessarily entangled in the material; as much as we agree that the angels are spiritual substances, subsisting forms, the flavor of matter haunts our consideration of the angels like a disembodied memory of a vague perfume. It is somewhat of a help to remember that the angel's normal existence is like that of the soul of a man after death and before the resurrection of the body; although, of course, the human soul has a lonely incompleteness about it in this state, which is altogether absent from the full life of the angels.

Their Incorruptibility

There is nothing in an angel that might fall out, come loose, or be cut off. An angel is totally incorruptible. Being completely simple, it cannot break up into parts; nothing of its nature can be lost for there is nothing composite about that nature. In simple terms, the angel does not go through that dress rehearsal for death, which we call a change; above all it does not have to play the leading role in the drama of death. Thomas, rightly, says that every change is a kind of death; for in every change some thing is lost, even although something is also gained.

Corruption, as we understand it, is the result of the separation of the principle of unity and life from the matter it unifies and vivifies. Obviously this implies at least the fundamental complexity of form, or unifying principle, and of matter. Looking at it in the concrete, we can destroy a fresco by scraping it off the wall or by tearing down the wall it beautifies; that is, either by destroying the thing itself or that upon which it depends. There is no chink in the armor of the angels into which we might plunge the lance of destruction. The angel cannot be taken apart or erased; it cannot be destroyed by destroying that on which it depends, for it depends on nothing but God. God could, of course, destroy an angel; not by a blow of an almighty fist or the roar of a thundering decisive command, but by the simple recall of the loaned existence the angel enjoys. In common with every other creature, the angel is not self-sufficient, its nature is not its existence; it lives by a borrowed, a participated existence. It too continues in being only because of the sustaining hand of God; there is no positive action necessary on the part of God to annihilate an angel, merely the withdrawal of that conserving hand without which an angel, and indeed a universe, falls into the nothingness from which it sprang.

Their Variety and Number

On the basis of their spiritual natures, we can spear of the angels as we would of members of the same family, emphasizing common characteristics such as immateriality, simplicity and incorruptibility. That generic sameness must not, however, betray us into conceiving of the angels as indefinitely numerous facsimiles of the one model. There is as much difference between one angel and another as there is between a horse and a man, for each angel is a distinct species, complete and entire in itself. In other words, angelic nature is not said of the angels in the same way as human nature is said of men; we differ among ourselves only by individual differences, specifically all men are the same. In each angelic species, on the contrary, there is only the one individual in whom the species is complete.

There is no point in a multiplication of individuals within an angelic species. In material things, such multiplication is absolutely necessary to assure the continuation of the species, for the individuals, reaching their allotted term of existence, cease to be; in the angelic order, the incorruptible nature of each angel is itself a guarantee of the permanency of the species. It might be argued that God's purpose in creating, the mirroring of His divine perfections, is better served through the multiplication of individuals within a species. Yet; as a matter of fact, it is by the variance of the species that finite creation achieves some little likeness to the smile of divinity, not through the material differentiation of individuals within the species.

With one exception, it is true that, throughout the created world, the individual is unimportant but for the part it plays in perpetuating the species. That exception is the world of man. There every individual is of supreme importance, for every individual is possessed of an eternally enduring soul, a soul that will outlast every other species in the material order. Really, the human exception is no exception at all. Throughout all of nature, it is the enduring, the permanent that is the object of nature's ceaseless care; because the individual's spark of life is such a momentary thing, it is unimportant in comparison with the constantly renewed existence of the species. It is on the basis of this identical principle that the human soul is so terribly important because it is not destined for the life of a moment, of a year or even of a century, but of all of an eternity. On the same grounds, men who see nothing spiritual, eternally enduring, in themselves arrive, with devastating logic, at the tragic conclusion that individual human life is a cheap, common, unimportant thing.

Even if there were some point in multiplying angelic individuals within the one species, it could not be done. Let us say we are discontented with our human souls and decide to do something about it. If we remember that our soul, being spiritual, has no parts, we can readily understand that there can be no question of trimming rough spots or rounding off curves. That soul, like all forms in matter and like all substances in the spiritual order, is utterly simple; if we could induce any change whatsoever, however small, we would have changed the whole thing. We might have produced something very pleasing but we would have destroyed a man. The slightest variation in a substantial form results in a substantial change; and the rational soul of man is precisely that substantial form by which he is differentiated from every other creature in the universe. The angels are subsisting substantial forms; any slightest differentiation would not mean multiplication of individuals within a species, but a specific, a substantial change. There is, in fact, a possibility of multiplication within a species only when an essential element of that species can suffer modification that is not a substantial modification; or, in plain language, the principle of individuation can be found only in matter. The angels are completely independent of matter.

The implication of this specific character of every angel, taken in conjunction with the number of the angels, is staggering. For their number is beyond all computation. The Sacred Scriptures hint at this in such passages by, "thousands of thousands, of angels ministered to him, and ten thousand times a hundred thousand stood before him." It is right, eminently right, that the number of angels should dwarf the number of all other created things. The beauty of creatures is an imperfect image of the beauty of God and the whole purpose of creation was to mirror in creatures something of that divine beauty; the more perfect the creature, then, the greater the image, of divine beauty; the angels, as the most perfect of all created beings, are the most perfect image of divine beauty. By their multiplication the divine purpose in the universe is most effectively attained. Each angel portrays an angle, a shadow of the divine beauty, each much more distinct than the fragrance of the locust tree from the blossom of a cherry tree.

The white light of divine beauty is only partly appreciated by us when it passes through the prism of creatures. There it is broken up into the thin rays of color, which alone may seep through to our mind and senses. The terrifying numbers of the angels give us some little idea of the streaming rays of beauty that pour from the world nearest divine beauty, the world of the angels.

Consequences of the Angelic Nature, in Relation to Bodies

Perhaps it was some vague appreciation of this angelic beauty that introduced the words "angel" and "angelic" into love's vocabulary. Actually, to look like an angel is a dubious accomplishment; at least to human eyes, an angel is not much to look at. Insisting on their independence of the material, we have already made plain the fact that bodies in no sense belong to angelic nature; angels are immaterial, completely spiritual substances. Yet angels stood, sword in hand, at the gates of Paradise, they came walking down the road to Abraham, made the long journey with the young Tobias. These angels certainly had bodies. Where did they get them?

Obviously, these bodies could not have been the angels' own bodies; angels do not have bodies. Since they did have them, they must have taken them for the particular occasion, somewhat as a man might hire a dress suit in the penury of college days. As to where they got the bodies, well, any answer is no more than a guess. After all, this particular body was only for appearance's sake; it was not necessary that it have a back as well as a front, that it be complete, a *human* body. In their search for the kind of body they needed, the angels were not reduced to grave robbing. Thomas suggests, timidly, that the angels used compressed air as the material of these bodies. He was, of course, only guessing. There are many questions relative to these angelically assumed bodies more important than their source. Could, for instance, these bodies produce vital acts, could they see, take nourishment, grow, grow old, rheumatic and creaky? The angel Raphael, declining the hospitality of Tobias, gave the answer, "I seemed indeed to eat and to drink with you; but I use an invisible meat and drink, which cannot he seen by men." No, these bodies were not capable of vital acts. Only living bodies, bodies informed by a substantial form proper to them, can do these things. Without bodies, devoid of matter and consequently of all quantity, an angel cannot be in place as we are; the surface of our bodies is, in a sense, surrounded. How can an angel be surrounded? It cannot be locked in a closet or folded up in the ectoplasm of a medium. Yet angels must be some place; they do not enjoy the ubiquity of God. The difficulty comes, as it so often comes, from our effort to conceive of everything in human terms. The angels are in place, not by a contact of quantity as we are, but by a contact of power. In other words, an angel is where he is at work. The philosophers have put all this in two words by saying that men are *circumscriptively* in place, while angels are *definitively* in place.

In Relation to Place

However we phrase it, the fact remains that an angel can operate in four corners of a room at one time; yet these four corners will be but one place for an angel. For an angel's place is where he is working, it may be that one material place exhausts the angel's power and then the material and the angelic place coincide; but it may also be that a dozen material places do not exhaust the angel's power and then, because our minds are so wedded to the material, we begin to insist that it simply cannot be so. The truth becomes plainer, and more startling, when we push it further. The fallen angels, who chose the swine for then next habitation, were speaking literally when they told Christ their number was legion. An angel, you see, does not need a defined space; there is no danger of any number of angels crowding each other, tussling for the same strap, or blocking a doorway. There is no limit to the number of angels assignable to any one material place for the crucial question of quantity is one that does not come up in the angelic world.

In Relation to Movement

The manner in which the angels move, then, represents little difficulty since it follows their manner of being in place. If this particular angel has assumed a body, then, by reason of the body, the angel moves locally, step by step, trudging up one hill and down another. Otherwise, that is, without the assumed bodies, the angels are in place by their operation, which is by intellect and will; they move as they change operation, with the speed, the ease and completeness of thought or desire. Gabriel was not out of breath on his arrival in Nazareth. It is true that the angels sat on the tomb of Christ the morning of the resurrection; but we must not read fatigue into that position. What could be more natural, having a body handy, than to sit down. We might almost say that the process of sitting down might well be one an angel could take pride in. For no one having a body merely sits down, they may drop themselves into a chair and heave themselves out of it in open confession of aging bones; they may collapse into a chair as although from the sudden disintegration of bones, and drape themselves over it as formlessly as a rug; or they may make of the process a demonstration of suave serenity, sitting down as smoothly as a cat stretches, as bewilderingly as a mirage disappears, as swiftly graceful as the glide of a swallow. From the practical point of view, it was unfortunate there was no twentieth century commentator on etiquette present to discover just how one *should* sit down.

Conclusion, Companionship of the Angels, An Inspiration

Undoubtedly we can accomplish the complicated operation of sitting down without angelic help; but to eschew the companionship of the angels entirely is to suffer a serious loss that may well lead to a misunderstanding of human nature itself. For a man is a cosmopolitan being alone in a provincial-minded world; he alone is spiritual, which is to say that he alone is impatient of matter, that only his thought scales the barriers of the universe, only his love holds fast to the dream of an eternal surrender, only his soul is dedicated to a task that only ceaseless energy and unending duration can possibly finish. It has never been good for man to be alone; it has always been good for a man to be in the company of those who cling to finer ideals, are possessed of greater talents, who strive for higher goals. His play in the game of life is steadily worsened if he meets only equals or inferiors; it is steadily improved if he moves in faster company where he has something to learn, something to imitate, something to urge him on every minute of the game.

An Acceptance of the Limits of Man

Alone in the material world, a man is apt to develop eccentricities as absurd as the quirks that twist the recluse into a caricature of a man. He has, as a matter of fact, made the absurd mistake, looking about the world, of thinking that his was the supreme intelligence, his the supreme love, his the supreme achievement; he has made an angel or even a god of himself and then, reasonably, given in to despair. He has missed the companionship of the angels that would have opened his eyes to the feeble stumblings of his slow mind, the waverings of his love, the ready fatigue of his energy; he has missed a realization that would have given him hope, pride in the intellectual family of which he is the humblest member, and confidence in his efforts, knowing he did not work alone.

An Insistence on the Excellencies of Man

On the other hand, from this same loneliness, he is apt to make, and in fact has made, the mistake of completely underestimating himself. His supremacy to the material world was too great to be believed, its responsibilities too heavy to he carried by his narrow shoulders, so he brushed aside that supremacy and plunged to the level of the things beneath, a level that seared and withered his lonely soul. He missed the companionship that would have opened his eyes to his own incorruptibility, the speed of his thought, the timelessness of his love, the height of his goals.

The Appeal of the Angels

In other words, being alone, man has taken himself apart; and, as so often happens, one of the parts was lost in the reassembly of his powers. It is not, however, men as men, but philosophers or scientists who take man apart. Men do not break themselves into parts; they take man as a whole. Perhaps that is the secret of the universal appeal of the angels to the mind of men. In that angelic world, the soul of man is at home as it can never be at home in any lesser world; there the soul of a man finds the common language of the spirit, the ready understanding, the quick sympathy and unquestioning helpfulness that allow him to be completely himself, relaxed but intense, at home. For this is the world of the spirit.

Room for the Angels

There is room enough in the world of nature for the angels. It would be a narrow, confining place without them. Additionally, room will be made for the angels as long as a man trudges the length and width of the world knowing his loneliness, humbly conscious of the limitations of his powers, awed by his superiority over the material world in which he moves. The hope, the vigor, the inspiration and the comfort of the companionship of these big brothers of humanity will not easily be surrendered; to one dedicated by nature to a search for the beauty and goodness of God, there will be slight challenge to the angels who most perfectly mirror that beauty and goodness. There is room enough in the world of nature, there is room enough in the heart of a man, for an angel who takes up no room.

CHAPTER X – THE ANGELS' VISION
(Q. 54-58)

1. The angels' vision a dream of men
2. From the beginning

(a) Among the first philosophers

(l) The fact

(2) Reasons of the fact

(3) Dual results of the fact

2. The dream and the moderns

(a) Descartes' angelism

(b) Its legitimate descendants

3. The dream of men a natural gift of the angels, perfect knowledge in a perfect way,

A. In a perfect way, i.e. innately, intuitively, independently,

(1)This knowledge is innate

(a) Relative to angelic essence

(b) Relative to angelic existence

(c) Relative to angelic intellect

(2) It is intuitive

(3) It is independent

(a) Source of the angelic ideas

(b) Source of the angels' knowledge of God

(c) Source of the angels' knowledge of self

B. Perfect knowledge

    1. The objects of angelic knowledge

       A. Spiritual object

         1. Other angels

         2. Thoughts and desires of men

         3. Mysteries of grace

       B. Material objects

      2 Infallibility of the angelic knowledge

Conclusion,

1. The dream of men is not without its excuse

2. It is not without its divine reason

3. Nor is it without it fulfillment

◫ CHAPTER X ◫
THE ANGELS' VISION
(Q. 54-58)

There is little of idleness in the universe; what little there is, is not for long. For the penalty of idleness is frustration and, shortly, extinction. Apparently, men can indulge in idleness with more impunity than any other creature of the universe; but the appearance of un-penalized idleness in the human world is an illusion. Actually, man is one with the rest of the world in the possession of that inner drive for the fullness of perfection that so ruthlessly stamps out the idle; he not only has this same drive, in him it exists in a degree so intensified that it seems to demand that he outstrip himself. H is possessed of a yearning for goodness and truth that pulls the heart out of him.

The Angels' Vision a Dream of Men

Unable to satisfy this quenchless thirst, men have, from the beginning both of individual life and the life of the race, been haunted by a dream; the dream of quick, easy, complete quieting of the remorseless demands of their very nature. Sometimes they have mistaken the dream for a reality, for the port itself instead of the guiding beacon; but, mistaken or not, the dream has persisted. Thus children go to school with lagging steps and race out of the classroom; vacation time is a release from prison and September is approached with the listless resignation of a doomed man's steps to the gallows. Yet "why" is never far from their lips; they want to learn, insist on learning, but easily, quickly, satisfyingly. It is as although the dream was born within them.

From the Beginning

In the very beginning of the race, satanic ingenuity could devise no temptation so seductive as the promise to materialize this dream, "you shall be like gods, knowing good from evil." Awed by the splendor of that dream, the strong, unimpeded intellects of the first human couple became as credulous as a child listening to a ghost story on a stormy night. Even after that first terrible lesson had been learnt, after men had seen what might be expected from grasping at shadows and deserting reality, they still started their tower of Babel that they might look into heaven.

Among the First Philosophers, the Fact

It is not so surprising, then, to see men, in the first baby steps of philosophic thought, tottering towards the bright tinsel of the unceasing dream. The fact is beyond dispute. Hindu philosophy tried to reach the utmost boundaries of wisdom by one proud thrust. Impatient of the material world, the Eastern philosophers denied it; their intellects would be independent of all else and, by a kind of natural contemplation of self, would pierce into and be absorbed by the absolute. The Chinese philosophy of Lao-tse embraced a kind of wisdom through contemplation together with an esoteric principle of revolution; the two added up to a sort of self-hypnosis, aided by opium, whose goal was complete cessation of activity and re-absorption in nothingness, to become one with the first principle.

Reasons of the Fact

To eyes made sympathetic by the vista of crumbled dreams that stretches the length of a lifetime, reasons for this fact of philosophical history do not have to be laboriously excavated from the ruins of the dream. Unquestionably glimpses of quick, sure, easy knowledge are given to men from time to time. A man's position in the units verse is a perch on the peak of an alp from which he can exult in the scoured cleanliness of sun-drenched clouds and the mysterious depths of the sky, depths that are above him not below him; or be sobered by the shadows, the fog, the ready darkness of the valley that lies at his feet. He stands nicely balanced between the spiritual and the material world. Standing on tiptoe he can almost peer into the city of the angels. Just as in himself he sees the gray modeled from his own bestial potentialities, so also in himself he sees an occasional flash of angelic beauty and perfection. It is not hard to understand a man dreaming of the wings of an angel or the claws of an animal.

Dual Results of the Fact

Then, too, just as there is no one so impatient with stutters as a stammerer, so there is no one more impatient of human intelligence than an intelligent man. Its weakness, its sluggishness, its inaccuracy, its dependence on the material world and material conditions are all a constant exasperation to him. If this is true despite the immense intellectual deposit we have inherited from the ages, how much more true must it have been in the early days of man's philosophic thought. Along with these two factors, there was a pride of intellect that was almost diabolical, as, in fact, is most human pride. It was a pride that could not, would not, stoop to the things love inspires. We look in vain for any mention of love among the Eastern philosophers. Love, you see, has a way of being satisfied with the crumbs that fall from the table. It is astounded at having so much, however little be given it; the haughty gesture expressing personal excellence is caught in mid-air by love's paralyzing glimpse of the excellence of God shining forth from the loved one. Love cannot be proud, so the early philosophers ruled out love.

The Dream and the Moderns

The results of this personification of a dream, this enthronement of the pride of intellect, were cataclysmic and, strangely, uniform wherever this dream took to itself a body. In Brahmanism, in Buddhism, in Taoism the goal of wisdom was always the same, denial of the reasoning process, denial of reason's efficiency outside itself, finally, the destruction of reason itself; under such circumstances, the ultimate destruction of man, the surrender of personality and individuality through absorption in the absolute, was a foregone conclusion. If men were to be angels, then they would in fact become neither angels nor men.

Descartes' Angelism

Beginnings are always difficult things; perhaps that is why man is always so impatient at the beginning of things. At any rate, he is much more inclined to indulge in a dream than to swing an axe, even an intellectual axe. It was almost natural, then, that at the beginning of the modern scientific age some one should take refuge in the age-old dream of an angelic short cut to knowledge. The modern father of angelism, which destroys both angels and men, was Descartes.

Its Legitimate Descendants

In its modern form, the dream restricted the material world's contribution to man's mental life to being man aged by human reason; as it turned out, this was an insistence on the complete independence of reason that later brought forth that astonishing child, pragmatism. The slow, plodding steps of reasoning were impatiently brushed aside in favor of the rapier-thrust of angelic knowledge, which would contain all else that was to be known. Additionally, this knowledge was made a practically innate affair; indeed, if it were to be so independent, there was nothing else to do but insist on its innate character. After all, it had been completely cut off from the material world in which it existed.

The Dream of Men a natural Gift of the Angels, Perfect Knowledge in a Perfect Way

Even in this very early stage of the modern resurrection of man's favorite dream, there are some seeds of catastrophe. Obviously, the denial of the reasoning processes and of the contact of reason with the material world isolates and perverts the mind of a man. The children of Descartes carried on his tradition boisterously plundering the intellectual level of man's life like so many vandals bent, not so much on booty, as on destruction. Destroy they did, first intellect itself and finally, reaching the inevitable result of a dream made to walk, the humanity of man. Rationalism trod its suicidal way through Locke, Berkeley and Hume; then Kant rushed to the rescue of reason but his aim was bad and reason died from the shot he fired. From this orphaned home where philosophy was a beaten waif, there came forth idealism and naturalism, the first, linking up the old dream with Neo-Platonism and the Hindu philosophies, thus sinking man in the unnatural depths of the world of pure spirit; the second, our American favorite, breaking up into the thousand and one varieties from pragmatism to evolutionism, in all of which reason is a thing of the past and man a creature with no future.

The dream has remained unchanged since the beginnings of the human race; it has appeared in philosophic dress again and again since the first puzzlings of the first philosophers. Its results have remained uniformly tragic; now, as always, the dream crashes in the unsounded depths of pessimism. And the lesson the dream teaches is still unlearnt. We still do not agree that it is not by casting away the bone we have that we shall find food, it is not by trying to become something other than ourselves that we can accomplish anything but our own destruction. It is as true now as it was in the beginning that we do not improve nature by destroying it; that originality does not consist in being different but in the astonishingly humble courage to be ourselves. We do not attain perfection by pretensions to the angelic but by being most thoroughly human.

In a Perfect Way, i.e. Innately, Intuitively, Independently

Through the ages, the promise of this dream, which has haunted men was perfect knowledge in a perfect way. What man strove for, even at the cost of his humanity, the angels have by their very nature. Their knowledge is had in a perfect way. Knowledge comes to the angel in the first instant of its existence, without loss of time or energy, without labor, and completely free of any dependence on the world of creatures beneath the angelic world. To put it briefly, so extreme as to demand further explanation, we could say that the angels' knowledge is innate, intuitive and independent.

This Knowledge is Innate, Relative to Angelic Essence

Innate knowledge in the angels means precisely what one would suspect, that the angels are created with their knowledge, as men are born with their faculties of intellect and will. There is no worry about it on the part of the angel; knowledge is an integral part of the angelic nature. Yet this does not mean that the angelic knowledge is the angelic substance, the angelic essence. Angels are not large masses of knowledge wandering about the courts of heaven; nor are they subsistent intellects. The intellects of the angels, as the intellects of men, are faculties, potentialities; their knowledge is an act of that intellect. If, indeed, their intellects were identical with their substance then the angels would be identical with God; they would he subsistent intellects and intelligence is one of those perfections that of themselves are infinite, utterly Perfect. Subsistent intelligence, as we have seen, is a property of God.

Relative to Angelic Existence

Nor does this innate character of angelic intelligence mean that the angelic nature is given life by angelic knowledge the angels' knowledge is not its existence. This should not be obscure. After all, it is plain that a non-existing dog does not bite, nor is the bite of an existing dog the dog itself. So the existing angel is presupposed to the knowing angel; it does not know until it exists, nor does it exist by the fact of knowledge. As a matter of fact, the angelic existence, marvelously perfect as it must be to match the angelic nature, still falls short of the wide scope of angelic knowledge. Angelic existence is limited to that one angelic species, that one angel, while angelic knowledge is free to roam from God to worms and back again.

Relative to Angelic Intellect

In both men and angels, intellect is a power, a faculty, an accident perfecting nature. Yet the angel's intellect does not grub about, among material things gathering its knowledge; hence its intellect is a single faculty, utterly, free of dependence on the phantasm of imagination or any other material thing. In us there must be both an active and a possible intellect, as we shall see more thoroughly later on in this book. The first finds the potentially intelligible material in the products of the imagination and makes it actually intelligible to the possible intellect, bridging the gap between the material and the spiritual; the second, actually understands. In this same way, to somewhat a degree, the infra-red ray camera and the human eye cooperate; the camera, on its film, making actually visible what formerly had been only potentially visible, then it is the eye that sees.

In the angels, the intellect is never merely a blank sheet waiting for knowledge to be scribbled on it; it is never merely potentially intelligent. Nor are the objects of the angels' knowledge wrapped around with the bandages of matter, which hide their faces, only potentially intelligible. Their knowledge is innate; so the objects of their knowledge, from the very beginning, exist in them immaterially, in an actually intelligible way.

It will, perhaps, help us to grasp the immateriality of the angels and their knowledge if we remember that the whole field of imagination, which so enriches human life, is completely missing in the angelic world. The angels have no imagination. If they had imaginations they would not be angels. For imagination is the function of a corporal organ, part of our sensitive or animal equipment; it is one of the links that bind us to the animal world, like a spinal column, hunger or death. Without a body, imagination is altogether impossible.

Angels, then, have never felt the sleekness of velvet or the hard gaiety of silk, the rush of wind on a spring day or the softness of a rich turf. They have never had the feel of clean clothes, the agony of tight shoes or a ragged collar. In fact they may know how these things feel, but their knowledge of them is purely intellectual; they have no sensitive knowledge, for the simple reason that they have no senses with which to know. This is the quite apparent reason why their knowledge must be innate; there is no way in which it can be gathered from the material world. On this same ground of their absolute spirituality, we must exclude all passions from the angels. Some of the early Fathers explained the wiles and craftiness of women on the grounds of a quite reprehensible carnal familiarity with the fallen angels, but this was a very bad guess in a somewhat vague cause. Angels do not tremble with fear, pace the floor with anxiety or boil with anger. This sort of thing belongs in our world, not in the world of the angels.

It is Intuitive

The intuitive character of angelic knowledge is much more readily grasped by our minds than its innateness; we ourselves have some little taste of that mysterious intellectual action of intuition. It is in us, quite normally, as the very first of our acts of knowledge; we know such things as tree, or a dog, man precursorly to our judgment that "this is a tree, dog or man." In other words, we have these concepts, not by the slow scrutiny of judgment and reasoning, but before these processes, by the first glance of intuition. In its higher forms it is the brilliant flash that illumines the minds of men of genius, the mystic penetration of the saints and the deep understanding of the simple faithful relative to the mysteries of faith.

It is Independent

The angels' intellect is a cup capable of holding the overflowing knowledge of all created things; but the cup does not fill itself. That intellect is a faculty or potentiality; it must be fulfilled by some act, by some form. Certainly it is not filled by the angels' own substance, perfect as that may be; for the angelic substance is only one drop in the steady flow of creatures from the Creator, a picture of one mood of God which cannot represent the drawling splendor of all His other images in the world of creatures. This cup must be filled by something other than the angel itself; if the angels' knowledge of them created world is to be perfect, some medium other than the angel itself, some other form must fulfill the potentiality of the angels' intellect. That other form, that other medium can be no other than the intelligible species, the ideas, the mental similitudes, the intentional existence of created things. There is no other possibility, God could give supernatural knowledge proper to Himself, as He does in the vision of His essence, but this would still be a gift, not a natural knowledge for an angel; the angel itself is inadequate to represent the whole created world; every inferior creature is not only inadequate, it is physically incapable of affecting the angelic intellect. The angels must know as we know, through ideas; where do these intelligible species come from?

Source of the Angelic Ideas

Certainly they cannot come from created things. We could as easily paint a mathematical point or wrap up the substantial form of a rose in cellophane as give an angel an idea of a flag by waving at the vault of heaven. Material things cannot act directly but only through a medium on spiritual things; in knowledge that medium is the phantasm of the imagination. There is, then, no way in which an angel can acquire ideas from created things, for it has no imagination.

Moreover, the thing is plain from the very manner in which the angel exists. We would be reasonably astonished to find a cabbage slinking up behind us with the grace of a leopard; cabbages move, but not precisely in that way, for movement follows the manner of existence. If that existence is a plant existence, then the movement is a plant movement; if the existence is animal, then the movement is animal. So our thoughts do not come together with even so slight a jar as that felt by the teeth meeting well cooked asparagus. The mode of existence of the angels is quite independent in material; their action or movement of understanding, then, is a smoothly intellectual thing. Let us look at the whole picture. Man has an intellectual potentiality unfulfilled by nature; God has no potentiality but perfect intellectual fulfillment, perfect act; in the middle, the angels, half-way between God and man, possess an intellectual potentiality perfectly fulfilled from nature, and so, of course not from the material world outside their nature.

The only source of these angelic ideas is God Himself giving them to the angels by directly infusing them into the minds of the angels. No higher angel will do for this first knowledge, as will be apparent from a later chapter on the speech of the angels. Here it is enough, by way of explanation of the incapacity of the higher angels, to point out that the angelic intellect and will, like the human intellect and will, are intrinsic accidents of the angelic nature; they are utterly unbreakable, theirs is the sacred territory from which everyone, everything is barred from a violent entry. This is the garden where only God and the individual possessor of that intellect and will can walk freely.

The angel, then, has intelligible species from God; about how many? No, the question is not nearly so absurd as it sounds; in fact its answer is decidedly illuminating. In our own case we do not base our judgment of intellectual acumen on the number of species, the amount of knowledge a man has acquired, but rather on how much a man can see in this or that particular species; it is not quantitative knowledge but penetrating wisdom that is the mark of excellence. Thus, a worker, who knows that he can get a brick off a roof by throwing it and sees nothing of the possibilities of its hitting someone on the head, is stupid. Thomas, in a comparatively few theological principles, could see the whole field of theology; a mathematician, in a few principles, can see the unfolding of the whole complicated area of mathematics; while a student, sitting under either Thomas or the mathematician. Must be satisfied with little bites from the edge of the pie of knowledge.

Our judgment in this case is entirely reasonable. The closer a creature is to God in the natural order, the more it participates in the divine perfections, the more perfectly it images God. Those nearer God in the intellectual order will then, participate more closely the divine mode of knowledge; and God understands everything in the one species, which is His divine essence. The angels as a class, have fewer and more universal species than men, being so far superior to them; the superior angels will have fewer and more universal species than the lower angels, precisely because of their superiority.

The angels' intellectual content is thus seen as an infused intelligible species, which are fewer and more universal the higher we go in the angelic order of perfection. How does it use these ideas? What is this intuition, which is the normal manner of knowing for the angels?

Certainly the angel has no period of cooing and gurgling infancy while it awaits the age when ideas are possible to it; it undergoes no tortuous school days in which ideas are gathered one by one. The angel is in no way in potency as to the acquiring of its ideas; these ideas are had from the beginning. Nevertheless, the angels, like ourselves, cannot consider more than one species at a time. These species are forms actuating the intellect; to have the mind consider two of them there at the same time would be like having a man run in different directions at the same time, and with much the same results. In scholastic language, the angels are always in act as regards the possession of these species, they are in potentiality as regards the actual consideration of this or that species. In other words their knowledge, like the knowledge of God, is always actually possessed; but, like the knowledge of man, it has its potential element, it is only successively used. For a man, no matter how much affection he may have for the multiplication table does not spend all his time thinking of it.

Although an angel cannot consider more than one of these species at one time, yet it can know many things at one time accordingly, as many things are contained in this or that particular species, much as a man, looking into one mirror, can see all the many things reflected in that mirror. In one species the angel sees all that it contains in just the one penetrating glance, as the eye of a camera in an airplane catches the detail of the city of New York as it paces restlessly between its confining rivers far below.

An angel can do this because the angel is a step higher in the intellectual order than men. The precise imperfection of the human intellect is its nearsightedness. It can only see one corner of the picture at a time; the world is a map too huge to be seen all at once by a human mind which must, instead, go slowly over the whole surface inch by inch, because of the weakness of our minds, we must come down from principles to conclusions like an old man cautiously feeling his way down a flight of steps; only when we reach the bottom, the conclusion, do we have a clear notion of all that might have been seen from the top by a stronger eye. Like children with a Christmas package, we must open things up, tear them apart and put them together again before we know what is in them. The one who made up the package or who has information from that original source knows the whole story by merely identifying the package.

Source of the Angels' Knowledge of God

The angels do not reason their way down from principle to conclusion, not because they cannot, but because they do not have to. Their position between God and man demands the absence of the essential imperfection of the human intellect, the imperfection, which makes reasoning, piece-by-piece judgment, necessary. It is, indeed, just this absence of the necessity for reasoning and judgment that males it impossible for an angel to make a mistake in natural knowledge. There is nothing peculiar about this; it is the way intuition works. As a matter of fact, we make no mistake in our first act of intellect, our intuition of tree, dog, man; our mistakes come in our judgments and reasonings, in our hooking the wrong things together. "John" and "crank" may both be representative of objective truth; but when we hook the two together to say "John is a crank" we run the risk of error and rash judgment. Objectively, the steps down from principle to conclusion may be sharply cut and broad enough; but if we miss one of them, we tumble down to erroneous conclusions with a battered head.

Source of the Angels' Knowledge of Self

Its own brilliant, purely spiritual, utterly immaterial essence is immediately present to the angelic intellect and is, in itself, completely intelligible. Consequently, it is immediately known by the angel without the necessity of a medium such as we must have. For it must be clear to every man that he knows his soul only through the revelatory character of his spiritual acts penetrating the material wrapping of his body. In this intimate, immediate knowledge of itself, the angel has a natural knowledge of God, as it also has in its knowledge of all other creatures; for nothing is fully known until God's part, the part of the cause and the exemplar, is known. The intelligible species by which the angels know all other things come only from God; they are the first copy of the ideas of God, the first participation of that supreme truth, the blueprint formed directly from the mind of the divine Architect.

St. Augustine put this beautifully when he maintained that the things of the world poured forth from God in a double way, intellectually into the minds of the angels; and physically into the world of things. In this account, the angels are looking, from the wings at the drama played on the stage of the world. He who wrapped up this great package, which is the physical world, has given His own first hand knowledge of it to the angels.

Perfect Knowledge

The natural knowledge of the angels is a vast sea that touches the shore of every created thing, with one exception. There are no natural secrets hidden from the piercing intellectual eye of an angel, except one; spiritual and material, all are laid open and naked before their eyes, except one.

The Objects of Angelic Knowledge
Spiritual Objects, other Angels

On the spiritual side, they know themselves, immediately, by their own substance. Even more so, they know every other angel in heaven or in hell in spite of the terrifying number of angels; of everyone each angel can say with perfect confidence "I knew him when." These other angels, too, have come forth from the creative hand of God, of them there exists, too, a perfect model in the divine mind; and as they came from God in their physical natures to exist in the universe, so they came from God intellectually to exist in the mind of the lowest angel.

Thoughts and Desires of Men

All material things are known to the angels for exactly this same reason, that is, because these material things are also creatures of God, effects of the first cause; a detailed account of them exists in the divine mind and is communicated to the minds of the angels. The mysteries of grace are completely above the powers of the angels. These supernatural secrets of God's own life and the share in that life He has planned for men and angels are totally beyond the entire powers of the natural order, which, of course, includes the angels. What knowledge the angels have of these things is a free gift of God by a special revelation to each particular angel; or, in the case of the good angels, in the beatific vision, the sight of the essence of God.

Mysteries of Grace

However, there is one natural phenomenon that is without the scope of the angels' knowledge that escapes the otherwise universal sweep of the angels' intellect. There is one thing too sacred for the eye of any but God, one private room where man, devil or angel cannot enter in; that is the realm of the thoughts and desires of intellectual beings, men and angels. Only God can enter into the house of our soul; and even God cannot violate our sovereignty there if there is to be desecration there, we must be the guilty ones; if there is to be the perfume of sanctity pervading the soul, God and our selves must pour the fragrant oil of consecration

An angel can know future things that come about necessarily, as an astronomer can know of an eclipse of the moon years beforehand; an angel can guess very accurately as to future contingent things, as a weather forecaster can predict the path of a storm with reasonable accuracy; an angel can know singular things in their most precise singularity, as a housewife knows the price of bread or milk. Yet, as to the movements of our intellects and wills, the angels have no grounds for more than a very poor guess until we have manifested such movements by our external actions. Even then, with the external actions there for all to read, they, and anyone else short of God, cannot be absolutely sure of the motives which inspired the actions Really the devil has a most uncomfortable time of it in the pursuit of his devilish profession He goes to the window, endlessly placing his bets on no more than a hunch; his mixture of hopefulness and despair must endure until the race is all over and the judges have handed down their decisions.

There is an obvious difficulty in this angelic knowledge of human affairs. If an angel does not know what Jim Jones is going to do at three o'clock on Wednesday afternoon, how does it find out on Thursday what actually took place? We have insisted again and again that the angels have all of their intelligible species from the very beginning of their existence; they receive no more natural knowledge, either from the world or from God. Yet, these past things are surely known, although as future they were not known. The difficulty is not so insuperable as it appears at first sight. After all, the ideas of God are eternal yet they are effective as divine decrees only in time; it was not just a few months ago that God decreed the creation of the soul of the Smith's newborn baby, but the decree was from all eternity. Even although the angels possessed all their intelligible species from the first instant of their existence, these species caused knowledge only after the existence of these future things in the material world. In other words, given the species from the beginning, the angel, by a decree of God, was barred from the use of this particular species until the event had occurred.

Infallibility of the Angelic Knowledge

All of this angelic knowledge is had without the possibility of misinformation, for God is the informant. There is no possibility of misjudgment, for there is no judgment involved in this knowledge; nor is there any chance of mistaken reasoning, where there is no reasoning. An innate, intuitive, independent, infallibly certain and perfect knowledge; a view of the universe second only to that of God; a perfect insight into the beauty, the variety, the perfection of the vast mirror which images the eternal splendor of the infinite, such is the angels' vision.

Conclusion, The Dream of Men is not Without its Excuse

As you can readily see, that age long dream of men is not without its excuse. There is such a perfect knowledge, which can be had in such a perfect way. Those momentary glimpses of incredible brilliance and penetrating simplicity were not illusions. The tales told by explorers of the intellectual world, the tall stories of the men of genius, the dark illuminations of the mystics that gave such a relish even to gall and vinegar, those solemn moments when our own minds are struck by this lightning from above, all these may sound like the exaggerated ravings of a returned Marco Polo of the intellectual world. In actual fact, however, they are deficient only by reason of the poverty of the pictures they paint for us, an inadequacy as hopeless as a tin-type of the living beauty of a woman of the last century.

It is not Without its Divine Reason

The dream did, indeed, have its excuse. It also has its reasons, for of course, we still dream. Its purpose is not to tease us with the cruel humor that dangles the bottle just out of reach of a screaming baby. It is not to humiliate us to the point of despair while we batter our brains out against a stone wall, as the old and the new philosophers did. The dream does not exist to tempt us to the rashness of presumption, moving us to cast away the crutches of human reason before we can walk or to play truant from school before we have learned to spell out the humble script of the material world. Rather, its purpose has been, and is, to keep alive in us that "unappeasable hunger for unattainable food," to fan that fire of divine discontent that never gives us rest, and to give us some little natural idea of the goal that never lacks inspiration, the goal of life close to God.

Nor is it Without it Fulfillment

The dream has its excuse; it has its divinely wise reasons; and it has its divinely generous fulfillment. True, we are men and men we must remain; there is no possibility of a fulfillment of this dream by natural means. However, through the goodness of God, Who has not yet found the limits of generosity, the dream comes true supernaturally, by a wave of the fairy wand of grace and glory; it comes true, dimly now, through the share in divine life, which grace brings to us, but with all the brightness of divine, not angelic, life in its fullness through the infinite reaches of eternity.

CHAPTER XI

ANGELIC SAINTS AND SINNERS
(Q. 59-60; 62-64)

1. Sanctity and sin in an emotional world.

2. Enthronement of emotion,

    (a) The fact.

    (b) Its excuses.

    (c) Its reasons.

3. Emotion and the appetite of man.

4. Appetite of the angels,

    (a) Its nature – free will.

    (b) Its distinction from nature and intellect.

    (c) Its denial of emotion.

5. The love of the angels,

    (a) Its nature, necessary and elective.

    (b) Its objects.

    (c) Its goal.

6. The sin of the angels,

    (a) Possible sins.

    (b) The actual sin,

(1) Its object.

(2) Its sponsor.

(3) Number of angelic sinners.

(4) The punishment of the sin.

Conclusion,

1. Human nature seen in the light of angelic saints and sins
2. Potentialities for good.

   (a) Potentialities for evil.

3 Consequences in men of angelic virtue and sin,

   (a) Humility.

   (b) Fear.

   (c) Self-respect.

📖 CHAPTER XI 📖
ANGELIC SAINTS AND SINNERS
(Q. 59-60; 62-62)

Sanctity and Sin in an Emotional World

Our modern world has enthroned emotion as the ruler of life and day-by-day new subjects throng to the palace to be presented to life's royalty. Some men make their bend towards the brutally and rough emotions that answer arguments with blows, that glory in butting against a tree instead of sidestepping it. Additionally, relax to the crunching of bones; others bow their heads to the squishy variety of emotion, the soft, deadly things that keep a man in a state of collapse before uncouth life.

Enthronement of Emotion

This emotional surge has not been a purely popular outbreak incited by sensational journalism. It goes much deeper than that. In fact, from the intellectual beginnings of the modern era to our own day, it has come from the top down; it is the logical outcome of subjectivism in religion and rationalism in philosophy. Surely the ordinary run of men can, to some extent, be excused for accepting the distorted photograph of a purely emotional man. They have been led into this thing by their leaders; coaxed, bullied, laughed, argued, threatened into it. As a result, however innocent of his plight the individual may be, man today finds himself in the strangely inhuman world where sanctity and sin are obsolete words faintly recalling the time when religion was not a matter of feeling, conversion a kind of epileptic fit, salvation a matter of that good feeling that comes from digestive perfection. From the very existence of the words sanctity and sin, one gathers that once upon a time men did not know they were ruled by biological necessity, thought they were possessed of a free will that gave them command of their lives, that moral codes were not a societal fashion and that men were different from animals.

The Fact

If the world were such as our moderns paint it, sanctity and sin would have no more place among men than they have among puppies or roses; for sanctity, like sin, is the fruit of a controlled appetite making its choice under the deliberate direction of one who is in command of his actions. That emotion plays a supreme role in the life below man is beyond question; but this life is below man. That emotion plays a large part in man's life needs no demonstration; but that we should come to think of emotion pushing man, willy-nilly, from birth to death, almost defies explanation.

Its Excuses

Perhaps it would not have happened, in spite of philosophy's attempted assassination of the intellect, religion's metamorphosis of faith from an intellectual virtue to a feeling, and the constant barrage of the sensible laid about the heart of a man, if we had held fast to the antidote for this over-familiarity with the material world. Unfortunately, we allowed ourselves to become strangers to that spiritual world of the angels, relegating it to the region of myths, fairy tales and poetry. As a result, we have concentrated on one side of our nature to the complete neglect of the other and become as lop-sided as slaves perpetually chained to the same side of a Roman galley.

Its Reasons

Our nature entitles us to a welcome on both sides of the railroad tracks. We cannot spend all our time with the angels under penalty of becoming so queer that even the angels, for all their charity, will have nothing to do with us; we cannot throw in our lot with the animals without becoming so bestial as to frighten the beasts. The animal has a place in our lives, as the angelic also has; but neither the one nor the other can carry on a war of extermination without destroying itself. If the truth be told, we are nearer to the angels than to the beasts, for it is the spiritual within us that is in command; familiarity with the angels, consequently, carries none of the immediate threats involved in rooting with the animals.

Emotion and the Appetites of Man

Certainly the place of the emotions, the movements of his sense appetite, within man it is made startlingly clear by a consideration of the appetite of the angels. For, of course, the angels have appetite. In an earlier chapter, treating of the will of God, it was pointed out that will is to intelligent beings what sense appetite is to the animals, the mainspring of action. Absolutely everything has within itself a tendency or inclination to its full perfection and to all that pertains to that perfection; an inclination that finds its expression either in straining to the attainment of that perfection or in enjoying that perfection once it is possessed. The general term for the faculty from which this inclination proceeds is appetite. Our long, intimate acquaintance with and respect for the world about us moves us courteously to extend the term to things incapable of knowledge and call it natural appetite. Still, the extension of the term is sheer courtesy; for these things do not move so much as they are moved, inexorably following the course laid out for them by the knowledge of God.

In the animals, this appetite is sense appetite; in intelligent creatures it is will. In both, this faculty of desire is completely blind. Nor is it to be pitied or sneered at in its blindness. It is supposed to be blind. Its work is not to know but to desire; if it does that, as it always does, we can ask no more of it. It makes no attempt to take over the work of the faculty of knowledge it does not peer into the future with sightless eyes or plunge ahead before a guiding hand offers its absolutely necessary direction. Nor can it improve on the light thrown before it by the faculty of knowledge, a dog does not dig his paws deeper in dry weather as a plant does its roots. The dog simply looks for a shady spot; a man does not dig for bones or eat a special kind of grass, but he does seek for truth, for love and for happiness, a quest that never disturbs the contentment of a dog. In other words, the appetite of any creature is of the same caliber as its knowledge.

Appetite of the Angels

When the creature in question is a complex combination of the material and spiritual, possessed of sensible and intellectual knowledge, as is man, there will, of course, be two appetites present, the sensible and the intellectual, which is called the will. The noise of battle within the household of his soul will not let a man seriously doubt the presence of these two appetites; for they get along much less equably than the jealous wives of a polygamous chieftain. When the creature in question has the splendid immateriality of an angel with its unadulterated intellectual knowledge, its appetite will be the intellectual appetite or will with no rival quibbling about its choices.

Its Nature – Free Will

To say that the will of the angels is a free will is to say no more than must be said of will wherever it is found. A noisy child with a penchant for hammering the furniture may indeed turn out to be an excellent boiler maker when he grows up; but because he can see the impediments to pleasant chit-chat involved in such a vocation, he can, if he likes, refuse to follow his natural bent. For intellectual knowledge can know supreme truth and thus open the way for the will to desire supreme goodness; but the intellect can also know particular truths and the reasons for their particularity, their limitations. Because of these limitations the will can and does accept or reject them, that is, the will is free. Not everyone who likes putting out fires becomes a fireman, quite possibly because one so heartily dislikes being doused with water in zero weather. The point is that an intelligent creature. In the face of particular goods, can always choose because he can always see not only the goodness but also the particularity, the limitation, of that goodness.

Its Distinction from Nature and Intellect

The angelic nature must definitely stay at home, eternally bound within its own limits; the angelic intellect is a hostess that sees all the world but only within the walls of its own house; while the angelic will is a visiting vagrant that wanders the length and breadth of the fields thrown open to it by angelic knowledge. The angelic intellect, like all intellects, is eternally at home, but in a home filled with a cosmopolitan group of guests, all of whom must follow the rules of the house; the angelic will goes out to the objects desired uniting itself to them. It is this characteristic of intellect and will that is so trenchantly expressed in the statement that an intelligent creature becomes what he desires but makes what he knows a part of himself. *He can know muck without soiling the intellect, but he cannot desire it without smearing himself.* Obviously, then, the free will of an angel is something quite distinct from the angelic nature and from the angelic intellect.

Its Denial of Emotion

While it is true that an angel can know and will, it is also unquestionably true that an angel cannot feel the excitement of racing blood, tragedy's sudden stab in the heart; it cannot be carried outside of itself with anger, faint at the sight of a snake or be overwhelmed by a rush of sorrow. For there is no room in the angels for emotions in the sense of passions or feelings. The angels, you see, have no bodies; and these passions are distinctly sensible or animal, movements of the sense appetite.

Lest we rush to the conclusion that angels are cold, clammy, impersonal creatures, it would be well to remember that an angel's joyous song heralded the Savior's arrival in Bethlehem, that an angel shared the agony of Christ in the Garden and comforted Him; that the archangel Gabriel minced no words in reply to Zachary's disbelief of his message and did not hesitate to rap him sharply on the knuckles with that severe sentence, "you shall be dumb." Yet it was this same severe angel who immediately appreciated Mary's fear and surprise, and his first words were words of assurance to dispel that fear; the archangel Raphael was a matchmaker of the first order, smoothing the way for the seemingly impossible marriage of young Tobias. These are not the actions of living icebergs.

The doubt about the warmth of the angels, however, persists. We think a man or woman without feelings, as fishy-eyed as a gambler, has something missing, is somehow perplexing, inhuman. As a matter of fact, we are right, such people are perplexing, as astonishing as a man without a head, for something belonging to human nature is not there. Lack of emotion is not at all virtuous; it may be a misfortune, making a man a monstrosity; or it may well be a vice. For man has not only a soul, he also has a body; he is not only rational, he is also animal; he has an intellectual appetite, but he also has a sensitive appetite. The movement of that sense appetite towards sensible objects, coming from the imaginative picture of good or evil and involving a physical or corporal reaction, is ordinarily called emotion, feeling or passion. So, for example, an actress who throws herself into a part can actually produce the corporal changes that mark out the path along which the sense appetite is running, she can weep, blush, turn pale, tremble, gasp.

These passions, amoral in themselves, are of immense value to man. By their help a man can muster up the courage to ask for a raise in salary, by the simple trick, for instance, of getting himself angry enough; the atmosphere of a church or a few minutes on our knees can awaken the will's desire to pray. These passions, in a word, react on the intellectual appetite, spur it into action or, being deliberately aroused by the will, complete the circle and make the action of our will that much more intense. Using these passions of ours, the cunning of God not infrequently coaxes us into greater spiritual activity by doling out sensible sweetness and consolation to His children, coddling them a little or bestowing a pat of encouragement and reward.

By reason of this intimate interaction between the will and the passions, these latter can also be an immense danger to a man. They can overwhelm the intellectual appetite and put a man at the mercy of the same motive power that dictates the actions of beasts; in opposition to the will they can terrify it into paralysis, weaken its action, cool its intensity to a vapid, lukewarm, nauseous thing. The men who succumb to the terror of persecution, the seduction of sin's occasion, the respect of men, the despair of life are all living witnesses of the danger of passion out of control. On a milder scale, the steady death rate in good resolutions is eloquent testimony to the existence of a rival appetite, which the will cannot regard lightly.

The Love of the Angels

Of course these sensible emotions are not in the angels. Angels have no bodies, so they can have no sense appetite, no imaginative pictures, no corporal reactions. Now this does not mean they are cold, unloving and unlovable creatures. They have an intellectual appetite and its movement is as proportionately more perfect than ours as the angels themselves exceed us in perfection. That angelic appetite has also met with good and evil, with triumph and defeat. There is joy among the angels in heaven; and there is sorrow, hate and despair among the angels in hell. Some have desired great things and now delight in the possession of the objects of their desires; others have chosen rather the petty than the great and now are tormented by the possession of the objects of their desire. Still, these emotions of the angels are not physical movements of passion; they are something infinitely superior, something whose nature opens our eyes to some of the possibilities within ourselves, for we, too, have an intellectual appetite.

Its Nature, Necessary and Elective

To understand something of those possibilities, and their limitations, we must see clearly the great difference between the knowledge and love of the angels and the knowledge and love proper to men. Quite naturally, and with no effort, we know some things perfectly; such things as that today is not yesterday, that we are not someone else, that happiness is the supreme value and so on. Still, we do not know all things naturally, easily, perfectly. Our love has the same split personality, some things we love naturally, necessarily; others we are free to embrace or reject, towards them we can be niggardly and cautious or recklessly generous. Yet, the reason is not the same for this similar characteristic of our knowledge and our love. Our intellect sees valley after valley, but only after climbing the intervening hills; its imperfections are due precisely to the fact that it does have to climb hills and clamber down the other side. Our will is like a woman who tries on hat after hat, finding none that does her justice; it grasps one after the other of the goods offered to its choice, not finding any one that includes all good, one that forces its choice on the will.

Its Objects

The angels, too, love their own good, their own goal, their own perfection naturally and necessarily; they cannot help themselves any more than we can. As in us, the angels' natural and necessary love is the spring from which proceeds that free, deliberate love of other things; because somehow, in some way, these things are bound up with their goal, their perfection, their happiness. Thus, loving themselves naturally and necessarily, they love the same qualities in other angels, just as we love the common human characteristics of human nature in other men. We can dislike a man because he is mean, unjust, successful, generous or virtuous; but it is completely impossible for us to hate a man because he is a man, because he has a soul or a mind. The same is true of the angels.

Its Goal

Like ourselves, the angels love God naturally and necessarily even more than they love themselves; for, loving their goal, their perfection, they are loving a similitude, an image of God. They are God's, they belong to Him, as we do; naturally and necessarily they work back toward Him, Who was their beginning. If they did not, there would exist a purely natural love in the angels that would be a perverted, twisted thing, loving to a greater degree something that was less lovable. Moreover, God Himself would be the author of this perverse love, as He is the author of nature; and this natural love would have to be destroyed by the supernatural love that was designed by God to perfect men and angels, the love that loves God above all things. Freely and with full choice, the angels love themselves, as we do; moreover, their love, like ours, extends to everything that is good. Their will, like our own, does not need to be coaxed out of doors; the only invitation necessary is a hint of goodness.

In all this there is a great similarity between angels and men; that similarity must not lead us to make the mistake of identifying angelic and human activities in the fields of knowledge and love. The similarity in love comes from the objects of that love; the angelic love in itself is something to make us gasp. In contrast to it, our passions seem like tottering steps of an infant compared to the smooth, consuming stride of a runner.

The love of the angels is not a spark slowly developing into a flame; it is an instantaneous bolt of lightning. The angel's will moves as does its intellect, like a rapier thrust straight to the heart of goodness. This love does not last for a day or a year; it is a lightning bolt caught in mid-air in all its burning splendor, for an eternity. It cannot change, as ours does, by discovering unlovable characteristics in its loved one; it has all the knowledge from the start. An angel cannot fall in love with a face and then discover the face was false; it cannot become uninterested, disloyal, fluttering from one love to another. The angelic embrace cannot end. That love cannot be halfhearted, lukewarm, timid, cringing before obstacles. An angel does not fall into love; it plunges in with crushing force. This love is a drive not to be stopped by obstacles, it is a consuming fire devastatingly complete; it is a surrender that is eternally unconditional. It is the dream that is buried in every human heart, the closest approach to divine love in the created universe. Can an angel have joy, delight, sorrow, despair and hate? Ah yes; and to a degree that, like the divine, terrifies us.

When God looked at the work of creation and found it good, He might well have been concentrating His gaze on the angels. From the first moment of their creation they possessed perfect natural happiness. Their intellects were perfect, their knowledge complete; their appetites, following in the footsteps of this perfect knowledge, were also perfect and in perfect possession of their natural goods from the very beginning. Indeed this work was good; even a divine artist could stand back from this masterpiece smiling that quiet smile of a master surveying his perfect work. The angels were perfect.

However, they were not perfect enough to satisfy the infinite generosity of God. There was still something that could be given to these creatures, a perfection above nature, a goal beyond the goal proper to angelic nature, a share in a life beyond the perfection of angelic life; they could still be raised to the height of supernatural happiness, to a share in the life of God, to an admission to the vision of God, which is heaven. Such a goal of love is not to be lightly had. It must be earned, earned by personal efforts. Such efforts, even when put forth by a nature as perfect as the angelic nature, ate utterly worthless of themselves; this goal is above nature and nothing nature can offer serves as a ladder to reach that end. The angels, also, needed grace, faith, hope, charity; the tools, that is, with which to carve out an eternal life with God. The tools were given to them from the first instant of their creation; but the goal had to be won by a use of those tools. Even of the angels it is true that divine happiness is not forced upon them; if they would live forever with God, it must be through their free choice.

The Sin of the Angels - Possible Sins

This was the trial of the angels, the choice between life with God or without Him. This was their term of probation, their opportunity to make a success or a failure of their lives. The issue was soon decided, for the angelic choice moves with swift directness to its object never to relinquish it. The choice was made irrevocably, eternally. By one good act the angels merited heaven, some of them; and the issue of heaven or hell was closed forever as far as they were concerned.

The victorious angels, as they stepped into heaven, brought with them the fullness of their natural knowledge, losing nothing on the way. From that time on they were eternally incapable of sinning, not merely because of the unchangeable nature of their love, but because any appetite in possession of the infinite good is not to be lured away from that adequately satisfying lover by the fetching smiles of anything else. Nothing can be more attractive; everything else is only a participation a mirroring of the beauties of that infinite goodness. This was the end of the angels, the final halt of the march to goodness and truth, the end of the road. From here on, what progress was made would be purely secondary, accidental, as inconsequential as a flower slipped into the lapel of a coat, and as absurdly pleasing as a totally unnecessary testimony of divine thoughtfulness.

The Actual Sin

It was a long road, yet the angels some were modeled in an incredibly short time. In fact, it was much too long for some of the angels; not all reached the end of it. There is not only love in the angels, not only the sublime perfection of that love in its elevation to the supernatural plane; there is also the abuse of love, which is sin. At first sight, it is difficult to see how an angel could sin. A man can stumble into sin when ignorance makes his vision defective; but there is no defect in the angel's knowledge. An angel cannot be rushed into sin by a storm of passion, for it has no passions. There can be no question in the angels of the long, bitter discouraging battle against habit that a drunkard faces; for bad habits were certainly not infused by God and there were no preceding acts by which such habits could be built up. This was the angels' first sin.

In a very real sense, it *was* difficult for the angels to sin. So difficult, in fact, that to the mind of Thomas, (although not all theologians agree with him) it was completely impossible for the angels to sin in the purely natural order. The immediate, intrinsic and natural rule of morality for them was their own intellects; these were perfect and were perfectly followed by the will of the angels. If they had not been lifted to the supernatural order, they could not have sinned, could not have gone to hell; but then neither could they have gone to heaven. There would have been no angelic sinners; nor would there have been any angelic saints. That has always been the risk of the high goals; the low, level places are safer, so safe indeed as to be worthless. It has always been dangerous to make "reckless leaps into darkness with hands outstretched to a star."

Its Object

Even in the supernatural order, an angelic sin it a difficult business. Even there, no imperfection is possible in the angels preceding sin, no darkening of the intellect, no absence of knowledge, no refusal of the will to follow the intellect; the angels could not choose evil, thinking it good. Yet they could choose good evilly. True, that statement throws no glaring light on the mystery of the angels' sin; but the truth that does dispel some of the darkness is wrapped up tightly in that brief statement. For while it is true that there could be no imperfection in the angels before sin, it is equally true that imperfection before sin was not necessary in order that the angels should turn away from God.

In treating of angelic knowledge, we saw that the angel received its full consignment of concepts at the very first moment of its life; but an angel, like a man, can consider only one concept at a time. What concept is considered at this precise moment is a matter to be decided entirely at the taste of the particular angel. It can consider this one, or that one, or none at all. In this precise power lies the key to the solution of the mysterious sin of the angels. In the concrete, it is not difficult to determine what sin the angels committed. They really had no such dazzling variety of evil as is displayed before the human tentative purchaser of evil. Only two sins were open to the angels, for only two sins directly appeal to spiritual nature, the sins of pride and envy. Moreover, envy could come about only as a consequent of pride. Concretely, then, the angelic sin could be no other than a sin of pride. How did that particular sin actually come about? We have a rather accurate picture of the process if we can imagine the modeled girl of the year, looking her very best as she prepares to step out of her room, stopping, as she naturally would, for one last approving glance, and standing transfixed by her own beauty. So the angels, considering their own beauty and perfection, were enchanted. There they stopped, captivated refusing to let their minds consider the further supernatural end to which that lustrous natural beauty was ordered. In this sense they wished to be like God, nothing could be more beautiful, nothing more perfect, they would be sufficient to themselves, placing their happiness, their final end, in themselves to the scorn of the supernatural happiness, which was the beatific vision. The splendor of the angelic beauty fascinated them, they refused to look beyond it to the infinite splendor of the vision of God.

The modeled girl's rapt admiration of herself could hardly be morally serious. Certainly it would not be an eternal choice; eventually her ankles would get tired or her stomach would demand some food. Yet in the angels, this fascination was a deliberate mortal sin.

It was mortal for it involved turning away from God, rejecting the final end for the created good, which was the angelic nature. Moreover, it was sinful. True, it is no imperfection in the angels not to consider this or that idea, generally speaking; just as it is no sin in a Catholic to refuse to wonder what day of the week this happens to be. Now if the Catholic fears this may be Friday, and be refuses to wonder about it lest he discover that he must subsist that day on the hated fish, he sins. So, too, with the angels; the faith in them, it is an imperfection and a sin not to consider this or that idea when they are obliged to consider it. The whole thing was deliberate, that is free and finder control. Surely the consideration of their own beauty and the embrace of that beauty was entirely voluntary; nor was the refusal to consider the vision of God, or the lack of all such consideration, a forced, necessary thing. In the angels, as in us, the mind turns to this or that subject of consideration as we wish it to; the euphemistic phrase, "a wandering mind," carries with it the pleasantly flattering, but completely false, implication that our mind is busy at one thing or another all the time. Our imagination wanders, but our minds work at the task we assign them. In the angels, that is even truer. In this case, then, the angels directly and expressly willed the consideration of their own beauty; the lack of consideration of the vision of God was willed indirectly and implicitly. They put themselves in the position of a man who refuses to listen to his own faults and limitations because he is so heartily in love with himself.

It seems clear that this sin demanded no imperfection in the angels *before* the sin. This lack of consideration of the final end was not before the sin, it was a part of the sin. The sin began in this inconsideration and was consummated in the evil choice of themselves made by the angels. To put the whole thing in strict theological language, thereby showing mathematicians that they are not alone in their esoteric terminology, we could say that the inconsideration of the final end was first in the order of formal cause, since the judgment of reason is the rule of choice; but in the order of efficient and final cause, the angel's evil choice of themselves was first since the free will moves the intellect to act.

The angels' sin was a rebellion, a wild, hopeless, stupid rebellion. Yet, it did have a splendid leader. Lucifer, who headed the rebellious hosts, was, in the natural order, the greatest of all the angels, good or bad. In other words, the most perfect nature that God has ever produced was the first to rebel against Him. Any of the other angels had only to look a step above to see a creature more beautiful than himself; but there were no creatures more beautiful than Lucifer. He was the most perfect image of the splendor of God; to realize he was only an image, he would have to look to God Himself. Pride was the sin of the angels, not weakness, ignorance or passion; and surely the greatest of the angels had the most reason for pride.

In the angelic world, the defection of Lucifer had a considerably greater effect than would the apostasy of a Pope in Christendom. He did not drag any of his fellows to hell with him by the scruff of their necks; but by way of example, suggestion or even, perhaps, persuasion he mustered quite an army. Scripture gives us an indication of this by declaring that all the devils are subject to Lucifer; according to Peter, speaking of sin, "by whom a man is overcome, of the same also is he a slave." It would seem to be the order of divine justice, that we are subject in punishment to him to whose suggestion we have consented in sin; him whom we choose as a leader in evil we shall have for a master in punishment.

Number of Angelic Sinners

To assign a number to the legions of revolting angels is, of course, sheer guesswork. No tally sheet of the devils has been given us and there is no other way in which we could know how many-followed Lucifer. Since, however, sin, of its very nature, is against intelligence and a violation of natural inclinations, it would be rash indeed to suppose that, in a nature so perfect it allowed for no mistakes, the majority fell into sin. It is much more probable that not as many of the angels sinned as conquered.

At any rate, these sinful angels, forever after known as devils, had committed supernatural suicide. They were, from then on, supernaturally dead, as helpless to climb back to the heights of the supernatural as a dead man is to scramble out of his grave. They had thrown away that participation of divine life, which is sanctifying grace and were, from there on out, incapable of producing any work worthy of heaven. Their intellects were stripped of all that supernatural affective knowledge, such as would produce love; the gift of wisdom had been tossed aside; and the speculative intellectual knowledge that might have come to them by future revelations was cut down to a dim, vague light. Indeed, from then on they would receive only such knowledge as was necessary for the working out of the divine plans; even such knowledge would be, for them, a suspect, torturing, uncertain thing stripped of the infallible certitude that comes from the supernatural virtue of faith.

For all that, they were a splendid lot as they trooped from heaven. Sin, of itself, does not destroy the integrity of nature as rebellion destroys the integrity of an empire; and theirs was a splendid nature. Their intellects retained the full perfection of natural knowledge, the complete freedom from the impediments of ignorance and passion. Their wills were still the splendid instrument of desire, which recognized no impediment to its attainment and no solvent of its embrace. Yet these splendid wills were forever confirmed in sin. The devils had no opportunity to repent, no second chance to remedy an initial mistake. In the first place, such a second chance depended, in them as in us, on the purely free gift of divine grace; of themselves they were helpless. Now over and above that supernatural helplessness, repentance is naturally impossible to the angels. An angel cannot turn back. The act of its will, like that of its intellect, is one swift, eternally enduring act. Whether it is to good or to bad, the angel must stand forever committed to its first choice, eternally loyal even although that loyalty is to the standards of hell.

The Punishment of the Sin

Such inescapable loyalty brings no joy to the devils. There is sorrow in hell, penetrating, despairing sorrow proportionate to the great joy of which the brilliant wills of the devils were capable. Their wills can and do resist the things that are in place of the things that might have been; the salvation of souls, the joy of the blessed, their own misery in hell are constant sources of unceasing sorrow. In fact, if this sorrow were not in the devils, it would be absurd to speak of their punishment, for punishment means, essentially, something against the will, something undergone with regret. Now, of course, there is no physical pain, no passion of sorrow in the devils; horns, tails, pitchforks and leering grins are no part of the diabolic equipment. These are, after all, angels; and angels are purely spiritual beings.

The instant their sin was committed, the devils were hurled into hell, the place of their eternal punishment. Evidently the fires prepared for them there could not physically torture them; a spiritual nature cannot be made to sizzle over a fire. Yet this fire can, supernaturally, be a real punishment; if, for example, it was endowed with the supernatural power of limiting the activity of a spiritual nature (as Thomas thought), it would place the particular devil in somewhat the same humiliating position of a strong adult confined in a baby's playpen. From time to time, some devils are allowed to wander the world for the exercise of human virtue, itself a humiliating and infuriating occupation; although there are some who have never been outside the gates of hell, as there are angels who have never left heaven. Whether in hell or on this earth, every devil carries the essence of hell with him, the despairing knowledge that all is lost forever. It may be that the fire of hell accompanies these wandering devils to humiliate their proud power, or perhaps it is only the humiliating thought, that they must return to that infantile enclosure which is forever in their minds.

Conclusion
Human nature seen in the light of angelic saints and sinners

This is the field of angelic love, the stupendous natural beauty and power of it, the heights to which it climbed and the depths to which it plunged; ringing through every instant of it is that mysterious, somehow terrifying note of forever, of eternity. This is the race to which we are kin. This is the love upon, which ours is modeled; for we also, have an intellectual appetite, a will capable of these heights, of these depths, and for an eternity.

Potentialities for Good

Now, because of that will of ours, we too can attain to the beauty of that angelic vision that was too much for the pride of the angels, it is so dazzling; we can go this far and further, to the heights which some of the angels did not climb to the vision of the eternal splendor, the life of God Himself. Our love, too, is capable of just such loyalty, plot such wholehearted surrender. In fact, it is only in proportion to our approach to this love of a spiritual nature that we are worthy of our own immortal souls. This is the love that can and must dominate the emotions, the passions, that we have in common with the animals. This is the love that is betrayed by the emotionalism of our day. For, in a sense, we can go down a bit lower than the angels we can not only lose God, we can do what the greatest devil cannot, we can give full rein to emotion and put ourselves on a level with the beasts.

Consequences in Men of Angelic Virtue and Sin
Humility

Familiarity with this love of the angels, giving, as it does, a knowledge of our unsounded potentialities for good and evil, is a source of virtues that are strangers to a world of emotion. For it brings a man face to face with the truth about himself. In the face of that truth he may well be humble. Emotion, uncontrolled passion, is not humble but greedy, self-centered and strangely, satisfied only with its own destruction. It is good to realize, when we stride along in the pride of life, conscious of our strength and bolstered up, perhaps, by a long escape from sin, that the greatest of the angels fell. It is a distinct deterrent to the rash inclination to flirt with the occasion of sin to know that, without such obstacles as the passions present to reason and will, the most perfect nature God ever made was plunged into hell.

Fear

Knowing the truth of himself and the angels, a man might well cultivate a healthy fear. For indeed devils are not mere myths. They are terrible realities; they are enemies with natures intact in their superiority and perfection, on fire with a hatred of God and all that smacks of God. Their very hate drives them on to focus their splendid intelligence on the destruction of God's kingdom on earth, His friendship in our hearts and our eternal life with Him. Our salvation may well be worked out in fear and trembling.

Self-Respect

Yet the truth about himself makes no molded coward of a man. We are of the race of the angels. Our lives, our love are not mere biological accidents, individually of no importance. Like that of the angels, our life and our love can escape corruption, dimming of activity, the rusty wearing down and weary, groaning of a last moment of life. We are above the common, the ordinary, the transient; we are of a long line of spiritual nobility. Our name is one to be kept honorable; for, like the angels, we must live with that name forever.

📖 CHAPTER XII – THE KINGDOM OF MAN 📖
(Q. 65-74; 90-93)

1. Scriptural account of the kingdom of man,
2. Modern rejection of the story.

3. The two elements of the story,

   a) The fact of creation.

   b) Account of the distinction and adornment of the universe.

4. Unreasonable rejection of the fact of creation,

   a) Résumé of proof of creation.

   b) Different senses of the word "evolution,"

      (1) A scientific hypothesis.

      (2) A pseudo-scientific solvent on a universal scale.

      (3) A philosophical explanation of the universe.

   c) Interrelation of creation and evolution.

5. Unjust rejection of the account of distinction and adornment,

   a) The purpose of the account.

   b) The language of it.

   c) Injustice of its rejection.

6. Origin of the kingdom of man,

   a) Thomas' approach to the question,

(1) His three principles.

(2) His chief interest.

(3) The science of his time.

(b) Causes of the kingdom of man.

(1) The work of distinction – the first three days.

(2) The work of adornment – the last three days.
(3) The rest of God – the seventh day.

7. Origin of the lord of the world,

a) His soul.

b) His body.

c) His partner,

(1) Time and manner of the production of woman.

(2) Her relation to man.

Conclusion,

1. Pertinence of the question of the origin of the world,

a) To the mind of man.

b) To the life of man.

2. Contrast of the answers,

a) From the appraisal of reason.

b) From the consequences of each.

📖   CHAPTER XII   📖
THE KINGDOM OF MAN
(Q.65-74;90-93)

Scriptural Account of the Kingdom of Man
Modern Rejection of the Story

In the Book of Genesis there is an account of the beginnings of the world that has amused the scholars of our age. In fact, their amusement was so huge that they shared the joke with the man in the street. The story was pleasant enough in its way, hardly plausible, still it was taken seriously by millions of men before the clear light of science exposed it for what it was, a myth among many similar myths. In that bright light, it looks as ridiculous as an actor caught in broad daylight with his make-up on. Such amused tolerance is the product of a sense of immense superiority, superiority so great as to make it unnecessary to bother about details. In any field, such superiority is dangerous, for it is the sort of thing that topples an experienced lineman from a telephone pole that makes a drunkard challenge the world. Superiority is a heady drink to be sipped, not gulped; however enticing its bouquet, clear its color and warming its taste, it too easily brings on early morning regrets. Perhaps our moderns are only gay, not really drunk, although they have proved steady drinkers of this dangerous drink; they have not yet reached the morning-after stage, but they have been careless, they have laid the bases for the groans of regret.

The Two Elements of the Story:

The Fact of Creation, The Account of the Distinction and Adornment of the Universe

Along with the story of the world's distinction and adornment, they have, extravagantly, carelessly, blindly, thrown out a momentous fact, the fact of the origin of the world. They have tossed the whole thing out like an old rag doll. Perhaps nothing stamps Thomas as so completely out of date, in the eyes of the moderns, as the fact that he took this story seriously, Surely, nothing so clearly marks him off from modern thinkers as the fact that he saw the two elements in this story, the momentous fact of creation and the simple account of the distinction and adornment of the world. His intellect bowed before the first of these, as an unimpeded intellect must always do homage to solid truth, and he could mete out justice to the second because of his firm grasp of the first.

Unreasonable Rejection of the Fact of Creation

Rejection of the fact of creation is unreasonable, not in the sense a man is unreasonable because he is slightly pig-headed or extremely meticulous. This rejection is unreasonable because it is an open flaunting of reason.

Résumé of Proof of Creation.

In a former chapter we have treated the matter of creation quite thoroughly, insisting that the world was brought into existence by a first cause creating it. However, a brief restatement of that reasoning will not be out of place here. A first cause means no more than an utterly independent cause; that is, a cause that has nothing or no one before it, that is in every sense first. To be independent in this full sense of the word means to be completely self sufficient as well as to be the first source of all else. Creation is commonly defined as "making something out of nothing;" more profoundly, it is the production of something independently of any pre-existing subject. In a word, it is the production of the whole being not merely a part of it, not disposing for it, or bringing it forth from something else.

So that creation, the truth so eminently clear to reason and so solidly taught by faith, means simply that the world was produced by the first cause, in the way proper to that first cause, that is, with complete independence. If we postulate anything on which this first cause depends, we are simply denying that this is a first cause and we push the problem just that much further back; we do not solve it. For it will always remain true, that where we discover someone leaning, depending, there will be something to lean on, to depend on; and the stability of this latter will not be the product of the feeble one who drapes himself on it. Complete independence in act means the production of the effect from nothing.

The reasons given for this explanation of the universe are those given for the existence of God. These can be put briefly by saying that either this was the way things were produced or there is nothing that lasts, is evidently false. There is no other way to account, not only for the universe, but also for the very least thing in it. The question here is not merely of mountains, continents and planets; but of even a speck of dust or the wink of an eye. One cries out the existence of the first cause as loudly as the other, or of all together. An endless chain of dependent causes does not explain any one of them or all of them, for their very dependence precludes the possibility of their being self-sufficient, the source or the first; that dependence demands something upon which to depend. There is an either, independent or first cause, or there are no effects; either that first cause created, if it acted at all, or it is not first. The fact of creation, with its strict adherence to the facts of the world, is not something a man needs to feel self-conscious about or to apologize for. Rather, it is something demanded in the name of all that is reasonable.

Different Senses of the Word "Evolution"

Reasonable or not, this fact of creation has been swept out of men's minds along with the rest of the account given in Genesis. Still, the house does not need to remain empty; in place of creation we can have evolution, either all at once or on an installment plan that eases the pain of its acceptance by spreading the burden over millions of years. Lest such a statement bring on, with the promptness of an echo, the charge that we are anti-scientific, ultra-conservative or behind the times, let us investigate the meaning of the world "evolution."

Such an investigation is important for the word designates a strange set of triplets; one or the other may enjoy the confusion of a stranger who cannot distinguish them, but each will indignantly resent having the faults of one of the others attributed to her, especially the faults of the weak sister of the three.

A Scientific Hypothesis

Most properly, the word is taken to refer to a scientific hypothesis. As such it was, and is, advanced as a scientific record of the development of life. As a scientific hypothesis, and within its own field, it has immense value. The mass of cumulative evidence supporting it certainly classifies it as a first class working theory; and this is all the scientist seeks. It is not, nor is it in this sense intended to be, a final explanation of the universe. The object of science is not an explanation but the uncovering of a universal; it does not seek the last cause, but a general law; its reasoning does not terminate in conclusions or explanations, but rather in the generalizations which are called scientific laws.

In this proper sense, no philosopher or theologian can have any objection to it. To contrast an adherent of the creation explanation and an evolutionist in this sense is as silly as it would be to consider as mutually exclusive terms the words "democrat" and "modeled." The only possible source of conflict here would be the extension of this scientific working hypothesis to the origin of the human soul. That would be stepping outside the field of science immediately, for it would be to step outside the field of experimental observation; moreover, it is a step not taken by the scientist.

A Pseudo-Scientific Solvent on a Universal Scale

The word "evolution" is also widely used for a pseudo-scientific theory that is in the nature of a patent medicine to remedy all intellectual ills by resolving all difficulties. It is considered applicable to nearly all fields and is actually wielded with the recklessness that formerly characterized the use of arnica or camphor. It is, for example applied to comparative religion and adduced as the explanation of the present existence of monotheism; to sociology and hailed as the explanation of the alleged development of monogamy from promiscuity; to ethics as the explanation of Christian ethics developing from a completely amoral condition and so on and on and on.

This approaches the ridiculous. If a man concludes, from the fact that the theory of relativity works beautifully in mathematics and explains many phenomena in physics, that everything is relative, he might, at any moment, logically start to use a pair of shoes for a handkerchief. These pseudo-scientific statements are quite groundless from a purely scientific point of view. As a matter of fact, the evidence shows no development of monotheism from polytheism or atheism; there is much more evidence for the conclusion that monotheism was the primitive form. A promiscuous society has yet to be discovered; and again the evidence of anthropology, insofar as it allows of a conclusion, points to monogamy as the primitive form of marriage. An amoral condition of men is a modern nightmare, not a scientific fact; some of the most surely primitive peoples we have yet discovered hold a high moral code and practice it. These things are flatly unscientific; yet they are solemnly advanced day after day, in publication after publication as although no scientific discoveries had been made since first the theorists started their castle building untrammeled by the brick and mortar of evidence.

For these things, there need be no sympathy whatever. They are without justification. They have none of the beauty of a fairy tale, the utilitarian efficient of a swindler's story, the venerable dignity of a myth, the plausibility of a lie or the humor of a whopping joke. Least of all have they any of the characteristics of a fact. They have only the ugly repulsiveness of intellectual degeneracy.

A Philosophical Explanation of the Universe

In its third sense, "evolution" is seriously advanced as a philosophic answer to the question of the origin of the world. This philosophic theory, which denies causality and finality, assumes that the process of change is a self-sufficient explanation both of itself and of the perfection of the universe. One form of this explanation declares that the story reads like this, some primary stuff, very imperfect, eternal or mysteriously coming into existence of itself, has slowly developed, thanks to chance and environment, with the force of inexorable law into the complicated world as we know it today. A scientist would have a graphic picture of all this if, in the vacuum he has created, there should suddenly appear a puff of smoke fragrant of a blend of Virginia and Turkish tobacco; and then, under his astonished eyes, the smoke took form, developing into a perfect ring slowly floating off (without air to float on) ,and as a last delicate touch, sporting just the suspicion of a bit of lipstick to support the illusion that there had been a smoker's mouth and a cigarette in back of the whole thing.

Another form of this explanation pictures a mysterious life force, again utterly imperfect, necessarily surging its way up through matter (which is unexplained, and indeed is not a reality at all) into the perfections we know today. In this opinion there is no material world, for only the process of change is real and that does not stop long enough for it to be recognized, let alone given a name. The words seem obscure, but the idea becomes perfectly clear when you picture the change of expression from joy to sorrow on a man's face, first blotting out the joy, the sorrow, the face and the expression. Both these forms of the philosophic explanation called by the name of evolution are extended to include man, body and soul. Both deny the idea of a cause, or a starting point, outside the process of change. Additionally, both necessarily deny an intelligent finality to the whole affair.

Interrelation of Creation and Evolution

All three of these senses of evolution, the scientific, the pseudo-scientific and the philosophical, must be seen in relation to creation if there is to be any dissipation of the confusion that has come from using the one word in three distinctly different senses. Quite evidently there is no possibility of conflict between evolution as a scientific hypothesis and the fact of creation. Creation is explicitly a statement of the last cause, the ultimate explanation of the universe; and, just as explicitly, science is not interested in last cause or ultimate explanations but only in the uncovering of general laws. Science has no professional interest in the source of these laws or in the nature of the lawgiver, or, indeed, in the very existence of such a legislator.

In the sense of a pseudo-scientific theory, there is no possibility of honest conflict between evolution and creation, or indeed between evolution and anything else, any more than there is a possibility of the babbling of a child clashing with some eternal truth. This theory is a positive insult to human intelligence; the audacity of its proposal assumes that we know nothing of the actual state of science, that we have heard nothing of the findings of science for the last twenty years.

In the sense of a philosophic explanation of the origin of the universe, evolution dashes head on with the act of creation, and it is just too bad for evolution if reason be the witness of the accident, or even the undertaker. In this sense, evolution is nothing more than the process of change on a grand scale, the change from potentiality to actuality, the realization of potentialities. To use some examples from an earlier chapter, it is the becoming of the statue from a marble block, the becoming of the surgeon from the butcher, the becoming of the masterpiece from the paints and canvas. To claim self-sufficiency for such a process, to posit it without explanation and blandly declare that it explains itself and everything else, is contrary to reason, unintelligible and so patently false.

Let us look at it a bit more closely. It is frankly a denial of the principle of causality and finality, that is, it makes the world a lustful brat that was unborn but is growing, a play unfolding without beginning or end, a book without a starting point, plot or finish, a motion that not only did not start and is not going anywhere but which has absolutely nowhere to go. This denial is reducible to the contradiction, which is an identification of opposites and it brings the mind up sharply against a dilemma. Either there is no difference between the potentiality and the actuality, between the canvas and the masterpiece, for the potentiality is the producer of the actuality by the mere process of change, by merely moving itself, of itself, to that perfection; and this amounts to a denial of evolution itself for it is a denial of change. Or, the other horn of the dilemma, this latest perfection produced by evolution is not the same as the potentiality from which it developed; in this case, it came from nothing of itself. This gives us something from nothing with no other cause adduced; more simply, it staggers the mind with the incredible contradiction that nothing is something.

This may seem much too brutal a simplification of evolution, since nothing has been said of the million of years involved, the power of the process of change, environment and chance. In a sense, the charge is just; this is a simplification of evolution. It has disregarded the table decorations, the hors d'oeuvres and the liqueurs to concentrate on the meat and potatoes of the meal. Yet, and as a matter of fact, millions of years do not help or hinder the problem; time has nothing to do with the central difficulty, it is merely a measure of the method of development not the explanation of that development. The process of change is merely a statement of the method of development, of how the change was brought about, it is not an explanation, not a statement of cause, it does not tell us why there is a world at all.

Now then, look at the part environment plays in the scheme; and necessity; and chance! Well, look at them. What produced the environments? What is the source of the necessity? What is chance, in this case, but the mathematician's "x", a statement of a common factor. The whole thing has been succinctly put in these words, "When there is change, there is reason for change, and the reason for change can be found only in something not involved in that change. It follows that if there is such a thing as a process of change with a definite and discoverable law which embraces the whole of physical reality, the whole physical reality must have a non-physical environment." For change and evolution presuppose the environment and the environed interacting on one another.

Unjust rejection of the account of distinction and adornment of the universe.

The Purpose of the Account

The rejection of the fact of creation is a violation of the reason of man; it is unreasonable in the sense of being mad. The rejection, on scientific grounds, of the Scriptural account of the distinction and adornment of the world has a petty meanness about it for it is definitely unfair. The purpose of Moses in writing the account given in Genesis was to instruct an unlettered people in the fundamental truths of the religious and moral order. He wrote that they might know the obligation of adoration and gratitude to Jehovah, the author, governor and conserver of all things; that he might preserve his people from idolatry in recalling to them that every Creature has its reason of existence in a superior cause, that every creature is destined to serve man, the Crown and masterpiece of creation, and not to be served by man.

The Language of it

Moses did his work in a masterly fashion. His language is necessarily one of great simplicity; but its grand figures speak vividly to the imagination, it pictures the sweeping lines of the universe in terms that slam against the senses. In fact, the account often approaches the grandeur and rhythm of sublime poetry.

A hundred and fifty years ago men were smiling at the tale of Moses because it said nothing of the nebular theory of the generation of the planets, the physics of Newton or the optical theories of Descartes. Today the smile comes again because there is nothing there of relativity, no statement of the principles of thermodynamics or of evolution. A hundred and fifty years from now another generation will continue to enjoy the huge joke of Moses not stating the scientific theories of that future time. In other words, the account is rejected primarily because Moses was not a bungler, because he did not fill a lesson in religious and moral truths with a scientific jargon that would meet the approval of all ages.

Of course it is vain to look for chemical formulas or mathematical statements in this account; there is no display of geological evidence and no anticipation of biological discoveries to be found in it. It was never intended as a scientific account; if it had been, it would have completely failed of its purpose, leaving the Hebrews of the desert glassy-eyed and slack-jawed in astonishment. It is unjust to look for contradictions to modern science in an account that was avowedly non-scientific. The very nature and language of the account made it so evidently elastic that the earliest Christian commentators could find hardly a word that was not open to widely different interpretations in the factual field, thus "day" might have meant twenty-four hours, many such days, an indefinite period of time or even a stage in knowledge; the creation of plants might have meant the instant establishment of perfect species or only the establishing of these species in germ for development; light, firmament, earth and many another word were seen, from the beginning, to be of this same indefinite character.

Injustice of its Rejection

Briefly, the account of Moses is an account that admirably serves its purpose, and that does not serve a purpose foreign to it. It is unjust to tie it down to the science of any one time, and unjust to cite it as contradicting the science of any one time. It can and does oppose pseudo-scientific theories that are at bottom philosophical, for it is avowedly expository of the philosophical truths that are at the roots of all being.

Origin of the Kingdom of Man, Thomas' Approach to the Question, His Three Principles

Thomas, approaches the account of creation from the vantage point of his faith, in doing so, he laid down some common sense principles. To him it was obvious that the truth of Holy Scripture must be held un-violated; after all, it is the inspired word of God and so there is nothing of truth, which can be surer. It also seemed clear to him that when it is possible to expose the Scriptures in many ways, no one position or interpretation should be so narrowly held to that, if it is certainly established that such a position is false, a man would nevertheless presume to maintain it. Such a man would justly be held in derision by the infidels and thereby block the infidels' way to belief. Thomas saw the necessity of remembering that Moses spoke to an uneducated community; condescending to their ignorance (*imbecillitas* is the word Thomas uses) he proposed only those things that were manifestly apparent to the senses. After all, man did not lose the knowledge of natural things by his sin, nor that science by which the necessities of the flesh are provided. In Scripture, then, man is not taught these things, but rather the science of the soul, which is the science he lost by his sin.

His Chief Interest

Thomas, in other words, makes it plain at the beginning that he is not approaching this account in search of scientific explanations. His interest, as a theologian, was centered on the metaphysical truths, that account, which affirmed and advanced for the Hebrews, creation as a fact and as an act proper to God; the first cause of all things, and the final cause of the world. Thomas was not particularly interested, then, in this account as scientific; nevertheless, in exposing it, he was obliged to make use of contemporary science, as we are today. Thomas knew the science of his time well; in this treatment he did not try to investigate that science, to improve it or modeled it. He merely used it.

The Science of His Time

To understand his exposition of the account of Genesis, it will be necessary to have at least a nodding acquaintance with the physics of Aristotle, which was the science of the thirteenth century. To the minds of the men of that time, the universe was made up of seven concentric planetary spheres contained within an eighth of the spheres of the fixed stars, containing in their turn the earth as the center. Above the heaven of the fixed stars began the invisible world, that is, the crystalline heaven, or heaven of the waters, which was the source of rain and the Empyrean heaven, or the heaven of light, which was the abode of the angels. The matter of these celestial spheres was strictly incorruptible because their forms completely exhausted the potentialities of the matter. To each sphere a moving intelligence was assigned; its work being to direct the circular motion of the particular sphere, not to inform it or vivify it as a soul vivifies a body. Below the lowest sphere, that of the moon, are arranged the spheres of the four elements, namely, fire, air, water and earth. By rights, each of these should be gathered up in a natural site with a resultant perfect equilibrium; but, in fact, they are intermingled. Since their natural tendency is to strive for their natural site, there results the distinctive movements of the elements, thus fire goes up, earth goes down.

Causes of the Kingdom of Man

With these ideas in mind, we already have a fair notion of Thomas' treatment of the account of creation. The first efficient cause was, of course, God, for Thomas had none of the modern madness about him. God is also the final cause or the end of the universe. The eternal ideas in the mind of God are the formal cause in the sense of exemplary cause. Additionally, since all things come from God, both the matter of things and their intrinsic forms are from God, existing, of course, only in conjunction as composites.

The Work of Distinction – The First Three Days

The act of creation was an eternal act of God. As to the unfolding of that eternal act in time, these were two phases, one of distinction and one of adornment. The first three days of creation were occupied with the work of distinction, for obviously there can be no adornment until there is something to adorn. The first day saw the distinction of light and darkness; the second day brought the distinction of heaven and earth, the firmament dividing against the waters; on the third day the waters of the earth were gathered into seas, dividing seas from dry land. The land carried its quota of plants as a man wears his clothes, for the plants were not so much an ornament as an ordinary and decent covering for the bare earth.

The Work of Adornment – the Last Three Days

The last three days were filled with the pleasantly creative labor of decoration, God appearing as the interior decorator of the universe facing a crucial test of His divine good taste. Thus, on the fourth day He concentrated on the heavens, adorning them with the sun, moon and stars. On the fifth day the waters received their bewilderingly various adornment of fishes, the air its fragmentary beauty of birds; the sixth day was dedicated to the adornment of the earth with its animals, among which was man. Yet he is so important that his production deserves, and gets, special treatment.

Throughout this exposition, Thomas Aquinas is content to coast along, explaining the natures of the different products in terms of the science of his time, modeling the great differences in the interpretations of the Fathers, assigning reasons for the precise order in which these things were produced. Some of these reasons are penetrating and humanly interesting to an extreme, the reasons, for example, for the production of the stars. Every corporal creature has three ends, itself, a nature above it, and the universe. Moses, in accounting for the stars, considers only the second, the utility of man, the stars serve man by giving light for the direction of work and the acquisition of knowledge; by furnishing a change of seasons to destroy the ennui of an unchanging climate, to conserve health and to allow the necessary food to be raised, things that could not happen in an eternal winter or an eternal summer; by furnishing opportunities for business and work by allowing the forecasting of dry and rainy seasons.

The Rest of God – the Seventh Day

By the end of the sixth day, creation was over and done with. Everything that was ever to exist was made by that time, either actually or virtually, that is, in its full perfection or potentially, in germ; as for human souls, they existed at least in their exemplar, in the mind of God. Creation was an accomplished fact; God then rested. Yet the rest of God by no means implies that God's action in the world ceased on the sixth day, there was no question of a Florida trip or an ocean voyage on a divine scale to get away from it all. He operates unceasingly in conserving and governing the world. The seventh day, marking the repose of God in this sense, is fittingly kept holy; for the sanctification of everything consists precisely in its reposing in God as God did in Himself on the seventh day.

Origin of the Lord of the World

To come to the creation of man, we find him destined to occupy a peculiar position linking the material and spiritual world in himself; consequently, it is necessary to consider the element of the spiritual and that of the material in him separately. Really, the spiritual offers no rational difficulty, although it has been the stumbling block of intellectuals for hundreds of years; but then what could be more fitting than that a professed intellectual should stumble over a block that was not there.

His Soul

It is immediately evident, and also a doctrine of faith, that the soul of Adam was certainly not an emanation of the substance of God, an outpouring of the divine stuff. From what has already been said of the infinite perfection and ceaseless act of God and what is quite evident of the limitation and imperfection of our own souls, there can be no question of identity of the two. The soul of Adam must, then, have been produced; and there is only one way to produce a spiritual substance, that is, by creation. It cannot be knitted, woven, grown or manufactured. It cannot be made from any material stuff; the attempt to maintain that it can promptly involves the contradiction that the soul is both spiritual and possessed of parts. Nor can it have been made from any preexisting spiritual substance; such a substance, precisely as spiritual, is devoid of parts and thus cannot have anything taken from it without being destroyed. The soul of man is created; and that means that God produced it immediately, for the utterly independent mode of action, which is creation is proper to the only utterly independent agent. Even although the angels were willing to take on a little extra work, God Himself could give them no part in this labor, which is possible only to omnipotent power. It is the common teaching of the Fathers and Doctors of the Church that the human soul was not produced before the human body, although philosophically there is no impossibility involved in such a previous production. Yet then, neither is there any reason to be found for such a previous existence. Certainly, if Augustine is right and the body was only virtually produced during the six days of creation, there is no reason why the soul must necessarily have come into actual existence in that period.

It is plain, then, that on the question of the soul of man both faith and reason stand diametrically opposed to the theories of complete evolution. Because the human soul is spiritual, it can come only from God and must come directly from Him. There can be no question of its slow development, or, indeed, of any development of it; not only because there is nothing from which a spiritual substance can be developed, but also because, being devoid of parts, the soul is had all at once or it is not had at all. In any question of the evolution of man, if we are to stand on reasonable grounds, his soul must be excluded from the discussion; otherwise we place him on the level of material creation in violation of the evident fact that his acts exceed the limits of the material.

His Body

In the production of the body of man, St. Thomas says no one element (fire, air, earth, or water) was exclusively used. As God had all things *eminently* in Himself, as the angels had all things *intentionally* (that is, by knowledge) in themselves, so man was a kind of microcosmos, having almost everything in his composition, spirituality in his soul, a likeness of the heavenly bodies in the stability of his make-up, and the earthly elements in his physical constitution. The question of the production of the body of man was really a question of disposing the material for the fit reception of the human soul.

Certainly that disposition could not have been accomplished by other human beings, as it is today; there were no others. Nor could it have been, naturally, the work of some other animals any more than a pair of tigers, let alone a pair of mountains, can dispose the material for the generation of a mouse. It was the work of God, perhaps immediately, by the direct divine formation of the body; perhaps immediately, that is, through lower animals to which such poster had been specially given or, as Augustine would have it, the body was only virtually produced in the work of creation.

Thomas Aquinas, opposing Augustine, inclines towards the immediate production of the body of man by God because of the absence of any sufficient natural factors for such production. Now, he agrees that there is no philosophical reason militating against the gradual preparation of the material for such a body by other forces acting through powers given them by God. In any case, it is never a question of any other than God producing the final human composite made up of body and soul; the question is merely one of the preparation of the material for the infusion of the soul by God. In a word, as far as the body of man goes, there is no reason for serious opposition to the theory of evolution; on the other hand, there is no compelling reason for an enthusiastic embrace of every evolutionary theory advanced. A good many have gone by the board already; probably a good many more will follow. So far it is not at all proved that the body of man actually did develop from some lower form.

The actual design of the human body was an artistic triumph worthy of divine ingenuity. What defects there are in man's constitution come from the nature of the material that had to be used if man were to be the link binding together the material and the spiritual worlds; no amount of skill on the part of the craftsman can make a sword durable if he is confined to tin as to his material, nor can divine ingenuity find any natural escape from the defects of matter when matter must enter into the essential composition of a creature. As we shall see later on in this book, and again in the second volume, these natural defects were remedied by the preternatural gifts given man for his life in the Garden of Eden.

It is true that some animals have keener smell than men, others keener sight, and so on. Yet this was because man's senses were ordered to his higher knowledge so that a nice balance was struck lest any one of his senses interfere with his reason; not many human ears are so keen that a man cannot think because of the racket made by a cat tramping over a rug. In the fundamental sense of touch, and in those internal senses, which so immediately serve reason, imagination, memory, appreciation, man far excels the animals.

We have no horns, claws or covering of hair and, normally, our hides are not too thick; in other words, man is shorn of the weapons and coverings naturally given to other animals. He does not have even a speck of fur or just a few of the porcupine's spikes. In place of these natural protections, man has his reason and his hands, by these he can prepare weapons for himself, provide himself with covering and the other necessities of life in an infinite variety. It is only the human female that does not have to wear the same coat of fur for a lifetime.

Man stands erect while the other animals normally go about on all fours; and for very good reasons. His senses are ordered primarily to intellectual delights, not to the search for sensible delights; he should not have his face to the ground as although concentrating on sensible things but rather high up where he can get a broad view of the sensible world, seeing it from all angles. To give his interior powers full play, it is right that his brain be placed above all the other parts of his body, that nothing might weigh heavy upon it and interfere with its operation. If man did not stand erect, he would have to use his hands for front feet, thereby seriously interfering with their usefulness; if he went about on all fours, he would have to take his foods with his lips and mouth, dispensing with all books of etiquette but at the same time thickening his lips, hardening them and roughening the tongue to the impediment of his powers of speech. Moreover, as the superior part of a creature is that by which nourishment is taken, the stature of man accurately places him in the world of creation, the plants have their superior part (the roots) pointed toward earth; the animals occupy a neutral position; while man points towards heaven.

His Partner

In the very beginning, God Himself noticed that man needed a helper; a fact that has been observed by, or called to the attention of, many a man since. It was fitting, then, that woman should have been created from the very beginning of things. However, the fact that Adam needed a helper did not imply that woman was created that she might crawl into overalls and go out into the fields; for such purposes Adam might better have been given a hired man. Now, obviously the human race would not have lasted very long if God had created only a man.

Time and Manner of the Production of Women

According to the medicine of his century, which, of course, Thomas did not correct, woman was an incomplete man, a half-baked male, whose unfinished characteristics come about through some weakness in the parents, some disposition in the human material or some extrinsic cause such as, for example, a strong south wind at the time of conception. Nevertheless Thomas thinks it is unjust to consider woman a cosmic accident; she was not an accident, this creature was made on purpose, deliberately planned by God. Furthermore, he insists that the notion of subjection of woman to man be properly understood. It by no means signifies that woman is the slave of man, subject to man for his utility; rather, the domestic subjection is an ordinary requisite for order; it is subjection, not inferiority. Of course, when more than one free individual are living together and working for a common end there must be someone in charge, one governor, one director. Certainly this subjection is not inferiority; above all, it is not inferiority in any subjective sense, woman is not less human than man, her soul cannot be denied equality with his, and so on. Rather, this subjection is a statement of difference, of unequal gifts that counter-balance each other, making of man and woman a balanced whole. Among the peculiar gifts of man Thomas mentions discretion of reason, which beyond doubt means excellence in speculative reasoning; leaving the obvious corollary to be drawn, namely, that woman excels in practical reasoning.

Her Relation to Man

There are many reasons why woman was fittingly formed from Adam himself. Among others might be mentioned the preservation of the dignity of the first man as head of the whole human race, by way of likeness to God, Who is the head of the whole universe. This also served to augment and conserve the love of man for woman as for one who came from himself, giving it some what the note of the love of a parent for a child; this increase and protection of love was of great importance in the human species where the union of the two sexes was indissoluble. As in the domestic life man is the head of the woman, it was fitting that woman come from man as from her principle; into the union of the two there was introduced, from this moment of origin, a note of sanctity and consecration from the fact that woman, proceeding from the side of man, was the figure of the Church proceeding from the side of Christ.

It is to be particularly noted that woman came from the side of man, formed from his rib. She was not taken from his head, lest she get the notion of dominating man; nor from his feet, lest she is despised by man as being subject to him by way of a slave. To Thomas it was obvious that woman's body was immediately produced by God; for certainly no one else could produce such a masterpiece from such humble material.

Conclusion, Pertinence of the Question of the Origin of the World To the Mind of Man

In concluding this chapter it is very much to the point to insist that this question of the origin of the world is not a purely speculative or academic affair the outcome of which makes no difference to individual men and women. The human mind is simply not made to shrug off a question as fundamental as this. That innate, driving insistence to know the why of things that gives the mind of man no rest is hardly likely to be content to know what this or that wheel is for while the meaning of the whole vast machine of the universe is hidden. The human mind has to have an answer to this question, however many others remain unanswered; and it will have an answer, although it concocts it from the monstrous materials of falsehood offered it by a world afraid of truth.

To the Life of Man

After all, a man has to live in this world, use it or be used by it year after year. Is it of no importance to him to discover that the whole is devoid of meaning and his puny life is a kind of vital insanity? Is it of no importance for him to be given a meaning that is totally false; that, for instance, reduces him to a part of a process, an accident in a biological experiment, a moment in the life of some organistic monster that uses him to his own destruction? Is it not important that he should find that the world he lives in is an intelligent product of a supreme intelligence, that he is its peak, that all beneath him is for the carving out of an eternally enduring personal life? It is hardly likely that men, embracing these different answers to the question of the origin of the universe, will live their lives with the same hope, the same intensity, the same courage, the same strong effort, for men, however ignorant they may be, are not universally fools.

Contrast of the Answers, From the Appraisal of Reason

In our time, the answers to the question of the origin of the universe boil down to two, the answer of creation and the answer of evolution; that is to say, there is only one answer given, the answer of creation, for the other denies the necessity of an answer for a universe that is without cause or purpose. On the grounds of reason the modern man is hardly offered a choice, at least in this sense that there is little choice for the human mind between madness and sanity. The one, on the basis of a self-sufficient universe with no trace of its self-sufficiency, offers a man a process in place of an explanation, a contradiction in place of truth, fiction in face of facts, disorder as the explanation of order. The other, on the basis of a supreme cause whose existence can be demonstrably shown, faces the facts and bows to the inherent dependence of all that is not God; it gives man an explanation, challenges him with the truth, and commands his respect for the order he cannot hide from his eyes.

From the Consequences of Each

There is much more to the apparent choice than the intellectual aspect of truth or Falsehood; there is the difference between despair and hope, between a livable human life and a life that is completely shorn of livability. For if there is no personal end to human life, there is no point in personal concern with the means of living that life, means that can be means only in name. If there is nothing above that man, there is no ground for his hope, no sense to his sorrows, no excuse for his efforts, no reason to his courage; love, triumph, success, justice and all the rest are catchwords coined to lure man into a struggle where he loses even although he wins. However, if he comes from the hand of God and goes his way to God, if every hair of his head is numbered, every moment of his life under his command, and ultimate success or failure not only a possibility but a certainty, then, indeed, man has something to live for. He can, and will, face the risks, take the blows, struggle to his feet after defeat, refuse to quit and scorn to bow his head to the things that are his servants. Yes, it does indeed make a difference what answer is given to the question of the origin of the world; the difference, in a word, between a human and an inhuman life.

📖 CHAPTER XIII – THE LORD OF THE WORLD 📖
(Q. 75-80)

1. The unknown lord,
2. Essential knowledge about man.

(a) Essential ignorance about man,

    (1) Its varieties.

    (2) Its origins.

    (3) The escape from it.

3. Life of the lord of the world,

    (a) Principle of life.

    (b) Its immaterial and subsistent character.

        (1) Its immortality.

        (2) Its incompleteness,

    (c) General notion of matter and form.

        (1) The soul the form of the body.

4. Is Equipment for action of the lord of the world,

    a) In general,
        (1) Distinction and number of the potencies of man.

        (2) Their subject.

        (3) Their duration

    b) In particular

(1) Some lower potencies,
(2) Vegetative potencies.

(b) Sensitive potencies,

(c) External.

(d) Internal.

c) Higher potencies of knowledge,

(1) Active and possible intellect.

(2) Reason and intellect.

5. Volitional equipment of the lord of the world. (Next chapter.)

Conclusion: Philosophy based on ignorance of man is a philosophy of degradation.

b) It is possible only by a distortion of one side of human nature.

c) Its result is the destruction of the whole of human nature.

d) Its goal is despair.

⊞ CHAPTER XIII ⊞
THE LORD OF THE WORLD
(Q. 75-80)

The Unknown Lord

A great deal has been made recently of the things we do not know about man. A best seller of not so long ago spent many dark pages on detailed statements of the damage our ignorance has done, institutes of human relations have been set up in great centers of learning to weave our piecemeal knowledge into a durable fabric; scientists are busy with every detail of man's physical life. For all our awakened interest in the study of man, the cardinal point has been overlooked, namely, that the essential thing to know about man is what he is.

Essential Knowledge About Man

We must at least know the nature of man before we can intelligently discuss any detail of his life. If this much is not known, there can be no real knowledge of the powers of man, we may be impatient at them, as a child is angry with a toy bird because it will not sing; or we may overlook them, as a starving man might sit down to die on a priceless antique chair, not knowing its value in terms of money and food. Without this essential knowledge, a man can be satisfied to eat the husks of swine when he might have been dining on the fare of kings or he can be straining after the impossible, surely he cannot know the boundlessness or the limitations of his hopes. The very necessity of nature itself guarantees the different actions of a pet monkey and a canary bird, but man has to know what he is and where he is going; he must choose a goal for his actions and point them at that goal, for his actions are deliberate. Only by knowing such a goal, fitted to the kind of nature he has, can a man determine whether his life has been a success or a failure, for it is only in terms of a human goal that a human life can be judged.

Essential Ignorance About Man

The essential ignorance about man, then, is the defect of this essential knowledge. Man must know himself, must know at least *what* he is, if he is to live a human life. In spite of the essential importance of this fundamental knowledge, men from the beginning, and perhaps more so today, have made serious mistakes about the very nature of man.

Its Varieties

He has been seen as pure spirit, an angel or a god, with the disastrous results of despair or the tragically comic results of childish pretense. He has been judged to be a mixture or conglomeration of spirit and matter, a lost spirit imprisoned in the flesh or a wandering mind; a strange monster whose constituent elements are more incompatible than oil and water. In our time, the tendency has been to exclude the spiritual from man altogether; from this premise, the steps have led steadily downward until there is now no further step to be taken.

In this materialistic light, man has been seen as a mere animal, a nice, bright, friendly animal, to be sure, but no different essentially from the rest of the animal world. Some of those who see man this way think he should make the most of his animality; others advise him to try, for appearances' sake, to forget it; still others ask him, while insisting on his pure animality, to act as although he had a spiritual soul. Another group sees man as merely a chemical compound. His essence, will some day be reduced to a chemical formula, his dreams are no more than the things that happen in a test tube. Meanwhile he is not to be too upset by the action and reaction, the explosions, the precipitations and strange flavors that mark his life, since there is, after all, nothing he can do about it. This would seem to place man low enough in the scale of things to satisfy his bitterest enemy; but another group has found a still more insulting estimate of man. Man is only a machine, necessarily producing the acts he does, the thoughts he thinks, the struggles he puts up, the illusion of love much as a sausage machine turns out its product if the right material is fed into it.

Its Origins

These truly terrible estimations of the nature of man might have come as a numbing shock to our age if we had not been so well prepared for them. As a matter of fact, they are not even a surprise; they are the inevitable result of a refusal to take the whole of man into consideration in determining his nature, the willingness to take the frosting or the cake, but not both. Then, too, this insulting ignorance of man did not happen today or yesterday. Very early in the history of mankind the attempt was made to get along without the material world. A no less energetic denial of the spiritual world dates from the Greek materialists and is almost universal in America today. Naturally, if either matter or spirit is denied in human nature that quiet, peace-loving creature we call man is replaced by a monster. Modern philosophy eased into the denial of the spiritual by quietly assassinating the intellect. With that out of the way and man's knowledge completely limited to the field of the senses, there is little to differentiate man from the physical world in which he moves.

The Escape from it

Not infrequently, the denial of the material or the spiritual in man has been motivated by cowardice, a flabbiness of heart that sought escape from the difficulties of human life by denying the humanity of it. For there are difficulties in the material side of human nature that no shocked rolling of the eyes, no amount of deep breathing or self-hypnosis can obliterate; just as there are terrific responsibilities in the spiritual side of man's nature that no amount of pleasure, no constant round of activity, no self-induced forgetfulness can wipe from the mind of a man. To men and women who shudder to mix with the rough reality of physical existence, an easy way out has been to deny it; just as those who preferred to cast their lot with the animal, or even with the inanimate, world, made their path easier by denying the spiritual. The pity of it has always been that these men could not follow their chosen paths alone but have always attempted to justify themselves in their own eyes, and in the eyes of men, by preaching their foolishness from the housetops to ensnare the simple, silly ones of the world.

Life of the Lord of the World

There is no need to set up a super-science and dedicate it to a life-long search of hosts in order to get some hint of what man is. The knowledge of human nature is not so difficult to come at. All we need do is to look at the human activity that goes into the living of human life all about us, or, indeed, within us. We may whip a puppy for chewing up shoes, but we are not silly enough to whip a tree for crashing through the roof in a storm; we know one little bit about these different natures by the way they act, at least we perceive that the whipping may do the puppy some good and that it will have no effect on the tree whatsoever. We are not surprised that lilacs do not sing, although we expect a song from a bird; and we are sure that no amount of careful watering or fertilizing will make a sidewalk any longer. In all this, we are proceeding on a judgment of different natures reached by a knowledge of the activities of those natures. It always remains true that activity follows the same line as the nature from which it proceeds; things have specifically different activities because of their specifically different natures.

Principle of Life

So we can tell immediately the difference between the living and the dead. To ask what is a man is only to ask what does a man do, what is his particular specific activity, what can we expect from a man that we can expect from absolutely nothing else in the world. If he is alive, he must be active, for, as we have seen in an earlier chapter, life is immanent activity. That activity avid mirror the nature of the principle from which it flows in man, just as it does in a bird, a tree or a horse.

Its Immaterial and Subsistent Character

One of the obviously distinctive things a man does is to know. From the objects with which this knowledge deals we have an immediate indication of the nature of man. Just from these few pages, it is clear that man knows cake, frosting, puppies, trees, canary birds, sidewalks and lilacs; as a matter of fact, man knows all material things, or he can know them, something he could not do if his faculty of knowledge had anything of material in it, any more than his faculty of vision can see all colors looking through green glasses. In other words, all corporal natures are fixed within corporal limitations; if the mind of man were corporal, then that corporal limitation would impede its knowledge of other corporal natures, just as a bad taste in a man's mouth affects his relish of everything he eats. From the point of view of its objects, then, one action of man, the act of intellectual knowledge, is immaterial, which is the same as saying that it is spiritual.

Its Immortality

We are thus forced to admit, from the ordinary activity of man, that man has an operation independent of corporal nature. If the activity is independent, of course the principle from which that activity flows is of that same nature; it is independent of corporal nature; it is spiritual. This independent principle of activity, since it can operate free of corporal nature, can exist free of corporal nature; for always the operation follows in the steps of the nature from which it proceeds.

To look at the matter from the point of view of man's activities themselves, rather than the objects of those activities, the very fact that man reasons is evidence that the principle of his reasoning is independent of corporal nature. At first sight, this statement looks obscure; but if we take it apart, see it step by step, its full force is clearly seen. Reasoning is no more than the comparison of judgment with judgment; and a judgment is normally a comparison with an abstract idea. In other words, the independent nature of reasoning has its first foundation in our possession of abstract ideas. We may grumble at wetness or marvel at beauty, but we shall never drown from falling into wetness or be injured by bumping into beauty. We can know not only this thing, but *things* in the abstract; a feat that surpasses the concrete character and singularity of the corporal world. This is an activity explicable only by a principle that itself surpasses the corporal, for, as the non-lethal blows of an infant's fist will clearly show us, the effect is not greater than its cause the activity does not surpass the manner of existence.

Many consequences of man's possession of abstract ideas are advanced in proof of the spiritual character of his soul. It is noted, for instance, that man alone speaks, has a moral sense, holds to religious ideals, can learn, cook his food, concoct weapons and so on. To these are added the long list of outstanding human achievements. Yet, as a matter of fact, these additional arguments are quite unnecessary; from the basic arguments of the objects of man's activities and the activities themselves we have a clear insight into the fundamental differentiation of man's soul from the souls of the brutes.

Animals, as living creatures, also have innate principles of life and activity, they have souls. In their activity, however, the brutes betray no operation that is independent of corporal nature; their activities are the activities of sense life. Consequently, the principle from which this activity flows, since it cannot act dependently, and cannot exist independently; again that central truth must be insisted on, activity is an indication of the nature of the soul, as an effect is an indication of the nature of its cause. The very intensity of these brute activities is distinctly limited; noises too loud will deafen them as lights too bright will blind them, for the corporal change demanded in every sensitive operation corrupts the sense which it affects. On the contrary, the object of intelligence, as it is more perfect, rather than corrupting the intellect, perfects it for other and more intense operations. To put the whole thing simply, it is enough to point out that even in their knowledge the brutes do not know *things*; they know this or that thing, not the abstract. It is not surprising, then, that they have never reached to the consequences that have followed in man from the possession of abstract ideas. It has been well said that the "animal is a strange mixture of stupidity and natural accomplishment; of cleverness and unteachableness; of natural ability and no development." These same things cannot be said of a man.

To conclude, from the independent existence of the human soul, that the soul was the whole man, would be a serious mistake. A man is, or at least should be, no less human when he eats than when he thinks. It would be much less tiring if a woman could accomplish her shopping in the few seconds it takes the mind to run through a department store, while her body was tossed into a corner or laid out comfortably on a bed; but it cannot be done. It is the same person who walks, laughs, talks and thinks. Man is not to be defined by his soul alone. That human soul, great as its prerogatives may be, is still only a part of man, an essential element of the composite that is man. It is no less a deformity to exclude the body from the notion of what man is than to exclude the soul; whether you make a god, an angel or an animal of man, you have destroyed man. This point need not be labored, if man's nature is indicated by the objects with, which his activities deal and by those activities themselves, it demands no philosophical cleverness to see that he has a body as well as a soul.

Its Incompleteness

In fact, we can push this further and say that even although that immaterial soul is spiritual and immortal, it is still incomplete without the body. Obviously the human soul is simple. For, lacking all material, it cannot have parts. The very notion of parts postulates quantity, a divisibility that is inseparable from matter and so unthinkable in a substance that is immaterial. Moreover, the fact that it is utterly simple and at the same time capable of subsisting of itself (as it quite evidently is capable of operating of itself) is a definition of its spirituality; a subsistent principle of activity independent of matter is spiritual. It is immortal, for there is no way to destroy it. It cannot unravel, it cannot come apart; it cannot be separated from that which gives it life, for it is itself the principle of life; it cannot be swept into oblivion by the destruction of another on which it depends, as a lamp might be destroyed by the collapse of the stand on which it has been placed, for it is independent. In other words, it is incorruptible because there is no possibility of either intrinsic or extrinsic corruption.

It can, of course, be annihilated by God, nevertheless, this is not so much a question of God's reaching out to strike it into nothingness, as of God's not reaching out to conserve it, cutting off the supply of existence from the human soul. For the soul of man, like everything created, merely borrows its finite existence from the infinite existence of God; it is not independent of the first cause either in its entry into existence or in the continuation of its existence. In common with all created things, the human soul has the metaphysical composition of essence and existence.

Yet this soul without its body is incomplete; it is not fully itself unless it is united to the body. It is not an angel, assuming a fictitious body for an occasion; it is the lowest substance in the intellectual world and ordered, by its very nature, to union with the body. Left to itself, it could discern nothing; its mind would remain a blank sheet, radically incapable of completing itself by its own strength, sterile and inactive without the complement by which alone it enters into relation with the objects it can know and assimilate.

It is an extremely grave mistake to look upon the soul's presence in the body as a punishment, making the body a prison in which the soul serves its time. The body is good and a source of good to the soul joined to it; it is the one link by which the soul can attain its complete perfection. Nor is this an oddity in the universe. Rather, it is a continuation of the harmony that runs through all the work of the divine architect, the imperfect is always for the perfect, the eye for the whole man, vegetative life for sensitive life, sensitive life for intellectual life, all for the sake of the whole. On a larger scale, each creature is for its own act, its own perfection, the less noble for the more noble, all for the universe and the universe for God. The soul, then, is an incomplete substance tending to complete itself; and by this very tendency, it is a principle of operation. It is a perfection crying for its fullness; and that fullness is obtained through union with the body.

Its Incompleteness, General Notion of Matter and Form.

The difficulty is how to unite such a splendid spiritual substance with the matter, which thus united, becomes the human body. A mere mixture of the two will not do. An utterly simple soul cannot be stirred into matter as sugar is in coffee, any more than a mathematical point can be dropped into a glass of wine. It is not sufficient merely to throw them together, as so many rocks in one pile; for the secret of this creature man is his unity, he is precisely one whole and all his acts testify to that unity. Nor is it enough to postulate a mere association of the two, like a rider in a saddle or a motor in a boat. These two incomplete substances must be united in a way that will result in one complete unit, one complete whole. In other words, the soul must be the substantial form of the body.

To a man who is not a philosopher, the words "matter" and "substantial form" look as formidable as a mechanic's tool kit does to one who lacks mechanical ability. If we describe matter as the determined element and substantial form as the determining element of physical things and then look at the two in the concrete, their terrifying aspect vanishes for then they cease to be strangers and we recognize them as old, familiar neighbors. It is obvious, for instance, that before the soul's coming, there is only the possibility of a man, the seed and the ovum, not a man; after the soul departs, there is nothing left but a corpse. It is clear, then, that if is the soul that determines the matter of the body to its human status; it is the soul that gives the body its specific note, making it human. It gives the body being and is the source of the body's human activities; we should be quite right in being frightened, astonished or utterly incredulous if a corpse sat up and guffawed in the face of the mourners.

The same truth is evident if we look at it from the side of the specific operations of man. It would be pointless to sit hour by hour by a corpse trying to argue with it, waiting for an inspiring word or a flash of genius to come from the dead man's mouth. It is the soul that is the principle of intellectual operations, that is, of the operations by which man is distinguished from every other creature, his specific operations. It is, then, the determinant of the species in man, his substantial form.

Substantial forms are an active, domineering race. The common note of their work has left a common mark on all of them, however low or high they may be, they are as easily recognized as officers of an army drilled to the perfection of precision. Not one of them, for example can tolerate doing its work through an underling; not one of them will give an equal a word to say in its work; everyone is much too self-sufficient to travel in pairs; all are fussy enough, and capable enough, to keep every inch of their domain under their thumb every single moment.

The Soul the Form of the Body

Of course, the soul of man, being a substantial form, shares these common characteristics. It is not united to corporal matter through a medium, an underling, such as a sensitive soul, one other body, or some other accidental or substantial form. Its union is immediate; and it leaves no room for any other soul in man. The soul is the unique cause of man's being, of his living, his animality, his human characteristics. Nor is this particularly surprising. It is a common fact of nature that the more powerful forms have more extensive activity. Thus, in the hierarchy of forms, the inanimate have the very minimum of activity, that of being; plant forms embrace the activity of the inanimate forms and add their own; animal forms include the activity of the inanimate and the plant forms, and add their own; and 50 on. To put it another way, the higher forms have a greater quantity of being; they have shared more fully, participated more completely in the supreme being. They imitate God more closely and exclude all inferior forms as superfluous; they themselves have all that the inferior forms possess, and more. Like every other substantial form, the soul is present in every part of the matter it informs, in every part of the body; and it is whole in every part of the body. The tail is not less feline than the head of a cat, nor is a finger less human than the head of a man; yet what there is of humanity in every part of man comes from the specific principle of humanity within man, from his soul. Instead of thinking, as we ordinarily do, of the body, containing the soul, it would perhaps be more accurate to thinly of the soul containing the body.

Man, then, is a composite made up of matter and form, of spirit and matter. Neither of these constitutes the species, both are incomplete; but from their substantial union comes that lord of the material world which we call man, the creature whose form is supreme among all forms in matter, reaching that peak of domination of things physical that brings us to the borderland of angelic independence. So much for the nature of man, for we know now that he is not divine, not angelic, not bestial, but human.

Equipment for Action of the Lord of the World, in General, Distinction and Number of the Potencies of Man.

A glance, however, at man's actions will show us at once that we have not investigated all of man's equipments The soul is the radical principle of all action; but then, the locomotive is the principle of all motion of the train, but it moves *by* its wheels. That is, the soul does not directly produce these actions of man; a man walks but *with* his feet and legs, he talks but *with* his tongue, he thinks but *with* his intellect. As a matter of fact, God is the only one whose act flows directly from his essence, He alone rather *is* His intelligence than *has* His intelligence. This truth seems obscure, but actually it is so obvious that it is hard to see. A man's soul is a substantial form, it acts directly in the substantial line to complete the substantial composite. Now, patently, man's actions are not substantial things, his laughs do not clutter up the house his thoughts do not have to be bathed, fed and sent off to school; they are accidents in the philosophical sense of existing only in something else, not in themselves. Their immediate cause, then, is one proportioned to them, an accidental form, not a substantial one. Supposing the contrary were true, suppose the soul did produce all the acts of man directly. By its very essence the soul is a determining principle, it is the active, the moving principle; it cannot take a day off, demand a sick leave, or retire for a siesta for its very nature demands ceaseless determining activity. Of it is the direct cause of our actions, then we never stop talking, thinking, willing, hearing, seeing and all the rest; which, thank God, is completely false.

If we are to act, we must have proximate accidental principles of action. Being what we are, we shall have to have a great many of them. Creatures below man reach a moderate perfection by few movements; man himself reaches a very high perfection by numerous and complex movements; the angels reach complete perfection by very, very few movements; while God has infinite perfection without any movement at all. Perhaps the full significance of this can be grasped from a parallel in the human order, some men maintain a precarious health by many remedies; some maintain perfect health with a few remedies; while others, have perfect health without ever entering a drugstore or consulting a doctor. In other words, the multiplicity of our accidental forms is at the same time a statement of our perfection relative to the material world, and a statement of our imperfection relative to the spiritual world.

Their Subject

For all their number and complexity, there is no difficulty distinguishing these proximate accidental principles of operation, which are called the powers or faculties of man; we have only to look at their destination to escape the misfortune of trying to we the ear for sight or the eye for sound. There is, in fact, a distinct hierarchy of these powers of man nicely graduated according to the universality of the objects at which they aim. The vegetative powers act only on man's own body; the sensitive powers work on all sensible bodies; while the intellective powers extend to all being. The same hierarchy can be traced if our measuring rod is the degree of immateriality of the object at which the different powers aim. Thus bare life transcends the inanimate character of matter; sense knowledge receives material things within the knower, stripping them of the ragged clothes of matter, but leaving them with the familiar material conditions; intellectual knowledge completely strips its guests of all matter and material conditions, insisting that they put on the bright garment of immateriality before they enter the house of the mind.

Their Duration

Neither is there much difficult in determining, in a general way, the location or place of residence of these faculties in man. The inorganic powers of intellect and will, which operate with intrinsic independence of matter are to be found in the only inorganic element of the human composite, in the soul of man. It is only the soul that can act with intrinsic independence of matter. The vegetative and sensitive faculties of man are clearly not to be found in the soul alone, for they are intimately involved in matter; neither are they to be bound in the body alone, for the body alone cannot produce the acts proper to these powers. Rather they are powers subjected in the composite of soul and body; not in either of the constituents of this composite. From this it is evident that the faculties of intellect and will endure as long as the soul endures, that is, forever; on the other hand, the vegetative and sensitive faculties endure only as long as the composite, which is man, endures, that is, until the separation of the soul and body in death.

In Particular

Coming down to an examination of these powers of man in particular, we encounter somewhat the same difficulty as would be found in a complete survey of the life of the universe. Man is a little universe in himself; certainly he has, in himself, a summary of the life of the universe and consequently, a multiplicity of faculties that is all bewildering, in its way, as the spectacle of the varied life in the world in which we live. To inspect each of these faculties in itself, without relation to anything else, would seem to serve no purpose beyond increasing our bewilderment, just as a study of the individual parts of the universe, with no attempt at correlation merely packs a man's head so full of facts and his eyes so full of sights that he can neither think nor see. We must, then, throughout this, try to see these faculties of man in their relation to man himself and to the rest of life in the universe; we must read them in their context, not in isolated texts; they must be seen in the grandeur of the whole picture, not in violently extracted sections.

Some Lower Potencies

From this point of view, man has powers in common with the plants, others in common with the animals, and still others that are entirely distinctive to himself. In all three we meet again that harmonious flowing of one into the other that marks the whole genius of creation. There is a union between these different faculties so close as almost to defy an attempt to mark clearly the line that distinguishes them; it is this close harmony that has been, too often, the cause of the eager attempts to conclude that man is only a plant or only an animal, or that all animals and plants are intelligent beings as man is.

Vegetative Potencies

The vegetative powers, common to man and plants, have, as their primary purpose, the inception of life and the protection of that life; this purpose is accomplished through three distinct operations, namely, generation; growth or increase to the point demanded by the perfection of the body; and finally nutrition or the conservation of that life. Of the three, generation is supreme and intimately approaches the activity of the animal or sense faculties; it is the only vegetative faculty that operates on a body other than its own.

Sensitive Potencies

The sensitive powers of man parallel the same powers in an animal. A teacher, who was not at all sure of himself, facing a class that was far too inquisitive for comfort, could hurry past these by stating dogmatically that these powers are of two kinds, external and internal, frowning heavily the while to snuff out any question before it could break into flame. But, of course, this would be cheating; for it would be ignoring the fact that there are five external senses and four internal ones, for a grand total of nine. Still, the teacher certainly would have his reasons for sidestepping a subject as complex as this.

External

The whole picture of the five external senses in operation can be obtained by observing so commonplace an affair as a man coming home from work and wandering into the kitchen as dinner is being prepared; providing, of course, that the man is normal, that he does take a taste of this and that, drop a comment or two and then get out from under his wife's feet. If he spent the long moments that intervene before the serving of dinner in analyzing that little jaunt of his into the kitchen, he would discover something like this. Two of his external senses had made a contact with sensible reality as real as a contact of a fist with a face, and with the same consequent material modifications, on a much milder scale, to be sure, his sense of touch had been struck by the warmth of the kitchen; his sense of taste was affected by the nibble which did things both to the sense itself and to the food he had so cautiously pilfered. Ruminating further, he would notice that two other external senses, while not smashing into sensible reality, had definitely been in contact with it through a medium, he had smelled the cooking food and heard his own words to his wife. The last of his external senses, his sight, had accomplished its purpose without direct contact, without material change either in his eyes or in the objects of sight, his eyes had not actually caressed his wife, she had not climbed into his eyes, nor was the food mangled by his greedy glance.

Internal

A great help in drawing up his analysis was furnished by his internal sense, which goes by the name of common sense, discriminating between the work of the external senses, protecting him from using his eye for tasting and so on. For each of the external senses is nailed down to its particular object; consequently some common model of sense perception is necessary, some clearing house which distinguishes between the external senses and their operations. This man was led to the kitchen in the first place by another of his internal senses, his imagination; for obviously, viewing these senses now purely from the animal or sensitive angle, it is only by the power of retaining a sense species gathered by the external senses that an animal can set itself in motion to obtain an absent good. His retreat from the kitchen was dictated by his estimative faculty with its power to directly apprehend the harmful or beneficial qualities of sensible things that are certainly not the object of the eye, the ear, the nose or any of the other external senses. These are not strictly sense qualities. Finally, as he sat there thinking it all over, he would be regaled by his memory, the last of his internal senses, which is a storehouse of the sensible species; from it are spontaneously revived species precisely as *past*, a non-sensible quality that escapes the imagination and so demands another faculty or power and which is so particular, so contingent, as to demand that it be taken care of by the sense powers of man. It is to be noted that the estimative power and the memory approach analogously very close to the operations of the intellect, being differentiated from it by the particular character and material limitations of their objects.

Higher Potencies of Knowledge

Over and above the vegetative and sensitive principles of operations, man's distinctively human faculties are the spiritual powers of intellect and will, of knowledge and volition. These are so complex in their operation, and so very important that they will receive separate treatment in the two succeeding chapters of this volume. In this chapter, however, a few rough strokes must be added to complete the picture of man's specific equipment at least as regards knowledge.

Active and Possible Intellect

Two intellectual faculties are distinguished in man, one that can know but as yet does not, the possible intellect; the other, which does not know but makes knowledge a proximate possibility. This distinction is really no more than our recognition of the fact that man does learn and that he learns of abstract things. He has, then, a faculty that acquires knowledge. Yet the objects of our knowledge are universal or abstract (as we have already seen to some degree and will see more thoroughly later) and universals are not to be found wandering about the streets, hiding in woods or swimming in streams. If only the possible intellect existed, only the faculty, which acquires knowledge, nothing would ever be known. Another faculty is necessary to make these concrete, existing things of the world fit subjects of our knowledge; the faculty that universalizes these concrete things, that makes them abstract, is called the active intellect.

Reason and Intellect

What we ordinarily call intellectual memory is really not a separate faculty at all; it is merely the act of our intellects retaining the intellectual species. Certainly it does not retain these species precisely as past, for that is a concrete, limited, material connotation, which is proper to the sense faculties and impossible to immaterial, universal objects. Neither do the words "intelligence" and "reason" denote different faculties, but rather different acts of the same faculty, the one, a simple direct knowledge of truth, which approaches the mode of angelic knowledge; the other, the labored acquisition of truth by way of comparison which is proper to man. "Synderesis" and "conscience," too, must be ruled out as distinct faculties, the first is no more than the habit by which we hold to first practical principles; the second is merely a practical judgment of the intellect as to what is to be done or avoided, what is right or wrong.

Conclusion

1. Philosophy Based on Ignorance of Man is a Philosophy of Degradation

From even this superficial glance at man, it is evident that he is a composite of body and soul. Within himself he contains the powers of inanimate, plant and animal creation; and surpasses them by his distinctively human power. He is not an animal, although he has a body, he is not an angel, although he has a spiritual soul that cannot be destroyed. He is a man, the connecting link between the material and the spiritual worlds. A philosophy that is blind to this essential knowledge of man is necessarily a philosophy of degradation, however sincerely its authors intend to defend man's humanity, however high they hope to elevate man, however desperately they champion human beings.

It is Possible only by a Distortion of one Side of Human Nature

These are not merely large statements that can be supported only by fragmentary evidence and loose interpretations. They are facts evidenced abundantly in both the theoretical and practical sphere of twentieth century life. On the theoretical level, for example, modern philosophy, neglecting the spiritual in man, degrades man to the level of an animal, a chemical or a machine; or, neglecting the material in man, degrades him to wraith-like proportions and exiles him from the world in which he must live. In either case, there has been an ignorance of man and so an ignorance of man's life. He has been tricked into attempting to live the life of an animal or to parody angelic or divine life; but it has been made consistently more difficult for him to lead human life.

Its Result is the Destruction of the Whole of Human Nature

In the practical spheres if man is an animal obviously he can demand no more from himself than he demands from other animals; if made, such demands are hopeless of fulfillment. High ideals, noble goals, respect, honor, enduring love, self-mastery, justice and all the rest are illusions he is foolish to take seriously. Under these circumstances, why should not a man plunge into gangsterism to the contempt of the rights of all others; why should not a government be contemptuous of the human individual, of the human rights of its own subjects, what is there to hold it back from sheer brutality modeled on the most immediately advantageous scale? Or, to go to the other extreme, why should men not despair in the evident hopelessness of trying to live an angelic life devoid of angelic equipment, why should they not mock at themselves as they absurdly pose on the throne of divinity? What motive is left, for a man to struggle for success, for mastery of himself, for virtue and a goal worth reaching for?

Its Goal is Despair

To ignore one side of man is to make a monster out of him. To make him all angel or all animal, we must destroy half of him. Additionally, man can no more live in that condition than can a horse that has been split in half. His very animality becomes a thing of disgust to the animal world; his angelic parodies, a shock to the invisible world. The end of either mistake can only be a complete loss of the notion of a human individual, a sacred person, not to be sunk in a mass, a race, a nation, not to be debarred from contact with a world into which he has been born. That is, the end of either mistake must be despair. Man has one end and he was given a nature equipped for the attainment of that end, and adequate to no other. Of course he must fail miserably if he is made to aim at an inhuman goal by reason of his conviction of inhuman powers to achieve a goal.

CHAPTER XIV

THE WILL OF THE LORD OF THE WORLD
(Q. 81-83)

1. A disturbing fact,

2. The mystery of the human will.

(a) Irritation at the mystery.

(b) Facts of the mystery.

3. The appetite of man,

(a) Fact of his appetite.

(b) Its harmony with universal order.

4. The humanity of man's appetite,

(a) of his sensitive appetite

1) The fact of it.

2) Its varieties.

3) Its relation to reason and will.

(b) of his intellectual appetite – the fact of it.

5. The nature of man s will,

(a) Universality of its object.

(b) Necessary objects.

(c) Free objects,

1) The nature of freedom,
2) Freedom and necessity.

3) Freedom and law.

(d) Proofs of freedom,

    1) From the nature of human knowledge – proximate source of freedom.

    2) From conscience.

    3) The moral argument.

    4) Argument from divine government of universe – radical source of freedom.

6. Relations of will and intellect,

    (a) Mutual movement.

    (b) Mutual superiority.

Conclusion,

    1. Facts of man's appetite.

    2. A disturbing fact in the universe.

    3. A disturbing fact in human life.

📖 CHAPTER XIV 📖
THE WILL OF THE LORD OF THE WORLD
(Q. 81-83)

A disturbing fact

The last chapter, this one and the next are dedicated to answering the question, what is man? In the last chapter, it was the essence of man and his faculties in general that were principally concentrated on. In this chapter, we shall examine in detail one of the faculties of man that easily stands out as one of the most momentous facts in the universe, the motive power of man's human actions, his human will.

The Mystery of the Human Will

From the beginning this human will has been one of the great mysteries of the universe; and it will remain so until the end, particularly to those who are committed to a statement of the universe in terms of physical formulae. To this clerkish mind, the will is a fractious pupil disgracing the whole institution by its wanton irregularity. It escapes all measurement, all calculation. As although it were a grinning imp tossing the clumsy giant of the universe about with a kind of spiritual ju-jitsu, the will expends, with insolent ease, enormous energy in ruling the complex kingdom that is man and his possessions; yet no trace of that energy has been recorded. In a world bound by strict necessity, the will alone is totally unpredictable; in a systematic universe, it stands out incorrigibly individualist. It remains an unknown quantity as far as physical science goes; it cannot be managed but only carefully coaxed and yet, while itself so utterly intangible, it is quite capable of managing the physical world about it.

Irritation at the Mystery

No wonder it has driven the wise men of our time to despair. It simply does not fit into the kind of orderly picture our times demand; so it has become necessary, to save the picture, to destroy the will, to banish it from the earth by a scientific *fiat*, which exasperatingly, itself is a product of a human will.

As a product of the human will, this very banishment has the will's refreshing variety about it; as although to underscore the huge joke of the will reading the decree of its banishment in a terrifying voice and at the same time listening to it in an attitude of abject terror, trudging off in heart-breaking loneliness and at the same time cozily sitting at home surrounded by friends. Some men have accomplished this banishment by reducing the will to mechanically monotonous regularity and necessity, which they insist, is the universal movement of all that exists. Man does what he does because he cannot help himself, rising and falling, scurrying to escape or rushing to attack drifting or driven but all the while jammed compactly into the serried ranks of the physical where no one gets out of step. This is the camp of the determinists, no little group even in our day although they belong, properly, in the nineteenth century.

Another group effects the banishment by a wave of the wand of science to make all things in the universe as unpredictable as the movements of the will of man. This is the modern school of indeterminism, which insists there is no necessity whatever in the world; the apparent regularity is the product of our mathematical minds. The technique, however, is far from modern; for it has been an old, old trick, when faced with a problem, for men to solve it by denying first one then the other extreme of the dilemma.

A much more widespread type of banishment today aims at a kind of compromise by making man merely an animal, enjoying no more freedom or responsibility than the others, but no more machine-like than the others either. These are the evolutionists who have carried our popular journals and newspapers by storm and have taken charge of educational philosophy to corrupt the foundations of Christian civilization utterly.

Finally, a group less bold than the others, destroys the human will by insisting that human knowledge is limited to particular, sensible things. We can know only what can be measured and weighed and observed scientifically; so man's appetite is limited to particular, sensible things to the exclusion of freedom.

All this makes for as orderly a picture as that of a city which insists that there be none but green traffic lights lest the citizens become confused. Still, it is not a pretty picture any more than a completely gray world would be a pretty world; nor is it a true picture, a fair representation of either the world or of men. These pseudo-scientific philosophers have falsified the accounts, writing down "identity" for "order" to obtain a neat result at the expense of facts.

Facts of the Mystery

The facts must be met if we are to understand human life, if we are to understand and direct our own actions. It will not do to excuse ourselves from murder on grounds that would excuse a tree from growing or a cat from stretching; as a matter of fact, we know the act is entirely our own. The facts are that we have a common relationship with the animals; and, no less clearly, that we have the unique gift of freedom. No matter how these two appear to confuse the orderly world we have drawn up for ourselves, both must be faced, for we are not trying to lull ourselves to sleep with bedtime stories but rather to light our anxious steps with the lantern of truth.

The Appetite of Man, Fact of His Appetite

Man's motive power is certainly not that of a machine, he has an appetite. In an earlier chapter, appetite was described as the driving force of every creature in the universe; its object was pointed out as the good, possessing the smack of desirability that draws all things to action. In irrational nature, it is called natural appetite, the obedience to natural physical laws; in the animals, sense appetite, or obedience to natural physical laws operating through animal instincts; in man, it is human appetite.

The necessity for a distinctly human appetite will be clearer if we understand the close connection between the inclination of appetite and the form or determining principle. Every inclination follows some form; it may be on a least of woven steel links or the leash may be as physically intangible as a divine command, but inclination must, of its very nature, be tied up with a form. A moment's thought makes the thing obvious; surely inclination, if it means anything, means a tendency in a determined direction and the principle of determination is precisely form. A difference in forms, then, demands a difference in inclinations to desirable objects, that is, a difference in appetite. Thus, inanimate creation and plant life possess only their own physical form, their own substantial principle of unity and life, with the result that they follow, necessarily and rigidly along the lines of that one form in entirely predictable fashion.

A creature that can know, however, possesses more than its own form. It cannot, of course, have many substantial forms, many principles of unity and life; but it can have, over and above its own substantial form, the forms of other things, forms received into itself by knowledge, determining knowledge and appetite over and above the determination given them by their own substantial form. The animal, for instance, by his sense knowledge receives particular forms, the form of a bird, a bone, a man; by that knowledge, a wider scope, a greater difference of object is immediately given to the animal's appetite. Man, by his intellectual knowledge, possesses the universal, the specific, form of things and immediately has an infinite horizon thrown open to his appetite. To reach out to that infinite field of good revealed by the universal character of intellectual knowledge, there must be a distinctly human appetite, an appetite distinctly proportionate to the knowledge of man.

Its Harmony with Universal Order

Nor is this an upheaval of the universal scheme of things. This is not making a special exception from nature for man; rather it is an insistence on facts as the manifestation of an order worthy of the supreme wisdom of the architect of the universe. Man is different in his appetite, precisely because he is different in his nature. Why should he be moved as the stones or animals are since he is neither a stone nor an animal? There is the same beautiful hierarchy in appetite that there is in being, in perfection, within the universe; the same gradual revelations of the beauty and perfection that is God's.

The Humanity of Man's Appetite, of His Sensitive Appetite

This is really the key to the apparent contradiction of man's appetites, are often insisted on war between the flesh and the spirit. As a matter of fact, man has two appetites for his nature is a complex of matter and spirit; he receives the forms of other things, not only in an intellectual, universal fashion but also in a particular, sensible fashion as the animals do. He has two appetites, a sensitive and an intellectual appetite; but both are human, both belong to man, neither is in any way a detraction from his human nature. Indeed, the denial of either one is tantamount to the destruction of the humanity of man.

The Fact of it

Now because it is so hard to deny the fact of wet feet or too salty food, there are few today who question our possession of sense knowledge. We do see the difference between a brown hat and a purple one, we hear a flat note in an otherwise splendid aria, we do smell the toast burning much too late to do anything about it. In other words, we, also, possess those particular species that come by the way of sense, the particular forms of things other than ourselves. As appetite marches in the footprints of knowledge, as the inclinations follow the forms possessed, there can be no doubt of our possession of a sense appetite. We can, and do, dislike burnt toast or flat notes, brown hats or purple ones; we can, and do, enjoy the brisk air of a fall morning or the lazily relaxing rays of a summer sun. You may, here and there, find a philosopher today to deny this; but there is a very good chance of your meeting him in Florida for the winter or in Maine for the summer.

The sense appetite, like all appetite, has to do with good as its proper object, either it sits back in lazy enjoyment of the good possessed, like a stuffed puppy dozing by a warm fire; or it watches with nervously alert eyes for a chance to seize the good that is not yet had but must be had. In the latter case we have the reason for action; man's inclinations ate no more than appetite's gentle hints or nagging demands that leave him little doubt as to what he still lacks and that give him little peace until he sets out on the long quest for the good.

Its Varieties

This is the general object of the sense appetite. There is, however, a striking difference in the particular objects of sense appetite. A starving man will fight for a scrap of food just as readily as a well-fed man will relish the last dainty delicacies of a banquet; a man will, in other words, not only reach out for and enjoy the good things, he will do the hard bitter things that seem to go flatly against his inclinations for good and pleasant things. There are, then, two faculties of sense appetite, one runs after the good precisely as good or runs from its opposite; the other is the fighter of the sensual side of our nature, the champion of the milder (concupiscible) appetite and its objects. This faculty, the emergency (or irascible) appetite, deals with good but precisely as difficult; its work is the conquest of difficulties and the overthrow of impediments to the milder appetite.

A detailed treatment of these two sense appetites is proper matter for the second volume of this work. Here it will be enough merely to catalogue them. Thus, from the mild appetite there spring such fundamental inclinations as, love and its opposite, hate; desire and aversion, relative to an absent good or evil; and delight and sorrow, the first of which is rest in the possession of good, the second, repugnance to the presence of evil. From the emergency appetite come hope and despair, daring and fear. Finally anger, it is sufficient, for the purposes of this volume, to note the distinction of these appetites and the common source of all the inclinations in the fundamental ones of love and hate. The whole subject of the passions of man, that is, of the movements of the sense appetite, is taken up in exhaustive detail in the next volume.

Its Relation to Reason and Will

None of these are evidences of intellectual appetite. In fact, there very often is sharp conflict between the intellectual appetite and these sensual appetites as many a man can testify when, holding desperately to his moment of high resolve, he refuses a cigarette although his mouth is watering for it, our attitude towards this conflict of appetites raging within us is a penetrating indication of the interrelation of these appetites; the fact is, we are not neutrals, not even belligerent neutrals, we are intensely interested in seeing the intellectual appetite come out on top. Thus, when a man becomes violently angry he is "beside himself"; a man is "crazy with pain," "paralyzed by fear," and so on; that is, these sensual appetites have usurped complete control with the result that this man is no longer a man, he is not himself, he is, for the moment, an animal. We naturally expect the sense appetites to be subjects in the kingdom of man; wizen they are not, their victim is in the grip of animal appetites, the supreme motive power of his actions is not that distinctly human appetite that is will, but one of its subjects.

These sense appetites do, as a matter of fact, obey reason and will. Normally we do not fly from evil as a sheep does from a wolf, in blind panic; we do not run in out of the rain as a cat does. We might even deliberately stay out in the rain for reasons that never occur to a cat. The movements of our sense appetites are not the instinctive reactions of an animal; when they are, we do not boast of them, we are ashamed. They are made to follow the reasoning of an intellectual being; that is what we mean by self-control and why we are rather proud of it as evidence of our more thorough humanity, of our having lived up to ourselves.

Not that the sense appetites always obey reason. Anger can flare up so suddenly as to take control in a surprise rebellion; animal love can gnaw away the foundations of resistance so slowly and imperceptibly that the fort caves in on its defenders when at last they rush to the defense. The soul has an utterly despotic control over the members of the body that move at its command; a hand or a foot does not rebel against the soul's orders to move. Yet, the reason and will exercise only a kind of political control over the sense appetites; these latter can rebel, and they do.

The reason for this difference is fairly obvious. The members of the body are executing faculties, they fulfill orders; of themselves they have no sovereignty, no power of movement. However, the sense appetites have a kind of sovereignty of their own. They are made to move at the command of man's deliberate will; they are also moved by sense objects and phantasms of the imagination. A man can awaken chagrined at having his dream-banquet interrupted by an alarm clock before he had taken a bite, or he can awaken with a sigh of intense relief at escaping the horrors of a nightmare; and all this, after he had tucked his mind away for the night in, the heavy blankets of sound sleep.

Concerning his Intellectual Appetite – the Fact of it

Man has his own substantial form to which his natural appetite responds; he has the sensible, particular forms gathered by sense knowledge to which his sense appetite responds; and, finally, he becomes all things, he possesses the forms of all being, by his intellectual knowledge and to this his intellectual appetite or will jumps to answer. Again, this appetite, like all appetite, deals with good, that alluring perfection that spurs to action or that, once possessed, quiets the clamors of appetite. Now, since it follows the universal, intellectual knowledge of man, its proper object is that universal good that is known by the intellect. It can, of course, reach out for any particular good; but only the universal, the supreme good is worthy of its mightiest efforts and this alone quiets all the will's desires.

The Nature of man's Will - Universality of its Object

Good in general, or, to give it another name, what fulfils desire, happiness, is the adequate object of the will. By its very nature, the will must march under this standard. Absolutely nothing can be done precisely under the aspect of evil; the murderer must see his crime as somehow good, the lonely schoolgirl must get some good out of her prolonged homesickness or there would be no murders and no blues. Whatever the particular goal to which the will runs, it must be painted in the colors of happiness; once a set goal is chosen, then the means necessarily connected with that goal take on some of its necessity and must be willed. If a man sees happiness in wealth, in pleasure or in God, then the things necessarily leading to wealth, to God or to pleasure cannot be objectionable to him, they cannot take second place until the goal itself has been changed. To put it in the concrete, it is impossible for a man to commit mortal sin without abandoning God as his ultimate happiness and final goal; that is precisely the terrible tragedy of mortal sin, that it does involve abandoning God for some glimmer of His beauty in the pool of the world.

Necessary Objects

Over and above this natural and absolute necessity of willing our end, our perfection, the necessity, which is the starting point of all voluntary action and which is itself entirely agreeable to the will, there is another necessity to which the will is entirely subject. A graphic statement of this necessity is seen in the willingness with which a man abandons his wardrobe in order to escape from a burning hotel. The necessity is, of course, hypothetical; he could have remained on guard protecting his clothes until he was burned to a cinder, but if he wanted to live, the clothes had to be left behind. Undoubtedly there is an element of unwillingness in this; but, at the same time, there is a very complete Willingness; he does not make his exit from the flaming hotel like a sulky boy but like a scared cat. He willed this particular end of escape, and, willing that, he necessarily willed all that was involved in the task of escaping, even to the abandonment of a hard-won wardrobe.

Free Objects - the Nature of Freedom

There is something of this element of unwilling willingness in man's embrace of any particular good, for one can not be had without the exclusion of others; it is only in the embrace of the infinite good that a man abandons all else and gains everything, only in that supreme good is every other good to be found. Experience is witness enough, however, that the note of reluctance is not a serious impediment to man's choice from the glittering counters of goodness. In both the natural and the hypothetical necessity, there is a thorough voluntariness that tones down the strong, severe lines of necessity's stern face. In coercive necessity, the necessity of brute force, sternness is changed to savagery. There is nothing here to attract the will. Yet, for all that, it is a puny thing; for neither is there in it anything strong enough to bend the fragile will of the weakest of men. A man can be beaten to a pulp, tossed into a gangster's automobile, hustled into a concentration camp or even nailed to a cross; he cannot be forced to will these things. For one of the mysteriously strongest things about the human will is that it cannot be moved by any force in the world; there is an inherent impossibility in the notion of applying leverage to a spiritual thing and no one knows this better than a sinner. No one but himself and God knows how absurd is the plea that he has been forced to commit sin.

Freedom and Necessity

Granted that there are some things that must be willed necessarily by a man, it is quite clear that not everything he chooses has been willed necessarily. In other words, man, in regard to some things, enjoys a gift unique in the physical world, the gift of freedom. Let it be well understood, however, that freedom here is not used in the same way in which it is proudly displayed today in such modern catchwords as "freedom of speech," "freedom of the press" or "freedom of conscience." Freedom does not mean the ability to do anything, say anything, believe anything; that is not freedom but freedom's abuse. That this is an abuse and not freedom itself is readily recognized when the thing is brought down to the concrete; it is not freedom that allows an orator to harangue a crowd into committing adultery With this man's wife; nor is it freedom in whose name newspaper advertisements and full powered propaganda urge men into an abuse of love and a flouting of nature; neither is it freedom's privilege to undermine the very social structure without which men cannot live. Freedom does not mean that a man has been turned loose on the world, released from all order, all direction, from all purpose; that is not a privilege, it is a condemnation to a bestiality far surpassing the animality of the brutes.

Freedom and Law

To apostles of license, every law is an insult to every individual citizen; every restriction is a cause for rebellion and men can live only so long as they have the physical force to maintain that life against all their fellows. Freedom, rightly understood, means no more than the right to choose between means to an end. There is no question of freedom relative to the end of man's activities, just as there is no question of freedom relative to that end once it has been attained in heaven. Freedom is man's badge of responsibility; it is a consecration to obligations rather than an exemption from all that demands courage and sweat and tears in its accomplishment. Freedom revolves entirely around the means to an end. Consequently the things that are not means, the things that lead a man away from his end rather than to it, have no place in the essential notion of liberty but in the description of its degradation and abuse. It is true that a man can commit murder, but that does not mean that he is free to murder; in committing his crime he is not exercising his liberty, he is abusing it.

For free will, like every other faculty of man, was given him that he might attain his full stature, his full perfection; that is, that by it he might attain his end. A deliberate aversion from that end is as revolting a perversion as the

Epicureans' resort to the vomitorium after a full meal. This faculty of will was not created to make a mockery of order but to make order's perfect accomplishment a personal achievement.

Nevertheless it is true that freedom does denote the absence of necessity. Is it necessary that we have a choice between two objects? Does, for instance, the fact of my town possessing only one newspaper destroy my liberty relative to newspapers; or, if there is only one theatre in town, is my liberty done away with? Evidently if there are more than one newspaper or theatre, I am free to choose between the competing purveyors of news and amusement. Nevertheless, I am no less free even when there is only one, I can read or refuse to read, I can go to the theatre or stay at home; in other words, the fundamental liberty of acting or not acting remains. The theologians call this the liberty of exercise, in contrast to the liberty of specification, which involves two or more objects; it is this liberty of exercise, which is absolutely essential to freedom. This is the freedom that we enjoy before every act and even during that act; for always we have the power to stop willing. It is, then, not at all necessary that the choice between good and evil be offered a man if he is to retain his freedom; indeed, there is much more opportunity for freedom's exercise when evil does not enter into the picture at all, much less chance for it when evil is rampant.

As an immediate consequence of this we are driven to a sane view of law. For in this light, law is not an infringement of liberty but rather a guarantee and protector of it; the Ten Commandments, for example, ruling out the things that draw us away from our end, do not destroy the material of liberty but concentrate our attention upon it. A police force, which effectively operates against crime, protects liberty. License, unrestricted action in whatever field, be it license of the press, of the radio, of speech, of morals, is the most serious menace liberty has to face; for license not merely abuses the freedom of the one guilty of it, it directly and immediately interferes with the freedom of others, preventing their steady progress to their end by their free choice.

Proofs of Freedom

If this freedom of men were being attacked by some jealous race that did not possess the gift itself, such an attack might be understandable. But when men themselves are eager to deny this faculty, when they battle with all the energy of fanatic strength, with all the ingenuity that can be commanded by wealth, educational advantages and institutions to champion the abuse of this gift, then we are facing a perversion that outdoes the excesses of paganism.

Today it is extremely necessary to defend the freedom of man from a vast army of intellectuals in America. What proof do we have of freedom?

From the Nature of Human Knowledge - The Proximate Source of Freedom

The immediate source of man's freedom is to be found in the intellectual character of his knowledge. By this knowledge, man is the only spectator on earth of the drama of the universe; he can enter into the inmost nature of everything else and he can step outside of himself, his is not the provincial view of the animals, but the cosmopolitan outlook that knows values and their limitations because it has the material for comparison. All appetite follows in the steps of knowledge and is proportionate to it, for appetite of itself is necessarily blind. All the universe moves to a goal, some of its creatures with slow, plodding steps in the dark, guided by the knowledge of the governor of the universe; others move from object to object as the flashlight of sense knowledge lights up the beauty of this sensible thing and leaves the rest clothed in the darkness of mystery; but men, with the floodlight of intelligence lighting up the whole scene see clearly the obstacles of evil, the helps of particular goods, but over and above they see the goal to which they race. The appetite proportioned to this intellectual knowledge can be satisfied with none of the attractions of the roadside stands; it drives on to the goal of all, the universal good that only man can know.

To look at it from another angle, the fact that we can know the universal enables us to appreciate the limitation, which is to say the imperfection, of the particular. We can see the good in the particular and take it to ourselves; or, seeing its limitation, its undesirability, we can pass it by. It is precisely this limitation of everything less than the supreme good that makes it as impossible for the particular goods to force the will as it is for a thimbleful of water to fill a twelve-gallon pail. It is only a good without limitation, without weak points, without undesirability that is proportioned to the will; only this is an adequate object, only this can move the will necessarily. Faced with anything less, the will is free.

The Moral Argument

On the moral side, an obvious argument for freedom is offered by several commonplace facts. Clearly, it is silly to fine a man for speeding if he is not the driver at all, but one driven by necessity. It is a stupid gesture to reward bravery if courage is merely the violent interaction of chemical reagents. It is absurd to exhort man to control his passions, to strive for goals, to hold fast to ideals if in all this he has no choice. In other words, the advice, counsels, exhortations, commands, rewards, punishments, the whole juridical process presuppose the freedom of man.

In fact, the whole question of morality and moral standards is irrational without the fact of freedom. If a moral law means anything, it means a law that does not force but obliges, a law whose subjects are capable of violating it in contrast to the subjects of a physical law. A legislature does not rule on the size of the ears of subjects, although it does insist on the payment of taxes. A modern philosopher, insisting that man is an animal, a chemical or a machine and at the same time talking of right and wrong, decent and indecent, noble and disgraceful is stultifying himself; the college student, accepting the principles of such teaching, is doing the rational thing when he throws all morality overboard.

From Conscience

A much more intimate proof of our freedom comes from the undeniable fact of our realization of that freedom, from the testimony of psychological conscience. Before a man lights a cigarette, he knows he does not have to light it; while he is smoking, he is sure he can stop at any time; when the smoke is all over and done with, the conviction of his freedom remains. He knows he has not been pushed about by cosmic forces. A man knows he is guilty of wrong because he is so sure he could have done right; he knows this thing should be done here and now, but he is just as sure that he can refuse to do it.

Nor is he an eccentric, queer and lonely in his eccentricity. The same convictions are quite universal among men. Consequently, when a criminal pleads for mercy on the grounds that he could not help committing his crime, he is actually advancing a plea of insanity, at least of temporary insanity. A professor can hold forth on the theory that the heritage of society dictates human action or that modeled or reflex arcs are the real movers; but he will probably report to the college authorities any student who laughs aloud or strolls out in the middle of the lecture.

Argument From the Divine Government of Universe, the Radical Source of Freedom

There is, finally, the proof of freedom from the beauty, the order of the divine government of the universe. Everything else in nature is moved according to its particular nature; a cat never barks, nor does a tree bite. Why, then, should man be the sole exception? Why should man be moved like a thing that is not human when he has human nature? Why should he not be moved in the human fashion, that is, freely? Why should man be subject to the necessary movement that regulates those whose knowledge is limited to the particular or which have no knowledge at all, when he has a universal horizon that is an image of the divine horizon? Why should his appetite, capable of the universal. The supreme, be forced to desire what is so plainly imperfect? In other words, as we saw in the chapter on the divine will, God is the radical source of our freedom by His divine government of the universe; we are free because the power of His will reaches out to all that is real, not merely to the creature, not merely to the action, but also to the mode in which that action is placed, to its freedom or its necessity. The first mover, when it is a question of moving man, moves him according to his human nature, freely.

An interesting point comes up here indicating the power of a lie if it is big enough and told often enough. Of recent years, it has become the fashion to look upon modern philosophers and educators as the champions of man while the Church is considered a reactionary enemy of all that is wholesomely human. Yet, if one were to run down the list of truths that every Catholic must hold as infallibly true, he would find such things as this, man is a creature of body and soul, his intellect is valid, it can certainly know truth, his will is free, he is in command of his life, one might well wonder, who is my neighbor?

Relations of Will and Intellect

The interrelation of intellect and will is a matter to be unraveled at length in the second volume of this work It must, however, be mentioned here because the intimacy of their interaction is obvious from what has been said; and the fact of that interaction presents the mind with a difficulty that cannot be slurred over. Since every appetite is blind and follows the steps of knowledge, evidently the will depends on the intellect for the object of its movement; a man cannot, for example, desire God as his supernatural happiness until he knows God by faith. Yet the will is the principle of all movement in man, so that the intellect moves to its considerations under the motion of the will; it is entirely up to the girl herself whether she will consider her big feet and be downcast or her pert nose and be considerably cheered.

Mutual Movement

The will cannot move until the intellect has shed its light, yet the intellect is moved by the will; certainly, this has the appearance of a vicious circle. Really, there is nothing vicious about it. The circle is broken by the admission of the obvious truth that the movement of one or the other must be first; granted that first movement, their interaction goes merrily on. That first movement is from the intellect, for it is fundamental that we must know what we are to desire. What moves the intellect to its first consideration? That first movement must come from an outside agent; and the only outside agent who can act directly on the soul is God.

Mutual Superiority

In his comparative estimate of these two faculties, St. Thomas considers the intellect the nobler, at least in the abstract and in the perfect state of heaven. His reasons are solid. From the point of view of their objects, it is clear that the object of the intellect is more simple, more abstract; which is to say that the intellect's object is less tainted with particularity, and has, therefore, less of limitation, of imperfection about it. From the angle of man's goal, which is the beatific vision, the direct, intuitive knowledge of Cod, the nobility of the intellect stands out boldly; for the perfection of man, like the perfection of anything else, consists in the highest act of his highest faculty. The enjoyment or fruition of God, the will's part in man's happiness, comes by way of consequence, it is a kind of corollary of that beatific vision.

In this life the action of the will may well be nobler than the action of the intellect by reason of the very nature of their objects. For truth, the object of the intellect, is in the intellect, while good, the object of the will is in things. The practical consequences of this fact are momentous. Thus, Thomas could be an angel of purity while possessing an expert knowledge of impurity; a detective can have an exhaustive knowledge of methods of robbery and still be an honest man. In other words, the intellect takes everything in on its own level. What we know exists in us in our way, whether it is worms or God; knowledge does not elevate or degrade us, rather it levels things to the one human plane.

The will, on the contrary, does not take things into itself; it goes out to things. We become what we desire. If that is infinitely above us, we are lifted out of ourselves to that superior height; if it be beneath us, we are dragged down to the level of what we crave. If we place our goal in God, we soar to divine heights; if we revel in the pleasures of the animals, we are dragged down to the mire of animal existence and further, for we can think of ways of being more animal than the animals.

Conclusion, Facts of man's Appetite

From this survey of the appetites of man we can understand that these appetites do upset the pretty pattern of uniformity modern philosophy has pieced together. They are disturbing factors in the universe and in individual life; they always will be. In fact, they are supposed to be. The divine architect plans them as restless springs of action that would allow a man rest only when the walls of heaven had been stormed and divine life itself shared. The aim of life and of the universe is not dull stagnation, but high attainment; and these appetites are the motive forces driving us on to that high goal.

Our sensual appetites are not a den of iniquity, nor a holy of holies. It is as much of an injustice to man to look upon these appetites as gods to be honored in clouds of incense as it is to throw up our hands in horror and view them as unclean things. They are neither one nor the other; they are the very homely, very human equipment of that image of God, which is man. They are capable of great heights and equally capable of great depths, but only at the instigation of a higher authority, which alone is to be blamed or praised.

That higher authority is the deliberate will of man; a source of terrific potentialities and responsibilities, opening up terrifying prospects of failure, driving on to actions that only a courageous human heart could dare to try. However, it is also the source of sacrifice, of the extravagance of love, of success, of virtue, of heaven. By that will, God can be ours, but by it, too, we can throw in our lot with Satan.

a Disturbing Fact in the Universe

The human will is a disturbing fact in the universe. Perhaps, because it is the supreme Fact. The crowned head can never rest easy; a subject world, whether within or without man, always holds possibilities of rebellion. Nevertheless, it is precisely this deliberate will that gives man dominion over the whole of creation, including himself. It is the key link in that beautifully forged chain of being that stretches from the crudest form of existence up through the glory of the angels to the splendor that is God.

a Disturbing Fact in Human Life

Of course it is a disturbing fact in human life. It is a constant reminder that we are human; and sometimes that comes hard. It would seem so much easier to look on our selves as machines, to lose ourselves in the dreamy softness of emotionalism, to let down the barriers to animalism very easy, very weak, and very cowardly. However, if it is a constant goad driving us on to be worthy of our humanity, it is also a constant defense against the horror of despair and the filth of license. It boldly stamps all of human activity with the human trademark, "mine"; the mark of control, of proprietorship, of pride as well as of responsibility.

The human will is disturbing for it makes us full sharers in the divine perfection, capable of knowing and acting as God does, through intellect and will; of sharing in the work of divine providence as no other member of the physical universe shares, completing that image of God in the physical universe. We alone, of all these creatures, have the power to rise to direct possession of God, For we alone, of all these creatures, have the power to rise in open rebellion against that God and continue in that rebellion for eternity.

CHAPTER XV

THE MIND OF THE LORD OF THE WORLD
(Q. 84-89)

1. The puzzle of heights and depths.

   (a) Natures bases for mystery of knowledge.

   (b) Pertinence of the problem of knowledge.

2. Modernity and the problem,

   (a) History of the modern view.

   (b) Position of the moderns.

3. The defense of knowledge.

4. The nature of knowledge,

   (a) Its characteristics, immaterial, immutable, universal, necessary.

   (b) Its source,

      (1) Negatively.

      (2) Positively from sensible things.

      (3) Its manner and medium,
      (4) Abstraction

         (a) The results of abstraction – the intelligible species.

         (b) The order of knowledge.

         (c) The accuracy of knowledge.

5. The objects of knowledge,

   (a) In the sensible world.

   (b) In the soul.

   (c) Above the soul.

6. Knowledge in separated souls,

   (a) Distinction from earthly knowledge.

   (b) Objects of this knowledge.

Conclusion,

   1. The shock of the problem.

   2. Significance of the answer,

   3. Relative to the universe.

   (a) Relative to human action.

   (b) Relative to participation in divinity.

☐ CHAPTER XV ☐
THE MIND OF THE LORD OF THE WORLD
(Q. 84-89)

The Puzzle of Heights and Depths

Mountain climbing and deep-sea diving appeal to only a sporting few among men. There is a considerable danger in each, increased, perhaps, by the hint each carries of the tragic character of extreme height or depth to the human individual. He knows if he goes down deep enough he will be crushed by outside pressure; and if he goes up high enough he may suffocate from lack of oxygen before he explodes from lack of outside pressure, but suffocation is small comfort. Indeed, it is probably the element of comfort rather than the fear of danger that keeps most men on the prosaic level of smooth earth. Whatever can be said of the thrill of heights and depths neither can compare in sheer comfort with a sleepy street on a summer evening or a soft chair and a warm fire on a wintry night.

The most comfort-loving man cannot dodge all heights and depths; but he can dislike them wherever he meets them. Usually that dislike is prompt and unmistakable. Even although we have stepped into an express elevator of our own free will, its almost instantaneous plunge down thirty stories leaves us with a sense of incredulousness and blurred fright. It is not so much a matter of danger or discomfort as it is that we have simply come down too fast; we are not built on the express model, we labor up step by step and come down even more cautiously. Our minds work that way, our wills work that way and, as far as we can arrange it, all the details of life follow the same pattern. Put our arrangements are by no means sufficient to cover the whole span of life. With no warning whatsoever, we look into the eyes of another and suddenly realize there has been a mutual plunging into the depths of a human soul, we are numbed and stumble away in a kind of dazed unbelief. Genius may labor over stubborn material for hours on end, then suddenly there is a Hashing insight that sends the mind into the heights like a frightened angel scurrying home; even genius is slightly dazed, incredulous, although its disbelief be hidden in a competent silence.

If we look down from the heights through the window of a speeding plane, railroads, ships, cities and forests look like toys; they can hardly be real, again that note of dazed disbelief. If you can picture a man getting that same view without moving a foot off the ground, you have some idea of his incredulousness before the fact of his own knowledge. His mind puts him off to one side of the universe, or above it, giving him a plane passenger's view of the whole as if he were no part of it. Without any warning, that human mind plunges past the surface of men and things down to the very depths to reveal, not something about men and things, but men and things themselves; and in a fraction of time that defies analysis with an absence of intervening steps that jars us out of our apathetic plodding. It is no wonder that this thing of knowledge has been a prime problem for philosophers from the beginning; it is no wonder that they have approached the problem in a somewhat sour humor, irritated, almost angry at the speed, the mystery, the heights and depths of it.

Nature's Bases for Mystery of Knowledge

Moreover, the problem has an immediate and crucial interest for every individual. For if it is true that appetite must follow knowledge, then it is precisely because of this mysterious, far sweeping, universal knowledge of man that human appetite surpasses that of the animals. It is because man can search the heights and the depths that he can be satisfied only by the supreme good. It is, then, the universal, abstract knowledge of man that is the immediate source and explanation of his freedom in the face of limited, imperfect goods; it is this distinctly human knowledge that gives him dominance over the physical world and himself; it is this that ultimately explains the responsibilities of human life, the possibilities of personal success and failure, of victory and defeat, of moral life and its ultimates of heaven and hell as being within reach of human activity. In a word, it is because man has a distinctly human knowledge that he has distinctly human desires and so distinctly human acts; that human life lies on a plane just below the angels and far above the brute world of matter. This, then, is no mere academic problem, this problem of knowledge; it is not to be shrugged off, but to be painstakingly investigated.

Modernity and the Problem, History of the Modern View

It is not strange that the philosophy of our day has lost no share of the universal interest in the problem of knowledge. What is surprising is that the activity of modern philosophy should be centered chiefly in denying the humanity of man's knowledge rather than in trying to explain it. But the fact is plain. This opposition to the humanity of man's knowledge is one of the chief grounds for the rejection of the scholastic answer to the problem, the so-called notion of the scholastics that the knowledge of man exceeds the content of sense knowledge yet takes its rise from the senses and the sensible world. The moderns have rejected one or the other of these two elements or the conjunction of the two. One school will insist that the world of sense is a world of illusions, it is the mind that we are projecting and playing with when we play the game of knowing the world about us; the other completely disregards intellectual activity, or tries to, reducing such activity to the world of the sensible, automatic, blind, instinctive forces. In this way the heights and the depths, the mystery and speed and all the rest are done away with by the simple expedient of blowing up the sensible world or of strangling the mind of men; quite a high price to pay for the comfort of level territory.

Position of the Moderns

The technique of escape from the problem of knowledge is by no means new. It was tried when philosophy was young and many a time since, still the world goes on and the minds of men go on. Still, a man who is trying to run away is not to be discouraged by previous failures; inevitably the technique would be tried again. The modern attempt can trace its intellectual roots to the beginning of the modern era when Descartes assumed his artificial chasm between the mind and the world of reality, an assumption that forced him to build the fantastic bridge of totally unwarranted parallelism. A fantastic bridge to span an assumed chasm seems fair enough; but men took it seriously.

Kant gave this assumption a philosophical flavor by apparently justifying it, when, with typical modern clumsiness, he rushed to the "rescue" of the humanity of man's knowledge against the positivistic attacks of Locke, Berkely and Hume. Murdering the victim effected the rescue. Kant proceeded by assuming that what is not given *formally* in experience comes *wholly* from the mind; such an unqualified statement as "sugar is sweet" is obviously not given formally in experience for all sugar cannot be experientially tested for its sweetness, so the statement must take its rise wholly from the mind. Both of these elements of Kant's original assumption were then developed independently to their logical conclusion of naturalism and idealism. The problem of knowledge was escaped again by the same technique of denying or disregarding one or the other of its constituent elements, the world or the mind. Still there were the stubborn facts remaining unexplained, both the world and the mind refused to be snubbed.

Coming down closer to our own day, Bergson made a polite gesture towards intellect as he stabbed it in the back by his contention that the intellect was not an instrument of valid knowledge and reality was so fluid a thing that it could not be known without being stopped in its flow and so falsified. The result was that we had neither a worthwhile mind nor a world with which we could come into contact. The intellect of man was not a valid investigator of the world of reality; it was a falsifier, a maker of useful (not true) concepts whose whole purpose was action. William James accepted the Bergsonian gesture with open arms, developed his Pragmatism (or disregard of truth in favor of utility), thus turning a valid scientific method of inquiry into an immensely popular and thoroughly worthless system of philosophy.

Today we reap the fruits of this wild sowing. For it is our age that has come sharply up against the express attempt at a thorough invalidation of the intellect and its activity or even a downright denial of the existence of the intellect. That means that we are heed with a denial of human knowledge, with all the consequences of such a denial for philosophy, science, human activity and human life. We are the victims of a modern "rescue" of men by modern "champions" of man's humanity.

The Defense of Knowledge

In an earlier chapter, it was shown that the Church had been forced to come to the rescue of the humanity of the very nature of man and to defend the freedom of human action. The same is true of man's knowledge. Just as the Church insisted that man was human, not animal, not angelic, not divine; just as she insisted he was master of his own actions, not the slave of blind forces within or without himself; so she insists on the humanity of his knowledge, the validity of his intellects. Man's knowledge is not the mere sense knowledge of the animals, it is not the innately perfect knowledge of the angels, it is not the sum total of all knowledge as is God's; it is the knowledge proportionate to human nature, to a spiritual soul informing a material body, a rational knowledge taking its rise from the senses and the world of the senses.

The Nature of Knowledge

In this matter, the difference between these two, both claiming championship of man, is that the one not only admits the existence of the spiritual, it sees the spiritual, not as something extraordinary, not as supernatural, but as an integral part of the natural order; the other, impressed by the vividness, the size, the multiplicity and the constancy of the sensible world and sense impressions, cannot tear its eyes away from this fascinating part of nature and so can see nothing else. The nature of man is a startling thing in the universe; it is a fusion of the material and the spiritual, the link binding together the spiritual and material world. But man is not, from that fact, a supernatural creature, a freak in nature, an upstart that must be reduced to a lower level. His knowledge, too, is a startling thing, taking its rise in the physical world and reaching to spiritual heights that far surpass anything in the world beneath man; but it is not, from that fact, an unnatural, preternatural or supernatural phenomenon, it is not to be treated as necessarily an illusion or an absurd paradox that defies understanding. It is entirely natural; and quite naturally it possesses such spiritual characteristics as immateriality, immutability, universality and necessity.

Its Characteristics, Immaterial, Immutable, Universal, Necessary.

A man's knowledge of a stone, a tree or another man immediately leaps far ahead of the particular notes of this stone, this tree or this man and presents the knower with a concept that is universally valid, one true of all stones, another true of all trees, another true of all men. It is coin of the realm of truth that is accepted even in eternity. It is not only universal it is as necessarily stable as the natures of those things known, because it is precisely those natures that are known. As long as a circle cannot have its nature changed and still be a circle, as long as man remains man, that is, as long as the essences of things cannot be falsified, this knowledge remains immutable.

That knowledge exists in a spiritual soul, in the immaterial faculty of intellect, in the only way in which it can exist there; that is, freed from the limitations of matter. It outstrips the contingency, the changeableness, the singularity of the physical world, taking on the characteristics of the spiritual world, yet faithfully representing the world with which it brings a man into immediate contact. There is indeed truth in the concepts of wetness, of beauty and of humanity, although it is not wetness but wet things, not beauty but beautiful things, not humanity but humans that have physical existence in the sensible world.

Its Source, Negatively

Yet, in spite of its decidedly spiritual nature, it is a serious error to trace this knowledge to any but a source proportionate to that composite nature that is man's. Certainly we do not know things, as God does, by simply looking at ourselves, knowing our own essence. A concentrated and exclusive study of ourselves may teach us some surprising things, but the number of things it will not teach us is positively staggering; and, if we continue this one-sided study long enough, we shall end up by not even knowing ourselves. We are men, not gods. We could know all things in our own souls only if the things existed there beforehand to be known. They do exist in God, the divine exemplar; the model to which all things were made. We have only the norm proper to our nature, the substantial form, which is our spiritual soul; it has the capacity to receive unlimited forms of other things by way of knowledge, but only the capacity. A savage of Tierra del Fuego can search his soul from now until doomsday, go into a very trance of introspection, and never come up with the knowledge of an automobile. In other words, we cannot know all things by simply knowing ourselves because we are not the cause of all things.

To a man whom the Lord has delivered up to study, the story of Catherine of Siena receiving profound knowledge through a miraculous infusion of ideas has an appeal that may well be tinged with envy. Not an hour of study went into her knowledge, no single difficulty kept her mind in turmoil for weeks, no book wore down her eyes, no error shook her judgment. Think of it! Now, do not think of it as the ordinary mode of acquiring human knowledge; that is the way the angels get their knowledge and men are not angels. It hardly seems necessary to argue the point, yet some men have been captivated by the joyous ease of innate ideas and argued that so men knew the world. If this were true, we would never be potential knowers for we would have our knowledge from the beginning. Then, too, there would be the insurmountable difficulty facing us, namely, that men born blind cannot know color and men born deaf cannot know sound. It might also be pointed out as somewhat strange that all men should forget all they naturally know.

Positively – from Sensible Things

Our knowledge does not come pouring into our heads from some outside source such as Plato's separated ideas. Any teacher will testify that nothing can be poured into a student's head, nor even hammered in; the student has to reach out and feed his own mind. As a matter of fact, in such a hypothesis there would be no excuse whatever For man having a body; it would be at best an obstacle and at worst a prison, rather than the essential constituent of his very nature.

Its Manner and Medium

The strongest argument against these dreams of easy human knowledge is the facts, which clearly indicate that our knowledge takes its rise from sensible things. The apprenticeship of childhood is an absolute requirement for the mastery of adult knowledge. The sensible world acts upon our senses giving rise to that sense knowledge we have in common with the animals, writing its permanent record in the phantasms or images of the imagination. So far sense knowledge carries us, and no farther. It is the gay knowledge of children, full of vivid colors, rippling sounds, swift movement, and delicious odors and lingering tastes with none of the animal's fear to tone down its gaiety.

Abstraction

From this highest level of sense knowledge, intellectual knowledge takes its rise. That transition from the sensible to the intellectual, however, is not made simple by saying it quickly; it represents difficulties that have been too much for many a philosopher. For the phantasm is sensible, particular, concrete; moreover, no sensible thing can act on a spiritual substance, cannot bump it, squeeze it, tickle its fancy, or take it by the throat. How, then, explain the immaterial, universal, necessary concept in the spiritual intellect coming from such a sources.

Admittedly men start off with their minds a blank page; such knowledge as we have, short of a miracle, must take its rise from the senses. It is also unquestionably true that everything in the world of experience is singular and concrete, not universal, while our knowledge is obviously universal. Yet St. Thomas denies that the universals are wholly from the mind, as Kant would have it. That denial is precisely the refusal to admit an identification of "what is not given formally in experience" with "wholly of the mind." Much that we know is not given formally in experience, such a prosaic thing, for example, as the sweetness of sugar; but this does not make it wholly a product of mind. The universality of man's knowledge has some root in the concrete, singular world of experience.

The specific nature of this dog is the same as that of another dog or, indeed, of all dogs. It is precisely the common nature enjoyed by all dogs, which makes this creature a dog and not a horse. In technical language, this means that the specific nature, or essence, of the concrete thing is negatively universal. The scholastics called this ratio or absentia; let us use a word with which we are now familiar and call it a form. It is differentiated in each dog by individual elements, the elements that contribute the "thisness" of the particular dog. This form of a sensible thing cannot exist in the physical world without individuating elements supplied by matter, a fact that experience forces on our mind; we are not chased by a universal dog or introduced to universal human nature. Nevertheless, it is evident that the specific form itself is not averse to universality; it does, as a matter of fact, exist in many dogs at the same time.

To have this form in its universality, then, means no more than to have it without the individual elements matter has given it; the *universal form does exist fundamentally in things*. Can it be unearthed in some way from particularity, from the "thisness" of the concrete things. This is the work of the intellect, by the process of abstraction, to make formally universal what was only fundamentally or potentially so.

Since scholasticism has been put in the stocks, this process has become famous; it is one of the missiles most frequently hurled at the hapless scholastic head. All rumors to the contrary, it is not a surgical operation cutting apart the individual and universal elements; it is not a matter of slapping a universal tag on a patently concrete thing at our own subjective pleasure or necessity.

Abstraction is in no sense a separation; it is simply a distinct consideration of the form to the disregard of the particularity of this thing, somewhat as a man might regard the redness of an apple without consideration of its sweetness, or the softness of soapsuds without regard to their taste. It is the same trick mathematics uses in considering quantity without regard to beauty; or that art uses in considering beauty without regard to the mathematician's quantity. Obviously the scholastics have taken out no patent on the process.

We have a faculty of intellect, called the active intellect, whose sole work is to throw light on the sensible image or phantasm to make the universal stand out from the particular as a spot-light makes one girl stand out from a chorus. This light, focused on the specific nature in the phantasm, enables the intellect to concentrate on its proper objects the universal nature of the thing, to the disregard of the particularizing elements of it.

the Results of Abstraction – the Intelligible Species

The result of this distinct consideration, or this process of abstraction, is the intelligible species or form, representing the essence, ratio or form. More strictly, it is certainly not the universal nature existing in the mind in the same way as it exists outside; but it is the same nature existing in the mind in a different way. Whereas in the concrete thing, the dog, for instance, it exists physically, in the mind it exists intentionally; whereas in the dog it was only fundamentally universal, potentially intelligible, in the mind it is formally universal and actually intelligible.

The intelligible species or form is not a sheer luxury; it is indispensable for distinctly human knowledge. This concrete thing is certainly singular and our knowledge is just as certainly universal. If this concrete thing is ever to be known intellectually, it must be made actually universal, actually intelligible. Without such a universalization, the possible intellect (our other intellectual faculty) cannot produce the positive act of knowledge. Let us put it this way. Precisely because the possible intellect is capable of knowing all things, it is not determined to any one, just as the eye, because it is capable of seeing all colors, is not determined to any one. Without such determination there can be no knowledge, just as without some color there can be no sight. The determination of the intellect is by the intelligible species or form. Just as the form or essence gave the universal nature in the physical order resulting in the concrete dog, so it gives the universal nature in the intellectual order resulting in our knowledge of the dog. We might see the whole picture as a double sharing in the ideas of God, physically, in the order of existence, and intentionally, in the order of knowledge. A common mistake that has turned many a philosopher against scholasticism centers upon the intelligible species. The notion has somehow got around that the scholastic is never in contact with the world he knows an intelligible species, an idea, but not the world of reality. As a matter of fact, the intelligible species is not the object known; rather it is that by which we know the thing. It is not the object but the medium; just as light is not that which is seen but that by, which color is seen, so the intelligible species is not what is known but that by, which a thing is known. We can, in fact, sail serenely through life without ever suspecting that we have a species, and be none the worse for it; but if we have no suspicion of possessing knowledge, we cannot sail through life, we shall have to be towed. It is only by the reflective, that is, the philosophic, consideration that we advert to the presence of species at all.

Nor does this make our knowledge exclusively universal, barring us forever from an intellectual knowledge of singular things. The *direct* object of our knowledge is the universal; the singular is no less an object, but it is seen *indirectly*, as we might see something from the corner of our eye without looking at it directly. It is, in fact, quite impossible for us to make use of any one of these intelligible species without adverting to the phantasm from which it was abstracted; so that in using any one we must indirectly, obliquely, consider the singular from which it arose. It is by direct intellectual knowledge that I know "man"; but it is also the fruit of intellectual operation that enables me to say, "John Smith is a man." The knowledge of the concrete individual "Smith" is intellectual, but indirectly so.

There is no chasm between the intellect and the sensible world; rather there is identity. To know is, in a sense, to become the thing known; it is to have ones own form physically and the forms of the known things intentionally. Knowledge is a vital action, not a mere passive reception or an automatic response. It is a union so intimate that we cannot so much as consider our act of knowledge without considering the object known; we do not know the act of our intellect knowing, but the act of the intellect knowing *something*.

the Order of Knowledge

As it starts off on the long, hard road of knowledge, the baby knows a puppy long before it recognizes the genus brute; for the first things we know are singular things, no universals. Sense knowledge must come first, furnishing the material for intellectual knowledge; and sense knowledge is of particular, singular things. Really, the infant has some vague, blurred knowledge of things at rest, things in motion and things colored, before it begins to play with the puppy. It passes from the mere potentiality of knowledge to actual knowledge; the medium between those two extremes is imperfect or confused knowledge. Thus a man standing on a hill and peering down a long road will first see something approaching; then he will be able to distinguish it as some animal, then as some man and finally he will recognize the individual modeled. The process is the same if considered from the angle of the time element; the child will distinguish a man from other animals before it distinguishes one man from another. In the intellectual order, the same holds true, first we get the more general notion; and only as knowledge gets more perfect does it become less general.

Our progress is necessarily slow, step by step, because the door of our minds will not admit more than one intelligible species at a time; some one or the other may contain many interrelated notions, as one mirror may reflect a roomful of people, but the intellect can no more be actualized by different forms at the same time than a man can run in different directions at once. If we were to store this consideration of intellectual knowledge right here, we would not have gone beyond what the scholastics call "simple apprehension," that is, the knowledge of things immediately perceived through intelligible species.

Of course we cannot stop here; this is only the first of three steps. First we grasp the essences of things; then we compare these forms one with another, tack on or deny certain properties, accidents, habits, circumstances, a process that is called judgment, the fertile field of everyday mistakes; finally, a comparison of judgments gives us the act which has given its name to our type of intellectuality the act of reasoning and it is here that philosophers are weighed and, not infrequently, found wanting.

the Accuracy of Knowledge

Until we get past the simple apprehension of the essences of things, there is no chance for error in our knowledge. The healthy intellect can no more make a mistake about the essences of things than a healthy eye can about color or a healthy ear about sound. The essences of things are the proper object of the intellect, the reason for which it exists; it is made precisely to know them.

Error in judgment and reasoning is not only possible, it is a fairly common fact. At least, many people, other than ourselves, frequently make mistakes. Judgment and reasoning involve composition or division; we can and do put the wrong things together or refuse to put the right things together. There is truth in the concept of a grumbler, as there is truth in the concept of man; but it may, in this particular case, be totally unjust to judge that this man is a grumbler in other words, we cannot make a mistake about the essences of things but we can be mistaken about the properties, the accidents and the circumstances of this or that essence. The bases of our mistakes in judgment are much the same as the leases of our mistakes in conclusions, although the principles from which we argue be correct; that is, we make the comparison too quickly, without consideration, without grounds for such a union, or through prejudice rather than on evidence, and so on.

Some men do make more mistakes than others, if for no other reason than because some men do not understand as well as others. It is not merely a matter of better physical equipment, more apt organs of sense, keener imaginations and better memory; but because of a distinct difference in the quality of the intellect itself. We can improve our minds. Still, no bit of magic can change them from the tabloid class into the intellect of an Aristotle or a Thomas Aquinas.

the Objects of Knowledge

The field of knowledge thrown open by intellectual activity seems almost limitless in comparison with the feeble knowledge enjoyed by the animals. If we keep our eyes fixed on the brutes, we might be able to persuade our selves that there is no knowledge superior to our own. The fact is. However, that human knowledge has its limits; rather than approach the question from this deflating angle, let us inquire just what we do know.

In the Sensible World

As we have seen, we know particular things indirectly with an intellectual knowledge, by a kind of reflection on the phantasm of the imagination. We know necessary things, like first principles, laws of the physical world; and contingent things, like grandmothers, and school days. We can even know some future things, like eclipses or next week's blizzard; but we know these things, not in themselves, but in their causes as a man knows there is trouble in the offing from the scowl on his wife's face. As for future things like a laugh, a sin, a yes or a no, they can only be guessed at by us at a great risk of having our guess turn out wrong. To see in themselves the future things that proceed from free causes is not the prerogative of men but of God.

In the Soul

We can know our own soul, its nature and faculties, not by meeting them on the street or by abstracting them from ourselves, but from the acts they produce. The acts, for instance, of the intellect and will are known by reflection, we know that we know by considering the act of *knowing something*; we know that we will by considering the act of *willing something*. This reflexive power is our special gift, a gift proper to intellectual nature alone; we are the only ones who can stand aside and look at ourselves and our acts critically, with an almost disinterested objectivity, as an angel might look at the earth.

Above the Soul

Things above us, like the angels and God, because they are completely free of all material are evidently not the proportionate, natural, direct objects of our knowledge. There is no point to our standing on tiptoe trying to snatch them into our minds directly; we must be satisfied to learn about them the long, hard way, by reasoning up from the material world we know so well. In this way we can know them, not comprehensively, not directly but, as in the case of God, by tracing His effects for the clues they give us as to His nature, stripping off the imperfections of the created world to get a glimpse of the uncreated, attributing all perfection to the one possible source of that perfection. This was, in fact, the procedure we followed in the very beginning of this book in treating the nature of God. Briefly, then, the direct object of human knowledge is the essences of things abstracted from singular, concrete things. From this basis, all judgment and reasoning proceed.

For a complete survey of the problem of knowledge there still remains the question of knowledge after death, for the soul of man does not die and it is precisely in the soul of man that his knowledge is centered. Separated from the body by death, the soul has lost its medium for investigation of the physical world, indeed of contact with that physical world. The helplessness of the soul seems even more striking when we remember that we cannot make use of a single intelligible species without referring to the phantasms of the imagination; and, of course, these phantasms cease to exist with death.

Still, this separated soul is the same soul with exactly the same nature it had before death, retaining possession of all the intelligible species amassed during life; it is consequently a rational soul, proceeding on the path of knowledge by that process of comparison which is judgment arid reasoning. To deprive an artist of color or a musician of all sound would be not nearly so tragic as to leave such a soul in a blank oblivion after death; it would be the most despairing, most frustrated of creatures. But how can it know?

Knowledge in Separated Souls

The answer to the difficulty is to be found in the fundamental truth that the mode of activity is determined by the mode of existence; thus the form of material things, when it enjoys a physical mode of existence, acts as the substantial form of a concrete thing, but when it enjoys an intentional mode of existence in the mind of man, it acts as the intelligible form of the intellect, causing knowledge. The separated soul has a different mode of existence than it enjoyed on earth; it exists without the body. Consequently, it should have a different mode of knowledge that, while not supernatural, is yet not the natural mode of knowledge of the soul when it is actually informing the body.

Distinction from Earthly Knowledge

The mode of existence the separated soul has is that proper to such separated spiritual substances as the angels. It therefore knows not only by the species gathered in life, using them as the angels use their concepts, but also by new species infused by God. Not that this new way of knowledge elevates the soul to a more perfect knowledge; in fact, this knowledge is inferior to that which was had and used by reference to the material part of man. The separated soul is like a little boy wearing his father's clothes, or a street peddler sitting in on a conference of European diplomats. This soul is sporting its big brother's mode of knowledge and is not quite capable of handling it.

The angels understand through fewer and more universal species, and quite perfectly; the soul, confronted by such a species, is like a man, totally ignorant of philosophy, forced to use the metaphysical principles of St. Thomas. He sees something in them can make some use of them; but nothing like what St. Thomas could see in them and do with them. Yet, precisely because these species are such angelic things, coming directly from God, they have the advantage of doing away with the necessity of physical contact with the sensible world, of being totally independent of distance, free of the necessity of reference to the phantasms of the imagination.

Objects of this Knowledge

In that state of separation from the body, the souls know other souls, just as the angels do. They have some knowledge of all natural things, but rather a vague, confused knowledge; whereas the angels, with the same kind of species, have a perfect knowledge of all natural things. This confused character of the separated souls' knowledge, due to the species being too big for them also limits their knowledge of particular things to a blurred vision, as although their intellects could not quite focus. Evidently more determination must be had than is to be found in the species themselves if a clear, distinct knowledge of particular things is to be enjoyed; there must be some other force focusing the intellect to the point where the details stand out clearly, such a force, for instance, as some preceding knowledge, some bond of interest, of love, of natural inclination to this particular thing, or a special ordination of God.

As a result, souls separated from their proper bodies have no natural knowledge of what goes on, on earth, They can know particular things clearly only through the determinations we have just mentioned; and such determinations cannot do away with the fact of separation from the physical world and the souls' lack of natural contact with it. That the curtain, which hides the doings of men might be drawn aside momentarily by a miracle is of course possible; that the blessed in heaven have a clear knowledge of the drama of earth supernaturally, through the essence of God, is quite true. Still, naturally speaking, this is impossible to the soul after death.

Looking out over the vista of human knowledge, we can understand something of the dazed unbelief, the frightened incredulity of modern philosophers. The thing is a distinct shock; it goes up too high, down too deep. Additionally, with a speed that jars us out of the plodding pace of the material world. It is even a little irritating in its mysterious intangibility. The temptation is to sulk a little. Like a man who sees something that simply cannot have happened but nonetheless does; he will not quite admit it, although he cannot deny it without admitting to himself that he is stubbornly fighting the facts.

Conclusion, the Shock of the Problem

The shock of human knowledge falls principally on the man who has focused all his attention on one part of the universe and made it impossible for himself to see the smooth harmony of the whole. He has studied the material side so expertly and intensely that he eventually becomes convinced that nothing else exists or can exist. It is almost too much to ask him to see the light of intellectuality as a great sun with rays streaming from it, for such a figure demands a view of the whole of the universe, not merely a part of it. Thus, in the very center, all things are understood by the one flaming sun itself, God knowing through His own essence; as we get further away from that center, the light becomes dimmer, less penetrating. The angels understand through a few of these powerful rays, and perfectly; man, as the rays get dimmer, needs many to light the way and then only imperfectly, finally, on the level of brute and inanimate creation, the light dies out altogether and things must be steered through the darkness by the hand of God.

To take the same universal view from the other side, we see the creatures, which work towards their perfection and that of the universe without knowledge of their own, but solely through the impress of the knowledge of God. Up a step we have the animals seeking their limited ends through a particular knowledge of the senses which precludes freedom; man stretches forth to his infinite goal through the universal knowledge of intellect, seeing the goal and each step towards it, but laboriously, step by step, with many an error; the angels dart to the same infinite goal easily, naturally, perfectly with a complete and infallible knowledge; God Himself is that goal, knowing Himself, possessing Himself by His very essence.

Significance of the Answer, Relative to the Universe

No, man's intellectual knowledge is not a freak in a physical universe; it is but another strip in the film unfolding the beauty and perfection of God, a corner of a blueprint which fits perfectly into the universal plan of the divine architect, a link in the chain that binds the meanest of creatures to the absolute perfection of God. Intellectual knowledge is not a freak but a demand of the humanity of man, the rightful trappings of his state as lord of the physical world, sharer in divine providence with the divine ability of looking ahead, considering his goals, providing for himself and for others in that kingdom.

Relative to Human Action

This human knowledge, because it is so intimately a part of man himself, is an indispensable condition for human activity, intellectual or otherwise. Without that universal, necessary, immaterial knowledge, the physical sciences, philosophy and the arts are impossibilities; without that knowledge of absolute, universal truth there can be no freedom, no morality, no striving for heaven, no ultimate union with God for eternity. Only the possessors of intellectuality survive the inevitable death, which stalks the physical universe. Only those who can know the wide stretches of the immaterial can taste eternal life with its eternal vision; all else must pass.

Relative to Participation in Divinity

It is only those who defend that intellectuality of man who can be counted among the friends of man and of truth; for only these are ready to face facts and to take up the burdens and privileges of humanity. Only those who accept the guidance of that intellectual beacon are worthy of the humanity which has been given them, only these take their place in the divine plans, and hold a valid claim to the title that belongs to man, the lord of the world.

☐ CHAPTER XVI – EVE'S FAMILY AT HOME ☐
(Q. 94-103)

1. World memory of an age of gold,

(a)Tradition and mythology of Greeks and Romans.

(b) Place of moral factors in this tradition.

2. Philosophical versions of this original age,

(a) A world of hate and strife (Hobbes).

(b) A world of unrestricted individualism (Rousseau).

(c) The modern world of mud.

3. Principles for the investigation of the original state of man,

(a) The integrity of nature.

(b) Cause and essential notion of superiority of the original state.

4. The individual in the Garden of Eden,

(a)His intellectual equipment and progress

(1) That of Adam.

(2) That of his children.

(b) His will his justice and his peace.

(1) His physical nature,

(2) His passions.

(3) Conservation of his life,

a) Food drink and vital actions.

b) Impassibility.

c) Immortality.

(c) His relation to other individuals—equality and inequality.

5. Domestic life in the Garden of Eden,

   (a) Difference of sex.

   (b) Generation of children.

   (c) Condition and care of children.

6. Social life in the Garden of Eden,

   (a) Necessity of political organization.

   (b) Slavery.

   (c) Dominion over the physical world.

7. Physical surroundings of the first man,

   (a)The situation of Paradise.

   (b) Its inhabitants.

   (b) Man's place in it.

Conclusion,

   1.) Difference from the account of Genesis,

   (a) In the pagan tradition.

(b) In renaissance philosophy.

(c) In modern materialistic philosophies.

2. The significance of these differences,

(a) For an estimation of the nature of man.

(b) For an appreciation of the work of God.

(c) For a determination of individual possibilities and goals.

CHAPTER XVI
EVE'S FAMILY AT HOME
(Q. 94-103)

World Memory of an Age of Gold

The statement of man's evolution has been hurled at our minds so constantly and from so many different directions that we are apt to overlook the fact that this idea is fairly recent. Men did not always maintain that man began from a woefully inferior status and gradually worked up to his present perfection like the hero of a success story. For centuries men cherished a precious memory. They told, with poignant regret, the story of an initial happiness and perfection that was only gradually lost as men descended step by step to the present miserable state; whatever the century this "present" represented, it was always a miserable state for the old days were always best.

Tradition and Mythology of Greeks and Romans

There are written records of such a memory dating back as far as nine hundred years before Christ, Hesiod's *Works and Days*. According to that first of the Greek poems, the days of men were fittingly divided into ages of gold, of silver, of brass and of iron That first golden age, an age quite distinct from the age of the heroes of Greek mythology, was a moral paradise; there way no sin in it, no injustice, no moral evil whatsoever, but all men lived in a delightful peace and harmony.

Much later, the Roman poet Ovid gave evidence of the vitality of this ancient tradition by recording the fume division of the days of men, insisting again on the golden age as an age of faith and justice. Of course physically it measured up to an Italian ideal an eternal spring with gentle breezes, rich harvests springing up spontaneously, with none of the unpleasantness of cold, ice or snow. The degeneration of man goes on steadily until the iron-age (the "present" of Ovid) is reached. He describes it thus, "The last age was of hard and stubborn iron. Instantly all kinds of wickedness broke out in this age, of a more degenerate turn, modesty, truth, and honor fled, in place of which succeeded fraud, deceit, treachery, violence, and an insatiable itch to amass wealth."

Place of Moral Factors in this Tradition

Throughout all these ages of the pagan tradition of an original state of perfection of men, the emphasis was steadily centered on moral factors. There was no question of man being driven down or up by blind, irresistible forces that left him stripped of praise or blame, even although the loss of the golden age was due to an overthrow of the reigning god, Saturn, and his replacement by Jupiter. The perfection of the golden age was seen as essentially a moral perfection; it depended on the absence of evil and was characterized by a profound peace and a harmony that echoed the deepest wishes of the human heart. In that age, men were happy because they were good; as that perfection became a memory, sin made its entrance on the stage of the world.

Philosophical Versions of this Original Age
A World of Hate and Strife (Hobbes)

The precious memory was definitely abandoned when the renaissance philosophers attempted to picture the natural state of man in such a way as to support a political theory. The exceedingly fearful and timorous Hobbes, championing the English monarchy's power and protection, insisted that all men are essentially bitter enemies because their happiness consists in exceeding their neighbors. By nature, all were equal, all self-seeking; so that the natural state of man was one of terror, war and a supremacy held by might, a condition of things that was particularly terrifying to a man like Hobbes. Men finally realized the futility of all this and the necessity of a common power to keep all in awe; they ceded their rights to the sovereign, not by a contract with the sovereign but by a contract between the subjects. They are now completely subject to the king.

A World of Unrestricted Individualism (Rousseau)

Rousseau went to the other extreme, insisting that men did not need a government to give them peace and happiness; all they needed was to be let alone. The theory of Rousseau might well have been expected. It was one of the periodic swings of the pendulum that had been throwing its shadow back and forth from the beginning. By one swing the position was reached that man was badly damaged somewhere along the line, some integral part of his nature had corrupted so that, as he now exists, he is essentially evil. At the opposite extreme, it was insisted that man had absolutely nothing the matter with him, needed no help from anyone in any line; he was in as good condition now as he ever was, as perfect as the day he was made. Rousseau, clumsy, ill at ease in society, plagued by complexes of inferiority and persecution, not only championed an absolute individual liberty and an emotional participation of life untrammeled, he attacked all authority. It is precisely because of authority, discipline and convention that man has been ruined; these things must be done away with. In his original state, man-was good, as was nature and God. Human institutions have destroyed man's original peace, goodness and innocence. Both Rousseau and Hobbes denied the social nature of man in his original state; the one picturing society as a corrupter of human nature, the other as an artificial savior of man from himself.

The Modern World of Mud

With the advent of a thoroughly materialistic modern philosophy, the happy memory of an original state of perfection of man was doomed. What perfection man can claim must find its source in a purely material universe that certainly did not produce effects above the material. Man was an integral part of a completely material world, to be explained, examined and evaluated as any other part of that universe. Thus man is pictured as a product of an evolving process within that material universe, a purely material product whose original state was at worst a primeval slime, at best a brute animality; his present position is not due to a degeneration or a fall, but to centuries of a steady climb that has left him qualitatively the same as his animal ancestors.

Sin, faith, justice, morality had no part to play in the origins of man, as they have no serious part to play in his present life. The change (for the better) that has taken place in man explains itself; for it was the very process of change that brought about the improvement. Man is the result of a blind necessity, of the interaction of natural forces that need no explanation. No credit can be given him for his present or past condition; no hope can be held out for his personal future. He is caught in a relentless tide of progress without a goal and without a beginning; in that progress he is an unimportant phase.

Principles for the Investigation of the Original State of Man

St. Thomas was familiar with the ancestors of the renaissance philosophers; he knew materialism in its earliest forms; the dreams and memories of the pagans were packed away on the shelves of his memory. But when he came to treat of the original state of man, he resorted to none of these; rather he was content to go to the factual account in the Book of Genesis, examine it, analyst draw out its implications, fill in its blank spots with reasonable hypotheses to give us a full picture of man in his first home.

the Integrity of Nature

Before plunging into the story itself, St. Thomas lays down some fundamental principles that give his whole treatment a unity, which makes its rational character stand out strikingly. The first principle he insists on is that nothing that was natural to man was lost by man's sin. When we speak of fallen nature or of the wounds suffered by nature through the sin of Adam, we do not mean that human nature suffered a bad smash-up and was condemned to hobble through the ages a hopeless cripple. True enough, human nature was injured, but in the same sense that a man is injured when he is left naked by the roadside. Objectively, he is in the same condition as a man who has never had any clothes, although he certainly feels a great deal worse. So human nature now is in the same condition it would have been had Adam never received any extraordinary gifts; but it has been stripped of those gifts, which Adam did receive. This is not a gratuitous assumption. There are sins enough in the world to give us material for a thorough check on the fact that sin, in itself, does nothing to destroy the integrity of human nature.

Cause and Essential Notion of Superiority of the Original State

By way of a second principle, St. Thomas points out that the cause of the original perfection of man was his original justice. That is, man was created in sanctifying grace with his soul completely subject to God; this subjection extended right on down so that man's sensible appetite was subject to his reason, and the physical world was subject to man. These two, original justice and original perfection, went hand in hand in Adam. They were, however, quite capable of separation, for one was within the order of nature, although not of human nature, while the other was above all nature. So, in the Blessed Virgin Mary, there was the same supernatural perfection and perfect justice as in Adam, with the same complete subjection of her soul to God; but without the accompanying extraordinary gifts of Adam's original perfection.

the Individual in the Garden of Eden

The extraordinary gifts that went to make up the original perfection of Adam were not supernatural but preternatural; that is, they were not entirely above the powers of all created nature but they did not belong to man by the principles of his nature. The immortality given to Adam, for example, was quite different from the immortality to be enjoyed after the general resurrection; this latter is something intrinsic, flowing from the body's participation in the spiritual qualities of the soul. While that of Adam was an extrinsic thing, supplied to the first man from an outside source. His immunity from suffering, or impassibility, was not that incapacity for injury which the blessed in heaven will enjoy because of the penetration of the body by the spiritual qualities of the soul; it was rather an escape from harm through prudence and providential care, an extrinsic rather than an intrinsic gift. Man's dominion over the created world followed the lines of his dominion over himself, as his sense appetite obeyed his reason, so did the animals obey his command; but, as he had no power of command over his vegetative powers, so neither could he command the vegetative and physical powers of the world, but he could use their help without impediment.

In other words, while the individual man in the Garden of Eden had considerable advantages over the individual man or woman of today, he was not in any way essentially different.

His Intellectual Equipment and Progress, that of Adam

Adam started off the human race on its long life; as its proper starting point, he represented that race in its perfection. Just as he began with physical perfection, without the bother of being born, growing up, developing his muscles and so on, so he also started off with an intellectual perfection. In fact, this latter perfection was quite necessary in view of his position as head of the race and, consequently, as teacher of all who should come after him.

As the first human teacher, Adam brought an equipment to his task that has never been modeled since by any member of that noble profession. He did not see God directly, seeing the divine essence, for that is quite super natural and, once had, cannot be lost; that is, if Adam knew God in this way, he could not have sinned. Rather, he knew God as we know Him, but more perfectly. After all, he had none of the worries about bread and butter clothing and housing, not to speaks of the family's future that distracts the mind of man today. Moreover, the clarity of his insight was not the least bit clouded by passion. From the effects of God, particularly from the act of the human intellect and the nature of the human soul, Adam's mind rose quickly and easily to a knowledge of God. His knowledge of the angels was had in the same way. But it is important to notice that Adam knew these things and all others as we know them, through intelligible species.

As for his knowledge of other things, well, Adam had to teach and govern the human family and, obviously, he could not teach what he did not know. His natural knowledge extended to all those, things that men are intended to know, that is, all those things implicitly contained in the first natural principles of knowledge. St. Thomas inclined to the belief that this knowledge, an extraordinary gift not to the individual Adam but to Adam as head of the human race, was an explicit, complete and perfect knowledge. Not that Adam knew every singular thing, that this stone would fall into this river at such a time, and so on. Nor did he know future free things, like the thoughts of men. His supernatural knowledge (his knowledge of the mysteries of faith) was limited to those things necessary for the correct government and guidance of human life in that original state of existence.

We do not have a full grasp of the intellectual stature of Adam unless we look beyond the rich deposit of knowledge given him to the use he could make of it. Many a deeply learned man is the answer to a swindler's fondest hopes; many an expert in one line is a simpleton in another. We make our mistakes through haste, prejudice, passion, insufficient evidence, in a word, because our reason is not in complete command of the situation. Adam's reason was in absolute command, command of his own kingdom and of the world, he seas incapable of mistakes in judgment and reasoning. He was, then, a deeply learned, very wise and exceedingly clever man.

That of his Children

If we were born in paradise, eve would have had all the advantages of reason in full command; but we could not have looked forward to such equipment as was given to Adam as head of the race. There would still have been school days, and plenty of them. We would have acquired our knowledge through the senses, we would have had to discover things for ourselves, be taught by others and so, bit by bit, pick up full knowledge. It would have been a much easier job, it is true, than it is today, or nothing, either in ourselves or in the outside world, would have interfered with the process of learning, no day dreaming, no laziness, no heat, cold, hunger, thirst or stomach-ache.

His Will, Justice and Peace

For all his cleverness, Adam might have been a very unpleasant person, even a holy terror in the Garden of Eden, if he were not also a very holy man. As he was created, his will was good. Moreover, there would have been no point to God's delaying the gift of supernatural life, keeping Adam cooling his heels as he dawdled about the meaningless tasks of a purely natural life; Adam was created in sanctifying grace and, as he was destined to glory as the angels were, there was no reason why he should not have started off earning his reward immediately. In fact, this sanctifying grace and consequent total subjection to God were the foundation of the whole perfection of Adam's state.

With sanctifying grace, he had all the virtues, although, indeed, those that implied some imperfection never flowered into action until after he had sinned. How could he be penitent who had committed no sin; or what field was there for mercy in a place that knew no misery? The virtues that did bloom into acts produced acts that, considered in themselves, were much more worthy of merit than ours are; for the perfection of his nature removed all obstacles to grace and all possible imperfection in his works, whereas with us there is the constant pull of the sensible world, the difficulty of attention, the flabbiness of our will. Still, because our acts are sometimes so difficult to place, the very doing of them indicates a much greater willingness, even eagerness, than if they were produced with an ease that made close attention entirely unnecessary.

It might seem difficult to understand how a man as intellectually and morally perfect as Adam could have sinned if we did not know that the sublime perfection of the angels was not proof against sin, and if we could scrape up any sufficient cause of our own sins other than our own free will. The sin of Adam will be treated at length in the second volume of this work under its proper title of original sin. Here it is enough to notice that we are in no position to sneer at Adam. If we had been born in paradise we too would have been born in sanctifying grace, for that original justice of Adam's was a gift to the whole human species, it was not a personal thing for Adam alone; and grace was the foundation of original justice. We, too, would have had the fullness of virtue, as Adam had; and, like him, we could have lost it if we made up our minds to lose it. Heaven would not have been guaranteed, nor would hell have been an impossibility for us; such complete security comes only from the vision of God which is the end, not the beginning, of human life. Indeed, the odds are that some of us would have sinned even if Adam had never offended God; and our sin would have had the same tragic consequences for our children that Adam's had for his. We would have lost the extraordinary gifts for ourselves; of course we could not give to our children what we ourselves no longer possessed.

His Physical Nature, his Passions

During their short stay in the Garden, Adam and Eve got on very well together. Of course they had human passions; they were human, after all, and passion is an integral part of human nature. That they were buoyant with hope, alight with desire, urged on by love was entirely a matter of their own free will, for these passions were under the complete control of reason. It must be admitted, although, that only some of the passions of the milder or concupiscible appetite, love, desire, hope and joy, had any place in Eden; the other passions, anger, despair, hate, fear and all the rest, presuppose evil and there was no evil in paradise. The battle between flesh and spirit, then, did not get started until the reign of peace that was a part of paradise had come to an end. There were no gluttons or drunkards in Eden, no one cowered in fear or boiled with anger, men were not beside themselves with passion, their intellects clouded, their lives swayed by the sensitive appetite. This was not the way men were started off on their earthly life by God.

Conservation of his Life, Food, Drink and Vital Actions

It is not certain whether Adam and Eve used forks; but it is certain that they took time out, now and then, for a bite to eat and a sup to drink. They did not have glorified bodies; in all its essential actions, their human nature was not different from ours. The natural consumption of energy involved in physical activity, the burning up of cells and tissues, demanded constant repair work by way of food and digestion. Moreover in the children, if there had been any, the necessity of growth would no doubt have produced the same prodigious appetites we see in children today.

The first couple might have been vegetarians for the little while they enjoyed this original perfection; on the other hand, Eve might have been an excellent cook and exceedingly proud of her skill. There is no way of outlawing steak from the menu of the Garden, for the use of animals for his own welfare is only a vindication of man's dominion over the animal world, not a proof of savagery. It might be argued that Eve would not have been condemned to the drudgery of cooking; but that is to overlook the fact that cooking is drudgery only to a blundering cook and to draw a purely imaginative, and false, picture of Eve languidly posed against a fitting background for all the endless hours of the long days. No woman can keep that sort of thing up all the time.

Impassibility

The natural consumption of energy was taken care of by ordinary food; but the gradual running down of the physical organism of man's body is not prevented by food, even by very good food, as we well know. In heaven, this natural mortality is provided against intrinsically when the soul communicates to the body not only what powers it has as a substantial form but also some of the properties it possesses as a spiritual substance. In the Garden of Eden, this natural mortality was temporally staved off by a special food, a food with special properties given it by God, the fruit of the tree of life. The eating of this food from time to time was to have kept man in his prime until such time as God took him to his eternal happiness in heaven; for the gateway to heaven from paradise was not death.

Adam and Eve did not have tougher skins, arms and legs that could not be cut off or lungs that could not become infected. The thorns on the rose bushes of paradise were just as sharp as they are everywhere else; and man's skin was just as tender. Adam and Eve were incapable of injury and sickness; but not because their bodies were somehow different from ours. Rather, this impassibility was an extrinsic gift, one that did not flow from the nature of man but came to him from the outside. In plain terms, man escaped injury and sickness by his own prudence and by the action of divine providence, just as many of us do today; only in that original state, this was the ordinary, the universal thing. In other words, man then had sense enough to keep his fingers away from thorns, to avoid the injurious things; moreover, divine providence assured him of not being taken unawares. It can be safely said that many a stranger in New York keeps divine providence a great deal busier than ever Adam did. Adam, of course, had the distinct advantage of his command over the animals; under such circumstances, it would not be much of a trick for him to maintain his seat on a horse or to cow a savage dog.

Immortality

Though they would be very nice things to have at the present moment, the impassibility and immortality of Adam are not to be compared with that which awaits us in heaven. Neither of these gifts totally outstripped the powers of nature. They are not to be considered as supernatural but as preternatural, that is, in the same class with such a gift as might be given to a farmer enabling him to take off after a chicken hawk by merely flapping his arms. Flying, you see, is not above all the powers of nature; it just does not belong to the nature of man.

His Relation to their Individuals, Equality and Inequality

Let us suppose for a moment that Adam had not sinned and, after all these centuries, we, as tourists, were to take a trip to the flourishing cities of these perfect men, would it be as dull an affair as standing for hours to watch a mass production gadget roll out of a factory? No, indeed; on the contrary, we would be astonished by the variety in evidence there. One person would be brighter than another, one would have a stronger will, one would be bigger, another more beautiful, of different coloring, different individual attractions, more pleasing personality, and so on. Life would certainly not be dull; particularly as the minimum of any of these things would still represent the perfection that excluded all evil, all defect. There would be no beauty parlors or plastic surgeons. A girl would not have perfect eyes and a nose that had best be forgotten. No man would be so fat as to be too fat, or so thin as to look scragged. For perfection of types, it would be a kind of super-Hollywood, with none of the bitter tragedies of disappointment lurking under the surface. Human beings would, indeed, be unequal, different in sex, different its body, different in virtue, different in intellectual gifts. Yet no one would be deficient; all would enjoy that special equality that makes every man perfect and every man a sovereign being.

Domestic Life in the Garden of Eden, Difference of Sex

The diversity of sexes in man's original state is plain from the account in Genesis. That it should have been so is plain from human nature itself, with only one sex, the species would have been incomplete, indeed, the individuals would have been incomplete as the sexes complement and perfect one another. So Eve was given to Adam as a helper, particularly in the work of generation.

Generation of Children

There would, of course, have been generation in the Garden of Eden. Thomas thinks this is true beyond all doubt, although it might be argued that, since generation is for the maintenance of the species, it was unnecessary in this state where men did not die; or, at least, it would have been sufficient to restrict the generative act to Adam and Eve since they were to live forever. Such argumentation overlooks the fact that the individual man is much more important than as a mere means to the good of the species. Nature intends the enduring and each man and woman, by reason of an immortal soul, is a much more enduring thing than any species however complete. In other words, the purpose of generation is not only the duration of the species but the multiplication of individuals within that species. As for the notion of restricting generation to Adam and Eve, St. Thomas says that it is as much a part of man's nature to live the domestic life and have children as it is to eat; so much so, that in the Garden of Eden there would have been no sterility, no perpetual virginity, everyone would have married. To this end, it would have been necessary that there be as many boys born as girls; Thomas thought that the control of the sex of the child would have been in the power of the parents, thus eliminating months of maternal anxiety and guesswork. At any rate, there would have been children born in those days, and born in exactly the same way as they are today; for, from the very beginning marriage has been a holy thing. However, the physical difficulties and pain of childbirth would have been avoided by man's preternatural gift of dominating nature and of impassibility.

Condition and Care of Children

Certainly there would have been no danger of the domestic life of paradise going on the rocks through sheer ennui. Couples there would not be driven to non-existent divorce courts through the boredom of having nothing to do but look at each other. There would have been children, and that immediately accounts for many hours of work. For these children would be as children are today, helpless, in need of care, nourishment, education and training.

There would have been work outside the home, too, something to take care of Adam's spare moments. The biblical account tells us that our first parents were to guard and work the place of paradise. Work, it seems, is not something man was meant to escape; when he succeeds in dodging it, he is inevitably miserable. This work, whether of Adam or of Eve, would have been something like the born mother's joy in her children, the chef's artistic pride in a pot of stew, or the book-keeper's delight in his hobby of gardening. It would not have been laborious, distasteful and fatiguing; but rather a joyous source of pleasure. The reason for assigning work even in paradise seems quite obvious; man needs work for the fullest development of his powers and, indeed, for the full perfection of his knowledge, at least for the experimental discovery of just what man himself can do and what nature can accomplish under his guidance.

There would have been no private property in Eden; such a division of property is necessary for harmony, order and efficiency where there is the constant threat of dis order, confusion and laziness. There was no such a threat in man's original state. Man would not have been an anarchistic individualist; social and political life would have been real necessities for man even in his state of perfection. This is apparent from the very inequality of individuals in that original state, an inequality that even Rousseau found no way to deny. That one should excel another in knowledge and virtue would be unfitting such a state if that superiority did not itself contribute to the welfare of the inferiors. In fact, it is a general principle that such superiority imposes the obligation of direction and assistance to inferiors; virtue and knowledge, in other words, are not only assets, they are also liabilities, ordained to the welfare of others.

Social life in the Garden of Eden, Necessity of Political Organization

Moreover man is a social animal. His full perfection is not to be attained in a solitary state of life; true, he might succeed in existing alone, but he could not reach to the enjoyment of that full human life of which his nature makes him capable. In Eden, then, men would naturally have lived in society, that is, they would have united for a common end to be obtained by a common means; which, of course, implies common direction. Obviously ten firemen, following their individual ideas as to when and how to get to a fire and what to do about putting it out, would be a great curse to insurance companies; just so, a society without a governor would be no society at all but a cluster of individual outposts forbidding in their armament.

Slavery

The political society of Eden would always be the type that dominates a man or directs him to his own and the common good. The domination of one man over another, which we know as slavery, by which one man uses another exclusively for the proper ends of the first did not exist in paradise; indeed, such domination could not exist until the bond that kept man subject to God had been broken.

Dominion over the Physical World

Man's social, domestic and individual life was made much easier and more pleasant by the dominion he exercised over the physical universe, a dominion that was modeled on his own command of himself. He could call a tiger (if he wanted a tiger) and get immediate obedience, just as he could command his own animal nature and get immediate and complete results. But he had no such command over the plant and inanimate world. He could call a carrot (if he wanted a carrot) until he was hoarse; he would have to go to the carrot, it would not come to him. He dominated this part of the world as he did his own physical nature, using it without impediment, joyously and freely. He could not order a plant about, but he could escape the embarrassing labor of biting on hard celery in a quiet dining room.

Physical Surroundings of the First Man - the Situation of Paradise

Where was the Garden of Eden? St. Thomas, judging from the rivers that sprang from it according to the biblical account, thought it was somewhere in the East. Wherever it was, Thomas thought it had the physical characteristics of the more pleasant part of Italy on a perfect day. He did not exactly say this; but he did draw the line at snow and ice, holding out for an equable climate, being particularly insistent of the advantages of a warm sun. It was not to be too hot nor too cold, but in between with a pleasant variety that would not call the inhabitants' attention to their lack of clothes.

Its Inhabitants

Speaking of inhabitants, it may be worth noting that Adam was an immigrant to the Garden of Eden while Eve was a native; Adam, you remember, was made outside the Garden and brought in by God himself, while Eve was made on the spot, a fact that may or may not be significant. There were to be no dogs allowed in Eden, for this was an exclusively human habitation. The only animals there, normally, came at the express command of the human inhabitants. There a man could take a siesta and not wake up to find the cat asleep on his stomach or a visiting lioness surveying his tousled condition with a critical eye. However, the life there was by no means to be a continual siesta. There was to be work, man's work and woman's work. Plenty of it; a work that was to go on, joyously, until the "Master of all good workmen" would put an end to the labor, easily slipping man into his eternal home where he could see for the very first time what heights happiness could reach.

Conclusion, Difference from the Account of Genesis
In the Pagan Tradition

Many of the details of this chapter are supplied by St. Thomas, arguing sometimes strictly, sometimes only plausibly, to complete the full picture of man's original state. Putting aside those details and concentrating on the bare skeleton of the account in Genesis, it should be evident that this story is not to be shrugged off as just another myth, even although we do not take into account the infallible authority of the God of truth, Who inspired it. Unlike the pagan tradition, this is not the kind of story men think up about themselves, or even about their relatives. The pagans of Greece and Rome made the original state of man one of long duration, with long accounts of the idyllic life during all those years of perfection; its loss was attributed, not to the fault of men, but to the overthrow of a god. Genesis insists that this say of men in the earthly paradise was hardly a moment in the long life of the first couple, stating baldly the hard bet that was most unflattering; for the brevity of that stay was immediately due to the meddling of men themselves. The biblical account tells what glorious chances man had, and of how he immediately muffed them. Having muffed them, man was left, as he would have been in a state of pure nature; the trials, labor and difficulties of existence today do not offer material for self-pity or excuses on grounds of disability, man has his full equipment for life.

In Renaissance Philosophies
In Modern Materialistic Philosophies

The renaissance philosophers, in defiance of the facts, denied man's social nature, making of him a beast of prey or a paragon of virtue. Genesis makes no such mistake about our nature; God does not make mistakes. Nor, for that matter, can man fool himself about his very nature, although he may tell himself fables about himself by way of escape from reality. The materialistic philosophy that has such a hold on the world today specializes in denial of facts; it makes man merely an animal, thoroughly un-moral; it denies the undeniable facts of his immaterial, spiritual soul and even the more inescapable fact of his origin from a first absolutely perfect first cause. This version of man's nature, like all the others, cannot afford to sneer at the account of Genesis. An air of superiority cannot gloss over the stubborn facts of God's causality and man's nature as we undoubtedly have it today.

the Significance of these Differences,
For an Estimation of the Nature of Man

Indeed, it is only by facing these facts that we get a real appreciation of man's nature. Only thus can we see him as spiritual and physical, as enjoying a freedom that even God must respect, a freedom that can hurl him ashamed from the portals of an earthly paradise or rush him triumphant into an eternal one with God. Only by facing the facts can we see man as he is, a creature made for work, for love, for marriage and a family; made to learn, to perfect his virtue, to approach to God and ultimately to rest with Him. Moreover, only in appreciating these things can we be fair to ourselves.

For an Appreciation of the Work of God

Honesty before the facts enables us to appreciate the work of God, seeing Him remedying the defects that naturally follow from the very ingredients of human nature, even although such correction demanded the planning of extraordinary gifts by the all-wise architect of the universe. In the light of the facts we can see that the plans were spoiled, not by the architect, not by the builder, but by man himself.

For a Determination of Individual Possibilities and Goals

The present state of man is man's work, not God's; even that initial tragedy was made a thing of hope and inspiration by the Son of God's redemption of those mistakes of men which we call sins. Because of the insistent part God has played in the destiny of that nature of ours, we can hope, labor, pray, love and live life to the full; for there is a paradise to which we can attain that alone fulfills the longing of our nature, that alone gives human life meaning and purpose. The story of man's beginnings is a sad account of what might have been; but it is also a vague hint of the glories that yet can be.

📖 CHAPTER XVII 📖

– GOVERNMENT OF THE PHYSICAL WORLD
(Q. 103-105)

1. Nature and purpose of government,

(a) Its essential postulate.

(b) Its proper act.

(c) Its condition.

2. A modern paradox,

(a) Championship of this conception of government.

(b) Recognition of proper act of government in the universe.

(c) Denial of government in the universe.

3. Necessity of government in the world,

(a) Principles of solution.

(b) The proofs.

4. Details of the government of the world,

(a) The governor of the universe.

(b) The subjects of government.

(b) The nature of government of the universe.

(1) Its immediacy.

(2) Its universality.

(3) Its efficacy.

5. Effects of the government of the world,

    (a) Conservation.

    (b) Movement of creature,

        (1) Divine power and the effects of created causes.

        (2) Fact of divine operation in every created agent,

        (a) Necessity of this in general.

        (b) Necessity in particular – relative to human will.

        (c) Divine power and miracles.

6. Distinction of eternal law providence and divine government.

Conclusion,

1.Impossibility of the denial of divine government in the universe

    (a) On modern grounds.

    (b) From its consequences.

2. The truth of divine government.

3. Completion of the picture of God.

⬓ CHAPTER XVII ⬓
GOVERNMENT OF THE PHYSICAL WORLD
(Q. 94-103)

Nature and Purpose of Government

As far as equipment goes anarchy is a condition of affairs that is remarkably easy to set up. All it requires is a people content to live aimlessly, destructively and with what protection an individual can give himself. On the contrary, politically organized social life involves decided difficulties in its establishment and maintenance; for this men must live purposefully, constructively and under a common protective direction. In this matter, our times have not veered to the easy side; anarchy has no general appeal to the twentieth century. Government, on the other hand, may well become the idol before which all men bow. In its roots, the word government implies direction, piloting; we have held fast to that notion of pointing men at some goal, although we have at times gone too far in the manner used to achieve this pointing, even so far as to think it was permissible for a government to take all its citizens by the scruff of the neck to direct their steps.

Its Essential Postulate

At any rate, it is clear to our minds today that government implies something to be governed, something to be directed; so that, broadly, we mean by government the rule or direction of a community. The essential postulate of government, then, is a community and a community comes into existence precisely because individuals concur in a common end, in contrast to the exclusive pursuit of individual ends in anarchy. Anarchy means lawlessness, while government means law; the defect or collapse of law is the collapse of government, for law is government's proper act of direction. Anarchy needs no executive or judicial elements for, by nature implying indirection, it has no law to execute, no norm by which to judge; the equivalent of anarchy can be quickly achieved in any government by the simple oversight of the fundamental character of the legislature and the attempt to supplant it by executive or judicial action. For the executive and judicial functions are consequent to law which is the absolutely fundamental and proper act of government.

The primary paralysis, followed by discord and ultimately by open riot, that would result if a dozen onlookers of a chess game were privileged to make all moves along with the players is a faint suggestion of what would be the condition of society if there were no unified direction, no unity in legislation. If the hypothesis be extended a little further to the point where these onlookers and players huddle around a non-existent game, we have some idea of the impossibility of unified government and law without the fundamental unity of a common end among the citizens; for without that unity of end, which is the source of the common life, the root of the community, the brick and mortar that holds society together, there would be no game of politics to be played.

Its Proper Act

With this conception of government our time, and particularly our country, has no quarrel whatsoever. Perhaps this age will be outstanding in history for its universal acceptance of these fundamental notions of government; certainly never before in the history of the world has there been such a universal championship of government's proper act of law. As evidence of this we have the © faith in the power of law which has led us into a kind of mass production of law for a variety of purposes that staggers the mind. We have made use of law for the correction of every kind of evil, economic, financial, physical, moral and social, and this in such meticulous detail as to make ourselves somewhat ridiculous. We do, indeed, believe in law and the power of law. As a last, if perverted, tribute to this championship of government we have the world wide drift to the absolute in the state, even among nations who fight absolutism.

Its Condition

Our modern almost worshipful attitude towards science is a recognition of the proper act of government in the physical universe and on a worldwide scale. Surely, scientific procedure and scientific knowledge has never been held in higher esteem; we are even willing to go to the length of denying validity to any other procedure or certitude to any other knowledge, reducing all intellectual efforts to the level of science. Yet the goal of science is nothing more than the discovery of law; it seeks to uncover a common way of acting, a community of activity and thus a common end. To put it briefly, science is really a demand, with full assurance, of an order in nature. The highest moments of scientific adventure are those marked by the discoveries of just such laws. Science does not attempt to reach conclusions or offer proofs; its interest is in the universal or common law which tells the story of how things act, that is, it is concerned with a fuller knowledge of the laws of nature.

a Modern Paradox, Championship of this Conception of Government

In ordinary times we would say that law, order, a common way of acting, a common end all bespeak a community and a government of that community But these are no ordinary times. The educated man of today, holding fast to modern tenets, is in the anomalous position of championing cosmic anarchy yet of giving full confidence to a scientific search for the laws that rule that anarchy. He must insist, in an age that puts complete faith in the multiplication of laws and the power of government, that the universe must be lawless, without government since it is without a governor. The world-wide drift to the absolute in political power and state direction has for its basis a philosophy that denies direction to the world, and which upholds the attainment of world progress without direction By some mad paradox, we trace political and social ills to poor direction, poor government; while we trace perfection in the universe to a complete lack of direction, a complete absence of government.

Recognition of Proper act of Government in the Universe

This is hardly an intelligent position. Yet, then again, our age has had many a bitter quarrel with intelligence and the hard feeling has gone so far that we have decided to disown intelligence or even to prove that there is no such thing; perhaps it is expecting too much to look for intelligence in so bitter an enemy's camp. This modern absurdity in the face of the order of the world can trace its origins back to that first attack on direction, that first positing of the principles of anarchy in religious circles that has come to be known as the Reformation. If religion could get along nicely without direction, there is after all, no reason for other things to put up with the meddlings of government. What reformation was in religion was molded into philosophy, running the whole gamut from humble doubts to bold denials and reaching its smashing climax in our own days when the existence of a faculty capable of valid universal knowledge is hardly taken seriously.

Denial of Government in the Universe

When the philosophers had finished cutting their own throats and had come to the harmonious conclusion that they could not get anywhere since there was no intellect with which to philosophize, science was ready to step into the breach with definite indications that it, at least, could get somewhere; philosophers immediately rustled to stake out claims in the territory of science; somehow they made science the foundation of philosophy, forgetting that science itself had no foundation except on the condition that the modeled philosophers were wrong in the first place in rejecting the intellectual foundations of philosophy.

The confusion has become so much a part of modern life that today men can deny world government and uphold world law. In fact, we have become so oblivious of the absurdity of this position that we begin to feel a little superior about it, smiling pityingly on those who assert that if government is necessary for order and progress in the affairs of politics, anarchy is not the answer to order, law and progress in the universe. How droll!

Necessity of Government in the World

It may mean little to the modern that the truth of divine government of the universe is explicitly stated in Scripture and that Christ Himself hammered that truth home; but at least, in the name of rationality, the overwhelming evidence should not be passed over in silence. And the evidence is overwhelming. We saw something of it in the beginning of this book in proving the existence of God. There it was brought out that the fact of irrational creation constantly acting for its own good demands the existence of a directing intelligence; in other words, that the order in the universe demands a supreme governor.

In treating of divine Providence, the three alleged explanations of order in the universe, chance, necessity, some cause within the universe, were examined in detail. Each of the three were rejected, chance because it was not an explanation of order but a statement of the existence of an order, which in a chance case, had been clashed with; necessity because it demanded as much explanation as the order it was advanced to explain; while the fact that the universal order included everything in the universe made it impossible for any natural cause, itself a subject of that order, to explain the existence of the laws to which it bowed. It was in that same chapter on providence that it became evident that the internal finality of things, the order of the ear to sound, of the eye to sight, of the individual to the species and so on was, too, a created thing demanding further relation to the things around it. In other words, no one creature was an isolated being from this point of views but a part of a universal plan that existed in the mind of the intelligent first cause.

This truth of divine government has been like a haunting melody, which a man cannot drive from his mind. It came up again in the examination of creation and evolution when it was brought out that God, as a perfect agent,

310

acted quite differently than do His creatures. We must act to acquire some missing perfection, while God can only act to share His goodness since He has all goodness from eternity; the only possible end He could have, then, in creating must have been Himself, the sharing of His divine goodness, that is, the only goal to which the world could be directed was God Himself. Obviously such a task of direction demanded a supreme governor, a governor commensurate to the end for all the laws laid down would have to have that end in view.

In this chapter the melody is heard again. It cannot be silenced. Nor is this surprising. The fact of order and government in the world is so fundamental that it must arise again and again in any treatment of God or of the world. In this chapter we shall really get down to bedrock, digging deep enough to uncover the relation of the fact of world government to the very first principles of thought and being. Of course the job demands overalls, dynamite, hard labor and plenty of perspiration; but it is a job worth doing.

Principles of the Solution

To allay that insidious form of fear which bears the euphemistic name of laziness, it might be well to give this task an air of ease by stating at once that the principles, upon which the proof of the government of the world rests, can be reduced to just two, namely, the principles of sufficient reason and of finality. Both of these are immediately reducible to the first and absolutely fundamental principles of identity and contradiction. Without these latter principles there could be no thought and, indeed, no being.

Taken in the concrete, the principle of sufficient reason is made perfectly clear by the fact that dogs bark and chicken bones are very bad for puppies although bread and milk is an entirely harmless diet for either mongrels or thoroughbreds. In its theoretical form the principle reads like this, "everything that is has a sufficient reason for itself and for the harmony of other things with it, either from its very essence or from something else." Evidently those things that flow from the very nature of a dog, from the fact that it is a dog, have their sufficient reason in the nature of the dog. In this sense, the principle of sufficient reason is no more than an insistence on the principle of identity, this dog is a dog, this nature is itself, so of course a bark is to be expected from it. The things that do not come from nature itself but from outside cannot have their sufficient reason in the nature. The dog does, in fact, die; clearly, then, its existence did not come from canine nature itself. What does not come from the nature must come from somewhere else, that is, from outside the nature; and to say that the sufficient reason of anything is from outside the nature is no more than asserting the principle of contradiction. In other words, we insist that this dog is not something other than a dog, it is not a dog and a god at the same time, it cannot, at the same time, be a contingent being and a necessary being.

The principle of finality, which has the inestimable merit of brevity although it gives no rest to the world, is, "every agent acts for an end." A penetrating mind is not necessary to see that this principle is immediately reducible to the principle of sufficient reason; it is, really, no more than a statement of the fact that there is a reason for every action. Every nature has a determined, or specific, effect; thus a dog barks, a man laughs or thinks. There is then a sufficient reason for this constant way of acting, this specific determination whether that reason be from the nature itself or from some one else who communicates it to this nature; if there is not this sufficient reason, then do not be surprised if a dog laughs in your face or your model sits back on his haunches and bays at a romantically full moon. A denial of the principle of finality, you see, immediately involves a denial of the principle of contradiction; this lad may be a man and, at the same time, a dog. The effect of barking could exist with no determination or tendency in the cause of all, it could just pop out of a man's throat for no reason whatever and might change to the chirp of a canary bird just as it passed the soft palate. The same mad story would hold good for the act of which this is an effect, for the faculty which produced this act, and, ultimately, for the nature in which this faculty resides. All would lack determination, yet have it; be what they are and be something different; Alice would have a new wonderland.

In other words, an efficient cause is never a sufficient explanation for an action. The fact that a man throws a brick is by no means the whole story; when the police catch him they will be crude enough to ask a few questions, especially as to why he threw the brick. The fact that a lecturer does deliver a lecture is not a sufficient explanation of his talk; it might, in fact, be difficult at times to come at a sufficient explanation. If one act is placed rather than another (as happens wherever there is such order as we find in the world) then there must be a determination, a reason, an end for that action.

The Proofs

With these fundamental principles clearly in mind, we can advance to an investigation, let us say, of a very young cabbage plant that has just been set out. It spends no time trying to find itself, reading up on vocational guidance or waiting for the mood to strike it; without going off in a corner to sob in self pity, with no search for a soul mate, it promptly drives its roots down for moisture while it reaches for the light and warmth of the sun. Moreover, all the thousands of cabbages set out each year will do exactly the same thing. Here, certainly, we have un intelligent beings acting in a most intelligent way, with constant, orderly effort to attain their greatest perfection and the perfection of their species. Clearly that order comes from the very nature of cabbages; but the determination of the nature does not explain itself, for the nature did not give birth to the determination, it did not exist before the determination. The orderliness of this procedure comes from some one outside that nature. When it is remembered that not only cabbages but all of irrational creation portrays this same orderly action, we have evidence of the existence of an intelligence that guides the whole of that irrational creation.

It may be objected that this does not argue to a world order, but merely to an order within each species; just as an orderly, affectionate family does not necessarily argue to a well-governed state, or even to a state that has a moderately decent government. This is the old objection that internal finality does not argue to external finality, the modern illusion that scientific laws governing particular natures can be admitted while it is denied that nature as a whole is going anywhere. Granted that we cannot know the whole of the divine plans with our finite minds, it is impossible to grant order within the species and then deny order to the universe.

Details of the Government of the World
the Governor of the Universe

In the first place, no creature, no species, is isolated. They bump, clash, embrace, nourish and are nourished, they have relations to one another, which is to say there is an order between them, an order in the whole. This very order of one thing to another is a created thing; it does not exist of itself, does not explain itself, has not sufficient reason for itself within itself. It must, therefore, have that sufficient reason from outside, it must have a final cause outside itself, a goal that is not itself. In plain language, the governor and final end of the universe is something that escapes the universe itself that is without its limits; that something is God. For, as we have already seen, everything created, everything that has not sufficient reason of itself within itself, falls within the natural or created order; only God. Who is supremely self-sufficient, is outside that order.

The same point might be argued from a different angle by pointing out that the end or goal corresponds to the beginning or the efficient cause. Since God is the cause of the world, He is its final end and the sole possible director or governor of the world to that final end. More simply, every agent acts for an end; the very first, or utterly independent, agent upon whom everything else depends must act for Himself.

Many men have been deceived into thinking the universe is without government because they have overlooked the striking difference between the government of the world and human government or human direction in any form. Just as we cannot pour knowledge into another's head, so neither can we put a principle of action into any other being; we may train a dog to bark at intruders but we cannot claim to have instilled the bark into the dog. No matter how benign our direction or government may be, it is always a kind of violence, at least in the sense that it is always from the outside; it is never a match for that easy, flowing direction that comes from nature itself. The direction or government of God, however, is not violent even in this sense; it does not come from the outside because His causality, unlike ours, reaches to the depths of being. The particular nature itself is such because of the divine plans and the divine execution of those plans; He does put the bark into the dog. That His direction is followed easily, naturally, from the very principles of nature does not prove there is no government of nature; rather, it is a constant natural parade of the government of God.

The Subjects of Government

As for subjects, well, no census taking is necessary. It is as impossible to find a creature not subject to that government as it is to find a creature that is utterly sufficient to itself. God is the only self-sufficient being; from Him all depend and to Him all go as to their end. He alone is the governor of the universe; everything in that universe stands in need of His direction to Himself, that is, everything depends upon Him for its nature and for its existence. We shall see this dependence again and more fully in a few moments. Now it is sufficient to point to the universal application of natural laws as an indication of the universality of the government of God. Those laws are the proper act of His government, directing all creatures to the common end of the community, which is the universe.

Its Immediacy

This, of course, does not mean that if a man looks up quickly when he hears a landslide bearing down on him that he can see God slowly straightening up from the effort of putting His shoulder to the mountain. God does not have to move everything that moves in the world by a personally immediate movement any more than the President of the United States has personally to enforce every Federal law. As a matter of fact, the extreme perfection of the government of God is more manifest in His sharing of causality with His creatures. The dictator's technique, for all its appearance of strength, is a confession of weakness; such a ruler must destroy liberty, he must execute rivals and concentrate all power in his own hands for he is not strong enough to exist otherwise.

Its Universality

Nor is there any danger of some subordinate cause in this divine government exceeding orders and starting a reign of tyranny unknown to the central government. We have already seen, in treating of the knowledge of God and His providence, that no smallest detail escapes Him, indeed, it is because every detail exists in the mind of God that its existence is possible, for everything in the universe is but a reproduction of the model which is the divine ideas. A divine newspaper is an unthinkable thing; not that there need be anything wrong with newspapers, but there is simply nothing going on in the world that is news to God. Even divine patience could not tolerate a newspaper under such circumstances. Neither is there anything happening, in the universe to wreck His carefully laid plans. There is no danger of a coup d'état overthrowing the government of God, for everything in the universe is so utterly dependent upon Him. There is no cause that can impede His action, because there is no cause independent of Him.

Its Efficacy

Even the case of rebellion on the part of man does not escape the order of divine governments For, while the sinner throws himself outside the divine order to the end of the universe, he hurls himself into the divine order of justice which is no less a part of the plan of the universe. The rebellion of sin itself cannot he complete; for the physical act of sin, since it has real existence, must be traced to the first cause of all reality. It is only the missing palate the defect of order, the hole in the human act, that is the exclusive property of the human will.

Effects of the Government of the World - Conservation

Coming down to particulars, two effects of this divine government that must be stressed are the conservation of things in existence and the part God plays in the movement of creatures. That the hand of God is necessary for the support of things in existence is a truth of faith abundantly clear from the Scriptures and defined again and again by the Church. Its truth is clear by the power of reason alone; we need only to grasp the meaning of conservation to see its necessity. Taking the word in its most obvious sense, that of continuation of existence, these is no difficulty in seeing that a being is independent of conservation by another insofar as it is independent of an other for its existence. That means that everything in the universe is continued in existence by God.

Understand, this is not a matter of warding off a blow, or snatching a child from under the wheels of an automobile. There are things in this world that do not need touch conservation as this; it is not necessary, for instance, to put a soul in an oxygen tent nor to protect an angel from bombs. This is a question of moment-to-moment supply of existence somewhat like the question of moment-to-moment supply of air to a man to sustain his life. As we have seen in an earlier chapter, existence is one of those perfections that are not an integral part of nature, that in themselves have no limitation and that are, consequently, participated, borrowed, from the one source where they are had in their infinite fullness.

Perhaps it could be put more simply by saying that conservation is a continuation of the act of creation which first supplied existence; only that being is independent of all conservation which is independent of creation, which has the fullness of existence by its very nature, not animal existence, not human existence, not angelic existence, but existence without qualification. In other words, only a completely self-sufficient being is independent of conservation by others, that is, God Himself. Everything else that is continues to exist only because God immediately furnishes its existence.

To ask if God could annihilate a creature is merely to ask if God could cut off the supply of existence of any creature. The answer is obvious. The production of every created thing was a free act on the part of God; of course the continuation of that act of creation is a free act on His part. Annihilation would not demand any special activity on God's part but merely the cessation of Hid creative activity. In other words, if God were suddenly to become the static thing modern philosophers are willing to tolerate as divinity, the universe would plunge into nothingness.

It is quite another question to ask whether God will annihilate any creature, or all of the universe. We have it on faith that God will not annihilate human souls or the angels. But, putting aside the field glass of faith and squinting at the question with the naked eye of reason we can get a reasonable view of the probable durability of the physical universe. God, in His dealings with the universe, has not, after all, so much choice; He must act either naturally or supernaturally, that is, He must operate either within the laws of that universe as laid down by Himself or outside those laws. Within the laws, or naturally, God will certainly not annihilate spiritual substances, such as souls and angels, for the very good reason that there is absolutely no natural way in which they can be destroyed, there is no natural force capable of their destruction. As for material things, well, on purely natural grounds it would seem that matter itself remains enduringly as the subject of all change; it is the subject of corruption rather than the object of corruption. But, then, that means little more than maintaining that, on natural grounds, material things would always remain at least potentialities.

Supernaturally, or by operation outside the natural laws, the answer is quite easy. God works miracles to manifest His grace; and annihilation does not manifest grace, in fact, it does not manifest anything, for in itself it is a denial so absolute as to leave not even an echo by which it might be located. It is much more a part of divine power and goodness to preserve or conserve things than to annihilate them by utterly pointless miracles.

The effect of conservation is fairly easy material of investigation, perhaps because it is so far above us; at least it is not complicated by a creature's action, for existence is the proper effect of God. The effect of God's government, which is His movement of creatures is something else again; for here the creature enters intimately into everything but the miracles of God.

Movement of Creatures, Divine power and the Effects of Created Causes

God can, evidently, produce any effect that a created cause can, just as a bishop can produce any of the effects produced by powers he has delegated to a priest. For the causality of every created cause has its roots deep in God; it is a delegation, a participation, a sharing in the divine power. In particular, God can, without a secondary cause, move matter to form, can move bodies, the human intellect and the human will. What was said above about the government of God must be kept well in mind here, namely, that the movement of God in nature does none of the violence to nature that human movement does. Consequently, God cannot force the human will for that is to do violence to it; rather, He moves it freely, according to its nature. We shall see more of this in just a moment.

First we must touch on a type of divine movement that is taken up explicitly in the opening chapters of the second volume of this work. This is movement only in the sense of attraction; it is not the effect of a push or a command but the result of an allure, an enticement, the eager rush inspired by the perfection of goodness. The attraction of everything desirable in this world is only a traveler's tale of the wonders of the Supreme Good, leaving unsaid the ineffable delights that alone will satisfy the human will's thirst for the universal good.

So much for the possibility of the action of God in the universe. The actual fact of His movement is the foundation for the first two proofs already given for the existence of God. In its briefest form, the reason for the fact of divine movement amounts to this, the active principles of the created world – the forms of things not only depend on the first cause for their intrinsic natural qualities, their actual existence and conservation in existence, they also depend upon God for their application to action, for that transition from mere potentiality of movement to actual movement. After all, it is not only the nature, the existence and the conservation that are real; the movement to action and the action itself are also real and so must be traced to the source of all reality.

Fact of divine operation in every created agent

This is not to make God the only cause and all created causes mere figureheads, instruments of divine causality; when a burglar strikes his victim over the head, we are quite right in blaming the burglar. Confusion in this matter usually comes from picturing God and the created cause as two horses tugging a heavy load up the steep hill of actions. God and the created cause do not work side by side in tile same order; one is the first cause, the other the second cause, that is, one works through the other. Perhaps this will be more easily understood if we remember that the action of God falls on the created cause rather than on the effect of that cause; the proper effect of God is to move the secondary cause to its actual causing, to change it from a potential to an actual cause then to continue its conservative action of the causality of that created cause.

Necessity of this in general

This divine movement of secondary causes is absolutely universal; which is to say no more than that no reality escapes dependence on the first reality. In things, which cannot be moved necessarily by any created causes, such for example, as the human will, this divine movement must be immediate. Something of this has already been seen above where it was pointed out that divine movement not only does not destroy freedom but is the only possible source of it. Certainly, the will must be moved from its potential willing to actual willing if it is ever to make a choice, if it is moved by any set of circumstances, it is not free in the face of those circumstances; if it moves itself, then it is already determined, that is, it is not possessed of that indetermination necessary for freedom. It must be moved but in a way consonant with its freedom; only God can move the will freely.

Necessity in particular , relative to human will

This sounds very obscure; and it should, for it is a mystery, a great mystery. The apparent contradiction involved in it is not, however, difficult to resolve. The resolution is merely a matter of our keeping in mind that nothing real exists without the sustaining hand of God. The will is a reality that must have its sufficient reason in the first cause; the act of the will is also real and must also be reduced to that same source of reality; but the very mode of the act of the will, its freedom, is, too, definitely within the order of the real and, consequently, it is not to be absolved from dependence on God. The same note can be produced by a bird and by an opera singer; the freedom of the latter needs no less explanation than the necessity of the former. The only adequate explanation is God. How can God move the will freely? To understand this it would be necessary to comprehend the divine movement. Remembering that the divine movement is the same as the divine essence, it is clear that such a comprehension of the infinite is beyond the powers of a finite mind. There precisely, in the infinity of the divine movement, lies the mystery of human freedom; and a very good place for it, too.

Divine power and miracles

Over and above the action of God in the physical universe establishing its laws, conserving and fulfilling them, there is another type of action on the part of the divine governor, which we have come to call miraculous action. That there is such action, surpassing the established order of nature, can be immediately seen from the numerous accounts of miracles in Scripture, the truth has been solemnly defined by the Church, as, for example, in the Vatican Council, "If anyone says that miracles cannot be performed and therefore the Scriptural accounts of miracles must be relegated to the class of myths and fables, or that miracles cannot be certainly known or the divine origin of the Christian religion be proved by them, let him be anathema."

As a matter of fact, the possibility of miracles should be beyond dispute from the very nature of the government of the world. God did not tie His own hands by establishing the natural order; and a miracle is nothing more than

God's action outside of the natural order, which was freely instituted by Him and entirely subject to Him. Not that God can surprise Himself by a wondrous action exceeding the whole order of nature; we have no business picturing Him as standing back amazed and a little chagrined that He had not thought of such a thing earlier. The eternal knowledge of God includes everything that will ever happen be it natural or miraculous.

From the point of view of the created causes, a miracle is a work of wonder; but seen objectively, it is merely a manifestation of the evident truth that the establishment of the natural order did not exhaust or limit the power of God. That order is dependent on God, not God on the order. The natural order and miraculous works do not stand glaring at each other like irreconcilable enemies. A miracle is not a violation of nature nor a destruction of natural laws; such a thing is an impossibility involving the contradiction of God acting against Himself. The nature of things is left intact by a miracle, it does no injury to natural laws; but through a miracle, a power transcending all the limits of nature makes itself known.

Distinction of eternal law, providence and divine government

For the clarity of the record, it may be worthwhile, in closing this chapter, to note in passing the interrelation of eternal law, providence and the government of the world. In the second volume of this work the question of eternal law must be gone into thoroughly. Here it is sufficient to point out that eternal law is the first principle from which providence and divine government of the world flow as conclusions. Providence is the plan of God covering every detail of the universe; while the government of the world is no more than the execution of the divine plan. Eternal law and providence are, obviously, in the mind of God, and from all eternity; the government of the world is, of course, in the universe itself, it began with that universe, for its proper work is to direct that universe to its final end, God.

Conclusion, Impossibility of the denial of divine government in the universe, on modern grounds

From all this, it is evident that the modern denial of government in the world is nothing less than a denial of any end, goal or purpose for the universe; many a philosopher today will explicitly insist on such a denial. Yet modern philosophy's own efforts seem to be directed desperately at a foundation for unity in the world, efforts that range from pantheism through the organismic philosophies to rank materialism. That is, they agree that the universe is a unity, has some common bond, yet they deny the common bond that ties that universe together, the bond that ties every community together, the bond of a common end. The reduction of the world to matter does not give us unity but disparity; nor is a common origin sufficient to explain the harmonious interaction of the universe. Certainly, none of the modern theories explain the determined mode of action that rules the universe. This is law and law is the act of government; it is absurd to proclaim the unity of the world, to extol the discovery of its laws, to insist upon the preeminence of science, and, at the same time, to deny government. Government without a common end is a contradiction in terms; if the cosmos is an anarchy with no discoverable laws, then government can be called into question, but not otherwise.

From its Consequences

If government be denied by the denial of a common end for the universe, then there is no basis for science or philosophy; there is no reason for the way things happen, for reason, the why of things, is itself a statement of end, of order, of government. Why seek laws if there is no reason for laws and no source of them? Why seek the ultimate causes of things if there is no reason for any cause? The whole intellectual game men have been playing for centuries is the futile amusement of a child. On this basis, attempts at reasonable human life and human activity are an absurdity that approaches the proportions of a cosmic joke. Can there be a determined, an ordered, way of living and acting which we call human when there is no goal, no end to such a life, to such activity? Why do this rather than that, why live up to this or that standard, why differentiate between man and a clod of earth unless there be reason for that difference, unless there be determination, order, government?

The denial of the government and finality of the world sounds daring in a classroom or in a book that not too many people will read. But no one has dared to take it out of that academic atmosphere and put it to work in its destructive entirety in the practical details of everyday life except such thoroughly un-academic people as gangsters and military tyrants. Here and there a naively logical student makes a public expression of what he has been so solemnly taught, or actually puts it into practice in a concrete act, and he is crushed under a wave of horror and condemnation coming even from the very institution in which the madness was taught. This madness simply will not, cannot work in everyday life; in fact, it is the destruction of the foundation of all activity. It reduces life to an utterly insane dashing about in a circle whose only termination can be exhaustion.

The Truth of Divine Government

The truth of the divine government of the universe answers all the yearnings, which from the beginning of time have sprung from the depths of the human heart, the yearnings for unity, for activity for progress, for accomplishment, for hope, for peace, for perfection, for God. This truth gives the only solid ground for the science we prize so highly today, for philosophy, for ordinary human life. Its denial is a violation of reason, of humanity, which brings crashing to earth everything that humanity prizes. It cannot for an instant he separated from the details of everyday life without immediately ushering in confusion, anarchy, stagnation and ultimately despair. To put it briefly, this truth, as is the way of truth, meets the facts; the facts of the world and of life in the world.

Completion of the Picture of God

The truth of divine government completes the picture vaguely outlined by the divine architect in the perfections of the universe. Those shadowy images, those fragile mirrorings of divine perfection, attain a clarity that alone makes them intelligible when we see their relation to the original, when we see which way they point, to what direction they go. It is from this divine harmony of the community which is the universe and its steady progress to its final end that we see God, not as the dull, static being modern philosophers frigidly embrace, but as the living intelligence Whose intense activity penetrates to the last moment of time and to the utmost depths of nature. He is not a cold, uninterested, tyrannical ruler of a world, which He has forgotten, but the intimate director of the smallest actions of the world and of men. He is not the infinitely distant and humanly meaningless god that makes the modern shudder and hug himself the tighter, He is the immediately present first cause and prime mover to Whom our destiny will link us in a personal unity for an eternity. He is the governor of the world.

◫ CHAPTER XVIII ◫

GOVERNMENT OF THE SPIRITUAL WORLD
(Q. 106-109)

1.Communication as an essential of social life.

   (a) From the nature of government.

   (b) From difference of government.

2. Communication among the angels,

   (a) Its reasonableness.

   (b) Its double nature, enlightenment and speech.

3. Illumination and enlightenment in the angelic world,

   (a) Its nature.

   (b) Its mode of operation.

   (c) Its subject matter and effects.

   (c) Its characteristics.

4. Speech among the angels,

   (a) Its nature.

   (b) Its mode.

   (c) Extent and subject matter.

5. Angelic government in the universal order,

   (a)The notion of hierarchy,

(1) Human hierarchy.

(2) The angelic hierarchy.

6. Government and order in hell,

    (a) Necessity of harmony in hell.

    (b) Speech of devils.

    (c) Subjection of the devils.

Conclusion,

1. A prescription for utopia.

2. Place of man in the government of the spiritual world.

3. Social life of heaven.

☐ CHAPTER XVIII ☐
GOVERNMENT OF THE SPIRITUAL WORLD
(Q. 106-109)

Communication as an Essential of Social Life
From the Nature of Government

Political action consists in working together to the common end under a united direction. Notice the word "common"; for every time the note of common is struck in the field of politics, the fact of communication is solemnly announced. Men do not get very far in political union if they are enemies so bitter that they have built an impenetrable spite fence between their minds. For government supposes an end common to a multitude, since it consists in directing the many to that one end. That there must be a goal over and above the individual one is brought out by a contrast of anarchy with government, for anarchy is the acme of complete self-interest, the pursuit of an individual end to the exclusion of all else; logically, anarchy reaches its full maturity in a solitary inhabitant of a desolate island, at least a desolate spiritual island. A common end among men who cannot communicate with each other is unthinkable.

Try to imagine men existing with absolutely nothing in common, neither race, species, ideals, thoughts, and you have a picture of loneliness so desolate or of savagery so intense as to give the woes and wars of men as we know them a merry air. If, by an impossible hypothesis, government did exist among such men, it would be a sterile, stagnant, dead thing; for the proper act of government, the means by which that common end is reached, namely, law, is itself a communication from the governor to those governed, the flagship's flash to the fleet. Such a government might look well under glass or mounted on a signet ring; certainly it could serve none but a decorative purpose.

It is essential, then, that we investigate the matter of communication for the rest of this book will be engaged with the question of government. In the last chapter, we saw something of the government of the physical world in general and what God can and must do in the movement of creatures to their end; in this chapter and the succeeding ones, we shall investigate the part played in the government of the world by creatures, angels, men and irrational creation.

From Difference of Government

Before plunging into the question of communication among the angels, it might be well to dispose of the inevitable objection against the necessity of communication for government. It will unquestionably be pointed out, it always has, that chemicals and trees do not communicate with each other or with members of the same species, yet they follow immutable laws thus giving incontrovertible evidence of government. The objection is well worthwhile in that it brings out clearly the two distinct classes of creatures, which are directed by the divine law governing the universe.

One class is governed and in no sense governs itself, that is, the inanimate world, the plant world and the world of brutes. Plant and inanimate creation is completely devoid of communication; yet in that creation there is perfect unity of action, of end and of direction. The point to notice is that this direction is all one-sided. This plant and inanimate world is like a world of slaves whose slavery is so abject that their end, their direction, the very response made to direction comes from the governor. These creatures are passive participants in divine providence. The brute world has some kind of communication; at least there seems no hesitancy on the part of a mongrel in reading rightly the confidently low-pitched growl of a bull dog, a cat and her kittens succeed in making known their mutual needs and anxieties. Here the crucial fact is that the brutes have no communication as between subject and governor; that is, they have no recognition of nature's commands as commands, no knowledge of laws as laws, but only a necessary response to an extrinsic principle, which has stamped its directions in the essential principles of brute nature. This is but another form of passive participation in providence.

The other class of creatures are governed in the strictest sense of the term. They are not only governed, they take an active part in that government and, in a very real sense, govern themselves. They share in divine providence passively by obedience to physical laws and actively by acting as a principle of direction for themselves and others. These are the creatures of the rational and intellectual worlds, men and angels.

These creatures can do what they are told; but they know they are being told and why they are being told. If the reason for the command remains obscure, there is certain to be some discussion, sharp criticism and even open revolt. These creatures not only have communication among themselves but also with the governor and his government, they know the common end and the different means to that end, they are consciously aware of the laws directing them to that end. All of this has been said effectively in what has come to be an American symbol, the general store, with its cracker barrel and homespun politicians, is a declaration of the sharp difference between the role played by men and by the rest of the physical world in the divine government; when such gatherings become popular among fleas or birds, we can begin to feel uneasy about the reality of that distinction. Until such a time, men will proclaim that truth even although they gather to deny it.

Because of our intellectual nature, the angels and ourselves are free, we have a choice of means to that common end. That freedom establishes beyond question individuality of thought and action; it thus gives rise to the infinite variety of social life and, at the same time, makes absolutely essential the communication we call speech if there is to be any social life. For speech is the means by which those strikingly different individualities are molded into one social whole, which works coherently through government to its common end. The very first evidence of group action comes with the first evidence of communication in the brutes; but they are a physical whole rather than a moral unit, they are pushed by the will of another, rather than united to govern themselves to a consciously recognized common end. However, even such group action as they have would be impossible without at least a minimum of communication.

Communication Among the Angels

We must establish communication among the angels, then, before there can be any talk of government among them, and, since they are a part of intellectual creation and should have an active part in governing themselves, their communication must be not merely of subject to subject but also of subject to governor and government. The establishment of communication among the angels is exceedingly simple. For angelic nature is not the type to sit sullenly in a corner without a word to say, feeling all alone in the world. The angels are one step higher than men in mirroring the divine perfections; in comparison with their intellectual powers, our own minds are cripples, limping along on crutches. They are intellectual natures, which means that they must have a knowledge of the end for which they were created and for which they act, as well as of the means by which that end is to be obtained. In other words, by the very fact of being intellectual, they must know the purpose of government and the laws by which that purpose is achieved, if this be denied them they have been changed from angels into something considerably less than men.

On the same grounds of intellectuality, as we have seen, the angels must be conceded freedom, the choice of means to their end, for appetite follows knowledge and an intellectual appetite can be satisfied only by the universal or supreme good. Even although there are no vicious temperaments among them, they are strikingly different personalities who necessarily demand communication as a means of molding the multitude into a social and political whole. Anarchy, you will remember, cannot happen among the brutes; it is knowledge and freedom that makes anarchy possible and that also gives rise to that active share in government – but only on condition of communication.

One comforting thing about intellectual nature is that every individual has something to communicate all the time. The hushed silence of patients in a doctor's office is a ghastly thing, whereas the effortless chatter of women on a streetcar has a comfortable human air about it; it is true that we have nothing to say only when our minds, hearts and imaginations have been utterly inactive, it is never true that we must search desperately for an original thought, for any thought that is ours is original. The personal element that colors every thought, every emotion is so distinctively original that it has never been seen before in the world and never will again; no one can possibly get at it until we have brought it out and made a gift of it to the world. For all these things are not the result of response to mere external stimuli but the totally incalculable and utterly secret results of highly individual activity.

Unlike other creatures, members of the rational and intellectual world cannot reach their fullest perfection except through others, that is, through the medium of social life. Society, whether among men or angels, is not a luxury of civilization but a necessity of nature. The rest of creation has an elaborate equipment for life and needs it badly, for life there is a solitary, pioneer affair; man has only his reason, his hands and other men, the angels have only intellect, will and other angels. To deprive such as these of communication would be much more serious than pulling a lion's teeth or making a cat wear leather heels.

It is not only angelic nature but the whole scheme of the universe that cries out for communication among the angels. As we approach the perfection of God, the imaging of divine perfections is more perfect; we come up the steps of perfection through mere being, then life, sense knowledge, rational or human knowledge to the heights of the intellectual life of the angels. Each of these grades of perfection has its own proper activity flowing from, and in full harmony with, its particular nature. So the supreme and necessary divine action is that substantial communication which is the Trinity; its closest image is the communication of thought and its consequent awakening of love; then, running down the scale of perfection, there is the communication by generation in the brutes and plants; and, finally, only a faint vestige of the Trinity is to be found in the mere existence of the inanimate world.

It is only the man who is conscious of his weakness who dares not share his strength, the frail man who must conserve his health, the ignorant man who must be niggardly with his knowledge, and the fool who has nothing of wisdom to offer; for it is a universal law of perfection that it seeks to scatter itself, to communicate itself to others. A miserly man of great wealth is an object of contempt even to himself for, in a sense, he is so dull he has not yet realized his wealth; his heart is still the heart of a street gamin who must use teeth and claws in the acquisition and defense of every penny. Without any other argument than the perfection of angelic nature, communication between the angels is an obvious truth; such perfection must be scattered, must be shared and in the only way possible to an intellectual nature, that is, intellectually, by the revelation of a concept or truth to another mind.

Its Double Nature, Enlightenment and Speech

In general, this intellectual communication among the angels corresponds to communication between men; it may be described as the manifestation of the angelic concepts to another angel. Among ourselves communication takes the double form of teaching or just talking, of revealing a concept as dependent from the first and supreme truth or as dependent from the individual will of the talker; we can demonstrate the freedom of man or we can mention our love of the opera, a favorite restaurant and our preferences for the company of certain people. In the angels, this distinction is much more sharply differentiated than in us; to its parts theologians have given the imposing names of illumination (or enlightenment) and speech.

Enlightenment is nothing more or less than what we call teaching, understanding teaching, of course, as the manifestation of truth and not as the exposition of wild theories of a man bent on being different or the Panicky wanderings of an unprepared professor. The concept revealed in enlightenment or illumination does not depend on our will but on the first truth; that is, it corresponds; to things as they are. Obviously, we are not teaching others when we bore them with our dreams, impress them I with our good intentions or wheedle them with our wishes. Teaching among the angels is quite a different procedure than it is among men. For angels do not teach one another by unwinding a long chain of reasoning to drop the anchor of truth in another's mind; reasoning is a human necessity for a human weakness, the crutch on which our minds hobble to the truth. The angelic teaching is not flavored by a liberal sprinkling of images, illustrations or contrasts; these are products of imagination and imagination is totally lacking in the angels. For them, the task of teaching is one of complete simplicity; they bring about the knowledge of truth in another angel by fortifying the inferior intellect and then manifesting the concept they wish to impart, taking the lower angel by the hand and then turning on the light.

It is true that the fortification of another intellect is a somewhat mysterious action. It cannot be by any direct action on the intellect of the angelic disciple, tightening its bolts, throwing up a few supports, or pouring in distilled strength; only God can act directly on the intellect and will. It seems rather to be an indirect bringing out of a little better than the best that is in a disciple, spurring the pupil on to actions that would not be possible to him alone. Thomas gives an invaluable clue in his use of the word "comforting" to describe the superior angers action on the inferior's intellect. With this comfort, the inferior angel understands much better, as a small boy sleeps much better in his mother's bed on a stormy night although he must do his own sleeping, or as an infant walks with assured help handy but falls instantly when that help is not in reach; so boys are bolder and more mischievous in the comforting presence of the gang.

The real sense of Thomas' carefully carved word is even stronger than this. For the inferior always works better in union with the superior, as vegetable life in animals is superior to that in plants, and sensitive life in man is superior to sensitive life in animals. Though the parallel is not exact because we are specifically equal, this same thing can be vaguely seen in the activities of men, a man plays better golf when his rivals are his superiors at the game, a man does better thinking when he is wrestling with an intellectual opponent who has him outclassed. On the contrary, a few years in the gutter will be no help to the finish of a cultured woman, there is a distinct intellectual deterioration in the thinkers of the Church in the absence of real opposition, muscles that are not strained become flabby. Just the fact of working with a superior intellect is itself a strengthening, a comforting of the inferior angel's mind.

The second step in this teaching, the manifestation of the concept, is accomplished by simply breaking it up. We have seen that a superior angel understands by fewer and more universal concepts; to hand down these concepts unchanged to an inferior angel would be like giving a child his father's clothes. They might be much better clothes, but are much too big for the child; so, in themselves, these superior concepts are much better concepts. However, they are too big for an inferior intellect and result in only a vague, confused knowledge. They have to be cut and shaped to fit the intellect of the angelic disciple, made more particular, their universality shrunk.

None of the angelic doctors can really be called specialists. The subject matter for their teaching embraces the universe of created things. It has not to do with the essence of God or the beatific vision of that essence; after all, every angel sees the divine essence to its full capacity and, anyhow, that essence cannot be manifested through teaching for it cannot be contained within the limits of any concept however universal. This angelic teaching concentrates on the divine works, which are in God as in their cause, that is, with the plans of the divine architect, the ideas of God, and their execution. Naturally the superior angels possess those plans in a way most like the divine possession of them, being more perfect images of God and closer to the source of those ideas.

Perhaps the best example of this manifestation of truth among the angels would be a ray of light speeding from its source, broken up into its different colors here and there, but never stopping until it had reached the limits of creation. Just so the manifestation of a superior angel sweeps on, not merely to one angel but to all inferiors. Accommodating itself to the mind of each, but never stopping until the lowest angel has been enlightened. The ray of angelic light cannot penetrate the will of any other angel; that is sacrosanct. Not even the angels can do more than coax the will of another to act, enticing it with a lovable thing, but never exerting that infallible allure that is proper to the Supreme Good itself.

But that angelic ray of light does sweep over all the intellects of the inferior angels, illuminating them, purifying them of all nescience, perfecting them, like the rays of the sun removing darkness, giving light and revealing the object of vision to the sight. Of course, the sweep of this ray is always from the top down, from the superior to the inferior; for only those who know more can teach, at least among the angels. Here there is no question of one being more expert in one line and less in another, a potential teacher of one, a necessary disciple of another, for in the angelic world, the superiors are always closer to God, they are pre-eminent in knowledge and sanctity and thus know more of all things than those beneath them.

There is no slightest stinginess in the doctrinal illumination of the angels. The superior tells all he knows, fully shares his superiority with all other angels in response to that urge of goodness to diffuse itself; this is a constant spiritual generation, an intellectual begetting that is absolutely unstinted. Nor is the superior any the worse for it; he remains superior for this greater knowledge is proper to him, these intellectual clothes fit him alone. All others can participate in that knowledge, but imperfectly, each in proportion to its intellectual ability. Eon after eon this angelic teaching goes on; with no night to interrupt, the angelic suns pour their rays in an eternal day for always there will be new things revealed about the world of created things, revelations that come first and best to the superior angels. Even after the world has passed and judgment has been pronounced, there will be a constant necessity for this illumination, the inferior minds will always need the comfort and manifestation of the superior angels, for this angelic learning is only participated, borrowed, as the air borrows a note from the throat of a singer and cannot maintain it without the constant support of the singing throat.

Speech Among the Angels

Not all-angelic conversation is of this solemn doctrinal type; among the angels there is that intimately personal speech that runs gaily through the days of human life in the bright garments of chatter, gossip, hopes, dreams, wishes and experiences. For each angel has all that prices less treasure of richly original and mysteriously individual knowledge that is an inalienable possession of personality.

Its Nature

Thomas calls this type of angelic conversation "speech." Both illumination and speech run none of the hazards and labors of voice production, enunciation and articulation, not to speak of lisping and stuttering, that do such strange things to human conversation. Both these types of angelic communication are accomplished effortlessly and with absolute accuracy by a simple act of the speaking angel. With the angels, the mere fact of a concept being directed to another assures the understanding of that concept.

We possess a concept in three distinct ways, habitually, as we hold to the multiplication table, not using it oftener than is necessary; actually, when we consider it here and now and, in a sense, talk to ourselves; finally, as ordered to another, as when we put an idea to work building a house, revealing a truth or unveiling the privacies of our personality. It is by no means enough for us to ordain a concept so the mind of another; a gag will keep our thoughts tightly imprisoned within ourselves, deaf ears are barriers that keep us circling the mind of another, indeed, even words themselves conspire against us, refusing to bear the heavy burden of intense concentration or clumsily spoiling the fine shadings of a thought too fragilely perfect to suffer transportation. Our concepts can be hidden from others either because we refuse to reveal them or because the very grossness of our bodies make ineffable the beauties that so captivate our minds; we are obliged to use external words and signs, and, often enough, the very externality is a positive impediment. It is precisely this obstacle that is missing in the angels.

Its Mode

How does the listening angel know it is being spoken to? To us this seems decidedly mysterious, although se have hints of the answer when, now and then, we feel someone's eyes upon us, we grasp a thought before it has been uttered, a word before it has been formed. Thomas says, quite simply, that just as our senses are moved by sensible things, so the intellects of the angels are moved by intelligible things; just as sensible signs excite the external senses, so through concepts the mind of the angels can be excited to attention.

When we consider that one angel can talk to another across the whole width of heaven, it might seem that heaven would indeed be an eavesdropper's paradise. It is true that distance has no part to play in angelic conversation, for the intellectual operation of angels abstracts from time and place that so enclose matter, the impediments that cling to our conversation through its phantasms and external words. Yet, as a matter of fact, heaven would be hell for an eavesdropper; for, although all of heaven be between the two, one angel can talk to another in perfect privacy because the sole excitant to attention is the will of the speaker. In fact, no one need ever know that these two were talking at all; there is absolutely no way of plugging in on the conversation for it passes through no switchboard.

Extent and Subject Matter

In the case of illumination, it is the superior angels who do all the talking; but the same is by no means true of the intimately personal conversation of the angels. Interiors can talk to superiors, and have something to tell them, or even to God Himself; this speech, you will remember, depends on the will of the speaker and the personality that is proper to him alone. What does one of the lower angels say to God? Well, there is a colloquy with God that is uninterrupted, a lovers' chat, a constant expression of admiration, adoration and awe at His excellence; now and then there will be an occasional conference as regards the things to be done in the ordering of the universe.

Angelic Government in the Universal Order
the Notion of Hierarchy

The perfection of angelic communication, with its necessary exclusion of the misunderstanding and emotional prejudice that so mars human social life; indicates something of the perfection of the angelic principalities. These have been given the name of hierarchies, a name that is defined by Thomas as a "sacred principality" with the full implications of a prince, his subjects, the community or multitude directed by the prince to its end. God, the supreme prince, as the first cause, lord and governor, is prince of all the angels, as well as of all men and indeed, of all creatures. The universe itself is a principality whose prince is God, whose subjects are all creatures and whose common end is God.

Human Hierarchy

Yet hierarchy is a sacred principality, that is, it is a term reserved for a community capable of participating in the holiness of God, capable of virtue and victory or of sin and defeat, a free moral community. Of these free moral creatures whose common prince is God not all belong to the same state within the great divine empire; the mode of government of each group follows the nature and activity of the subjects governed, for God is a very wise prince. The human hierarchy receives the government of God under sensible similitudes and is a separate state; the angelic hierarchy receives this divine direction in its intelligible purity, without the medium of sensible things.

The Angelic Hierarchy

Since government, political and social life follow the natures and activities of the subjects, particularly when the governor is wise, it follows immediately that the social and political life of the angels is vastly different from our own. It will involve no temperance or uplift societies, there will be no athletic clubs or sewing circles in it; plays, games, sports will all be ruled out. All of these presuppose bodies and the angels have no bodies. They have only that double operation of a purely intellectual nature, the type of operation that is

God's own, the operation of intellect and will. Whatever differences there are within that angelic state will have to be based on these operations.

Each angel is an individual species, since there is no way of multiplying individuals within a species that excludes the individuating principle of matter; yet we find three main lines of intellectual activity within the angelic state, three grades of universal understanding constituting the three angelic cities or the three hierarchies of angels. The first knows the reasons of things as they exist in the absolutely universal cause, God Himself; they stand in the vestibule of God. The second, with a less perfect, less universal knowledge, knows the reasons of created things as they exist in the most universal created causes. The third knows the reasons of things as dependent on their proper created causes.

Just as in any city not all men can be traffic policemen or stenographers, so among the angels there must be a distinction of offices and duties if general confusion is to be avoided. So in each of the three angelic cities, three different orders are distinguished. The first angelic city centers its activity on God Himself, contemplating the essences of things in God. Within it are the Seraphim, the highest of all the angels, who excel in their immediate union with God and their flaming love for him; from this fiery love comes their name. Next are the Cherubim with the plenitude of wisdom, which their name indicates, excelling in the knowledge of the divine secrets, the wisdom of divine providence; they have a clear vision of the first operating virtue of the divine model. Last in this order are the Thrones who have a perfect knowledge of the end of all things and so of the disposition of the divine judgments. The Thrones have the note that is common to this whole order; the Cherubim retain this and add a special note; the Seraphim possess the note of both Thrones and Cherubim and add another still higher note. Indeed, this interrelation within each hierarchy is universally valid, the lowest order has the common note, which is possessed and surpassed by the immediate superior. The orders of this first hierarchy can be compared to men, all of whom are friends of a king, but one has the right to enter familiarly into the presence of the king, another knows the secrets of the king; the third is united to the king in a perpetual companionship.

The second angelic city, engaged with the universal created causes, has for its proper object the general ordering of means in view of the end and therefore demands the distinction of three orders. The first is made up of the Dominations to whom pertains the distinction of the things to be governed; then the Virtues to whom belongs the faculty of fulfilling the things to be done, imparting to general causes the necessary energy; and, finally, the

Powers who are busy with the details of how things to be done or commanded are to be carried out in detail.

The work of the third angelic city is primarily one of execution for its object is the particular causes of created things. The leaders in this city, the Principalities who deal chiefly with the beginnings of actions, are the leaders in that angelic work of execution, which consists of announcing divine things. Next are the Archangels whose work is the announcement of great things to men and the care of goods that are at the same time general and particular, such as the truths of faith and the divine cult. Finally come the Angels who announce the ordinary things and take care of the particular, individual goods.

Within each of these orders there are many, very many, individual angels. If we knew them perfectly we could distinguish all their proper actions to the last detail. But, knowing them only imperfectly and vaguely, we cannot know that each has this particular work and this particular place within his order, just as meeting a strange factory worker in an exclusively textile city, we can know no more about him than that he works in a mill. It is to be noted that the foundations of these orders are the different natural perfections of the different angels, perfections which we have seen are carried over into the realm of grace; consequently they endure even after there is no world to be directed to its proper end.

It would be a legitimate question here to ask how much of this doctrine on the angelic hierarchies is of faith. There is, in fact, very much of it that leaves no room for doubt. It is clearly of faith that the angels speak to one another and to God from the varied and numerous statements of such conversations in Scripture. The Council of Lateran has defined the existence of three hierarchies of angels in each of which there are three choirs; the names of these choirs are all contained in Holy Scripture. To this may be added the evidence from the liturgy of the Church, the Te Deum, the offices of the Guardian Angels, of Michael, Raphael, and so on. The detailed development and philosophical explanation are the work of St. Thomas, drawing upon the rich tradition of the Fathers, especially Gregory and Pseudo-Dionysius, the biblical functions of the angels and the philosophical tradition of movers of the heavenly spheres. He gives a new organic structure to the world of separate intelligences by his arrangement of them on the principle of lessening intellectual illumination, perfectly assigning their place in the universal order and keeping in perfect harmony the grades of participation of the divine perfection.

Government and Order in Hell
Necessity of Harmony in Hell

A treatise on the government of the spiritual world would be incomplete without a word on hell. For, of course there is government and some kind of order in hell; as a work of God, hell cannot escape the plans of the divine architect. There is a kind of perverse harmony in hell, a concord of wickedness such as we might find among thieves or murderers. It is a cooperation, not of friendship or social leanings, but of viciousness aimed at a common goal, not of achievement, but of destruction. The basis of that concord, that order of hell, is the natural gifts of the fallen angels, just as the natural gifts of the good angels make up the basis for their hierarchies. Natural gifts are not lost by sin precisely as sin, so Lucifer and his followers carried over a natural superiority and inferiority into the realm of sin. There Lucifer is supreme because he is naturally the most perfect of all the devils and because his sin was the greatest.

It cannot be much comfort to him, for there is no more potent cause of misery than the commission of evil, especially for a clear intelligence; to be a leader, to be supreme, in sin is at the same time to be the greatest in misery. What little satisfaction might be had from a sense of power is turned to ashes by the fact that the greatest of the devils is subject to the least of the good angels, for all order and dominance is originally in God and is participated by creatures in proportion to their propinquity to God. Indeed, often a little vinegar is added to the ashes as when, for instance, a mere man like the Curé of Ars is given complete superiority over the whole horde of hell.

Speech of Devils

Conversation is not lacking in hell, although it is undoubtedly far from edifying; for the devils still have their angelic wills and concepts. There is no illumination, no teaching, in hell, and not only because the devils are so wholly evil that they give no help whatsoever to another; the fact is that illumination is always in reference to the order of the first cause and they are completely in disorder relative to that first cause. However, now and then, the good angels tell the devils some things that it may be necessary for them to know for the working out of the plans of divine providence.

The perfect social life of the angels is not to be attained by men this side of heaven; but that does not stop men from dreaming. Perhaps it is because we are such close kin of the angels that even a momentary consideration of their lives afflicts us with a traveler's nostalgia; they seem like big brothers who have beaten us home by many a weary mile. We envy them a little, dream our dreams of homecoming, and try to make the shelter of the moment look something like the home at the end of the road That family yearning for perfection that drives men restlessly on has made itself felt no less strongly in his social life than in his individual life. Men have dreamed their dreams of the perfect society, put those dreams down on paper apologetically or belligerently, and tried, with an inevitable futility, to make the dreams come true within the walls of an earthly city.

It is not strange that some shadow of the angels should hover over those dreams and those gallantly conceived theories; the tragedy is that not more of the angelic pattern was woven into the plans; the stark fact is that men can never fill all of the angelic prescription for utopia. As a rule one or two aspects of the angelic society have been fastened on to the complete neglect of the rest. The community of goods among the angels, For example, has seemed a splendid ideal to men, that the wealthier should dispense all of their goods, unstintingly, constantly, joyously in a blaze of beneficence as life-giving and as dependable as the warm smile of a spring sun, that would make the ideal state among men. Or that the superiors should always be superior, that those who have most should continue to have it, that the more intelligent should always be rulers and the less intelligent always subject without a murmur of discontent, either of these would make for utopia among men.

Conclusion, a Prescription for Utopia

As a matter of fact, the angelic utopia is not made up of one or the other of these factors. It is true that there is a complete community of goods, an unstinted generosity on the part of the superiors; but that community of goods does not involve a classless angelic society, that generosity on the part of the superiors in giving is perfectly matched by the generous subjection of the inferiors in receiving. In this society, superiority is measured rightly by propinquity to God; the greater are those who most closely image divine perfection in being, knowledge and love; the generous are those who have most to give and the goods they scatter so freely are not lost to the givers although they are received by others. Superiority here involves a responsibility of constant teaching that others might be helped, subjection involves a constant docility that help might be received; order is thus perfect and government a benignly indispensable help.

Place of Man in the Government of the Spiritual World

That perfection has not yet been seen on earth; nor will it be seen, if for no other reason than that men are not angels but fallen men. The angelic hierarchy is, by its nature, distinctively different and more perfect than the human hierarchy; but it is not so different that a bridge of the supernatural cannot span the gap between the two. For in heaven, men will be like the angels and, indeed, will close up the ranks broken by the sin of the devils. The high dreams of men have roots deep in the plans of God; they are not to be pulled from the minds of men by disappointment, disillusionment or a failure so constant as to be habitual. Men will dream on; and, eventually, the dream will come true, and stay true.

Social Life of Heaven

However, the angelic doctors will have a teaching task of the first magnitude on their hands when men take over their part in the social life of heaven. We shall have much to learn, so much that we shall spend an eternity in the learning of it; not that we shall sit in absorbed silence drinking in knowledge while not daring to betray our ignorance by so much as an unguarded word. We shall have plenty to say and the angels will have plenty to learn; for each of us brings a mysteriously rich personality with us, a personality that yields to no explorer of truth but ourselves. In other words, the lines of communication between ourselves, and the angels will be wide open; it would be neither human nor angelic if immediate and constant advantage were not taken of such an opportunity to get a word in.

□ CHAPTER XIX □

THE ROLE OF THE ANGELS
(Q. 110-114)

1. The heavenly movers of the material world,
2. A modern denial.

    (a) An historical affirmation.

3. The fact of angelic activity in the world,

    (a) Its proof.

    (b) Its limitation.

    (1) Its consonance with the dignity of material causes.
    (2) Angelic action in the world of men

    (a) Indirect action, on the intellect and will.

    (b) Direct action, on the sense faculties.

    (c) Relation to human dignity self sufficiency and freedom

4. Angelic ministers to the material world,

    (a) Assisting and ministering angels.

    (b) Place of superior angels.

    (c) Limitation of ministering angels.

5. The role of angels in the world of men,

    (a) Of the good angels – guardianship,

---

(1) Subject of this guardianship.

(2) Dignity and distribution of the guardians.

(3) Effects on the guardians.

(b) Of the devils attack,

(1)The fact and causes of hostility.

(2) Its limitation.

(3) Physical attacks of devils,

    a. Infestation.

    b. Obsession.

    c. Permission.

(4) Moral attacks.

Conclusion,

1. Role of the angels and scientific thought.

2. Role of the angels and philosophic thoughts.

3. Role of the angels and moral thought,

    (a) Appreciation of supra-human aid.

    (b) Value of this appreciation.

☐ CHAPTER XIX ☐
THE ROLE OF THE ANGELS
(Q. 101-114)

the Heavenly Movers of the Material World

The modern rejection of the idea of angelic activity in the material world is a fact that need not be argued, least of all to the moderns. They are rather proud of it as evidence of the happy transition of the world from infancy to maturity, putting away poetic and mythical notions to subsist on the solid meat of facts. In reality, this denial of angelic activity is not due to the world's having grown up so much as it is to the world getting childish.

a Modern Denial

It is expected that a child will take a fable as a fact and miss the moral it makes, so the moral is carefully pointed out at the fable's end. Just so some delightful fantasy is taken seriously today and ridiculed; a Christmas card portraying tiny angels going about with tapers to light the stars or playing violins to put music in the wind is smiled at as a pitiful relic of a superstition that is long in dying. As a matter of fact, no one seriously supposes that the stars are like street lamps to be lit at night and extinguished in the morning by sleepy or yawning angels, nor that music is injected into the wind by a kind of super-broadcasting station; even if some men did harbor these fantastic notions, they would not be nearly so close to madness as those who suppose the light came from darkness and the wind from a vacuum. The fantasies, however, are not philosophical expositions or theological tracts; they are fantasies, beautiful fantasies that a normal child is quick to appreciate.

More often this denial of angelic activity is not so much a matter of conviction as of aversion, like a child's fight against an afternoon nap because it interrupts his play. This modern rejection is not a result of a conviction of the impossibility of the supernatural (absurd as such a conviction may be) but of an aversion to the supra sensible because it interrupts the game of exclusive concentration on the glitter of the sensible world. In speaking of the angels and angelic activity as such, there is never a question of the supernatural, for the angels, as created substances, are part and parcel of the natural order; but there is always question of the supra-sensible, for the angels are pure intelligences, devoid of all corporal qualities and characteristics. It is precisely because of this supra-sensible character of theirs that the angels have fallen out of favor with the modern world. A supra-sensible creature automatically puts a limitation on man's engrossment with the sensible world, it puts a stop to his childish pretense of having everything in his hands to make or unmake at his scientific hat. As soon as an angel comes in, man has to stop playing God; and he likes to play God.

It was just this absolute devotion to the game of materialism that turned modern philosophy so sharply away from the intellect and that now leaves that philosophy high and dry as neither philosophy nor science but only anti-intellectual.

an Historical Affirmation

Historically, this modern position is an infant in arms. Angelic movers of the universe immediately found their place in Oriental philosophy; Plato placed a spiritual substance over every corporal thing as an integral part of his doctrine of self-subsistent ideas; Aristotle, while disagreeing with the Platonic doctrine of separated forms, admitted the angelic presidency over the material world, although he restricted it to the more universal agents of the corporal world, the heavenly bodies. The Arabic philosophers, with Avicenna, held to the Platonic teaching, but made those spiritual substances a conglomerate whole, which was called the active intellect. The Fathers of the Church and the scholastics placed different corporal substances under the presidency of different angels, not because of any peculiar affinity in the angels, but because of a definite orderly arrangement on the part of divine providence. Yet, all retained the central notion of spiritual activity in a material universe. It was when the modern world went back to the childhood of Greek philosophy with the re-birth of materialism in the fifteenth and sixteenth centuries that all activity was centered in the material world itself; all existence, all life, all being were centered in the material world when that philosophy reached the full flower it is enjoying today.

The Fact of Angelic Activity in the World - Its Proof

The angelic activity in the material world is stated plainly in Holy Scripture; to take just one instance, when the modeled eunuch had been baptized, Philip was moved across the country with the easy speed with which a man's mind moves from one thought to another. As a matter of fact, this state of affairs is eminently reasonable indeed, it is demanded by the order of things all about us. In the political world we insist that particular power be ruled and directed by the universal so we carefully distinguish the gradually mounting powers of cities, counties, states and federal government. The idea was not a brilliant

343

inspiration unheard of before in the universe; it was merely another case of man's genius copying the artistry of nature. In the physical world the particularity of a form is a declaration of its subjection, minerals are subject to plants by reason of the plant's power to assimilate other forms to their destruction; the plants bow to animals which can assimilate forms by particular knowledge; all physical nature is beneath the dominion of intellect and its power to assimilate all forms.

Its Limitation

Every material form is, by the fact of its materiality, particular, limited to the here and now while the angelic forms are universal precisely because they are free of matter. Just as in the material universe the less particular directs and administers the more particular, so the universal spiritual forms should direct the determined and particular forms of material creation. In fact, such administration on the part of the angels seems to be demanded by the effects, which in an earlier chapter, we have called accidents, that is, the effects that are not the direct result of any one material cause but that come by way of surprise from the clash of material causes. In other words, there are things happening in the material world not wholly explicable by material causes alone; and this is particularly evident when we keep in mind the universality of the order in that material world.

Its Consonance with the Dignity of Material Causes

This does not mean that the angel's equipment for government includes an Aladdin's lamp. An angel cannot change a horse into a cow by a wave of a wand, or by a wave of anything else; in fact, an angel of itself cannot produce a single material composite, not a tree, a rock or an animal. The information of matter by its form is not an angel's work; that belongs to the material causes or to God Himself. We can think ourselves into a fit of sickness, or drive ourselves on by will power long after the point of exhaustion; but an angel can do no such thing to the material world. The difference is that our soul is immediately united to matter as the form of matter; the angels have no such connection with matter and so have no means of effecting a formal, intrinsic change. What changes they can produce in matter must be made from the outside, by extrinsic causality.

Of course, they can produce some changes in matter. After all, the superior has all the power of the inferior; if a bird can charm a man or a shark can take off his leg, these things are not to be denied to an angel. Indeed, the angel, being superior, has the power of all beneath him in a superior way; he will move corporal agents more smoothly, more efficiently, more powerfully than any material cause. There is no real reason for surprise when the angel produces effects with a material cause that the material agents themselves could never produce; we are not particularly surprised that a cooks working with such clumsy materials as a fire, a barnyard fowl and some stale bread, can produce a beautifully browned roast chicken stuffed with dressing, although we know well enough that the fire, the chicken and the bread could never achieve such perfection left to themselves.

The angels can move bodies with a corporal movement; nor should this have to be argued very seriously. We grant the power to a bull, particularly if the matador is a little slow or clumsy, and surely an angel is superior to a bull. Lt is inconceivable that a bull should toss an angel, but quite within the realm of possibility that an angel should toss the bull. Really, this angelic movement of bodies is just another case of the beautifully interlocking hierarchy of being in which the lower, in its supreme activity, touches the higher order. For local movement, as we have seen in considering the grades of life, is the supreme activity of a purely material composite and the activity which should naturally be immediately subject to a higher, a spiritual, nature.

What difficulty there is in this truth is a difficulty of imagination rather than of conception. We can easily understand men throwing a ball with their hands or bumping into doors with their noses; but the activity of the angels in regard to such things seems not so easily grasped. It seems a distinct disadvantage to lack a body, particularly in a game like baseball or football. The difficulty arises from our insistence on carrying over the imagery of human activity into the world of the angels. We argue that because a man cannot throw a ball without hands, of course an angel is just as helpless. The fact is that a body limits and contracts the activity of a spiritual substance rather than aids it; because of its union with the body as its form, our human soul cannot move other bodies except through its own body. The angel, not suffering this limitation to a particular body, can move other bodies freely, without the use of a corporal medium; the very absence of a corporal medium makes it impossible for us to draw imaginative pictures of the process, such as an angel getting set for a blow or swinging in a graceful arc before hurling a ball.

It must be constantly insisted that this angelic activity is within the natural order. It in no way conflicts with nature or the causality of secondary material causes; it is itself a part of nature and a secondary cause. The one thing it does to material causes is to make their operation more perfect through union with a higher cause.

It is completely certain that the angels, of themselves, work no miracles; that is God's proper field, for a miracle must exceed the whole order of nature. They do things that may seem wonderful indeed to a particular material cause; but then it would seem wonderful to a stone, could a stone enjoy wonder, that so small a boy could impart On it the preternatural gift of flying through the air.

Angelic Action in the World of Men, Indirect Action, on the Intellect and Will

Coming to the world of men, it should be immediately apparent that an angel can no more pour knowledge into a human brain than can a human professor; for the intellect is one of those intrinsic accidents, inhering directly in the substance of the soul, that no created agent can get at directly, either to read the thought hidden there or to put new thoughts alongside the old ones. If a man wants his guardian angel to know what he is thinking, he must speak out; not even an angel can read one's thoughts.

Direct Action, on the Sense Faculties

Angels can, of course, teach men in somewhat the same way in which they illuminate inferior angels. The process, however, is not exactly the same. There must be the same comforting or strengthening of the intellect and the cutting of the angelic concept to fit the inferior mind; but this is not quite enough. The human intellect cannot digest raw intellectuality. Its natural way of knowing is by abstracting the idea from the sensible image or phantasm; the angelic idea must be given a coating of the sensible before it can be swallowed by the human mind. It is not necessary that we know an angel has enlightened us for the fact to have taken place; although we must, of course, realize that we have a new idea. Much the same thing happens in human affairs and we think nothing of it; how many employees have dropped a thought on the boss's brain, then sat back patiently waiting, letting the idea sink in to such a depth that the boss will take it for his own and push it to the limit. Many of the good thoughts we have, the inspirations, resolutions, hopes, kindnesses are not the result of our innate goodness but of the patient labor of a teaching angel, thanklessly repeating the lesson over and over again.

Relation to Human Dignity, Self-Sufficiency and Freedom

Our will is no less sacred than our intellect. No natural agent, angels included, can force that will to action or move it directly. What is done with a will is done indirectly, coaxing, presenting lovable objects, desirable actions, threatening it, as we persuade a child with a piece of cake or frighten a criminal with the threat of the electric chair.

The dreams that warned Joseph against Herod were quite ordinary operations of an angel. Not that all dreams are angelic in source or material; but it should not be hard to see that the angels have the power to impress images upon our imagination or to present our senses with external stimuli. We can hurry, shivering, into a theatre in the dead of winter only to have the blistering summer day pictured on the stage so affect our imagination that the air seems sultry and perspiration pours from us. A fairly moderate stomachache can start our imagination off on the most woeful series of images; a single buzz of a mosquito is sufficient for us to imagine whole chunks of our legs being bitten off. If the necessarily clumsy make-believe of the stage, a bodily indisposition, or the faint stirring of one of our senses can so vividly affect the imagination, we can be very sure that the angels can do a better job with it.

Both the senses and the imagination are corporal, organic faculties, powers we have in common with the animals and so, of course, under the presidency of the spiritual world, open to spiritual activity. The exercise of angelic activity in these fields demands nothing extraordinary on the part of the angels; if they can move material things locally, they can stimulate our senses and imagination. Unlike the intellect and will, our senses and imagination can be obtained from the outside.

Angelic Ministers to the Material World

Nor is this angelic activity in the world of men an affront to our self-sufficiency, our dignity or freedom any more than the activity of a professor is an infringement on the dignity or freedom of his students. Rather, it opens up a much greater field to human minds, strengthening and uplifting them; this activity is a perfection of human nature within the purely natural field which human nature of itself could not attain.

Assisting and Ministering Angels
Place of Superior Angels

While there is no work to be done in the material world so great that the least of the angels could not take care of it, there is an orderly distribution of angelic activity according to divine providence that leaves the first hierarchy of angels exclusively engaged in the courts of heaven. St. Thomas makes the comparison with the regime of a temporal kingdom in which not all of the counselors of the king are ambassadors, some remaining permanently at the court as participants of the secrets and counsels of the king, others receive the royal commands and plans and pass them on to the actual messengers.

Limitation of Ministering Angels

In the court of heaven, the highest hierarchy (Seraphim, Cherubim and Thrones) are members of the divine household whose whole activity is centered on the divinity itself. The first choir of the second hierarchy (Dominions) serve as the medium between the heavenly court and its messengers; while the last two choirs of the second hierarchy (Virtues and Powers) and the third hierarchy (Principalities, Archangels, Angels) have the actual administration of the material world. From the supernatural point of view, inasmuch as all enjoy the beatific vision, all the angels are said to be assisting angels, assisting at the throne of God; but from the natural point of view, the first four choirs (Seraphim, Cherubim, Thrones, Dominions) are assisting angels; the last five (Virtues, Powers, Principalities, Archangels and Angels) are administering angels. Of the two groups, the assisting angels are far more numerous, a conclusion reached on the grounds that what is more perfect in the world, what is more directly and fully an image of divine perfection, is more directly the intent of nature and nature's author. Just as there are many more angels than there are corporal species, so there are many more of the higher angels than of the lower.

The Role of Angels in the World of Men,
of the Good Angels – Guardianship

The particular role of the good angels relative to the world of men is one of guardianship. This may sound a little insulting to the adult human for it implies protections direction, inspiration, comfort and encouragement. Why should all this be necessary? Isn't man able to take care of himself; why treat him like an infant?

Subject of this Guardianship

The assignation of guardian angels to men, a fact completely certain from abundant places in Holy Scripture, is not a peculiar exception for the case of men by way of precaution against their infantile debility; it is merely an insistence on man's integral place in a perfectly ordered universe. In that universe, the lower is ruled and regulated by the higher, the movable and variable by the immovable and invariable, the lower material things by the higher material things, the corporal by the spiritual. Certainly man, through his free will, can avoid evil but not perfectly as the constant victory of passion eloquently testifies so also the universal knowledge of the natural law can guide man to good, but the application of that law to particular cases gives man too frequent an occasion for a bad mistake. In spite of the help that comes directly from God, the help of grace and the virtues, there is plenty of room for the work of the angels in the practical perfection and application of these virtues. There is no need for pride stiffening our necks at the mention of guardianship; look at the human record.

Dignity and Distribution of the Guardians

Angelic guardianship is not limited to a group, a class or a race; it extends to every individual human being. If we find it hard to believe the extravagance of divine generosity in delegating a heavenly prince to every human being, it is principally because we so consistently underestimate the dignity of the human individual in the scheme of the universe and the plans of the divine architect. On the same grounds, the crucified Son of God was a stumbling block to the Gentiles.

In the material world, divine providence, while extending to the smallest details, evidently intends and extends particular care to that which is enduring. Thus, for example, we see the extraordinary precautions taken by nature to preserve the species and its seeming carelessness towards the individual when it has a spawning fish lay millions of eggs that a few might come to maturity. The human individual, from the point of view of perpetuity or endurance, rates higher than any material species; for his rational soul is by nature destined to an eternal existence. The enduring individual of the human species is the particular care of divine providence, a care which ex presses itself with at least the same emphasis as is given to the material species. Tile individual human being has a particular guardian angel because he is immensely important in the plans of the divine architect.

As a matter of fact, there is probably no man who does not have the help of more than one of these guardian angels because there is no man who is not a part of some larger body, some social organism. As these social organisms, like the laws that govern them, are of their nature perpetual, they have their own guardians; there is an angel guardian of a kingdom, a state, of a city, perhaps even of a diocese, a parish, a religious order or a monastery.

The angelic guardians of individual men are drawn from the lowest choir of the third hierarchy, the choir of the angels. Each angel, of course, differs from all others as much as a stone differs From a tree; for there is the gap of species between them. Within the choir which furnishes guardians for men there is the same graded order of perfection that is to be found in the whole universe; and that graded order is made use of in the actual assignment of guardianship. The more perfect angel is given the greater work, thus preserving the proportion between the perfection of nature and the perfection of function; for example, the more perfect angels are given as guardians to those men from whom more is demanded in the line of spiritual perfection, such as the saints, of intellectual labors, as the men of genius, of work for the common good, as statesmen, and so on. Where the object to be guarded is more universal, the guardian angel chosen is of a higher choir; so, going up the list of city, state, kingdom and so on, we pass up the line of the angelic choirs destined to guard the world of men.

Coming down to particular cases, St. Thomas denies that Christ had a guardian angel because He was, from the very beginning of His life, in possession of the beatific vision; and it is the work of a guardian angel to lead men to that vision which constitutes their eternal happiness, so the individual man has no guardian angel in heaven or in hell, but rather a companion reigning with him in heaven, or a persecutor punishing him in hell. Christ rather had an angel ministering to Him than a guardian protecting him. Man in the Garden of Eden had a real need of a guardian angel, even although he could suffer no danger from the rebellion of his sensitive nature or from the material world in which he lived. As the event proved, there was always the supreme danger of attack from the devil. The infidels, the thoroughly wicked, even anti-Christ himself will have guardian angels, as follows from the general ordering of the universe and of men. Nor is this guardianship in vain; without it, these men would be very much worse. In fact, the loss of a guarded soul is not to be laid to negligence on the part of the guardian angel but to the wickedness of the individual soul which is always free to plunge itself into hell.

The guardianship of the individual soul begins, in the opinion of Thomas, at the moment of birth, not at the moment of conception. While it is true that the child in the womb is certainly possessed of human nature, it so intimately belongs to the mother as to be almost a part of her, as the fruit is a part of the tree; during that time, the child is guarded by the guardian angel of the mother, not by its own guardian. Beginning at the moment of birth, that guardianship continues up to the moment of death when human nature is disintegrated by the separation of the body and soul. At no time during the span of human life is a man deserted by his guardian angel, at no time is he without the protection of that heavenly prince. No matter what he does with his life, no man suffers the loss of that unrelaxed vigilance and untiring patience of his angel.

Effects on the Guardian

How does the angel feel about it ally would it not be entirely reasonable if the angel of a first class sinner were to throw up the whole job in disgust? At least the angel would seem to be entitled to a little disappointment or even chagrin at the total waste of his magnificent efforts. As a matter of fact, the angel's peace of mind and happiness in no way depends upon the activities of man; it is not wearing its heart on its sleeve, that heart has been given to God. The guardian angel is in possession of eternal beatitude and so impregnably protected from all sorrow; its will is in perfect accord with the divine will so that whether man follows the order of merit to an eternal reward or the order of justice to eternal punishment, he cannot cause sorrow to an angel by stirring up a conflict between God and His messenger. There is, however, a real possibility of conflict between the guardian angels of different individuals or of different principalities, as for instance, in the case of war, when the aims or needs of these different subjects of guardianship are diametrically opposed. Here again the conflict is more apparent than real and certainly cannot result in bitterness between the angels involved. Both angels are perfectly united to God, in complete harmony with His divine will and, of course, that divine will is in harmony with itself; the conflict comes from an incomplete knowledge of the divine plans and ceases as soon as those plans are revealed. The angels know this; during the interval preceding such a revelation, they do not sever diplomatic relations, refuse to speak to each other, or contaminate the air with nasty innuendoes. Each does his utmost at his own task, satisfied to be fulfilling the task assigned by the divine Master.

This doctrine of the guardian angels is by no means merely a popular sentiment in the Church, as Calvin thought. The fact of guardianship is absolutely certain and of faith from the Scriptures themselves. That every one of the faithful has his particular guardian angel is quite clear from Holy Scripture and is the universal doctrine of the Fathers of the Church. That not only everyone of the faithful but every human being has his own guardian angel is the common teaching of the Doctors of the Church; that every kingdom, province and city has its own angel seems quite clear from Scripture. St. Thomas thinks that public persons, destined to work for the common good, have another angel commissioned as guardian for these specifically public works. That every parish, order, monastery and so on has its own angel is a probable opinion that seems to follow immediately from the principles behind the general guardianship of the angels.

Concerning the Devils – Attack

Besides the good angels there are also fallen angels; which fact would immediately lead one to suspect that angelic activity in the material world is not exclusively of a beneficent nature. These devils harbor no love either for God or man; their very nature gives them the power to act on the senses and imaginations of men, to coax the human wills and to feed human intellects with the material for knowledge. They have the motive for acting and the power to act; the fact is that they have acted in the material universe from the days of the first man.

The Fact and Causes of Hostility

Of course such activities are definite attacks on men, attacks whose history has its roots deep in the beginnings of the universe. There is first of all that terrifying hatred and envy of God that so consumes the devils now. Pride led them to ape the self-sufficiency of God; pride cannot now let them forget the shamed exposure of their insufficiency. As it led them to ape the divinity itself, so now it leads them to ape the divine government of the world; Satan's kingdom sends its own ambassadors into the material world to work to the ends of evil that divine beneficence might be thwarted. Over and above this pride and envy of divine things, there is a definite hatred and envy of men as participants of the divine life and divine happiness, an envy that drives the devils on to every effort to impede that union of God and men.

Its Limitation

The devils are not stragglers from a once proud army, plundering where and when they like; they are not guerilla bands that have escaped a pursuing army; nor are they an army of evil that has fought the legions of God to a standstill. They are by no means out of control; rather they are definitely and completely subject to God. The extent and power of diabolic attacks on men are themselves subject to divine ordination; the divine government is wise enough to fit even such things into the working out of the perfection of the universe, for it knows how to use evil by ordering it to still greater good.

Physical Attacks of Devils, Infestation, Obsession, Possession

Now and then, but rarely, the devil makes a spectacular display by attacking men physically. This might be of great importance for advertising purposes, if the devil needed advertising; it has little importance from any other point of view. Theologians, ascending to a climax of impotent fury, have distinguished three classes of these physical attacks. The first, called infestation, consists of an attack centering on the surroundings of man rather than man himself; noise-making, throwing things about, breaking articles of furniture, mysterious knocks on doors and walls, and so on. It was this sort of thing that plagued the Curé of Ars night after night for so many years during the pitifully few hours he could set aside for sleep. Obsession, on the contrary, is a personal attack, but essentially an exterior attack directed to physical injury and so to the instilling of terror; in its effects, it does not go beyond the attack that any man might make on another by blows or kicks.

The real crescendo in these attacks is reached in what is called possession. Here the devil approaches internal domination of the person involved for he takes over almost complete control of the lower faculties of the possessed person, imagination, senses, even purely vegetative and animal operations. So much is this true that during the time of possession, the one possessed has no control over these faculties. It must be remembered that this attack is also no more than physical, that it has no moral significance and is without the power to sway the will or act directly on the intellect; that is, it is incapable of forcing a person to commit sin. Sometimes possession is permitted by God with no fault whatever on the part of the one possessed; at others, there are definitely assignable causes from the side of the victim, such, for instance, as openly selling the soul to the devil, weakening the will by constant practice of hypnotism, flirting with the devil, or openly inviting him in, through spiritualistic modeled, frequentation of astrologers, fortune tellers and so on.

Moral Attacks

The moral attacks of the devils are really much more serious; but because they are much more commonplace and not at all spectacular, they are much less feared by men and women. We call them temptations. It is a mistake, of course, to comfort ourselves with the thought that all temptations come from the devil. As a matter of fact, temptations have entirely efficacious causes in the appetites, habits and companions of men; indeed, some of them may come from God Himself. For, after all, a temptation, strictly, is nothing more than an experiment, a trial, to determine the powers of the one tempted. It is this nature of temptation that shows so clearly the difference between temptation as it comes from God, man or the devil.

The temptations from God are rather to show a man himself and others of what stuff this man is made and of what he is capable. Thus, the terrible temptations and trials of the saints were evidences to the saints themselves and to others of how great things they must suffer for God and how utterly dependent they are on God. The temptations that come from men are normally for the purpose of the tempter, to discover things for himself and, perhaps, to obtain things for himself. Thus, for a man to tempt God is a sin because it proceeds from doubt or incertitude of God's power; a man may tempt other men either to help them or to injure them. When the purpose is injury, the spiritual seduction of others, the tempter is doings the devil's work for this is precisely the aim of the devil's moral attacks, to seduce man, to lead him into sin. The passions of man and the world about man are said to tempt man, but only materially, offering him the material for sin. Obviously they have no conscious purpose of temptation behind them unless they are used by a conscious agent such as the devil or another human being, as indeed they often are. Indirectly we might blame all sins and temptations on the Devil insofar as the exemplar of all sin and the corrupter of human integrity came about through the temptation of Eve by the devil. For the most part, however, we get along in sin very well without the devil, even without the help of anyone but ourselves. We cannot do the supernatural work required for heaven without supernatural help; but we suffer no such insufficiency in the order of evil, we are quite capable of sins that damn us to hell without any suprahuman aid. Not all sins are traceable to the devils; but there is no class of sins to which the devil does not tempt men and women.

In the course of such temptation, it is quite possible for the devil to work marvels, just as it is for the good angels to work marvels; but not miracles. The devils have lost none of their natural powers through their sins; but neither have they gained any supernatural powers as a result of their fall. The works of the devils are marvels only from the point of view of the material causes with which they are worked; the serpents produced by the Egyptian magicians, the fire from heaven that consumed the herds and family of Job, the crash of the house which killed his sons – these were not tricks but stern realities with the devil for their author. They were certainly not miracles.

It would seem, granted the natural cleverness of the devil and the clemency of God, that once the devil has been thoroughly beaten by a human individual, he would pretty well abandon that manner of attack on that individual. Usually it works out that way. After all, there is no sense in throwing armies against a fort that has proved invincible. On the other hand, once a weak spot has been found by the devil, it is fairly certain that there will be many future attacks on the same place and along the same line.

Conclusion, Role of the Angels and Scientific Thought

The role of the angels in the government of the material world is not likely to be the subject of a scientific paper within the next few years; it is to be devoutly hoped that no conscience-stricken American millionaire leaves a legacy to set up a laboratory for such an investigation. The results would be doomed beforehand to a most unscientific character. Science has nothing to offer by way of proof of the angelic governors for such a matter is simply not subject to scientific methods of inquiry. By the same token, there are no grounds for scientific attack on the role of the angels in our world. Science and the suprasensible cannot come to grips. If science thinks, at any time, that it is attacking or destroying the notion of angels and angelic activity, it is in the throes of a nightmare. Don Quixote was much more sane, attacking windmills with a lance, than is a scientist attacking the invisible, intangible, immaterial substances of the angelic world with a scalpel or a microscope.

Role of the Angels and Philosophic Thought

Nor can the role of the angels be disproved by philosophic thought. Some philosophers have thought they found a way around this by first strangling the outer guard of the angelic world, the human intellect; unfortunately, with the death of the intellect, philosophy ceased to breathe and the former philosophers were stripped of all but scientific equipment. Facing the facts of the existence of man's intellect, the order of the universe and the hierarchy of being, the angels and their activity in the material world are demanded; a demand that was recognized as genuine by generations of philosophers.

It is true that the activity of the good angels cannot be demonstrated by the human reason alone; any one of these effects could be produced directly by God Himself. Yet the activity of the devils seems to present us with definite proof of the presence and activity of spiritual substance. It is to be remembered that philosophy and science do not exhaust the possibilities of certain knowledge for man. He can still be told truth by one who knows all truth; he can still receive knowledge in unadulterated form directly from the first truth by way of revelation on the authority of the first truth, Who cannot deceive or be deceived, the role of the angels in the material universe is indisputable.

Role of Angels and Moral Thought, Appreciation of Supra-human Aid

The moral thinking of men offers an added source of conviction of the activity of the angels, for it brings home as nothing else can, the need of man for supra-human aid. Our own human weakness is a splendid reason for the strength and help of the angels. The realization of the hordes of far superior beings on the alert for the downfall of man makes the doctrine of the guardian angels a necessity if terror is not to hold sway over the human heart. With our eyes open to the weakness of man and the strength of the forces of evil, the way is clear for a full flowering of virtues essential to the living of human life. We are quite willing to exercise a healthy caution, not at all resentful of the truth of a wholesome humility; concretely, we are much less likely to flirt with sin, temptation or the occasion of sin on the false assumption that nice people like ourselves do not succumb to the things we are hardly likely to develop, in the moral order, that careless confidence that sends a veteran steelworker hurtling to his death; we shall cultivate a sound, rational fear.

Value of this Appreciation

The comfort and courage of the presence of the guardian angels is not an invitation to sluggish mediocrity of effort but an inspiration to outdo ourselves. The importance of man in the universe, underlined by the fact of angelic guardianship, is something to be held fast to as the solid ground of self-respect and evident refutation of the slimy theories that would sink man in a mass. Purity is not nearly so difficult in the presence of angels who stand continually in the presence of God. All of these virtues are obvious conclusions from a man's admission of the truth of the angelic government of the physical world. Perhaps the most obvious of all is the one that will be most slow in its growth, that graciously human virtue of gratitude. If the angels would only frown at us by way of reminders or stand conspicuously till we were forced to think of a tip, if they would cough, but no, they are entirely unobtrusive. It is entirely up to us to murmur a word of thanks, or go haughtily on taking their indefatigable service for granted.

📖 CHAPTER XX 📖

THE ROLE OF MEN AND OF FATE
(Q. 106-109)

1.A fundamental truth – integrity,

(a) The view of the slave.

(b) The view of the coward

(c) The view of a man.

2. Fact of the activity of corporal creation.

3. It the mode of this activity,

(a) Philosophic explanations.

(b) Principle of this activity.

4. Influence on human actions,

(a) Distinction of human action and acts of man.

(b) Direct influence on human action.

(c) Indirect influence.

(d) Influence on the spiritual world.

5. Fate,

(a) Its definition in general.

(b) Its harmony with and distinction from providence.

(c) Its inevitability and universality.

6. The role of man,

    (a) Physical action on the material world.

    (b) Strictly human action,

        (1)of man's intellectual powers,

            a. On the minds of others.

            b. On the material world.

        (2) of his generative powers.

        (3) of his nutritive powers.

7. Man's place in the government of the world,

    (a) Relative to divine and angelic action.

    (b) Relative to the material action of bodies and of other men.

    (c) Man's own power and place.

Conclusion,

        1. Summary of this volume.

        2. The Lord of the world.

        3. The divine architect.

☐ CHAPTER XX ☐
THE ROLE OF MEN AND OF FATE
(Q. 115-119)

Old things may be best but if so they are badly cheated, for we give them nothing like the proper attention excellence deserves. Old things become so familiar, so comfortable that they seem to mould themselves to our shape, abandoning their own, as although at the same time to wrap their arms about us and proclaim their surrender of themselves to be merged with us. They do really become a part of us to such an extent that we see as little of them as we do of ourselves; it is almost shocking to have an old thing brought sharply to our attention, as confusedly embarrassing as a suddenly realized excess of introspection. These are to be taken for granted, as we take our hand, our eyes, our minds for granted; which is to say, they are to be persistently overlooked.

A Fundamental Truth – Integrity

All through this book a fundamental truth has cropped up again and again; it is no surprise to meet this old friend in this final chapter we are so accustomed to this familiar truth by this time that it seems like an old friend; and, like an old friend, we can easily take it for granted, pass it by, overlook it, sure that there will be no recriminations, no enduring enmity as the result of our blindness. Perhaps we can best express this familiar truth by pointing out that a coward multiplies the dangers he must face and dies a thousand times; or that one lie must always be patched up by several others The reason for both of these is that one fact cannot be dodged without a hundred others crashing into us head on, one stone of truth cannot be crushed without an instant need for extensive repair work to prevent a collapse of the building. In other words, a man cannot toy with any part of the divine plans without defacing the edifice.

If through cowardice, aversion from unpleasant truths, ignorance, pride or any reason whatsoever, we take away any least thing from God, the universe, or any part of that universe, we reduce the whole to chaos; undoubtedly because the whole is so perfectly ordered on the model of divine truth that it is not patient of the least error. The fact remains that if we try to run away from the omnipotence of God, we throw ourselves into the remorseless maws of a heartless machine; if we exalt man above all else, we destroy him; if we attempt escape from the bitterness and struggle of a material world by fleeing from it, we become lost in a shadowy world of fantasy; if we exalt the material world, we are helpless before a monstrous divinity fabricated by falsehood.

In a word, there is no substitute for truth, the whole truth. There is no corner of the universe so distant that in it we can bury an unpleasant fact of that universe beyond all discovery. The facts must be faced, all of them. The truth must be admitted, all of it. In spite of himself, man cannot turn his back on a fact, a truth, a detail of the plans of the universe; he can only pretend to, shouting his pretensions the louder as the ominous tramp of truth's boots pounds down the avenues of his mind.

the View of the Slave

There is no cause for astonishment, then, in the fact that the view of men on the activity of material creation in the affairs of the universe profoundly affects their views of God and of man, particularly when the original view has something in it of fact dodging. In the concrete, the interrelation of our views of the material world, man and God is startling. Take, for example, the view that is almost universal among modern philosophers today, the view that cedes supreme activity to matter, in fact, insists that there is nothing else, no other source of perfection. This is a slave's view of the world, of man and of God; in such a world, man is just a part of an unthinking aggregation or process, without significance in his beginning, without hope in his life, with no goal to crown his death. God, in such a world, is non-existent.

The view of the coward

This picture is so monstrous it is no wonder men have turned coward in the face of it. It leaves no room for God or moral responsibility, thus apparently releasing man from burdens; but at the same time it leaves no room for order, for intelligence, for purpose, for value or for meaning. That is too much for a race whose first question is "whys", and whose constant quest is for happiness. Some men of today have tried to run away from this horror by denying its existence, much as a frightened boy on a lonely road will try to still his chattering teeth by assuring himself there are no ghosts. There is no material world, or, if it does exist, its activity is not its own in any sense but that of a spirit, preferably our own human spirit. Other men have not had the energy for even this much of a gesture of protest against the horror. In them, cowardice reached its supreme goal of abject surrender in the suicide of humanity when men said that while material creation did not exercise the only activity, its particular action was wholly irresistible. Material creation operates, they say, with a necessity and inevitability that admits of no control, no interruption, no escape; men, in the face of this inexorable movement of the material world, are helpless pawns.

the View of a Man

In contrast to this distorted view of the plans of the divine architect, there is the human view, which, since man is a shadow of divinity, is also the divine view. It sees in the material world a real activity, operating at the command of physically necessary laws; but an activity that is only a part of a world activity, a subordinate causality with its definitely subordinate place in the workings of an orderly universe. The material creation is subject, above all, to the supreme mover; it is controllable by those shaven in divine providence, the intellectual creatures we call men and angels. True enough, this is a hard view, it demands courage, insists upon responsibility, on action, on persevering effort, but it also gives room for meaning, for hope, for success, for *human* life. It is a view that has all the brilliance, the inflexibility, the suavity and peace of the whole truth.

Fact of the Activity of Corporeal Creation

If it is remembered that the activity in question here is not that of living things but of inanimate creation, the fact of material activity can hardly be seriously questioned. The activity of living things has already been treated at some length in this book. Here we are interested, not in that immanent activity that is within and for the agent, but in the transient activity that passes from the subject to the outside; the kind of activity that we see, for example, in a chemical reaction, radio-active substances, in the long, graceful sweep of the wind, the rush of the rain or the hushed falling of snow.

A few men deny the existence of such activity; but not many, perhaps for the very good reason that such a denial is much more than open violence to common sense. The denial is itself a reflection on the power of God, as although He were a weakling tyrant Who did not dare share any of His power, guarding His causality in niggardly fashion lest another, sharing it, should discover His fundamental weakness; to protect Himself, He made all creatures merely puppets of His omnipotence. The denial, if sustained, would mean that the whole order of cause and effect had absolutely no existence in the material world; with the result that the investigations of science were sterile, empty gestures fruitless of result, that the whole field of human activity, of moral responsibility and purposive action were no more than the hazy illusions of a mind too long locked up in solitary confinement.

Indeed, it would have results even wider than this. For it would mean that the material world had absolutely no reason for existence. The perfection of substance is in its function, that is, the reason for activity on the part of creatures is the attainment of perfection lacking to them or, in other words, they exist for the attainment of their ends. Deny this activity and you blast out the rational foundation for the existence of the material world. To put the thing in modern words, you destroy the dynamic character of the world, reduce it to stagnation, to decay, to ultimate nothingness.

the Mode of this Activity - Philosophic Explanations

By far the greater number of men readily admit the fact of the activity of the material world. In trying to explain this evident fact, philosophers have offered a variety of opinion that pretty well exhausts the possibilities and the impossibilities. So true is this, that practically every vagary of modern philosophers is reducible to the three following explanations of older philosophers. According to the Jewish philosopher, Avicebron, material activity was only an apparent activity; really that activity was the result of a spiritual power that penetrated all bodies. Plato and the Arabian philosopher, Avicenna, (with considerable difference of detail) explained this material activity by saying the part played by matter was only a preparation, a stage-setting, a disposition; the real activity was due to an immaterial, spiritual principle. The Greek materialist, Democritus, would have it that the action of the corporal creatures was merely a case of the flow of atoms from one body into another.

Aristotle and Thomas went deeper into the question and solved it by answering the question why bodies act at all, rather than the question of how they act They decided that the principle of activity was the individual perfection of the acting body; and very reasonably, too, for few men are seriously hurt by being struck by an imaginary automobile, it is only a real body that can act, and only insofar as it is real. The proportion, in other words, of the activity of a body corresponds to its possession of perfection, to the actualization of its potentialities; it can act on other bodies only insofar as these other bodies lack perfection, that is, have unfulfilled potentialities. To put this into the ruthless brevity of scholastic terminology, we would have to say that a body can act insofar as it is an act and according to the potentialities of the subject upon which it is acting.

To Aristotle and Thomas, this immediately brought to the fore a continuation of that hierarchy of being we have seen so often; for there will be a scale of activity in bodies corresponding to the scale of their perfection. If there exist bodies, which have completely realized all their potentialities, whose form has completely exhausted the possibilities of their matter, then these will be the supremely active bodies, the first corporal movers. The science of their times offered Aristotle and Thomas just such perfect bodies in the celestial bodies; these were then placed at the top of the scale of material activity, influencing all other corporal action.

Principle of this Activity

The scientific basis of this conclusion has long since gone into the discard; it has been decided scientifically that the stars and planets are not bodies of a different kind from those that exist here on earth. But the metaphysical principle explaining the activity of the material world, the principle of individual perfection, has lost none of its validity. The seeds of material activity are the potentialities, realized and unrealized, whose interplay works steadily to the ordered perfection of the material universe.

Influence on Human Actions

Although he believed the heavenly bodies were the first corporal movers, directly playing their part in the activity of every lesser material thing, Thomas made it plain that the influence of these bodies did not upset or destroy the field of human activity. These heavenly bodies, after all, were but another part of a well-ordered universe, as also is man; they have their specific nature, as has man. One does not destroy the other; rather, both take their proper, orderly place in the divine plans.

Distinction of Human Action and Acts of Man

To see the exact influence of material agents of the human order, it is necessary to understand that there is much about man that is outside his control; the growth of his beard, for example, his size, what he says in his sleep, the blunders he makes in his absent-mindedness. All these, as distinct from specifically human acts, are called "acts of man." The distinctly human acts proceed from man's intellect and will; of these man is the master. The distinction could be put simply by saying that the spiritually controlled acts of the human race must be distinguished from those that escape the spiritual control and which are material in their origin and fulfillment.

Direct Influence on Human Action

Stated in these terms, it is not difficult to see that human acts have no direct relation to the activity of the material bodies, much less any direct subordination. This is no more than saying that the material cannot act upon the spiritual, that a dust storm cannot soil an angel, a star cannot affect the free will of a man, nor can a planet pour ideas into a human mind. If it were otherwise, there could be no human actions. Man would act like the rest of material nature, following necessary physical laws; that is, he would have no free wills no Choice of action, no responsibility, no control over himself or anything else. In a word, the human world would no longer exist.

The direct action of the stars on the human intellect or will is a metaphysical impossibility and is in flagrant conflict with the unquestionable facts of humanity and human activity. Nevertheless the belief in the subordination of man's life to the stars has been for centuries a cowards refuge from the struggle of being human, and never more so than today. Thus, a famous American newspaper columnist, recently dead, could write that today astrology is no longer a dubious calling practiced by and for the shabby inhabitants on the fringe of the underworld. Today especially it is a straw for a sinking world whose following is in the highest stratum. One reader of the stars could leave a quarter of a million dollars at her death; another, of distinctive lineage and social impressiveness, makes her engagements for February in Palm Beach; for March, April and May in New York; for June, in London.

Indirect Influence

That the stars, or any other bodies, might well have an indirect influence on the actions of man is self-evident from the very nature of man. He is material as well as spiritual and his material side can, of course, be acted upon by any other corporal force; undoubtedly, his material side has an influence on his spiritual actions. This is news to no one at all. Lt has been no secret that a full moon and a smooth sea have done a noble part in arranging human romance.

Coming down to the particulars of the influence of these things on the intellect of man, it is evident that a man in physical agony does not do his best thinking, that the disturbance of his sense faculties by the racket of a boiler factory, the stormy arousal of his passions or the churning of his imagination all upset the workings of his intellect. The same things have an undoubted part in influencing or upsetting man's free choice. But no matter what the disturbance on the organic side of man's nature, the fact is that it is on the organic side, not on the spiritual side There is no question of direct action on the intellect and will; nor can the will be forced to act, disturbance or no disturbance, precisely because it is a free will. Its action is forced only by the universal, supreme good, anything less may present a seductive appearance, but never an utterly convincing one.

Influence on the Spiritual World

Of course the angels or devils do not have to scurry for cover in April showers or sigh sadly under a spring moon; floods or blizzards, stars or suns can have no influence, direct or indirect, on the activities of spiritual substances for there is no point for material contact. As a matter of fact, material activity is limited even in the material world. Even if there were such supremely perfect corporal movers as the ancients visualized, their action on purely material creation would not proceed with nearly such inevitability and necessity as astrologists would have us believe it does in the human field; for there still remain inexplicable from the point of view of order those accidents or clashes of material causes which cannot be reduced to any one natural physical cause.

Fate

The astrologic enthusiasts must be enrolled among the rationalists and modern fatalists who rather indignantly deny the idea of a divine providence as unworthy of either God or man and then, paradoxically, turn wholeheartedly, for a solid foundation of the world and of life, to a juggernaut called fate. If for no other reason than that the idea of fate plays so large a part in the lives of so many men, it is worthy of examination.

Its Definition in General

Generally speaking, fate might be defined as a hidden cause from whose activity nothing can escape. Actually, this definition is capable of widely different interpretation. In one sense, this hidden cause may be taken to be the disposition of the stars; from this disposition absolutely everything comes about necessarily, even the most intimate acts of knowledge and love. This is the sense in which the fatalist takes the word; and the sense, which has been roundly condemned as heretical by the councils of the Church.

Its Harmony with and Distinction from Providence

Another, and perfectly sound sense, identifies fate with divine providence, either with divine providence immediately or with the effects of divine providence, that is with the orderly disposition of all creatures and their activities in view of the end of the universe. In this sense, fate is no more than a restatement of the Catholic doctrine which we have already seen in treating of divine providence; and, in this sense, there is no question of an inescapable necessity that destroys human freedom, whatever is the infallible efficacy of divine ordination.

The attempt to read our fate is the mighty task of trying to read the mind of God; for, if we are looking for the reason of this orderly arrangement of the things of the world, the reason, the ultimate answer, is not to be found in the stars, in the entrails of chickens, in the turn of a card, in the leaves of a teacup or in any of the rest of the trappings of the readers of the future. It is to be found in the plans of the divine architect of the universe. The actual execution of those plans is to be found, of course, in the universe itself; that is, the formal carrying out of the divine plans, the formal disposition of creatures which is the effect of divine providence and might be called fate in a Catholic sense, is all about us. In foretelling the weather, then, we are not trying to climb inside divinity; in a very real sense, however, we are reading the plans of God as they are executed by secondary causes.

its Inevitability and Universality

If we keep in mind the distinction between causal fate, which is divine providence, and formal fate, which is the effect of divine providence, the degree of inevitability in fate, taken only in the Catholic sense, is easily and rightly understood. That causal fate which is divine providence is, of course, completely infallible and certain; God makes no mistakes and receives no news from the world. But it is the mysteriously omnipotent infallibility of an infinitely good God, whose every action is a guarantee of the integrity of every created nature. The formal fate, which is the effects of divine providence or the disposition of secondary causes and their activity, has no metaphysical inevitability in itself. Secondary causes are interfered with every day in the week; in fact, it is precisely to thwart a secondary cause that we carry umbrellas on rainy days and laugh at the rain. The purely material world produces its effects with a physical necessity; while the human world suffers only the moral rule of the law of God.

On the basis of this same distinction, it is not hard to determine the subjects of fate and the extent of its kingdom. For absolutely everything is subject to causal fate, the plans of the divine architect which are divine providence. To formal fate, or the action of secondary causes executing divine providence, only those things are subject, which are naturally subordinate to secondary causes; that is, God Himself, the angels and the spiritual faculties of man must be excepted.

The Role of Man, Physical Action on the Material World

Coming now to the last phase of the government of the world, the part man plays in cosmic activities, it is clear that the material side of man needs no special treatment. He cannot lift up a mountain, although he may lift up the baby; he can be drowned, shot, run over, suffocated or done away with in thousands of other more or less artistic ways. His material being and activity is subject to the same laws, the same limitations and enjoys the same possibilities as the rest of material creation. His distinctive activity is an intellectual one. A question of distinctively human activities in the workings of the universe it a question of what man can do about that universe with his mind.

Strictly Human Action
Man's Intellectual Powers - on the Minds of Others

Let us restrict the question still more and ask what man can do with his mind to the minds of others. More simply, can one man teach another? The fact of man's ability to teach another by sharing with them his ideas is solidly established by the routine experience of human life; if this teaching ability is not a fact but an illusion, then it is the grand illusion or modern life on which untold hours and incredible fortunes have been totally wasted. What is not so clear in this matter is how this transfer or communication of ideas takes place.

One explanation, that of Averroes, declared that one man taught another by giving the student the teacher's own ideas, much as one plane refuels another by giving away its own gasoline. The sense of this explanation was not that only the thing known was the same, that the subject matter of ideas was identical, but that the very intelligible species of both intellects were one and the same. Plato made education a kind of alarm clock; its purpose was merely to jog the memory of the student. For the ideas are all in every mind from the very beginning and have only to be aroused to be converted into actual knowledge. Aristotle, and Thomas after him, insisted that every man starts life with a blank mind; that each mind is a distinct, personal faculty to be perfected by distinctly personal ideas. This blank mind has potentialities; education is nothing more than the actualization of these potentialities, the reduction of the power to know to actual knowing. The teacher, in this case, is not a refueling plane, not an alarm clock, but a hod carrier bringing the materials to bricklaying students.

Moreover, as we have already seen at some length, the channel through which knowledge enters the mind is that of the senses, for the human mind, short of direct action by God, can gather ideas only from the phantasms of the imagination which, in turn, are the product of sense activity. The teacher's work then is not directly to place ideas in the mind of the student, that would be too much to ask even of an angel, but rather to furnish the material for ideas, to offer the sensitive and imaginative approach, or, as St. Thomas puts it, to take the student by the hand and lead him slowly, carefully from what is known to that which is as yet unknown.

Consequently, the very first condition for the teacher is knowledge of what he is trying to teach, he must know where he is going if he is to lead others to a goal of definite knowledge. His actual procedure, like the procedure of all art, must be modeled on the procedure of nature for, as St. Thomas points out, a man, left to himself, proceeds from the things he knows step by step to what he has yet to learn. He goes from the naturally known principles to the conclusions that follow from those principles. Nature is always the principal cause as well as the model; art takes the tricks of nature and then by them helps nature along.

To put it still more concretely, the teacher takes his student in hand, leading him on to the things to be known from the student's own slender stock of knowledge by proposing sensible examples, similitudes and contrasts, stepping up bit by bit from the less universal to the more universal truths, or stepping down the same way from the first principles to less universal conclusions. But his particular job as teacher is to show the connection between the principles and conclusions. In the trenchant phrase of Aristotle, proof (demonstration, teaching) is a syllogism causing knowledge.

The limitations and extent of this ability of man to teach are evident from this process of teaching. A garage mechanic, as such, cannot teach a statistician to play with figures; nor can the statistician, as such, enlighten the mechanic on the inner life of an automobile. Yet there is no man however wise who cannot learn something; nor is there any man, however ignorant who has not gathered some knowledge that another lacks. In fact, this can be pushed a little farther by saying that the humblest child with the use of reason can tell things to the greatest of the angels, things that the angel, of itself, could not knows for the mind of man is an inner sanctuary where only God enters freely, so that the thoughts of our mind can be known to another only through our condescension in revealing them. It would undoubtedly be presumptuous for the most learned of men to attempt to teach an angel natural truths; for one of the precise notes of angelic superiority over human nature is their absolutely perfect knowledge from the first instant of creation.

On the material world

The power of our mind over matter not formally joined to the human soul amounts to absolutely nothing; we can blow out a candle with a whiff of breath, but no amount of mental concentration will snuff out the flame. Even relative to our own body, the effects we can bring about by the use of the mind must be through the instrumentality of the material faculty of imagination; an imaginary ocean crossing can make us sea-sick or a broken thermometer make us shiver with cold in an overheated room. But imagination will never break one of our legs; nor will any amount of mental effort coupled with imagination knit a broken leg. This instrument of the imagination, in other words, has very definite limitations. It is possible for intense mental concentration to render us impervious to sensible stimuli; so St. Thomas could have an ulcerated leg cauterized and be quite unconscious of the pain and the cauterization. It is to be noticed, however, that the concentration does not destroy the external stimuli it ignores; Thomas undoubtedly would have been a joy to a very poor cook, but the spoiled food would still have been spoiled food.

Death's separation of body from soul rather than increasing the power of man's mind and will over material creation, naturally speaking decreases that power; by death, man loses his one medium of contact with the material world. From that time on, even such a relatively simple activity as local movement, like pushing an enemy downstairs, is beyond human power.

Concerning his Generative Powers

As for the other powers of man, well, they naturally have the same limitations as the physical world of which they are so intimate a part. Thus, the generative powers of man can have only physical results. In the lower animals, the sensitive or animal souls are directly caused by generation; after all, they are no more than material forms and are produced, as other material forms are produced, by the action of material causes. But man's soul is spiritual; and a spiritual substance can be produced in only one way, by the direct creative action of God. Certainly it cannot come from material causes, for it far exceeds them; nor can it come from the spiritual, which, by their very nature, are utterly simple, incapable of division, increase or diminution. To claim that human parents produce the soul of their offspring really amounts to a denial of the spirituality and immortality of that soul; which means, really, a denial of the humanity of that soul, putting it in the same class as the souls of plants and animals coming from material, dependent on material and corrupting with the corruption of matter.

The human soul, then, comes directly from the hand of God. However proud a young father may be of his child, he must give God credit for the greater work; the child is more God's than the parents'. The work of the parents is to dispose the material of the body, prepare the home for the reception of the immortal guest, which is the human soul.

Concerning His Nutritive Powers

On the side of nutrition, man, in common with every other living thing, has that extraordinary and mysterious activity by which food and drink are changed into integral parts of his nature. As the individuals of the human race increase, the original deposit of humanity is not split up or spread thinly to make it go farther; there is a definite and substantial conversion of nourishment into the human material which makes up the human bodies.

Man's Place in the Government of the World, Relative to Divine and Angelic Action

Before concluding this final chapter, it might be well to sum up the forces of the government of the world precisely as they affect men and women. We have seen that man is completely subject to the government, the movement of God. That movement, far from being an affront to his nature, is its guarantee and, indeed, the sole cause of man's existence, his life, his soul, his liberty, his fulfillment. The angels cannot directly act upon our intellects or wills. Whatever their power, they are helpless before the individuality of man's free will. The good angels exercise their power in guarding man, protecting him from external evils, teaching him subtly, anonymously, working effectively on his senses and his imagination, encouraging and comforting him. The devils use that same angelic power to tempt man or, sometimes, to attack him physically, but always within the limits placed by the mercy of God.

Relative to the Material Action of Bodies and of Other Men Man's own Power and Place

Physical creation cannot get past the barriers of man's spiritual nature any more effectively than can the angels; his intellect and will stand supreme in their privacy. But, of course, man's animal nature is open to the influence of material action; and so, indirectly, his intellect and will can be affected to some degree by this extrinsic, physical activity. The efforts of his fellow men leave a man serene in his independence; again his intellect and will acknowledge no master save God. His fellows can teach a man, ministering the materials of knowledge, they can act upon his physical nature; but no one, no thing, can take away his mastery over his own life and the consequent responsibility he bears for the failure or success of that life.

Conclusion

Summary of this Volume

The work of this volume might be stated with extreme simplicity by saying that it was devoted to a study of God and the world; broken down to its full significance, that certainly means that it studied almost everything. Obviously that is too much for any one volume to do; nor did this book attempt to study everything in all its details. Rather it kept a steady eye on the universal harmony of the world and its Creator, concentrating on the broad outlines of the plans of the divine architect, lest the beauty of the plans be hidden by a mass of details. Even those broad outlines of the architect and His plans are awesome. There was, for example, the question of the existence of God, then a study of His nature and attributes, as well as a glimpse into the inner divine life, which is the Trinity, the distinction of the three divine persons in one divine nature.

The next step was the processions of creatures from God, which included the production of these creatures, or creation, and their distinction into angelic, corporal and human. A study of the natures of each of these culminated in the question of their conservation and harmonious interaction by the universal government of the universe.

From this study two facts stood out in bold relief as a sharp challenge to modern thought, the fact of the importance of the human individual and the fact of the orderly planning of the divine architect.

The Lord of the World

These two are a challenge to modern thought. For the first is a sharp denial that man must reconcile himself to existence on a purely material plane where he it individually, totally unimportant; a part of a process, a moment in cosmic development, a unit in a mass whether of race, class, party or mere earth. It is a flat repudiation of the cowardice that would surrender rights, hopes, ideals, success, independence and control in order to escape responsibilities, disappointments, failure, labor and self-control. It is an indignant attack on the theories that urge a man to resignation, cynicism in all the fields of distinctively human endeavor, in knowledge, love, controlled action, attainment of a goal worthy of manhood. For from this study it is clear that man is indeed lord of the world and lord of himself; a provider for himself and for others, a governor of himself and others, a giant on the earth who, with no more than his reason and his hands, makes use of all the material creation and cannot be made use of by anything in the world. He is intelligent, he is free, he is responsible; his life has meaning, it is going to a definite goal that is intimately personal. And he alone, of all creatures in the material world, can say that he will or will not go along the path that alone will lead him home. He is the master; the rest, his servants. He is the lord of the world.

The Divine Architect

The second fact is an even more fundamental challenge to our times. It is an open revolt against the madness that holds for a world without meaning, a god without intelligence and a man without purpose. It refuses to keep submissive silence in the face of absurdities such as the assumption that order came from disorder, something from nothing, progress by chance or without explanation and government from anarchy. It challenges the modern world to attempt to put these absurdities into concrete living of human life; and scorns the intellectual dishonesty that preaches one doctrine and lives another. For from this study, it has become apparent that God exists, a supremely intelligent, completely omnipotent, infinitely wise, utterly perfect God. The imaging of the perfections of divinity in the world of creatures was nowhere seen more clearly than in the orderly hierarchy of perfection and limitation; on the basis of fact, of authority, of reason the order and wisdom of the divine planning and government stood out. While, on the same basis, the attempt to deny divinity, to explain the world without God, science without divine government, or philosophy without first truth was shown to be impossible. In other words, from the irrefutable evidence of His edifice of the universe, the existence and nature of the divine architect was shown to be visible to those images of His divinity to whom He consigned the lordship of earth.

രായ്ക്കരായ്ക്കരായ്ക്കരായ്ക്കരായ്ക്കരായ്ക്കരായ്ക്കരായ്ക്കരായ്ക്കരായ്ക്കരായ്

This Ends Book One of Three

രായ്ക്കരായ്ക്കരായ്ക്കരായ്ക്കരായ്ക്കരായ്ക്കരായ്ക്കരായ്ക്കരായ്ക്കരായ്ക്കരായ്

Books Two & Three will complete this masterpiece.

Credits:

Published in 1941
By
Walter Farrell O.P., S.T. Lr., S.T.D
Member of the Thomistic Institute

ക്കരാക്കരാക്കരാക്കരാക്കരാക്കരാക്കരാക്കരാക്കരാക്കരാക്കരാക്ക

Visit us at your local bookstore on the web at our web site:

http://revelationinsight.tripod.com/

E-Mail: Mystic@orthodox.com

Visit us at your local bookstore on the web at our web site

FREE BOOK offer for visiting our website: "His Daily Bread"

All works always at least 10% off retail, through our store

Works of the "Catholic Classics" Series

Volumes 1-5

1st segment

Explanation of the Rule of St Augustine	Hugh of St. Victor
Treatise of the Spiritual Life Books 1-3	Bishop Morozzo O.Cist
Imitation of Christ	Thomas a' Kempis

2nd segment

Little Book of Wisdom	Henry Suso

Note: vol. 2-4 are fraternal twins writings

Works of the "Desert Fathers" Series

Volumes 1-4

1st segment

Wisdom of the Desert   James O' Hanney

Desert Fathers Books 1 & 2   Countess Hahn-Hahn

Evigarius Essentials Book 1   Evigarius

Works for the Master

"Philosopher's Palate" Series

Vol. 1-4

1st segment

Divine Names   Pseudo Dionysius

First Principle   Duns Scotus

Boethius   Consolation of Philosophy

Pesenes   Paschal

Works for the Journeyman

"Great Christian Mystical Writings"

Volumes 1-5

1st segment

Ascent of Mount Carmel	St. John of the Cross
Dark Night of the Soul	St. John of the Cross
A Cell of Knowledge	Anonymous
Divine Consolation	Angelina Foligno

2nd segment

A Cloud of Unknowing	Walter Hilton

"The Contemplative" Series

Volumes 1-4

1st segment

Ladder of Perfection	Walter Hilton
Selection of Hugh of St Victor	Hugh of St Victor
Third Spiritual Alphabet	Francisco de Osuna

Works for the Apprentice

The Initial Series

"Pilgrim's Pantry"

Volumes 1-5

1st segment

The Kneeling Christian	Anonymous
Passion of Christ	Bro Smith SGS
Way of Perfection	Teresa of Avila
Augustine Essentials	Augustine

2nd segment

Ascent of the Pilgrim	Various Authors

Research Essentials" Series

Volumes 1-4

1st segment

Medieval to Modern English Dictionary	R /I Publishing Staff
Contemplative Life	St. Bruno
Ecclesiastical History	Bede
Church Creeds	Various

"The Monastic Series "

Volumes 1-6

1st segment

A Short Overview of Monasticism	Alfred Wishart
Monasticism from Egypt to the 4th Cent	W. Mackean

2nd segment

A Monk's Topical Bible in 4 Books.

The Thomas Aquinas Library

Volumes 1-6

1st segment

The Companion to the Summa   Walter Farrell O.P.

2nd segment

Contra Gentiles   Thomas Aquinas

Women of Faith Series

Volumes 1-4

1st segment

Teresa of Avila   Interior Castle
The Works   Julian of Norwich

Dialogues   Catherine of Sienna

All these works may be purchased through us directly or from
your local bookstore.

Each series will comprise of 12 volumes each.

Visit us at your local bookstore on the web at our web site

FREE BOOK offer for visiting our website:

"His Daily Bread"

All works always at least 10% off retail through our store

http://revelationinsight.tripod.com/

E-Books in

Kindle